Library of Congress
Subject Headings

RESEARCH STUDIES IN LIBRARY SCIENCE
Bohdan S. Wynar, Editor

LIBRARY OF CONGRESS
SUBJECT HEADINGS:
Principles and Application

Second Edition

Lois Mai Chan

1986
Libraries Unlimited, Inc.
Littleton, Colorado

LIBRARIES UNLIMITED, INC.
P.O. Box 263
Littleton, Colorado 80160-0263

Library of Congress Cataloging-in-Publication Data

Chan, Lois Mai.
    Library of Congress subject headings.

    (Research studies in library science ; no. 19)
    Bibliography: p. 485.
    Includes index.
    1. Library of Congress. Subject Cataloging Division.
Library of Congress subject headings. 2. Subject
cataloging. I. Title.
Z674.R4 no. 19   [Z695]   020 s   [025.4'9]   85-24115
ISBN 0-87287-543-1

In memory of

Kar K. and Sau N. Mark

TABLE OF CONTENTS

Part 1
PRINCIPLES, FORM, AND STRUCTURE

Part 2
APPLICATION

APPENDIXES

PREFACE

This second edition of *Library of Congress Subject Headings: Principles and Application* reflects developments since the first edition appeared in 1978. Since that date, use of the Library of Congress subject headings system has increased considerably, not only in the United States but abroad, and not only for library catalogs but also for periodical indexes and bibliographies. During the same period, there has also been a large increase in the number of online library catalogs and bibliographic databases accessible to the public, often with keyword or component word searching on titles, subject headings, and other data elements. In the next decade, public access to online bibliographic tools can be expected to grow significantly. In the light of this growth, librarians and other information professionals are now pondering the viability of the Library of Congress subject headings system in the changing environment.

This new edition addresses the questions concerning the place of traditional subject headings in online subject retrieval, the desirability of subject cataloging changes, and the need for a reexamination of the Library of Congress system in view of online subject retrieval. Its main purpose, however, is still to throw light on the current system, for now and for the future. The widespread use of the system has provided, to some extent, an answer to the viability question: more and more organizations in the United States and abroad are using or adapting it. That fact alone demonstrates the continuing need for information that will help the system's users understand its complex provisions. Furthermore, beneficial change in any system requires a thorough knowledge of the system's foundations.

No attempt is made to formulate rules. The book is written in two modes, analysis of principles and description of application; for the latter, the approach is to report rather than to prescribe. In order to avoid confusing what is with what ought to be, my own opinions are largely limited to Parts 1 and 3 of the book.

This book is primarily intended for librarians and information professionals, library and information science instructors, and advanced students; library technicians and beginning students using the book may require the assistance of experienced professionals or instructors.

I am indebted to many individuals and organizations for their assistance in the preparation of this edition. I wish to acknowledge my debt to the following: Theodora Hodges for her invaluable editorial assistance; Doris H. Clack and Pauline A. Cochrane for reading part or all of the manuscript; Nancy Dare, Donna Sykes, and Marlene Wallace for typing the manuscript and proofreading; and Theresa Kao for bibliographical assistance. Mary K. D. Pietris, chief of the Subject Cataloging Division at the Library of Congress, and her staff, particularly Eugene Frosio, principal subject cataloger, have been most cooperative and helpful in consultation and in providing information regarding recent policy changes and heading revisions.

The preparation of both editions of this book was supported by grants from the Council on Library Resources, for which I wish to make a special note of acknowledgment.

L.M.C.

Part 1

PRINCIPLES, FORM, AND STRUCTURE

1

INTRODUCTION

The Library of Congress subject headings system, developed originally for the Library's own collection, has been adopted widely by libraries and information services in the United States and, to some extent, abroad. It is one of the two standard systems used for subject cataloging in American libraries with general collections, the other being *Sears List of Subject Headings*.[1] An important reason for its widespread use is the fact that Library of Congress cataloging records have been available to other libraries throughout the twentieth century. The Library began selling its printed catalog cards in 1898. Use of Library of Congress cataloging information increased considerably when the Library began distributing its MARC (Machine-Readable Cataloging) records. Some libraries get magnetic tapes directly; others get much of their cataloging information through networks or bibliographic utilities that in turn have regular MARC tape service.

Outside the United States, the Library of Congress's list of subject headings either has been translated (more or less directly) or has served as the conceptual base for a number of subject access systems.[2]

Library of Congress subject headings are also used as the indexing vocabulary in a number of published bibliographies, perhaps the best known of which are *Subject Guide to Books in Print* and *Publishers Weekly*.

As the indexing vocabulary of the Library of Congress's MARC database, the headings have become an online retrieval tool both within the Library of Congress and outside. A number of bibliographic utilities allow searching by subject headings; RLIN (Research Libraries Information Network) and WLN (Washington Library Network) are prominent examples. Many individual libraries have their own online catalogs with access by subject, often with sophisticated search options; most of these libraries use the Library of Congress system for subject cataloging. The LC/Line database in the SDC/ORBIT system and the LC MARC and the REMARC databases in the DIALOG system bring the Library of Congress's subject cataloging to subscribers, along with flexible and powerful search capabilities. Finally, records in the *British National Bibliography* (BNB) and the UK MARC database carry Library of Congress subject headings in addition to the subject entries based on PRECIS (Preserved Context Index System), the subject indexing system developed for the BNB.

The adoptions just noted are all used for the subject cataloging of books. But the system also functions as a thesaurus for periodical indexing. For example, *Magazine Index*, a computer-based index to popular journals, bases its indexing on *Library of Congress Subject Headings.*

Responding to such widespread use and interest, the Library of Congress now solicits suggestions and recommendations from libraries outside its own walls when it is planning major changes or instituting new policies. The Library as an institution is aware of the fact that its subject headings system has become a de facto standard for subject cataloging and indexing in circumstances far beyond those for which it was originally designed.

In 1982, the Council on Library Resources sponsored a subject access meeting; one of the basic assumptions for discussion at this meeting was that "*Library of Congress Subject Headings* will be the basis for the controlled vocabulary in online access catalogs."[3] At the present time, the council is supporting studies of subject authority control in general and of the Library of Congress subject headings system in particular.

Information professionals, outside as well as inside the Library of Congress, recognize a whole new horizon in the use of *Library of Congress Subject Headings* as an online retrieval tool. Changes are inevitable; some changes, many would claim, are long overdue. Still, the system has clearly demonstrated its versatility in a wide range of conditions and is holding its own in popularity. A new look at the principles that underlie its features is in order. We turn first to its early history and then look at some other factors that determined its development.

HISTORY

The Beginnings

Shortly after the Library of Congress moved from the Capitol to its new building in 1897, the question arose concerning the form of the Library's subject catalog.[4] Two major decisions followed: first (in late 1897), to establish a new classification system; and second (in 1898), to adopt the dictionary form of the main catalog—in other words, to have a catalog with names, titles, and subject headings interfiled alphabetically. Charles A. Cutter's *Rules for a Dictionary Catalog*[5] had been published in 1876 and by 1898 was in its third edition; the dictionary catalog was well on its way to becoming the predominant catalog form in American libraries. The Library of Congress's move to such a catalog, plus the effect of its practice (begun shortly thereafter) of selling its printed cards, put the Library at the forefront of the development of both American cataloging practice in general and of the use of the dictionary arrangement as a catalog form in particular. Indeed, according to J. C. M. Hanson, the first chief of the Catalogue Division, one of the Library's reasons for adopting the dictionary form for the catalog was "a desire to be in a position to cooperate with the largest possible number of American libraries."[6]

During much of the 1800s, before the adoption of the dictionary catalog, the Library's subject catalog was in alphabetico-classed form; this catalog had been published in 1869. As the Library's subject headings came to be used more and more widely, many librarians asked that its headings list be published too. This was done, under the title *Subject Headings Used in the Dictionary Catalogues of the Library of Congress*; there has been a continuing series of editions and supplements (with a title change to *Library of Congress Subject Headings* at the eighth edition in 1975). The first edition appeared in 1914. The prefaces and introductions to the early editions provided information on the decisions that guided the growth of the system. The development of the list was the responsibility of the staff of the Library's Catalogue Division. Hanson and Charles Martel (whose tours of duty as virtually successive chiefs of the division spanned the years 1897 to 1930) have been formally recognized as the individuals who provided the initial guiding principles. The introductory pages in the first few editions of the list include the following passages:

> The organization of the catalogue to which the list in a measure forms a guide, the determination of the principles and methods to be followed in its construction and their successful application in the development of the subject catalogue are due to Mr. J. C. M. Hanson, Chief of the Catalogue Division 1897-1910, assisted by the labors of his associates. [second and third editions][7]

> Whatever measure of logic and consistency has been achieved in the headings is due to the continuity of oral tradition which stems from J. M. C. [*sic*] Hanson, who was Chief of the Catalog Division from 1897 to 1910, Charles Martel, Chief from 1912 to 1930, and their associates in the Catalog Division, and the occasional written instruction issued by them. [fourth and fifth editions][8]

In the introduction to the fourth edition of the list, David Judson Haykin, then chief of Subject Cataloging Division of the Library of Congress, presents his view of the beginning of the list:

> There was not, to begin with, a scheme or skeleton list of headings to which additions could be made systematically, completing and rounding out a system of subject headings for a dictionary catalog. Such a scheme could not have been devised at the time the Library's dictionary catalogs were begun, because there was no solid body of doctrine upon which it would be based; the guiding principles which were then in print for all to read and apply were very meager and concerned themselves with the form of headings and their choice. They did not provide the theoretical basis for a system of headings.[9]

At the time when the Library of Congress was making its first decisions on how to structure its dictionary catalog, Cutter's *Rules for a Dictionary Catalog* had been in circulation for more than thirty years; it had gone into the third of its four editions; it was well regarded in the profession. One would expect it to have had considerable influence on what the Library of Congress did in setting up headings for its new catalog. Yet Haykin talked about the inadequate theoretical basis of "guiding principles then in print." He appeared to believe that Cutter's rules had not been found sufficient for the Library's needs.

At any rate, there is no evidence that Cutter's rules were ever adopted officially by the Library of Congress. In fact, in Haykin's *Subject Headings: A Practical Guide*,[10] which was published in 1951 and acknowledged as the official guide in subsequent editions of the list, there are only a few passing references to Cutter's rules. Nor was Cutter ever mentioned in the preface or introduction to any of the editions of the list. Nevertheless, as we shall see in later chapters, Cutter's influence is quite obvious in Haykin's discussion of the fundamental concepts of Library of Congress subject headings: the reader as the focus, unity, usage, and specificity.

It is only many years later, in a paper presented by Richard S. Angell when he was in turn chief of the Subject Cataloging Division, that we find recognition of Cutter's role: "The final formulation of Cutter's objectives and rules was taking place at the same time that the Library of Congress was expanding and reorganizing the collections at the turn of the century. His work had a considerable influence on the founders of the Library of Congress catalog."[11]

Thus, although Cutter's influence on the Library of Congress's subject heading practice has yet to be acknowledged in a Library of Congress official publication, his subject heading principles are even now reflected in *Library of Congress Subject Headings* in spite of many modifications and compromises that have been made in the face of practical demands. As Francis Miksa puts it, *Library of Congress Subject Headings* is a reflection of the principles of Cutter "interpreted through Haykin."[12]

Actual work on the new subject catalog at the Library of Congress began simultaneously with the printing of the first author cards in July 1898.[13] At that time it was found necessary to begin an authority list for subject headings. Haykin's earlier quoted statement that there was not a "skeleton list of headings to which additions could be made systematically" might give the impression that the Library of Congress list was begun in vacuo. In fact, the *ALA List of Subject Headings for Use in Dictionary Catalogs* (1895), which was conceived as an appendix to Cutter's rules and was designed for use by small and medium-sized public libraries,[14] had already appeared. In a paper presented at the American Library Association Conference in 1909, Hanson recounts the beginning of the compilation of the Library of Congress list:

> While it was recognized that the A.L.A. list of subject headings had been calculated for small and medium sized libraries of a generally popular character, it was nevertheless decided to adopt it as a basis for subject headings with the understanding, however, that considerable modification and specialization would have to be resorted to. As a first step preliminary to the real work of compilation, a number of copies of the List were accordingly provided, a number of blank leaves sufficient to treble the size of the original volume were added, and the copies thereupon bound in flexible leather....
>
> New subjects as they came up for discussion and decision were noted on slips and filed. If the subject had already been adopted by the A.L.A. committee, i.e., had appeared as a regular printed heading on the List, a check mark was added to indicate its regular adoption by the Library of Congress.[15]

Hanson also indicates that, in addition to the ALA list, other works consulted included the Decimal and Expansive classifications, the Harvard list of subjects, the New South Wales subject index, Forescue's subject index, and numerous other catalogs, bibliographies, encyclopedias, and dictionaries.

Editions of the Subject Headings List

Almost from the beginning, as noted above, the Library of Congress took on the responsibility of giving other libraries an account of its cataloging practices. A brief account of the various editions of the subject headings list and of auxiliary publications on subject headings practice is appropriate here for the information it may convey on the development of the system.

Preparation for the first edition of *Subject Headings Used in the Dictionary Catalogues of the Library of Congress* began in 1909; there have been ten editions to date. The tenth edition was published in 1986. Supplements to the editions were issued on a fairly regular basis in the early days and have appeared at least quarterly since 1943. Table 1.1 provides a list of the editions and supplements.

A few additional comments on the last three editions are in order. The quarterly microform editions that began to appear with the eighth edition make the full current state of the list available outside of the Library of Congress, and they usually appear one to three months ahead of the printed quarterly supplements. The microform editions, however, do not include the front matter (i.e., preface, introduction, and list of major changes) that appears in the printed supplements. Nor are changes as clearly noted; the microform lists are thus less helpful to a library updating its subject authority records than are the printed lists. The ninth edition (plus its first two supplements) embodied a larger percentage of heading changes than had been the pattern in the past. Many of these changes were made in response to name heading changes called for in the new rules for descriptive cataloging, *Anglo-American Cataloguing Rules*, second edition (*AACR2*).[16] A 1979 report by the Library of Congress on these changes included a statement that a "top-to-bottom reconstruction of the philosophy or the structure of headings is not being planned."[17] The tenth edition, which appeared in 1986, contains headings that were valid as of December 1984. Consequently, changes that occurred since then are not reflected in this edition.

Table 1.1. Editions of and Supplements to the Library of Congress's
List of Subject Headings

Edition	Date	Title, Supplements, and Description
1st	1914	*Subject Headings Used in the Dictionary Catalogues of the Library of Congress*; included *see* and *see also* references; fourteen supplementary lists published.
2nd	1919	Same title; supplements in 1921, 1922, and 1924.
3rd	1928	Same title; cumulative supplements in 1931, 1933, 1935, and 1938.
4th	1943	*Subject Headings Used in the Dictionary Catalogs of the Library of Congress*; quarterly or more frequent supplements (some issued by the H. W. Wilson Company); separate list of *refer from* tracers.
5th	1948	Same title; *refer from* references incorporated into main list; use of symbols to denote type of reference.
6th	1957	Same title; format redesign.
7th	1966	Same title; production automated, making supplements easier to produce.
8th	1975	*Library of Congress Subject Headings*; also available in microform, with each quarterly microform issue a fully cumulated reflection of the full list; long introduction, featuring subdivision practice; separate list of headings for children's literature; introduction also published separately.
9th	1980	Same title; information on subdivisions not included; no theory-based changes but many changes in forms of headings.
10th	1986	Same title; basically a cumulation of the 9th edition and its supplements through 1984.

Auxiliary Publications

The long introduction to the eighth edition included a list of most commonly used subdivision terms, with scope notes governing their application. This introduction was much welcomed by librarians, catalogers especially, particularly because of the effect of the Library of Congress's 1974 announcement that subdivisions in the "most commonly used" list could be used without specific authorization—that they could, within the limits of their scope notes and as appropriate, be considered "free-floating." Information about subdivisions was omitted from the ninth edition, creating considerable demand for the separately published introduction to the eighth edition. When supplies of this publication were exhausted, a revised and partially updated account of the same sort of information was prepared. This was issued in 1981 under the title *Library of Congress Subject Headings: Guide to Subdivision Practice.**

A list of auxiliary publications on subject heading practice appears in appendix B of this volume. These publications began appearing in 1906 and continue to the present day, the latest being *Subject Cataloging Manual: Subject Headings* (1984).[18] Many of the publications concern subdivision practice; others give information on headings for language and literature, for children's material, and for music. Because most of the sort of information given in these publications is now incorporated in editions of *Library of Congress Subject Headings* and the *Subject Cataloging Manual*, the early lists are primarily of historical interest. Two publications issued by the Library of Congress on a regular basis also contain information on policies and actions bearing on subject heading changes. These are *Cataloging Service Bulletin* and *Library of Congress Information Bulletin*.

FACTORS INFLUENCING DEVELOPMENT

Literary Warrant

Early decisions on the basic source of the concepts represented in the Library of Congress subject headings list had an important influence on the nature of the list. Writers on controlled vocabulary subject access systems frequently point out that there are two fundamentally different ways to build such a system: from the top down, so to speak, deciding what topics constitute the universe of discourse and what terms and interconnectors should be used to represent them; and from the bottom up, looking at what is written and selecting terms and interconnectors based on what is found in the literature. The latter approach is spoken of as building on literary warrant, a concept first put forward by E. Wyndham Hulme.[19] It was literary warrant that governed

---

*Some of the information contained in the scope notes under the commonly used subdivisions has become obsolete. Currently, there are no plans for updating the notes except on a case-by-case basis.

construction of both the Library of Congress classification and the Library of Congress subject headings system. The subject headings list was developed in especially close connection with the Library's collection. It was not conceived at the outset as, nor has it ever been intended to be, a comprehensive system covering the universe of knowledge. This policy of literary warrant is stated in the preface to the early editions of the headings list: "The list covers subjects in all branches of knowledge so far as the cataloguing of the corresponding classes of books in the Library of Congress progressed."[20] Haykin comments further in the introduction to the fifth edition:

> [The list] includes only the headings adopted for use in the diction-
> ary catalogs of the Library of Congress in the course of cataloging
> the books added to the Library's permanent classified collections,
> and is not, therefore, a list of headings equally complete in all fields
> of knowledge. Neither is it a skeleton or basic list which could be
> completed in the course of years of cataloging.[21]

Systems based on literary warrant grow by accretion for the most part. As time passes, logic and consistency suffer in spite of conscientious maintenance efforts. As early as 1943, in the preface to the fourth edition of *Subject Headings Used in the Dictionary Catalogs of the Library of Congress*, Haykin notes failures in logic and consistency in the list and attributes them to the way the list grew. "The failures in logic and consistency are, of course, due to the fact that headings were adopted in turn as needed, and that many minds participated in the choice and establishment of headings."[22]

A further result of the list's growth by literary warrant is that it reflects the nature and size of the collection it was designed to serve, the collection of the Library of Congress. It has been criticized for showing a strong American bias; this bias simply reflects the fact that the de facto national library of the United States is naturally heavily oriented toward American materials.

Assumptions about Function

In any indexing system, policy decisions on structure and applications reflect the directors' ideas of what the system should do for its users. Different notions of a system's objectives lead to different results. Over the past 100 years many statements of what a subject catalog should aim at doing have been published, and some of them have been received with considerable acclaim. Unfortunately, when one analyzes the question of what these statements call for in practical terms, one finds a vague picture that at best reflects conflicting demands on the catalog.

Cutter's 1876 statement of "objects" has been cited often—and is still cited—as an articulation of the functions of subject entries:

1. To enable a person to find a book of which ... the subject is known [and]

2. To show what the library has ... on a given subject [and] in a given kind of literature.[23]

These two points are deceptive in the simplicity of their wording. Moreover, to the extent their meaning can be assumed, they make different demands on the catalog. The first point calls for a subject catalog to be simply a tool for location, to be a finding list for users who have a subject term in mind (and can map it onto the library's subject heading vocabulary). Paul S. Dunkin comments: "The first objective will be best served only if we have entry under the specific subject of the book, the one subject with which it truly tries to deal."[24] Cutter's second point, on the other hand, calls for collocation of material by subject and by genre—a much more demanding task, because here one is dealing with a group of entries together rather than individually.

Seventy-five years later, Jesse H. Shera and Margaret Egan spelled out eight "objectives for any form of subject cataloging."[25] They called for access by subject to all relevant materials, at any level of analysis, under precisely phrased controlled vocabulary headings that are further differentiated by subheadings and that take account of subject ramifications. They also called for a supporting structure of cross-references from variant terms and to affiliated subject fields (affiliated in several different ways), plus information that would allow patrons to make selections by various criteria. However, Shera and Egan recognized that it was impractical for all their objectives to be met, that limitations of personnel and finance would force modification.[26]

Cutter's statement was highly influential, yet it leaves fundamental questions unanswered. What is meant by the phrase "of which the subject is known" and "what the library has on a subject"? Or by Shera and Egan's "all relevant materials" or "affiliations among subject fields" or "criteria for selection"? How far should cross-references go in showing affiliations among subjects? To what units should subject cataloging apply: to books, to parts of books, to series, to individual titles in series, to serials, to journal articles, to nonprint materials of various types? How deep should the subject analysis be: many headings per item even for small items, or one or two—ideally one—to summarize its content? Except for general agreement on using headings to summarize, there has been little consensus, at the Library of Congress or within the profession in general, on the best answers to these questions.

Carlyle J. Frarey's comment from the 1950s is still basically valid:

> We do not know whether the subject catalog is doing its job or not; whether it is effective or ineffective; whether it is good or whether it is bad, for it has never been decided what the subject catalog is supposed to be. To some it is, or ought to be, a selected subject bibliography; to some, a subject index; and to still others, the subject catalog is no more than a convenient device for finding some good and useful material on a particular subject.[27]

The frequent criticisms of the subject catalog for being too specific or too general reflect the conflicting opinions on what the functions of the subject catalog should be.

Modern writers recognize in general two methods of subject representation: summarization and depth indexing. The former aims at displaying the overall subject content of bibliographic entities (books, journals, etc.), while the latter attempts to bring out the content of smaller units of information (chapters in books, articles in journals, etc.) within bibliographic entities. Many users are content to have the subject catalog fulfill the function of summarization and leave depth indexing to bibliographies and indexes. Wyllis E. Wright speaks to this point of view:

> If a reader really wants "all the material available" on a subject of any size, he is better served by bibliographies than by card catalogs.... I believe that, for general library use, subject headings are and will continue to be effective, if we confine them to the task of showing a reasonable display of subject materials for the use of a majority of our readers. The specialist uses bibliographies, for the most part, and we should not attempt to duplicate these bibliographies in the catalog.[28]

Frarey concurs:

> It is [the] failure to define the objective with sufficient precision which has contributed to the long, still unsettled controversy over the most suitable form for the subject catalog to take. It is this same failure which has led in our time to some confusion between the functions of subject cataloging and subject indexing, and to criticisms of the subject catalog because it does not provide the sufficiently deep analysis of the contents of our libraries required or sought by some users of library materials....
>
> There is need to recognize different levels of subject control, and within the hierarchy the bibliography serves one purpose, the subject catalog another, and the subject index still a third.[29]

In a survey of user studies of the subject catalog, Frarey comes to the conclusion that "there is very little use of the subject catalog to find all the material the library has, or to obtain comprehensive coverage of the subject under investigation.[30]

In the face of so many unanswered questions, and with many people acting over more than three-quarters of a century, variance in the product is unavoidable. The list and the cataloging done from it necessarily reflect the absence of professional consensus on the function for which it is a tool.

In the late 1970s and the 1980s, as the system was moving into the online age as a tool of subject retrieval in online catalogs and retrieval systems, similar questions relating to function were still being asked, and some of the answers have begun to come forth through catalog use studies. Other questions relating to the adaptability and viability of the Library of Congress subject headings system in the online environment are being raised. These will be discussed in Part 3 of this book.

Lack of a Code

As noted earlier, many inconsistencies and irregularities have crept into the Library of Congress subject headings system over the years. While the basic principles of the dictionary catalog laid down by Cutter and reinterpreted by Haykin have been adhered to in general, they have often been compromised in the face of practical constraints. In some cases, too, the same principles have been interpreted differently on different occasions, giving rise to another sort of irregularity. Many information professionals blame this uneven state of affairs on the fact that the system has grown by accretion without the guidance of a specific code or body of rules.

The need for a code for subject cataloging, corresponding to the one for descriptive cataloging, has long been keenly felt but never fulfilled. Interestingly, since Cutter, the only codification of subject heading practice for dictionary catalogs appeared in Italian, in the Vatican Library's *Rules for the Catalog of Printed Books*, completed in the 1930s and translated into English in 1948.[31] In essence, the subject headings portion of the Vatican code reflected the practice of the Library of Congress.

Over the years, the closest thing to a set of rules for subject headings since Cutter was Haykin's *Subject Headings: A Practical Guide* (1951). That work was officially acknowledged as a statement of principles for the choice and form of headings and references.[32] Still, Haykin's work is more an account and exposition of Library of Congress practice, with occasional apologetics, than a code.

A surge of interest and an intensified call for a code was apparent in the literature of the 1950s. Frarey's survey of catalog use studies[33] and other works on subject headings in the 1940s provided an impetus and could have laid the groundwork for a code. There is evidence that Haykin began work on a code in the late 1950s, but unfortunately his work was not completed; the remains of his attempt exist in an unpublished document entitled "Project for a Subject Heading Code."[34] Since then, there has been no effort either to continue his project or to begin anew.

In spite of its insufficiencies as a code, Haykin's 1951 work was a full and consistent treatment of the practice and guiding principles in operation at that time. But in the more than thirty years since it was written, there have been many changes in both the theory and practice of subject analysis. This work is an attempt to reexamine the basic principles in light of recent developments and changes and to describe current practice at the Library of Congress.

Because more and more retrieval options are available to library users now than formerly, there is a growing need to reexamine the part that retrieval through subject headings plays in overall subject access. Recent evidence indicates that subject searches make up a greater fraction of all searches than was measured in the catalog use studies of a decade ago.[35] If that is the case, especially if it should be determined that a significant number of subject searches are through subject headings, it is more important than ever to understand the theories and policies that determine current Library of Congress practices with regard to subject headings. Furthermore, we need a thorough understanding of the system to assess the impact of proposed improvements.

REFERENCES

[1] *Sears List of Subject Headings*, 12th ed., ed. Barbara M. Westby (New York: H. W. Wilson, 1982).

[2] Organizations that have used the *Library of Congress Subject Headings* include:

   o   the Library of Parliament of Canada, which prepared *Répertoire des vedettes-matière* (*Subject Headings Used in the French Catalogue*), published in 1963

   o   Université Laval, Québec, Canada, which published its *Répertoire des vedettes-matières*, 8ème ed., in 1976

   o   the Bibliothèque Nationale in Paris, which adopted the Laval list in 1980 and adapted it as the basis for its subject authority list; and the Bibliothéque Royale de Belgique, which used both Library of Congress subject headings and the Laval list as the basis for its trilingual (English, Dutch, French) thesaurus (see Suzanne Jouquelet, "A Network of Subject Headings: The Répertoire of Laval University Adapted by the Bibliothèque Nationale, Paris," *International Cataloguing* 12(2):17-19 [1983])

   o   the Organization of American States, which used the Library of Congress list as "a source for basic standardization" for the current Latin American project for subject authority entitled *List of Subject Headings for Libraries* (LEMB) (see Bertha Nelly Cardona de Gil, "Project: List of Subject Headings for Libraries [LEMB]: Problems of Translation and Adaptation" [Paper delivered at the 48th IFLA General Conference, Montréal, 1982])

[3] Keith W. Russell, comp. and ed., *Subject Access: Report of a Meeting Sponsored by the Council on Library Resources, Dublin, Ohio, June 7-9, 1982* (Washington, D.C.: Council on Library Resources, 1982), 68.

[4] J. C. M. Hanson, "The Subject Catalogs of the Library of Congress," *Bulletin of the American Library Association* 3:385-386 (July 1, 1909).

[5] Charles A. Cutter, *Rules for a Dictionary Catalog*, 4th ed. (Washington, D.C.: Government Printing Office, 1904).

[6] Hanson, "Subject Catalogs," 387.

[7] Library of Congress, Catalogue Division, *Subject Headings Used in the Dictionary Catalogues of the Library of Congress*, 3rd ed., ed. Mary Wilson MacNair (Washington, D.C.: U.S. Government Printing Office, 1928), iii.

[8] Library of Congress, Subject Cataloging Division, *Subject Headings Used in the Dictionary Catalogs of the Library of Congress*, 5th ed., ed. Nella Jane Martin (Washington, D.C., 1948), iii.

[9]Library of Congress, Subject Cataloging Division, *Subject Headings Used in the Dictionary Catalogs of the Library of Congress*, 4th ed., ed. Mary Wilson MacNair (Washington, D.C., 1943), iii.

[10]David Judson Haykin, *Subject Headings: A Practical Guide* (Washington, D.C.: Government Printing Office, 1951).

[11]Richard S. Angell, "Library of Congress Subject Headings—Review and Forecast," in *Subject Retrieval in the Seventies: New Directions: Proceedings of an International Symposium*, ed. Hans (Hanan) Wellisch and Thomas D. Wilson (Westport, Conn.: Greenwood Publishing, 1972), 143.

[12]Francis Miksa, *The Subject in the Dictionary Catalog from Cutter to the Present* (Chicago: American Library Association, 1983), 365.

[13]Hanson, "Subject Catalogs," 387.

[14]Carlyle J. Frarey, *Subject Headings, The State of the Library Art*, vol. 1, part 2 (New Brunswick, N.J.: Graduate School of Library Science, Rutgers—The State University, 1960), 17.

[15]Hanson, "Subject Catalogs," 387, 391.

[16]*Anglo-American Cataloguing Rules*, 2nd ed., prepared by the American Library Association, the British Library, the Canadian Committee on Cataloguing, the Library Association, and the Library of Congress, ed. Michael Gorman and Paul W. Winkler (Chicago: American Library Association; Ottawa: Canadian Library Association, 1978).

[17]"Changing Subject Headings and Closing the Catalogs," *Cataloging Service Bulletin* 4:13 (Spring 1979).

[18]Library of Congress, Subject Cataloging Division, *Subject Cataloging Manual: Subject Headings*, prelim. ed. (Washington, D.C.: Library of Congress, 1984).

[19]E. Wyndham Hulme, "Principles of Book Classification," *Library Association Record* 13:445-447 (1911).

[20]Library of Congress, *Subject Headings*, 3rd ed., iii.

[21]Library of Congress, *Subject Headings*, 5th ed., iii.

[22]Library of Congress, *Subject Headings*, 4th ed., iii.

[23]Cutter, *Rules for a Dictionary Catalog*, 12.

[24]Paul S. Dunkin, *Cataloging U.S.A.* (Chicago: American Library Association, 1969), 67.

[25]Jesse H. Shera and Margaret Egan, *The Classified Catalog: Basic Principles and Practices* (Chicago: American Library Association, 1956), 10.

[26]Ibid.

[27]Carlyle J. Frarey, "The Role of Research in Establishing Standards for Subject Headings," *Journal of Cataloging and Classification* 10:185 (October 1954).

[28]Wyllis E. Wright, "Standards for Subject Headings: Problems and Opportunities," *Journal of Cataloging and Classification* 10:176, 178 (October 1954).

[29]Carlyle J. Frarey, "Developments in Subject Cataloging," *Library Trends* 2:219, 221 (October 1953).

[30]Carlyle J. Frarey, "Studies of Use of the Subject Catalog: Summary and Evaluation," in *Subject Analysis of Library Materials*, ed. Maurice F. Tauber (New York: School of Library Service, Columbia University, 1953), 147-165.

[31]Vatican Library, *Rules for the Catalog of Printed Books*, translated from the 2nd Italian edition by Thomas J. Shanahan, Victor A. Schaefer, and Constantin T. Vesselowsky, and ed. Wyllis E. Wright (Chicago: American Library Association, 1948).

[32]Haykin, *Subject Headings*, 147-165.

[33]Frarey, "Studies of Use of the Subject Catalog."

[34]David Judson Haykin, "Project for a Subject Heading Code" (revised; Washington, D.C., 1957), 10 pp.

[35]Karen Markey, *Subject Searching in Library Catalogs before and after the Introduction of Online Catalogs*, OCLC Library, Information, and Computer Science Series 4 (Dublin, Ohio: OCLC, 1984), 77.

2

BASIC PRINCIPLES

The Library of Congress has yet to publish a statement of principles for its subject cataloging system. The principles that underlie the system, therefore, can only be inferred from practice and policy statements. As mentioned in the previous chapter, David Judson Haykin's *Subject Headings: A Practical Guide* (1951), which draws heavily on Charles A. Cutter's *Rules for a Dictionary Catalog* (1904), comes closest to being a statement of principles of the Library of Congress subject cataloging system. The following discussion is therefore based on Library of Congress practice and policy statements; the writings of Cutter, Haykin, and other chiefs of the Subject Cataloging Division; statements on subject analysis from authorities in the field; and the Library of Congress subject headings system itself.

THE USER AND USAGE

For Cutter, the foremost principle in cataloging was consideration of the best interest of the user of the catalog. In the preface to the fourth edition of *Rules for a Dictionary Catalog*, he states:

> The convenience of the public is always to be set before the ease of the cataloger. In most cases they coincide. A plain rule without exceptions is not only easy for us to carry out, but easy for the public to understand and work by. But strict consistency in a rule and uniformity in its application sometimes lead to practices which clash with the public's habitual way of looking at things. When these habits are general and deeply rooted, it is unwise for the cataloger to ignore them, even if they demand a sacrifice of system and simplicity.[1]

Haykin calls this guiding principle "the reader as a focus":

> ... the reader is the focus in all cataloging principles and practice.
> All other considerations, such as convenience and the desire to
> arrange entries in some logical order, are secondary to the basic
> rule that the heading, in wording and structure, should be that
> which the reader will seek in the catalog, if we know or can presume
> what the reader will look under. To the extent that the headings
> represent the predilection of the cataloger in regard to terminology
> and are dictated by conformity to a chosen logical pattern, as
> against the likely approach of the reader resting on psychological
> rather than logical grounds, the subject catalog will lose in effec-
> tiveness and ease of approach.[2]

What this principle means is self-evident, but how to make it operational is
not. The problem is delineating the user.

Cutter did not appear to have difficulty knowing users and usage. In a
recent study on the subject, Francis Miksa offers an explanation: "For Cutter,
... the public was notably regular in its habits. In fact, he spoke of the habits of
the public as being prominent enough to be observed and in a certain sense
charted."[3] Users of libraries in Cutter's time probably were more
homogeneous, as Miksa suggests, and more easily defined. However, the
continuing emphasis on the "convenience of the public" in spite of changing
historical context has led to difficulty in defining or delineating the user. As
users became more diversified, questions concerning them were being asked
constantly: Who is the user? Is there such a thing as a typical user? A number
of writers on the subject catalog have pointed out the difficulty.

Robert A. Colby: "A general obstacle to putting this principle into
practice, is the lack of axiomatic knowledge about readers' habits and of valid
methods to study the readers' use of the catalog. With the readers of interest
here, there is the additional problem of their heterogeneity."[4]

John W. Metcalfe: "[Cutter] did not see clearly or satisfactorily resolve
the conflict of 'usage' with a consistent 'grammar' of headings and
subheadings.... Obviously the usage principle is a confusing one for the
cataloguer to apply and for the catalogue user to follow."[5]

R. K. Olding: "Cutter's admission of the usage principle, or rather his
failure to define it adequately, has probably made for more inconsistency in
the dictionary catalogue than anything else."[6]

Marie Louise Prevost asks the most cogent question on this point:

> What is the "public" which we, in general libraries, serve through
> the catalog? Children, young people, adults; the expert, the inept,
> the illiterate, the savant; scientists, artists, authors, teachers, and —
> librarians. Once the diverse nature of the users of the catalog is
> recognized, it becomes a patent absurdity to speak of cataloging
> according to the "public" mind as if that mind were a single entity.[7]

Paul S. Dunkin also seriously questions the validity of such an approach:

> Is there such a creature as "the public," or are there many publics,
> each with its individual varieties and needs? Studies will, no doubt,

continue as long as cash can be found to pay for them. Suppose some study were to succeed; suppose it were to show that there is only one user and to identify that user and his needs and habits. Would we dare to build a catalog around those habits and needs? Perhaps not. Habits and needs change; this year's man will not be the same man next year. A catalog built on this year's public's habits and needs might hinder next year's public.[8]

In spite of numerous user studies and subject catalog use studies, it has never been made clear who and what kind of person this user is who is supposed to hold such powerful sway over the form and shape of the catalog. Yet the policy of the "convenience of the public" continues to operate, usually on the premise that the user is the kind of person catalogers assume he or she might be and might behave. Though a bit harsh, Dunkin's comment on the reason for following such a policy perhaps contains some truth: "On the one hand, it has a noble ring; who can deny that libraries exist to serve? One would as soon attack mother love or home. On the other hand, it is convenient; it gives us an excuse to do almost anything in the catalog."[9]

Until the early 1980s, the nature of the user remained elusive because of a dearth of scientific studies that focused on catalog users and their habits. In the 1980s, with the development of the online public catalog, a series of catalog use studies[10] has been undertaken. These studies have been conducted with scientific methods and more sophisticated instruments than were available to those conducting earlier catalog use studies. From these studies, new profiles of users emerge. A significant finding is that a majority of users use the online catalog for subject search.[11] Although the users remain diverse in their background, needs, and habits, many of them share a common characteristic: most have difficulty with the subject searching process in online catalogs. With increasing knowledge of how the catalogs are being used, improving the Library of Congress subject headings system in order to meet the needs of online catalog users becomes a challenge for the years ahead.

Related to the question of the nature of the user is the issue of linguistic usage. In naming the subjects in the catalog, Cutter proposes usage of the public as the guiding principle: "General rules, always applicable, for the choice of names of subjects can no more be given than rules without exception in grammar. Usage in both cases is the supreme arbiter, the usage, in the present case, not of the cataloger but of the public in speaking of subjects."[12] Haykin phrases the principle of usage in these terms:

> The heading chosen must represent common usage or, at any rate, the usage of the class of reader for whom the material on the subject within which the heading falls is intended. Usage in an American library must inevitably mean current American usage. Unless this principle is adhered to faithfully most readers will not find the material they desire under the heading which first occurs to them, if they find it at all.[13]

Thus, there are basically two approaches to the problem. The first, proposed by Cutter, is to consider usage as the supreme arbiter in the choice of form and language, having priority over logic or philosophy. However, the diversity of users and the difficulty and perhaps impossibility of defining usage make codification of cataloging practice extremely difficult. In the case of the

Library of Congress subject headings list, part of the difficulty arises from the fact that the list, which was originally designed for the Library's own collection, now serves also as a general standard for a variety of other libraries. Features and characteristics that were developed to meet the demands of a large general research collection may not always be suitable for the other types of libraries that also use the list. This makes the notions of user and usage even more amorphous and difficult to define.

The second approach is to attempt to develop a system that adheres to logic and strictly formed principles, assuming that a logical and consistent system can be learned by the user. Because of recent technological developments in cataloging, there is a need for a system that can be easily adapted to machine manipulation. In this context, there is an increasing demand for consistency and uniformity.

UNIFORM HEADING

The principle of uniform heading is most closely associated with descriptive cataloging. The entry for an author's name is made under a uniform heading so that all works by the same author will be grouped together in the catalog. This principle applies to subject entries also. In order to show what the library has on a given subject, each subject should appear in the catalog under one name and one form only. Haykin calls this the principle of unity: "A subject catalog must bring together under one heading all the books which deal principally or exclusively with the subject."[14] This principle is also explained in the introduction to *Sears List of Subject Headings*: "One uniform term must be selected from several synonyms and this term must be applied consistently to all works on the topic."[15]

The English language is rich in synonyms derived from different linguistic traditions. Many things are called by more than one name, and many concepts can be expressed in more than one way. Variant names for the same object or expressions for the same concept often occur in different geographic areas. There are also many near-synonyms that overlap so much it is impractical to distinguish between them and establish them as separate subject headings. In all these cases, one of the several possible names is chosen as the subject heading. If the name chosen appears in different forms, only one form is used.

The main reason stated by Cutter and other writers for grouping all material on a subject under one heading is to prevent the scattering of material on the same subject. Uniformity of terms was considered a remedy for the scattering that resulted from the earlier practice of catchword title entry, in which entry was made under a term used by the author of the work being cataloged. A true subject heading gathers all works on the same subject together, regardless of the author's choice of terminology.

However, the objective of listing all books on the same subject together can also be fulfilled by listing all works on that subject under each possible name or form. In other words, if the library has twenty books on a subject that can be expressed in five different terms, it is possible to list all the books repeatedly under each of the five possible headings. However, although this is physically possible, it is not economically feasible in a card or book catalog; it is expensive and it creates great bulk and congestion in the catalog.

Economy, therefore, was the other overriding reason for the adoption of the principle of uniform heading in a dictionary catalog.

As is the case for an author heading in descriptive cataloging, in establishing a subject heading, three choices are often required: name, form, and entry element. When a subject has more than one name, one must be chosen as the heading to represent all materials on that subject, regardless of authors' usage. For example, in *Library of Congress Subject Headings*, the heading **Ethics** is chosen from among these synonymous terms: Ethics; Deontology; Ethology; Moral philosophy; Moral science; Morality; Morals; and Practical ethics. **Oral medication** is chosen in preference to Drugs by mouth; Medication by mouth; or Peroral medication. Frequently, a word may be spelled in different ways, e.g., Esthetics or Aesthetics; Hotbeds or Hot-beds; Marihuana or Marijuana. Again, only one of the spellings is used in the heading.

When the name chosen for a heading can be expressed in different forms, e.g., a phrase, a term with a qualifier, or a subdivided form, only one may serve as the heading. For example, a choice must be made between Surgical diagnosis and Surgery—Diagnosis; between Cookery (Shrimp) and Cookery—Shrimp.

A further decision, on the entry element, may also be necessary if the term contains two or more elements and both or all could possibly serve as an entry point, for example,

Diagnosis, Surgical
Surgical diagnosis

Plants, Effect of light on
Effect of light on plants
Light on plants, Effect of

While in descriptive cataloging there exist detailed and elaborate rules governing the construction of name headings with regard to the choice of name, form, and entry element, there are no corresponding rules for subject headings. This lack of rules makes consistency and uniformity in the construction of headings extremely difficult to achieve. While the principle of uniform heading is observed in *Library of Congress Subject Headings* in general, there are many exceptions.

The principle of uniform heading renders *Library of Congress Subject Headings* essentially a single-entry (for each subject) system, as opposed to a multiple-entry (for the same subject) system, such as PRECIS (Preserved Context Index System, which is used in the *British National Bibliography*). In PRECIS, the principle of uniform heading is applied to synonyms. However, in cases of multiple-term headings, the system requires a separate entry under each significant term. In such a system, the problem of entry element, which is of extreme importance in a single-entry system, does not exist. For example, in *Library of Congress Subject Headings*, we find the heading **Differential equations, Partial.** The same heading appears in three forms in PRECIS:

Partial differential equations   515'.353

Differential equations
    Partial differential equations   515'.353

Equations
    Partial differential equations   515'.353

Because PRECIS has been developed for a bibliography based on an automated system, the display of multiple forms for the same heading does not entail the same kind of economic burden as in a manually operated cumulative catalog.

While the multiplication of entries in a card or book catalog has been a major concern, the problem must be viewed differently in an online environment. In a card catalog, a separate record must be created for each entry (subject, author, or title), and each record can be accessed through only one access point—the heading for that particular record. In an automated system, each bibliographic item requires only one record, which can be retrieved through multiple access points. A record that has been assigned the index term Partial differential equations can be accessed through any of the three words in the term, instead of only the beginning word. As a result, the principle of uniform heading must be viewed in a different light in an online retrieval system. (See chapter 11 for further discussion.)

In *Library of Congress Subject Headings*, a heading in the form of a phrase may be entered either in its natural word order or in the inverted form, but not both. In this type of heading, the principle of uniform heading is observed almost without exception. In other forms of headings, particularly headings with subdivisions, exceptions to the practice of uniform heading are occasionally made. Haykin mentions several types of "duplicate entry."[16] When two components of a heading are equally significant and a reasonable or logical choice of entry element between the two cannot be made, duplicate entries are often made, e.g.,

1.   **United States—Foreign relations—France.**
2.   **France—Foreign relations—United States.**

1.   **English literature—Translations from Chinese.**
2.   **Chinese literature—Translations into English.**

These are duplicate entries in the true sense of the term, i.e., entries that are conceptually the same. The two headings assigned in each case are identical or reciprocal in wording, though with different entry elements.

Another type of duplicate entry, Haykin explains, is used "when a heading for which local subdivision is not provided must be used for a topic which is treated definitely with reference to a place."[17] In this case, a duplicate entry is made under the next broader heading that admits of local subdivision. For a work about gnatcatchers in California, the duplicate entries would be:

1.   **Gnatcatchers.**
2.   **Birds—California.**

As a matter of fact, this practice does not really violate the principle of uniform heading, since these headings represent overlapping but different concepts rather than two different forms of the same heading. Figure 2.1 illustrates the difference between the two types of duplicate entry.

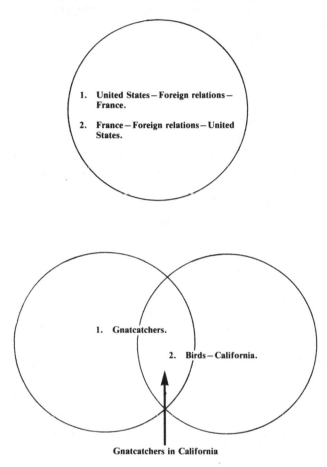

1. United States — Foreign relations — France.

2. France — Foreign relations — United States.

1. Gnatcatchers.

2. Birds — California.

Gnatcatchers in California

Figure 2.1. The two types of duplicate entry.

While the use of duplicate entries of the first type is relatively limited in Library of Congress subject cataloging practice, the latter type, using overlapping headings to represent the content of a document, is quite pervasive. (For details on assigning duplicate entries, see chapter 8.)

TERMINOLOGY

Subject headings are verbal representations of the contents of library materials. A great deal of the effectiveness of a subject headings system depends on the choice of terms used in forming the headings. The objective is to effect a perfect match between the term chosen by the user in search of information and the heading displayed in the catalog. In a system based on the principle of uniform heading, language — or the construction and display of the headings — is extremely important.

With the English language, three problems are of particular significance: (1) choosing among synonyms, (2) distinguishing between homographs, and (3) keeping up with changing usage. An object or concept can often be expressed by more than one term or in more than one way. A subject may acquire different names in different geographic areas or at different times. Conversely, the same word may carry different meanings. Both synonyms and homographs are problems that must be dealt with in the construction of subject headings.

Synonyms

Whenever a subject can be represented by more than one term, the principle of uniform heading requires that a choice be made among candidate terms. As stated earlier, the guiding principle in the choice has been common usage. Cutter, Haykin, and other writers have offered general guidelines* regarding choice of terms in the following categories: synonymous terms, variant spellings, English and foreign terms, technical (or scientific) and popular terms, and obsolete and current terms.

Choice among synonymous terms

Cutter's rule 169 states:

In choosing between synonymous headings prefer the one that —

(a) is most familiar to the class of people who consult the library....
(b) is most used in other catalogs.
(c) has fewest meanings other than the sense in which it is employed.
(d) comes first in the alphabet, so that the reference from the other can be made to the exact page of the catalog.
(e) brings the subject into the neighborhood of related subjects.[18]

---

*In the choice of proper names, the problem involves more than usage alone. Since most proper names used as subject headings also serve as main and added entries, a coordination between descriptive cataloging and subject cataloging is necessary. The choice and forms of proper names are discussed in chapter 6.

Choices (a) and (b) concern usage, choice (c) aims at providing a distinctive term for a subject, choice (d) concerns mainly the printed catalog and has been generally ignored in other forms of catalogs, and choice (e) betrays Cutter's desire to achieve, whenever possible, a degree of subject collocation in an alphabetical subject catalog. An example of a Library of Congress subject heading that conforms to Cutter's rule is the choice of **Church history** instead of Ecclesiastical history.

There is also the problem of near-synonymous terms, as Thelma Eaton points out: "Much more of a problem than synonyms are the near-synonymous terms.... There are other subjects that are not exactly the same, but they are closely related and it is easy to put them together under one heading."[19] Cutter's instruction concerning near-synonymous terms is: "In choosing between two names not exactly synonymous, consider whether there is difference enough to require separate entry; if not, treat them as synonymous."[20] There are many examples in the Library of Congress list of near-synonyms treated as synonyms. For example, Religious history is treated as a synonym of **Church history**, and Freedom is treated as a synonym of **Liberty**.

Choice between variant spellings

Needless to say, a current spelling is preferred to an obsolete one at the time of establishing a heading. The existence of some obsolete spellings in the Library of Congress list is due to the fact that the spelling changed after the heading was established and the heading has not yet been updated. In recent years, much effort has been devoted to updating terminology, for instance, from Aeroplanes to **Airplanes**. For variant spellings that are in use concurrently, American spellings are preferred, e.g., **Labor** instead of Labour; **Catalog** instead of Catalogue. In other cases, the choice follows *Webster's Third New International Dictionary*, e.g., **Aesthetics** instead of Esthetics; **Archaeology** instead of Archeology.

Choice between English and foreign terms

The choice would appear to be obvious. A catalog designed to serve English-speaking users should naturally rely on English terms. Yet there are exceptions. Cutter's rule concerning language states: "When possible let the heading be in English, but a foreign word may be used when no English word expresses the subject of a work."[21] Haykin states the rule in the following terms:

Foreign terms should be used only under the following conditions: (1) when the concept is foreign to Anglo-American experience and no satisfactory term for it exists, e.g., *Reallast, Précieuses*; and (2) when, especially in the case of scientific names, the foreign term is precise, whereas the English one is not, e.g., *Ophiodon elongatus*, rather than *Buffalo cod* or *Blue cod*; *Pityrosporum ovale*, rather than *Bottle bacillus*. Terms of foreign origin, which retain their foreign form, but which have been incorporated into the English vocabulary are, of course, to be regarded as English words, e.g., *Terrazzo, Sauerkraut.*[22]

Following the principle of common usage, the Library of Congress chooses English terms as a matter of general policy.[23] However, in a case where there is no English term for the concept and the concept is normally expressed in the foreign term even in English-language works and reference sources, the foreign term is chosen, for example, **Laissez-faire; Coup d'état; Tsunamis; Bonsai.** Also, a foreign term is chosen if, after proper authority research, no citation to the concept expressed by a foreign term can be found in any English-language source and the concept appears to be unique to the language of the work being cataloged, e.g., **Groupement d'intérêt économique.** In such cases, the headings will be replaced later if English-language equivalents are subsequently found.

Choice between technical (or scientific) and popular terms

Cutter states:

A natural history society will of course use the scientific name, a town library would equally of course use the popular name — **Butterflies** rather than **Lepidoptera, Horse** rather than **Equus caballus.** But the scientific may be preferable when the common name is ambiguous or of ill-defined extent.[24]

Haykin echoes Cutter's principle:

Whether a popular term or a scientific one is to be chosen depends on several considerations. If the library serves a miscellaneous public, it must prefer the popular to the scientific term. It may even prefer it, if the popular term is commonly used in the professional or scientific literature; in speaking of the genus bee in general, for example, even the scientists will use the term "bee" rather than *Apis.* However, the popular term must be precise and unambiguous.[25]

On another occasion, Haykin further explains:

The choice is not difficult because, obviously, in a catalog intended for a miscellaneous public the popular term must be used as the kind most likely to be resorted to by the largest group of users, whereas scientific terms, although usually more precise in their meanings, will be sought by the specialist in each field and are, therefore, suitable for a special library catalog.[26]

The user is the focus in both Cutter's and Haykin's statements. Both allow that the choice must be different in a general library serving a general public from that in a special library serving specialists.

In the Library of Congress list, popular terms are generally used, e.g., **Cockroaches** instead of Blattariae; **Lizards** instead of Lacertilia. However, for animals and plants, while the common name is preferred if it is in general use and unambiguous, the Latin name is chosen if the common name represents several levels (species, genus, family), if it is not in general lay usage, or if the organism occurs only in a foreign country or countries.

Choice between obsolete and current terms

In establishing a new heading, the choice between an obsolete term and a current term presents no problem, provided that one term is clearly more current than the other(s). The only problem is, how does one recognize an obsolete term? Personal knowledge of the language is a help but not always a reliable guide. Frequently, outside sources must be consulted. Dictionaries seem to be the natural tool, but Haykin expresses reservations about the use of dictionaries as the source of subject headings: "Dictionaries record both older terms no longer in use and terms in use at the time of the compilation of the dictionary. They do not usually indicate a choice on the basis of currency."[27] He considers periodicals to be the "surest sources" of usage because they carry the most current literature on various subjects. However, in dealing with new subjects, a heading is needed immediately, often before its terminology is settled. A new invention or concept is sometimes called different names by different people, and the cataloger is in the position of having to choose among several possible names without much help or guidance from outside sources. One example was the choice of Electronic calculating-machines as the heading for computers when they first appeared, a heading which has since been replaced by **Computers**.

A further problem is that common usage is not stable. Many terms once in common use become obsolete. Others acquire different meanings. For example, the terms Negroes and Blacks refer to the same ethnic group, but the former term, which was once the standard term used in subject headings, has acquired a pejorative connotation in the social context and is considered objectionable; it was replaced by the headings **Blacks** and **Afro-Americans**.

Theoretically, an established heading that has become obsolete should be replaced by a current one. Haykin points out the need for constant revision:

> [The cataloger] must use the term in the sense in which it is currently used, regardless of the older literature in and out of the catalog. This leads inevitably to a policy of constant change in order to maintain the catalog up to date. To put this policy into effect the cataloger must substitute the latest heading for the one which is obsolescent or obsolete and must refer the reader to the current heading from the headings which have fallen into disuse.[28]

However, in practice, economic considerations have played an important role. It is costly to change existing subject entries in a manually operated catalog, especially when a large number of items is already cataloged under the heading. The Library of Congress must consider not only its own interests, but also the needs of all the libraries that use the list. This is why until recent years it has been rather conservative in revising obsolete headings. This is why headings such as Electronic calculating-machines and Aeroplanes remained in the list long after they went out of common use. In the 1960s and 1970s, outdated terminology was the most criticized aspect of the list, much more so than structural aspects. An example of such criticism was Sanford Berman's analysis of subject headings relating to people.[29] Since 1975, the Library of Congress Subject Cataloging Division has made considerable effort to update obsolete terms.

Homographs

A corollary to the rule that a subject should be represented by only one term is the rule that each heading should represent only one subject. A problem arises when dealing with homographs. Cutter's rule states: "Carefully separate the entries on different subjects bearing the same name, or take some other heading in place of one of the homonyms."[30] Frequently, "some other heading" may not be available. In such a case, a modifier is added to differentiate between the homographs, e.g., **Cold; Cold (Disease)**, so that each subject or concept is represented by a unique heading. The principle of unique heading is an important factor in improving precision in retrieval, in other words, in reducing the number of irrelevant records retrieved.

SPECIFIC ENTRY AND COEXTENSIVITY

Specific and Direct Entry

In the literature, the concepts of specific entry and direct entry are almost always addressed together. For that reason, they are discussed together here. It is worth noting, however, that the two concepts are quite different in nature. Specificity is a many-faceted notion, used in talking about terms themselves and about the match between the meaning of a given term and the content of the document to which it is applied. The concept of directness involves the way a heading of given specificity is presented, by itself or in context. An entry with the heading **Creeping fescue** is a direct entry, while an entry with the equally specific heading **Ground covers – Lawn grasses – Creeping fescue** is an indirect entry. The difference between the concepts of specificity and directness is not always recognized, a fact that often makes it difficult to ferret out what writers mean when they talk about specificity and specific entry.

In *Rules for a Dictionary Catalog*, Cutter claims that the rule of specific entry is the main distinction between the dictionary catalog and the alphabetico-classed catalog. His explanation of the rule of specific entry is: "Enter a work under its subject-heading, not under the heading of a class which includes the subject.... Put Lady Cust's book on 'The cat' under **Cat**, not under **Zoölogy** or **Mammals**, or **Domestic animals**; and put Garnier's 'Le fer' under **Iron**, not under **Metals** or **Metallurgy**."[31]

The Vatican code states the principle of specific entry in these terms: "Works are recorded under their specific subjects, and not under the names and designations of the classes and disciplines to which they belong, e.g., **Poll-tax**, not **Taxation** or **Finance**."[32]

From these statements and examples, it would appear that the difference between the alphabetico-classed catalog and the dictionary catalog in the treatment of the subject Cats represents a choise between **Zoology** and **Cats** as the subject heading. Such is, in fact, not the case. In an alphabetico-classed catalog, the heading for a book on cats would presumably be **Zoology — Vertebrates — Mammals — Domestic animals — Cats**, and not **Zoology** alone. In terms of the degree of specificity, this heading is as specific as the heading **Cats**. The real difference is in the choice of the entry element, or the access point in the catalog. In the alphabetico-classed catalog, in order to find the subject Cats, the user must look under **Zoology**, while in the dictionary catalog, the subject is listed under **Cats** without intervening elements. This is what is meant by direct entry: the user looks directly under the term that specifically describes the topic rather than under a broader term that includes the specific term as a subdivision.

E. J. Coates analyzes the problem in these terms:

> The difficulty and confusion in Cutter's thinking about subject headings arises from his intermittent failure to distinguish between the criteria applicable to a complete subject heading on the one hand and to an entry word on the other.... He fails to distinguish two separate stages in subject cataloguing a work for the alpha-betico-specific catalogue. The first stage is the naming of the work's specific subject, the second is the selection of a particular part of a compound name to serve as entry word.[33]

With regard to the first stage, i.e., the naming of the work's specific subject, there is no fundamental difference between the alphabetico-classed catalog and the dictionary catalog. The difference lies in the arrangement of the headings in the catalog resulting from different entry elements for the same heading. In the alphabetico-classed catalog, headings are arranged to a large extent according to their subject relationships. Each heading begins with the broadest term and contains a hierarchical chain of terms leading to the specific subject, an arrangement that results in grouping related subjects together. In the dictionary catalog, subject relationships are abandoned in favor of alphabetical arrangement for the sake of ready or direct access.

Haykin clarifies this point by stating:

> In effect the headings for a given topic in an alphabetico-classed and a dictionary catalog are equally specific. The difference lies in the fact that in the former the specific topic is the last element in a complex heading, whereas in the latter it is named directly; what distinguishes the subject heading in a present-day dictionary catalog from other forms is that it is both specific and direct.[34]

Cutter refers to the effect of direct access as the "facility of reference,"[35] which he considers the primary objective of the dictionary catalog. In using an alphabetico-classed catalog, the user usually requires the assistance of an alphabetical index. The dictionary catalog combines the subject headings list and the index, thereby saving the user the extra effort of consulting a separate index, but losing the advantage of subject collocation.

Questions may be raised about the relative advantages and disadvantages of each kind of catalog. Cutter claims that the objective of the dictionary catalog is "to show at one view all the sides of each object; the classed catalog shows together the same side of many objects."[36] At the same time, Cutter also recognizes some of the disadvantages of the dictionary, or alphabetical, arrangement:

> The systematic catalog undertakes to exhibit a scientific arrangement of the books in a library in the belief that it will thus best aid those who would pursue any extensive or thorough study. The dictionary catalog sets out with another object and a different method.... Its subject entries, individual, general, limited, extensive, thrown together without any logical arrangement, in most absurd proximity, ... are a mass of utterly disconnected particles without any relation to one another, each useful in itself but only by itself.[37]

Cutter's views are echoed by Julia Pettee:

> The superiority of the alphabetical subject catalog over the classed catalog rests not only upon its direct access to specific subject matter without the intermediary of an index to a classification scheme, but also upon its ability to collect material from different fields under a topical name, and this is its supreme claim to distinction.
>
> Its disadvantage is, of course, that the alphabetical dispersion of topics makes it impossible to assemble logically related material brought together in a linear classification scheme.[38]

In order to achieve the benefit of direct access in the catalog, the advantages of subject collocation must be abandoned. However, in the course of the development of the dictionary catalog in American libraries, there seems to have been a constant desire to have the best of both worlds, especially in the earlier stages, when users as well as makers of subject headings were still accustomed to the classed catalog. The recognition of the advantage of direct access has often been accompanied by the desire to maintain as well the advantage of the classed catalog of grouping related subjects together. As a result, many headings that are characteristic of an alphabetico-classed catalog have been introduced into the dictionary catalog over the years.

This phenomenon is manifested in *Library of Congress Subject Headings*. The source of this development is analyzed by Richard S. Angell:

> For the most part, the subject headings used in these catalogs [of the Library of Congress] derive from statements of "objects" and "means" formulated by Charles Ammi Cutter in his *Rules for a Dictionary Catalog*.... While the early officers were in accord with Cutter and the majority of United States libraries in rejecting the classified or alphabetico-classed catalog in favor of the dictionary catalog, they were unwilling to contemplate the dispersion of headings that could follow from full adherence to Cutter's rule of specific entry, at least in its application to compound headings.

They preferred to combine elements of a dictionary and a classified arrangement. The fact that the Library's subject headings began as a mixed system opened the door to inconsistent decisions as the catalog grew.[39]

The cost of the compromise has been the loss of consistency and predictability of the forms of headings. There is a basic difference between the forms of headings in alphabetico-classed catalogs and in dictionary catalogs. Coates points out the incompatibility between specific direct entries and the alphabetico-classed entries: "Specific alphabetical entry designed to give the enquirer immediate access to his subject ... is incompatible with the assembly of entries on related subjects. The alphabetico-specific catalogue arranges headings by their affinities of spelling, the classified and the alphabetico-classed forms arrange their entries by affinities of meaning."[40] To intersperse alphabetico-classed headings in a dictionary catalog is to invite inconsistency, particularly when there are no rigorous rules or guidelines concerning the extent to which such headings can be introduced. This has been the case with the *Library of Congress Subject Headings*, particularly among inverted headings and certain headings with subdivisions. (These are discussed in detail in later chapters.)

Concept of Specificity

There is another source of difficulty with the principle of specific entry beyond the fact that it is often confused or melded with the notion of direct entry. This difficulty comes in defining the very concept of specificity. From Cutter on, there have been various attempts at definition.

Cutter: "Enter a work under its subject-heading, not under the heading of a class which includes that subject."[41]

Haykin: "The heading should be as specific as the topic it is intended to cover. As a corollary, the heading should not be broader than the topic."[42]

Sears List of Subject Headings: "The rule of specific and direct entry is to enter a work directly under the most specific term, i.e., subject heading, which accurately and precisely represents its content. This word serves as a succinct abstract of the work."[43]

Oliver Linton Lilley, in an inquiry into the meaning and nature of specificity, identifies at least four types of relationships that determine its nature:

1. Specificity is in part a function of a particular subject area.

2. Specificity is in part a function of a particular library.

3. Specificity is in part a function of a particular book.

4. Specificity is in part a function of a searcher's exact need in a particular moment of time.[44]

Later writers on subject analysis continue to search for a workable definition of specificity. Among the more successful recent attempts are the studies by John Balnaves and Elaine Svenonius. Balnaves[45] summarizes five inter-related but distinguishable aspects of the term:

1. The manner in which one term can be said to be subordinate to, and more specific than another in a hierarchical arrangement of terms....

2. The extent to which a characteristic which distinguishes a document class is precisely labelled by a descriptor....

3. The extent to which each descriptor provides direct access to the file for the class of documents which it labels....

4. The extent to which each descriptor is a precise and exact label for the smallest class to which a document belongs....

5. The extent to which descriptors are assigned to classes to which parts of documents belong, as well as to classes to which the whole document belongs.

His final conclusion is: "Whatever improves precision is specificity."

Svenonius identifies seven types of specificity. They are, in summary:

(i) Formal Specificity: Specificity can be defined in terms of the logical relation of class inclusion.

(ii) Extensional Specificity: In ordinary language the specificity relation (regarded as inclusion) is used with logical precision when it holds between classes that can be clearly defined in extensional or referential terms.

(iii) Phrase-length Specificity: One extension of the inclusion relation into the domain of non-referential language is when specification is regarded as modifying. There are exceptions but generally it holds that a word modified is more specific than the word unmodified.

(iv) Coercive Specificity: The specificity relation can be defined more or less well by enumerating all the pairs of objects (words) between which the relation is supposed to hold.

(v) Componential Specificity: A quantitative measure of specificity has been developed by Thyllis Williams. Roughly the specificity of a word is proportional to the complexity of its dictionary definition, where definition complexity is understood in terms of both the descriptive components and the syntax of the definition.

(vi) Consensus Specificity: Presumably there exists some partial consistency in different people's opinions about specificity, a consensus whose bounds are unknown but which might be measurable using sociolinguistic experimental methods.

(vii) Operational Specificity: Operational specificity is defined in the context of indexing, or assigning subject headings to books in a library. The operational specificity of an index term is the number of books in the collection indexed by the term. Operational specificity is decidedly relative, but it is so in a clear, mathematically measurable way. Its relativity reflects the very legitimate variability not of "specific", but of "specific (precise) enough for some purpose." Further, the definition of operational specificity goes some way to make explicit the concept of specificity as it is understood in the application of the specific entry principle. It does this insofar as the function of the principle is to regulate the number of entries that accumulate under any one heading. Moreover, an operational definition of specificity is useful in that it provides a method for systematically varying indexing specificity. That is, the definition makes it possible to approach experimentally the question: "How specific is specific?".[46]

Although these writers differ in their approaches and definitions of the concept of specificity, there appears to be a certain degree of agreement that specificity is a relative term and must be viewed in a particular context. The term takes on different meanings depending on the context. Some of the common frames of reference in which the concept of specificity has been defined are discussed below.

1) *Specificity in relation to the hierarchical structure of a particular indexing language.* This is sometimes referred to as term specificity, or what Metcalfe calls "subject specification."[47] The specificity of a term is defined in relation to other terms in the same indexing language. In this context, the indexing term on a lower level of a hierarchical chain is said to be more specific than one on a higher level. In this respect, the relationship between general and specific terms is similar to that of broad and narrow terms (or broad and close, with regard to classification). In such a context, **Cats** is more specific than **Mammals**, which in turn is more specific than **Vertebrates**. Although the specificity of a term can be easily ascertained in a two-dimensional hierarchical chain containing single-concept terms, problems arise when multidimensional hierarchies containing complex terms are involved. For example, it can be easily recognized that **Stomach** is more specific than **Digestive organs**, and that **Ulcers** is more specific than **Diseases**. It is not easy, however, to determine whether **Stomach – Diseases** or **Digestive organs – Ulcers** is the more specific

term. In such cases, the notions of specificity and generality become difficult to define.

Another problem relating to term specificity is how to determine the optimal level of specificity in a particular indexing language. On this question, F. W. Lancaster makes the following observation:

> However often a term is used in indexing, it is unjustified if, for instance, over a two-year period it has never been used in searching. This would indicate fairly clearly that the term is unnecessarily specific. Indexers use it because it is available and documents exist on the specific topic. However, requests are never made this specifically in this particular subject area so that a term at this level of specificity is redundant.[48]

An alternative to using frequency of use in searching as the criterion of term specificity is to view specificity in terms of frequency of application in indexing, as suggested by G. Salton and C. S. Yang:

> Term specificity ... may be assumed to be related to the number of documents to which a given term is assigned in a given collection, the idea being that the smaller the document frequency, that is, the more concentrated the assignment of a term to only a few documents in a collection, the more likely it is that a given term is reasonably specific.[49]

In her discussion of "operational specificity," Svenonius puts forth a similar view: "The operational specificity of an index term or subject heading is defined as the number of items in the collection indexed by the term, that is the number of postings made to the term; or in other words, the specificity of a term is its frequency of occurrence."[50] In this sense, the specificity of any term is relative to a particular collection of documents. As pointed out by Angell, the level of specificity should be determined "by the characteristics of the demands which are made upon an information system in a particular application or installation."[51]

This is certainly true of the Library of Congress subject headings system. Specificity in that system has been based on the nature and extent of the collection at the Library of Congress. New headings are established as they are required in cataloging the Library's collection, and subdivisions are often developed because of the large number of postings under a particular heading in the catalog. However, as the system has been adopted by many other libraries, the determination of the optimal degree of specificity poses a unique problem for those responsible for its development and maintenance. Because the list has become the standard one for all but very small libraries and some specialized libraries, it must now try to perform the impossible task of being all things to all people. The various demands placed on the system by other libraries, many of which are vastly different in size, function, and clientele, are often incompatible and even conflicting. As a result, it has been difficult to achieve consistency and uniformity in determining the optimal level of specificity throughout the system.

2) *Specificity in relation to the document being indexed.* In this case, a specific heading is one that coincides with, or corresponds to, the content of the document being represented. This appears to be what Cutter had in mind when he advised putting Lady Cust's book under **Cats** rather than **Zoology** or **Mammals**. Miksa interprets Cutter's definition of specificity in these terms:

> For Cutter, identifying the specific subject of a work was not an exercise in making the most complete description possible of a work's aboutness, using language as the ultimate measuring device. Rather, it meant to locate a work at the narrowest point possible in an already established order of subjects independent of the work. Determining a work's specific subject did not refer to assigning a label to a book that uniquely characterized its subject totality by some measure of entirety, but rather referred to assigning the work to a label that was the most appropriate one available in a system of labels already extant.[52]

Metcalfe uses the term *document specification*[53] for this aspect of specificity. Another term now often used to express this aspect of specificity is *coextensivity*. The degree to which this kind of specificity is achieved is partly the function of the indexing language and partly that of application in the indexing process. In this respect, the specificity of a particular indexing term is viewed in relation to the document to which it is assigned and not to its place in the hierarchical structure of the indexing language. A specific heading is not necessarily a narrow one, nor a general heading always a broad one. In other words, *general* is not synonymous with *broad*, nor *specific* with *narrow*.

The heading **Zoology** is generally considered broad, and the heading **Cats** narrow. The heading **Zoology** is general when applied to a work about cats. However, for a work of zoology, the heading **Zoology** becomes as specific as the heading **Cats** is for a work about cats. On the other hand, the heading **Cats** when applied to a work about Siamese cats is a general heading. In this context, a specific heading is one that corresponds to the content of the document to which it is applied, while a general heading is one that represents the class to which the subject content of the document is subordinate. With regard to the meaning of the term *specificity* in relationship to the document, the Library of Congress recently issued the following statement:

> Specificity means that subject headings should exactly cover the topic of the work cataloged, being neither broader or narrower than the topic.... Specificity is not a property of an individual term or subject heading, but is relative to the relationship between the term or subject heading and the work to which it is applied. The "broad" heading "Economics" is specific when applied to a general work on economics.[54]

In practice, the question is whether specificity (i.e., coextensivity) is always achievable or even desirable. Achievability depends partly on the indexing language; one cannot use a term if it is not in the list. Haykin comments on this aspect:

If the subject catalog were to consist of a predetermined number of more or less broad headings, a work on a specific topic would have to be entered under the broader one. The broader heading would thus be used for works as comprehensive as the heading, as well as for works on all the topics comprehended by it. To find out whether the library possesses a book on a specific topic, the reader would, in the first place, need to know how broad a heading might be used for it, and, in the second place, would have to scan all the entries under the broader heading in order to select those which are of interest to him. Even then, he would be able to identify only those of which the titles clearly indicate the subject; conceivably the titles might be cryptic, even misleading.[55]

The lack of specificity in this sense of the term results in generic posting, i.e., listing works under headings broader than their contents.

Whether specificity is always desirable is also open to question. There seems to be a general assumption that perfectly coextensive headings should be used if possible. The statements by Cutter and Haykin quoted earlier seem to imply precisely that. However, in practice this assumption has not always held. Haykin also states that "there are limits to the principle of specificity ... beyond which its application does not appear to serve the best interest of the reader."[56] For example, should a book about storm petrels be entered under **Storm petrels; Petrels; Sea birds;** or **Birds**? Should a book about the Volkswagen Rabbit be entered under **Rabbit automobile; Volkswagen automobile;** or **Automobiles**? The answers must necessarily vary with regard to the nature and extent of the collection and the needs of the users. Even in PRECIS, which aims at coextensive entries, the most specific term is not always considered the most useful. For example, the string assigned to a work entitled *Disruptive Behavior in Schools: The Report of a Working Party of the Essex County Teacher's Association* is:

Schools. Students. Behavior problems. Essex. Reports, surveys.
The particular kind of behavior is not specified.

In the application of the Library of Congress subject headings system, attempts are generally made to achieve coextensivity by assigning specific headings whenever they are available, by creating such headings, or by assigning several separate headings (each broader than the content of the document being cataloged) in order to cover various aspects of a complex subject. (This practice is discussed further in chapter 8.)

3) *Specificity with regard to the depth of indexing.* Frequently, the term *specificity* is used to refer to the depth of indexing. The degree of specificity may be at the summarization level, where the subject headings represent the overall content of the document, or it may be at a deeper level, where the terms chosen represent the individual components. Depth indexing results in a large number of headings assigned to each document in order to cover the individual parts or units within the document. The number of terms assigned is largely a matter of indexing policy rather than the nature of the indexing language; the same thesaurus or subject headings list can in most cases be used either way.

The degree of the depth of indexing is generally determined by the demands of the users and, not infrequently, by the availability of personnel and resources. The Library of Congress follows a policy of summarization rather than indexing in depth. (This aspect of Library of Congress practice is discussed in detail in chapter 8.)

Precoordination and Synthesis

Generally, the content of a document falls into one of the following categories:

a single subject or concept, or single subjects or concepts treated separately in a work, e.g., Flowers; Flowers and shrubs

aspect(s) of a subject or concept, e.g., Fertilization of flowers; Arrangement of flowers; Collecting and preserving flowers

two or more subjects treated in relation to each other, e.g., Flowers in art; Flowers in religion, folklore, etc.

It is clear from this list that except for single subjects, document content cannot always or even often be represented by single terms or simple adjectival phrases. When this is the case, if the principle of specificity is to be followed, document contents must be represented by headings formed with some sort of combining device. Mortimer Taube identifies two types of specificity: "The specificity of a specific word or phrase and whatever degree of subdivision is allowed" and "the specificity achieved by the intersection, coordination, or logical product of terms of equal generality."[57]

The first category listed above presents a problem only when a document treats a topic at a deeper level of specificity than is allowed for in the indexing vocabulary, or when users do not approach the system at such a level of specificity. Frequently with the second category (aspects) and always with the third category (relationships), a single term is not sufficient. In order to achieve the specificity required, two or more terms must be used. In many cases, specificity is achieved by using a phrase to combine two or more general terms, either of which is broader than the resulting heading, e.g., **Fertilization of flowers; Flowers in art; Effect of light on plants**. For example, for a document on the fertilization of flowers, both terms will be required in representing the subject. This is also true in the case of the subject Flowers in art.

Another way to represent complexity is to use two or more separate terms without indicating the nature of their relationship. Such an approach leaves it to searchers to track down documents indexed with terms reflecting all the aspects of the topics that interest them. The two different approaches are called precoordination and postcoordination. In a precoordinate system, terms for a topic and its aspects are linked at the time of indexing, with prepositions or other devices (punctuation or the structure of the string) showing how the terms interrelate. In a postcoordinate system, terms for the main subject and its aspects are simply listed separately. PRECIS is a highly precoordinate system; ERIC (Educational Resources Information Center) is a postcoordinate system. Many headings in *Library of Congress Subject Headings* show precoordination, and precoordinated headings are generally considered the ideal for complex subjects. But catalogers at the Library of Congress often take a postcoordinate approach. There have been complex headings in the Library of Congress list since the early editions, and the ratio of complex subject headings to the whole list grows with each edition—a circumstance that is perhaps a reflection of the increasingly complex nature of modern knowledge and the way it is presented. However, because of the lack of rules over the years to regulate specificity, the procedure used to combine terms has not been applied consistently. A recent statement from the Subject Cataloging Division of the Library of Congress acknowledges this: "Although *LCSH* is primarily a precoordinate system, practice under many headings requires postcoordination in order to achieve specificity. There are numerous cases in which we do not combine elements in the heading itself or in subdivisions in order to be specific. Decisions can be determined by looking at LC cataloging."[58]

In cataloging a book on a complex subject for which there is no coextensive heading in the *Library of Congress Subject Headings* list, the subject cataloger at the Library of Congress may either propose a new heading as required for the book being cataloged (a procedure currently preferred)[59] or choose to use several existing headings. There are many highly complex and specific headings in the list, such as:

> **Opening of the eyes of one blind at Bethsaide (Miracle)**
> **Church maintenance and repair (Ecclesiastical law)**
> **Suites (Clarinets (2), horns (2), violins (2), viola, double bass)**

On the other hand, for a work entitled *Zirconium Oxide Modes for Small Molybdenum Investment Castings*, instead of creating a new specific heading, the Library of Congress cataloger chose to use four separate headings:

1. **Molding material.**
2. **Zirconium oxide.**
3. **Precision casting.**
4. **Molybdenum castings.**

It is interesting here to review Cutter's solutions to the problems of complex subjects. With regard to Cutter's treatment of aspects of a subject, Jessica Lee Harris comments: "Nowhere in his rules does Cutter define specific entry explicitly enough to show whether he thought of it as including the aspect or point of view from which a subject is treated."[60] Cutter's classic example, Lady Cust's book entitled *The Cat*, has the subtitle *Its History and Diseases*, but these aspects are not reflected in Cutter's subject heading **Cats**. Nevertheless, there is scattered evidence that Cutter recognized the need for specifying aspects of a subject. Although he provides no explicit rules concerning subdivision, subdivision is implied in his rules for filing. The *Catalogue of the Library of the Boston Athenaeum*, for which Cutter was responsible, includes headings of the type **Cattle—Diseases**. In his rule for "compound subject-names," provisions are made by means of phrase headings for expressing aspects of a subject and relationships between two or more subjects. His rule 174 reads:

The name of a subject may be—

(a) A single word, as **Botany, Economics, Ethics,** or several words taken together, either—

(b) A noun preceded by an adjective, as **Ancient history, Capital punishment, Moral philosophy, Political economy.**

(c) A noun preceded by another noun used like an adjective, as **Death penalty, Flower fertilization.**

(d) A noun connected with another by a preposition, as **Penalty of death, Fertilization of flowers.**

(e) A noun connected with another by "and," as **Ancients and moderns.**

(f) A phrase or sentence, as in the titles "Sur la règle **Paterna paternis materna maternis**" and "De usu paroemiae juris Germanici, **Der Letzte thut die Thüre zu;**" where the whole phrase would be the subject of the dissertation.[61]

Although Cutter fails to distinguish between headings representing single concepts and those indicating complex relationships, it is clear from the rule that he recognizes the need for combining terms, or coordination, in order to represent complex subjects.

In dealing with a complex subject for which no single heading exists, it is sometimes difficult to predict which approach will be taken by the Library of Congress. In original cataloging, not knowing whether the Library of Congress will create a specific heading for the complex subject, and, if so, which form it will take, outside catalogers tend to follow the second approach and to use several existing, more general headings in order to bring out the various elements and/or aspects covered in the document. For example, *Library of Congress Subject Headings* contains the heading **Nuns as public school teachers,** but no single heading Public school teachers. Until such a heading is established—a likely occurrence when a subject cataloger at the Library of Congress encounters a work on that subject—subject catalogers outside of the Library of Congress will probably assign two headings, **Public schools** and **Teachers,** to such a work.

Means of Precoordination

Synthesis, the device used to express complex subjects by combining terms in a heading, takes several forms in the Library of Congress subject headings list:

o   Adjectival phrases

> **Economic forecasting**
> **Electronic marketing**
> **Plant diseases**
> **Plant inspection**

o Phrases containing conjunctions or followed by *etc.* (representing partial synonymy)

Boats and boating
Hotels, taverns, etc.

o Phrases containing conjunctions (representing relationships)

Church and education
Television and politics

o Phrases containing prepositions

Cookery for the sick
Deficiency diseases in plants
Fertilization of plants
Flowers in literature
Pantomimes with music

o Headings with qualifiers

Cookery (Chicken)
Finite fields (Algebra)

o Headings with subdivisions

Church architecture — Italy
Physics — Research
Plants — Identification

o Combinations of the forms above

Church and labor — Italy
Choruses, Secular (Unison) with instrumental ensemble
Clocks and watches in art
Piano, trumpet, viola with orchestra — Scores

There are no fixed rules concerning which form to choose in order to express a specific relationship. Usage, i.e., what may appear to be the form most likely to be consulted by the user, or existing patterns generally determine the choice of form. Over the years, preference and policies have varied. For example, in the past the geographic aspect of a subject has been expressed either by the phrase **[Subject] in [Location]** or the subdivided form **[Subject] — [Location]**. Recently, headings in the phrase form have been converted to the subdivided form, e.g., from Church and state in Bavaria to **Church and state — Germany (West) — Bavaria**; from Slavery in Matanzas, Cuba (Province) to **Slavery — Cuba — Matanzas (Province)**; from Catholic Church in Austria to **Catholic Church — Austria**.

With regard to use of the subdivided form, one must also consider the purpose. If, as Haykin[62] and Margaret Mann[63] claim, subdivision is a device for subarrangement, then it is required only when there is a considerable file under a given heading. If, on the other hand, the purpose of subdivision is to render the headings more specific, then subdivision is justified even if there is only one document under the subdivided term. (See further discussion in chapter 4.)

An important problem in forming precoordinated headings is that there are no fixed rules for the citation order in which terms are combined in headings. Because of the principle of uniform heading, only one term in a compound or complex heading is used as the entry element. The lack of a predictable order and of consistency among similar headings limits retrieval effectiveness, especially in manual catalogs.

There are indications that in some areas the Library of Congress subject headings system is moving toward a greater degree of term specificity and coextensivity. In music headings particularly, recent trends are toward more formularized coordination with fixed citation orders (see discussion on pages 272-274). As a result, many headings of similar types previously printed in the list have been removed because catalogers can now easily formulate the required headings according to the established patterns or citation formulae. The increasing use of free-floating subdivisions (see discussion in chapter 4) also provides a greater degree of synthesis than was allowed previously.

REFERENCES

[1]Charles A. Cutter, *Rules for a Dictionary Catalog*, 4th ed. (Washington, D.C.: Government Printing Office, 1904), 6.

[2]David Judson Haykin, *Subject Headings: A Practical Guide* (Washington, D.C.: Government Printing Office, 1951), 7.

[3]Francis Miksa, *The Subject in the Dictionary Catalog from Cutter to the Present* (Chicago: American Library Association, 1983), 74.

[4]Robert A. Colby, "Current Problems in the Subject Analysis of Literature," *Journal of Cataloging and Classification* 10:20 (January 1954).

[5]John W. Metcalfe, *Information Indexing and Subject Cataloging: Alphabetical: Classified: Coordinate: Mechanical* (New York: Scarecrow Press, 1957), 73, 77.

[6]R. K. Olding, "Form of Alphabetico-Specific Subject Headings, and a Brief Code," *Australian Library Journal* 10:128 (July 1961).

[7]Marie Louise Prevost, "An Approach to Theory and Method in General Subject Heading," *Library Quarterly* 16:140 (April 1946).

[8]Paul S. Dunkin, *Cataloging U.S.A.* (Chicago: American Library Association, 1969), 141-142.

[9]Ibid., 141.

[10]Carol A. Mandel and Judith Herschman, "Subject Access in the Online Catalog" (a Report prepared for the Council on Library Resources, August 1981); Charles R. Hildreth, *Online Public Access Catalogs: The User Interface* (Dublin, Ohio: OCLC, 1982); Joseph R. Matthews, Gary S. Lawrence, and Douglas K. Ferguson, eds., *Using Online Catalogs: A Nationwide Study* (New York: Neal-Schuman, 1983); Karen Markey, *The Process of Subject Searching in the Library Catalog* (Dublin, Ohio: OCLC, 1983); Markey, *Subject Searching in Library Catalogs: Before and after the Introduction of Online Catalogs* (Dublin, Ohio: OCLC, 1984).

[11]Markey, *Subject Searching in Library Catalogs*, 77.

[12]Cutter, *Rules for a Dictionary Catalog*, 69.

[13]Haykin, *Subject Headings*, 8.

[14]Ibid., 7.

[15]*Sears List of Subject Headings*, 12th ed., ed. Barbara M. Westby (New York: H. W. Wilson, 1982), 13.

[16]Haykin, *Subject Headings*, 57-60.

[17]Ibid., 59.

[18]Cutter, *Rules for a Dictionary Catalog*, 70.

[19]Thelma Eaton, *Cataloging and Classification: An Introductory Manual*, 4th ed. (Ann Arbor, Mich.: Edwards Brothers, 1967), 156.

[20]Cutter, *Rules for a Dictionary Catalog*, 70.

[21]Ibid., 69.

[22]Haykin, *Subject Headings*, 9.

[23]Library of Congress, Subject Cataloging Division, *Subject Cataloging Manual: Subject Headings*, prelim. ed. (Washington, D.C.: Library of Congress, 1984), H315.

[24]Cutter, *Rules for a Dictionary Catalog*, 70.

[25]Haykin, *Subject Headings*, 9.

[26]David Judson Haykin, "Subject Headings: Principles and Development," in *The Subject Analysis of Library Materials*, ed. Maurice F. Tauber (New York: School of Library Service, Columbia University, 1953), 50.

[27]Haykin, *Subject Headings*, 8.

[28]Ibid.

[29]Sanford Berman, *Prejudices and Antipathies: A Tract on the LC Subject Heads Concerning People* (Metuchen, N.J.: Scarecrow Press, 1971).

[30]Cutter, *Rules for a Dictionary Catalog*, 71.

[31]Ibid., 66.

[32]Vatican Library, *Rules for the Catalog of Printed Books*, trans. from the 2nd Italian edition by Thomas J. Shanahan, Victor A. Schaefer, and Constantin T. Vesselowsky, and ed. Wyllis E. Wright (Chicago: American Library Association, 1948), 250.

[33]E. J. Coates, *Subject Catalogues: Headings and Structure* (London: Library Association, 1960), 37.

[34]Haykin, *Subject Headings*, 3-4.

[35]Cutter, *Rules for a Dictionary Catalog*, 79.

[36]Ibid., 68.

[37]Ibid., 79.

[38]Julia Pettee, *Subject Headings: The History and Theory of the Alphabetical Subject Approach to Books* (New York: H. W. Wilson, 1947), 59.

[39]Richard S. Angell, "Library of Congress Subject Headings — Review and Forecast," in *Subject Retrieval in the Seventies: New Directions: Proceedings of an International Symposium*, ed. Hans (Hanan) Wellisch and Thomas D. Wilson (Westport, Conn.: Greenwood Publishing, 1972), 143-144.

[40]Coates, *Subject Catalogues*, 26.

[41]Cutter, *Rules for a Dictionary Catalog*, 66.

[42]Haykin, *Subject Headings*, 9.

[43]*Sears List of Subject Headings*, 12.

44Oliver Linton Lilley, "How Specific Is Specific?" *Journal of Cataloging and Classification* 11:4-5 (1955).

45John Balnaves, "Specificity," in *The Variety of Librarianship: Essays in Honour of John Wallace Metcalfe*, ed. W. Boyd Rayward (Sydney: Library Association of Australia, 1976), 54-55.

46Elaine Svenonius, "Metcalfe and the Principles of Specific Entry," in *The Variety of Librarianship*, 186-187.

47John W. Metcalfe, *Subject Classifying and Indexing of Libraries and Literature* (Sydney: Angus and Robertson, 1959), 278.

48F. W. Lancaster, *Vocabulary Control for Information Retrieval* (Washington, D.C.: Information Resources Press, 1972), 104.

49G. Salton and C. S. Yang, "On the Specification of Term Values in Automatic Indexing," *Journal of Documentation* 29:352 (December 1973).

50Svenonius, "Metcalfe and the Principles of Specific Entry," 183.

51Richard S. Angell, "Standards for Subject Headings: A National Program," *Journal of Cataloging and Classification* 10:193 (October 1954).

52Miksa, *The Subject in the Dictionary Catalog*, 53-54.

53Metcalfe, *Subject Classifying and Indexing of Libraries and Literature*, 278.

54Material distributed at Regional Institutes on Library of Congress Subject Headings, sponsored by ALA Resources and Technical Services Division, Library of Congress, ALA/RTSD Council of Regional Groups, 1982-1984.

55Haykin, *Subject Headings*, 9-10.

56Ibid., 10.

57Mortimer Taube, "Specificity in Subject Headings and Coordinate Indexing," *Library Trends* 1:222 (October 1952).

58Material distributed at Regional Institutes on Library of Congress Subject Headings.

59Library of Congress, *Subject Cataloging Manual*, H187.

60Jessica Lee Harris, *Subject Analysis: Computer Implications of Rigorous Definition* (Metuchen, N.J.: Scarecrow Press, 1970), 22.

[61]Cutter, *Rules for a Dictionary Catalog*, 71-72.

[62]Haykin, *Subject Headings*, 27.

[63]Margaret Mann, *Introduction to Cataloging and the Classification of Books*, 2nd ed. (Chicago: American Library Association, 1943), 146.

3

FORMS OF HEADINGS

INTRODUCTION

Subject headings in the Library of Congress system represent a mixture of natural and artificial forms of the English language. Single nouns, adjectival phrases, and prepositional phrases are based on natural forms and word order. On the other hand, headings with qualifiers, headings with subdivisions, and inverted headings are special forms that are not used in everyday speech.

Traditionally, forms of subject headings have been viewed in terms of their grammatical or syntactical structure, i.e., the way words are put together to form phrases or sentences. Charles A. Cutter names the following categories of subject headings in a dictionary catalog: a single word; a noun preceded by an adjective; a noun preceded by another noun used like an adjective; a noun connected with another by a preposition; a noun connected with another by *and*; a phrase or sentence.[1] In the Library of Congress system, the sentence form mentioned by Cutter is not used. David Judson Haykin identifies seven forms used in *Library of Congress Subject Headings*: noun headings, adjectival headings, inverted adjectival headings, phrase headings, inverted phrase headings, compound headings, and composite forms.[2] Richard S. Angell categorizes the forms as follows:

> Headings proper have the grammatical form of noun or phrase, the principal types of the latter being adjective-noun, phrases containing a preposition, and phrases containing a conjunction. Phrases may be in normal direct order of words, or inverted.
>
> Headings are amplified as required by 1) the parenthetical qualifier, used principally to name the domain of a single noun for the purpose of resolving homographs; and 2) the subdivision, of which there are four kinds: topic, place, time and form.[3]

Jay E. Daily,[4] in a thorough morphological and syntactical study of the forms of subject headings, divides them into the following categories: one-word headings, two-word headings, headings consisting of three or more words without function words, and those with function words. Variations within each group are also identified.

The use of nonverbal symbols in conjunction with the words in a heading is relatively simple in the Library of Congress system. The comma is used to separate a series of parallel terms and to indicate an inverted heading. Parentheses are used to enclose qualifiers. The dash is the signal for subdivisions, e.g., **United States — Air defenses**. The period is used to separate a subheading from the main heading and only appears in a name heading, a uniform title, or a name-title heading used as a subject heading:

> **United States.   Air Force**
> **Bible.   N.T.   Acts — Commentaries**
> **Aristotle.   Poetics**

Headings may also be categorized in terms of semantics. Most headings represent single concepts or objects. Compound headings contain more than one concept or object, some expressing an additive relationship, others representing phase relationships (such as cause and effect, influence, bias, etc.) between concepts and objects. Still other headings represent a particular aspect of a subject, such as form, space, time, process, or property.

In the Library of Congress subject headings system, there does not seem to be a relationship between grammatical form and semantic function. A heading representing an aspect of a subject is usually in the form of a subdivided heading, but it may also appear in the form of an adjectival phrase (direct or inverted), a prepositional phrase (direct or inverted), or a heading with a qualifier:

> **Factor tables**
> **Multiplication — Tables**
> **Squares, Tables of**
> **Plant inspection**
> **Fertilization of plants**
> **Plants, Protection of**
> **Cookery (Squash)**

The problem, then, is how to determine or predict the choice of a particular form in a given situation. Both Cutter and Haykin attempt to deal with the problem but fail to provide specific guidelines. Some aspects of the problem are discussed below.

CHOICE BETWEEN NOUNS AND PHRASES

When a choice is to be made between a noun and a phrase both of which represent the same object or concept, Cutter proposes that phrases "shall when possible be reduced to their equivalent nouns, as **Moral philosophy** to **Ethics** or to **Morals; Intellectual** or **Mental philosophy** to **Intellect** or **Mind**."[5] However, he also recognizes the difficulty in applying such a rule:

In reducing, for instance, Intellectual philosophy or Moral philosophy, will you say Mind or Intellect, Morals or Ethics? And the reader will not always know what the equivalent noun is, — that Physics = Natural philosophy, for example, and Hygiene = Sanitary science. Nor does it help us at all to decide whether to prefer Botanical morphology or Morphological botany.[6]

No satisfactory solution to the problem has been offered.

CHOICE AMONG DIFFERENT TYPES OF PHRASES

In his rules, Cutter[7] gives examples of the same subject named in different ways:

Capital punishment
Death penalty
Penalty by death

Floral fertilization
Flower fertilization
Fertilization of flowers

He feels that there is no way to formulate an absolute rule to ensure consistency in the choice, and that the best rule of thumb is, "when there is any decided usage (*i.e.*, custom of the public to designate the subjects by one of the names rather than by the others) let it be followed." Here Cutter immediately recognizes a difficulty: "As is often the case in language, usage will be found not to follow any uniform course." As a result, there is no uniformity in the choice among different types of phrases.

CHOICE BETWEEN PHRASES AND HEADINGS WITH SUBDIVISIONS

Topics that might be represented with phrase headings may often be handled by using a subdivision with a main heading. Cutter did not deal with this device: his rules do not mention subdivided headings, although headings with subdivisions are covered in his rules for filing. Haykin recognizes the problem of having to choose among forms that have equal standing in current usage, such as **Stability of ships; Ships' stability; Ships — Stability**, but offers no solution. In *Library of Congress Subject Headings*, any of the three forms may have been chosen with regard to individual headings:

Squares, Tables of
Factor tables
Multiplication — Tables

Recent practice favors headings with subdivisions over phrase headings. According to current Library of Congress policy, unless the proposed phrase heading is very well known by the informed public in exactly that form, it is considered more useful to establish the proposed new concept as a topical subdivision under the generic heading, e.g., **Butterfat—Fat globules** [not Milk fat globules]; **Greenhouses—Climate** [not Greenhouse climate]. Many phrase headings established earlier have been converted to the subdivided form:

Original form	*Converted form*
Social science research	**Social sciences—Research**
Color of birds	**Birds—Color**
Teachers, professional ethics for	**Teachers—Professional ethics**

Because of the lack of specific rules regulating the choice of forms over the years and because many people have participated in establishing headings, many inconsistencies still exist in *Library of Congress Subject Headings.* Nonetheless, there are certain predominant patterns in the usage and function of each form of heading. Recent efforts at establishing specific guidelines[8] will ensure greater consistency in newly formed headings. A discussion of various forms of headings in *Library of Congress Subject Headings* follows.

SINGLE NOUN OR SUBSTANTIVE HEADINGS

A single noun is chosen as the heading when it represents the object or concept precisely:

Chapels
Economics
Forgery
Humanism
Railroads
State, The
Success

When adjectives and participles are chosen, they are used as substantives or noun equivalents:

Advertising
Aged
Comic, The
Poor
Sick

In the past, as Daily points out, the article was used in some cases but not others even when grammatical usage would require it.[9] A decision was made a few years ago that, because of machine filing, no new subject heading is to be established with *the* in the initial position. Many of the original headings with an initial *the* have been converted to the current form:

Original form	*Converted form*
The arts	**Arts**
The Many (Philosophy)	**Many (Philosophy)**
The One (Philosophy)	**One (The One in philosophy)**
The West	**West (U.S.)**

On the whole, the plural form of a noun is used for denoting a concrete object or a class of people, e.g., **Airplanes; Churches; Florists; Teachers.** This is not a rigid rule and there are many exceptions. A deliberate exception is made for names of fruits for which the singular noun denotes both the fruit and the tree, e.g., **Peach; Pear.** Headings that represent biological species are generally in the singular, e.g., **Coconut palm; Japanese macaque; Rhesus monkey;** headings for larger taxa are almost always in the plural, e.g., **Palms; Macaques; Monkeys.**[10] In cases where both the singular and the plural forms of a noun have been established as headings, they represent different subjects: usually the singular form represents a concept or abstract idea and the plural a concrete object, e.g., **Essay** [as a literary form]; **Essays** [for a collection of specimens of this literary form]. However, in newly established headings, this distinction is no longer made. Another way of distinguishing between the concept and the specimens is to add a qualifier to one of the headings, e.g., **Biography** [for collective biographies]; **Biography (as a literary form).**

In headings for art, the former practice of using the singular, e.g., **Painting**, to represent the activity and the plural, e.g., **Paintings,** for the objects has been discontinued. Currently the singular noun, e.g., **Watercolor painting**, is used to represent both the activity and the object.[11]

ADJECTIVAL HEADINGS

An adjectival heading consists of an adjectival modifier followed by a noun or noun phrase. The modifier takes one of the following forms:

o   Common adjective

> **Military supplies**
> **Rural churches**
> **Nuclear physics**

o   Ethnic, national, or geographical adjective

> **Jewish etiquette**
> **American drama**
> **European newspapers**

o   Other proper adjective

> **Brownian movements**

o   Present or past participle

    Mining machinery
    Laminated plastics

o   Common noun in the possessive case

    Carpenters' square
    Children's art

o   Proper noun in the possessive case

    Carleton's Invasion, 1776

o   Common noun

    Ocean currents
    Lake streamers
    Landscape gardening
    Milk contamination

o   Proper noun

    Norton motorcycle
    Norway pine
    Lakeland terriers

o   Combination

    Real estate office buildings
    Gold-platinum alloys
    Copper Miners' Strike, Mich., 1913-1914

Haykin points out that it is important to recognize the distinctions between various types of adjectival headings because the type of *see* reference required varies with the type of heading: "In general, no reference needs to be made if the generic term, that is, the noun, serves merely as the vehicle for the modifier which gives meaning to the phrase. Conversely, a reference is needed if the adjective, or adjectival noun, serves primarily to modify or qualify."[12] The following examples illustrate Haykin's statement:

Electric capacity
    [no reference]
Electric cables
x   Cables, Electric

In current practice, new headings of the second type would be established in the inverted form to begin with, e.g., **Buses, Electric**.

    In the past, no distinction was made between an adjectival heading that represents a single concept, such as **Nuclear physics**, and one that represents a complex subject that can be easily converted into a subdivided form, e.g.,

Milk contamination [instead of Milk—Contamination]; **Mining machinery** [instead of Mining—Mechanical equipment]. As a result, different forms of headings exist for similar concepts. In current practice, the distinctions are made, and the subdivided form is used in newly established headings for complex subjects.

CONJUNCTIVE PHRASE HEADINGS

The conjunctive phrase heading (two or more nouns, with or without modifiers, connected by the word *and* or *or*, or followed by *etc.*) is used in the following situations:

1) When the concepts contained in the heading are affinitives, or sometimes opposites, that are usually treated together in works; the conjunction expresses an additive feature:

Good and evil
Crime and criminals
Reporters and reporting
Boats and boating
Libel and slander (Roman-Dutch law)
Library institutes and workshops
Literary forgeries and mystifications
Emigration and immigration
Emerald mines and mining
Children's encyclopedias and dictionaries
College and school periodicals
Mines and mineral resources
Open and closed shelves
Stores or stock-room keeping
Lamp-chimneys, globes, etc.
Hotels, taverns, etc.
Law reports, digests, etc.

Haykin calls these compound headings or composite forms. Library of Congress policy regarding headings of this type has been changed, with current policy requiring the establishment of separate headings for each of the elements in a conjunctive phrase heading. Many previously established headings of this type have been replaced by separate headings, e.g., the heading Textile industry and fabrics has been replaced by the two headings **Textile fabrics** and **Textile industry**; the heading Bicycles and tricycles has been replaced by the two headings **Bicycles** and **Tricycles**.

2) In compound headings that represent relationships (influence, cause and effect, and so on) between objects or concepts, e.g., **Religion and international affairs; Literature and society; Television and children**. The relationship in each of the headings is implied and distinguished by context rather than by form.

3)   When one noun serves to define another, more general noun, e.g.,
Forces and couples; Force and energy.

While previously established conjunctive phrase headings will continue to
be used in subject cataloging, newly established conjunctive phrase headings
are limited to the second instance, and only when the subject cannot be
expressed in the **[Main heading]** — **[Subdivision]** form, i.e., when the
relationship between the two concepts is discussed at a broad level and from
the perspectives of both topics,[13] e.g., **Education and crime; Feminism and the
arts**; but **Body temperature — Effect of drugs on** [not Drugs and body
temperature]; **English literature — Italian influences** [not English literature and
Italian civilization].

PREPOSITIONAL PHRASE HEADINGS

Prepositional phrase headings consist of two or more nouns, connected
by one or more prepositions:

Children as musicians
Community mental health services for children
Grooming for men
Jewelry as an investment
Photography of animals
Radar in speed limit enforcement
Television in health education
Transplantation of organs, tissues, etc.
Women in agriculture
Rodents as carriers of disease

Some of these headings express a single concept that cannot be named by a
single noun, e.g., **Divine right of kings; Spheres of influence; Stories without
words**. Still others represent a relationship between distinctive and otherwise
independent subjects, e.g., **Communication in library administration; Federal
aid to community development**. Many of the prepositional phrase headings
represent an aspect or facet of a subject that could be represented by a
subdivided heading, e.g., **Cataloging of art** [instead of Art — Cataloging];
Taxation of aliens [instead of Aliens — Taxation]. Previously, many of the
prepositional phrase headings contained phrases that brought out the
geographical aspect of a subject, e.g., Church and state in Italy; Italians in
Portugal; etc. These are now being replaced by the **[Topic]** — **[Place]** form,
e.g., **Church and state — Italy; Italians — Portugal.**
A large number of headings in the form of **[Class of people]** as **[Another
class of people]** represent the role of a certain class of people in an activity or
profession, e.g., **Children as actors; Artists as teachers**; etc. Previously, many
of these headings referred to women, such as Women as diplomats; Women as
missionaries; etc. They have now been replaced by headings in the adjectival
form[14], e.g., **Women diplomats; Women missionaries**. However, headings of
this type that refer to groups of people other than women remain valid, e.g.,
Physicians as musicians, and headings in the form of **Women in [discipline]**,
e.g., **Women in business.**

Current policy favors the subdivided form of heading, which has resulted in fewer prepositional phrase headings.

QUALIFIERS

A qualifier is a word or phrase enclosed within parentheses that follows the main heading. Many headings that contain qualifiers are jurisdictional or corporate name headings established according to *Anglo-American Cataloguing Rules*, second edition (see further discussion in chapter 6).

Over the years, parenthetical qualifiers have been added to subject headings for various purposes: (1) to distinguish between homographs, e.g., **Pool (Game); Cold (Disease); Rape (Plant)**; (2) to clarify the meaning of an obscure or foreign term, e.g., **Polyps (Pathology); Extra Hungariam non est vita (The Latin phrase)**; (3) to limit the meaning of a heading in order to render it more specific, e.g., **Olympic games (Ancient)**; and (4) to indicate the genre of a proper name, e.g., **Banabans (Oceanian people); DECSYSTEM-20 (Computer); Conquistadora (Statue)**; (5) to designate a special application of a general concept, e.g., **Cookery (Chicken); Environmental engineering (Buildings)**; and (6) to specify the medium of performance in music headings, e.g., **Concertos (Violin)**.

In a number of cases it is not clear why the qualified form instead of the phrase form was used, or why the qualifier was used at all, e.g., **Profession (in religious orders, congregations, etc.); Programming languages (Electronic computers)**. In many cases, the purposes indicated above can be achieved by using the subdivided or the phrase form, e.g., Chicken—Cookery; Ancient Olympic Games [or Olympic games, Ancient].

Until recently, practice was not consistent. In 1978, in order to ensure greater consistency in newly established headings, the Library of Congress developed guidelines[15] with regard to qualifiers. The parenthetical qualifier is to be used (a) to specify the intended meaning of the term if several dictionary definitions exist; (b) to resolve ambiguity if the main heading is similar in construction to other existing or possible headings; and (c) to make an obscure term more explicit. The parenthetical qualifier is no longer used to designate a special application of a general concept. For this purpose, the following forms are used instead:

o   Headings with subdivisions (preferred form)

> **Geography—Network analysis**
> [not Network analysis (Geography)]
> **Public health—Citizen participation**
> [not Citizen participation (Public health)]

o   Adjectival phrase headings

> **Combinatory enumeration problems**
> [not Enumeration problems (Combinatorial analysis)]
> **Industrial design coordination**
> [not Designs (Industrial publicity)]
> **Serial control systems**
> [not Control systems (Serials)]

o   Prepositional phrase headings

> **Information theory in biology**
> [not Information theory (Biology)]
> **Anesthesia in cardiology**
> [not Anesthesia (Cardiology)]
> **Abandonment of automobiles**
> [not Abandonment (Automobiles)]

INVERTED HEADINGS

Because the Library of Congress subject headings system was originally designed for the card catalog, in which each record possesses only one access point and is filed in one place in the catalog, the choice of the word to be used as the entry element in a phrase heading was a paramount consideration. When a subject heading contains only a noun, there is of course no question about the entry element. When the heading contains more than one word, a decision must be made about which of the terms should be the entry word.

Theoretically speaking, subject headings in a dictionary catalog based on the principle of specific and direct entry should be entered directly according to natural word order, e.g., Life insurance; Theory of knowledge. In practice, however, this has not always been the case. From the earliest stages in the development of the dictionary catalog, it has been found desirable to invert certain phrase headings so that they will be filed under a term other than the first. In *Library of Congress Subject Headings*, many headings have the noun brought forward in inverted form, e.g., **Insurance, Life; Knowledge, Theory of.**

There are no specific guidelines, nor discernible patterns, for inverting headings. In many cases, there is no way to predict the form of a heading in *Library of Congress Subject Headings*, as the following headings show:

> **Bessel functions**
> **Functions, Abelian**
> **Abelian groups**
> **Groups, Continuous**

In adjective-noun headings containing national adjectives, certain patterns based on subject categories have been identified.[16] Headings with national, ethnic, or language qualifiers are generally inverted, *except* those in the following categories: major literary forms (e.g., **American poetry; German essays**); certain headings in the fields of anthropology (e.g., **Chinese rites**), linguistics (e.g., **Arabic philology**), and social sciences (e.g., **Flemish movement; Roman emperors**); proper names (e.g., **Celtic Church; Oneida Community**); and headings containing adjectives that have lost their national, ethnic, cultural, or linguistic connotations (e.g., **Arabian horse; Chinese cabbage; English horn**). However, the same patterns do not seem to hold for the majority of headings containing other kinds of adjectives. Compare the following groups:

> Agricultural chemistry
> Biological chemistry
> Environmental chemistry
>
> Chemistry, Clinical
> Chemistry, Pharmaceutical
> Chemistry, Organic

The rationale for inverted headings is explained thus by Haykin: "When it is desired to bring the noun in an adjectival heading into prominence, either in order that it may appear in the catalog next to other headings beginning with that noun, or because the adjective is used simply to differentiate between several headings on the same subject, the inverted type of adjectival heading is used."[17] Margaret Mann advises using inverted headings "only when necessary" and offers the rationale for this form:

> A problem arises if a term such as pathological psychology is used. The general heading **Psychology** will lose all the books which deal with this subject in its application to medicine, because the two groups will not be filed together. In such a case, the term may be changed to bring the new subject into relation with the main subject heading to which it belongs; in other words, a term must be found which will allow the special application of the topic to be grouped with the main subject. Such headings are called "inverted headings." They are adopted when it seems desirable to keep classes together to maintain a somewhat logical arrangement....
>
> Several good reasons for grouping the various aspects of a subject in the dictionary catalog warrant the use of inverted headings. Such an arrangement (1) brings books on related aspects of a subject together; (2) ... results in a grouping that is frequently different from the classified arrangement on the shelves; and (3) ... relieves readers of the trouble of searching in a number of places in the catalog to find related topics.[18]

The reason given in these statements for the use of inverted headings is to bring related subjects together. Wyllis E. Wright comments succinctly: "The use of inverted phrases is usually a mark of attempted classification."[19] In practice, because some but not all phrase headings are inverted, the advantage of subject collocation is only partially realized. Compare the following groups:

> Insurance, Disaster
> Insurance, Life
> Insurance, Health
>
> Disaster relief
> Life insurance trusts [cf. also **Trusts, industrial**]
> Compulsory health insurance

While different kinds of insurance are grouped together by means of the inverted form, various aspects of the same kind of insurance are separated.

Looking back, one finds that this practice is sanctioned by Cutter[20] himself: "Enter a compound subject-name by its first word, inverting the phrase only when some other word is decidedly more significant or is often used alone with the same meaning as the whole name" (p. 72). The primary advantage of this rule is subject collocation. Cutter recognizes that "to adopt the noun (the class) as the heading is to violate the fundamental principle of the dictionary catalog" (p. 73) and that "the specific-entry rule is one which the reader of a dictionary catalog must learn if he is to use it with any facility; it is much better that he should not be burdened with learning an exception to this, which the noun rule certainly is" (p. 74). To invert a phrase heading in order to bring the noun forward is a concession to the alphabetico-classed catalog.

Concerning the order of words in headings containing more than one word, Cutter discusses three options.

(1) We can consider the subject to be the phrase *as it reads*, as **Agricultural chemistry, Survival of the fittest** (p. 72).

Cutter's objection to this form is that "it may be pushed to an absurd extent" (p. 72) in headings containing a noun preceded by an adjective. He offers an example:

A man might plausibly assert that Ancient Egypt is a distinct subject from Modern Egypt, having a recognized name of its own, as much so as Ancient history, and might therefore demand that the one should be put under **A** (Ancient) and the other under **M** (Modern) and similar claims might be made in the case of all subject-names to which an adjective is ever prefixed, which would result in filling the catalog with a host of unexpected and therefore useless headings (p. 72).

The interesting words in this statement are *unexpected* and *useless*. They evidently assume users who were accustomed to the classified arrangement. A user acquainted with the rule of specific and direct entry should not find these headings unexpected. In the same paragraph, Cutter hastens to add: "Nevertheless the rule seems to me the best if due discrimination be used in choosing subject-names."

(2) We can make our entry ... under what we consider the most significant word of the phrase, inverting the order of the words if necessary; as ... **Species**, Origin of the, the word Origin here being by itself of no account; **Alimentary** canal, Canal being by itself of no account (p. 72).

This form is reminiscent of the catchword title. The objection to it, Cutter sees immediately, "is that there would often be disagreement as to what is 'the most important word of the phrase,' so that the rule would be no guide to the reader. But in connection with (1) and as a guard against its excesses (2) has its value" (p. 72).

(3)   We can take the phrase as it reads ... but make a special rule for a noun preceded by an adjective ... *first*, that all such phrases shall when possible be reduced to their equivalent nouns ...; and, *secondly*, that in all cases where such reduction is impossible the words shall be inverted and the noun taken as the heading, as **Chemistry**, Agricultural; **Chemistry**, Organic (p. 72).

The objection to this rule is that "it would put a great many subjects under words where nobody unacquainted with the rule would expect to find them." Works on the Alimentary canal, Cutter observes, would hardly be searched under Canal (p. 72).

As a solution, Cutter offers the rule quoted earlier: "Enter a compound subject-name by its first word, inverting the phrase only when some other word is decidedly more significant or is often used alone with the same meaning as the whole name" (p. 72). Nonetheless, he recognizes immediately that this "combined rule" will not solve all the problems. On the contrary, it often compounds them. Cutter concedes "that this rule is somewhat vague and that it would be of doubtful application" (p. 72). Subsequent application of the noun rule in *Library of Congress Subject Headings* has borne out Cutter's misgivings.

As Francis Miksa[21] points out, Cutter probably intended that inverted headings were to be used sparingly, i.e., only if the phrase began with a "non-significant" word and could not be reduced to an equivalent noun. Cutter distinguishes between the adjective-noun headings in which the noun is the name of a class and the adjective indicates a subdivision (e.g., Comparative anatomy; Capital punishment), and the adjective-noun headings in which the adjective implies a subject and the noun indicates the aspect in which the subject is viewed, e.g., Ancient history; Medieval history [the historical study of the ancient world or the Middle Ages]. However, in determining the forms of headings for the alphabetical subject catalog, this distinction has not always been used as a criterion.

Entering a heading under the "more significant" word has always been, and is still, a general guideline in the Library of Congress system. However, because this guideline allows a great deal of subjective judgment on the part of catalogers in determining the significant word, many inconsistencies in form have resulted. In spite of repeated efforts since Cutter, no rigorous, objective criteria for determining entry elements have yet been developed. This is an area on which much has been written. Following is a summary of some of the discussions and proposals.

The Vatican code offers the following guidelines for adjective-noun headings: "The adjective usually precedes the noun in English when it conveys the specific sense, while it follows the noun when it only qualifies a concept that is already specific in itself or indicates a minor variety or division."[22] In practice, it is difficult to perceive how this rule would apply in the formation of the group of headings related to the subject Chemistry cited on page 56.

The Vatican code also provides rules for inverting prepositional phrase headings. Its rule 384 states:[23]

1) Prepositional phrases which represent a distinct concept are usually retained in their common form.

Conflitto di leggi	Conflict of laws
Piante nell'arte	Plants in art
Padri della chiesa	Fathers of the church

2) The words are inverted when the first word represents a vague and indistinct concept, while the second term indicates a specific topic.

| Animali, Leggende e racconti di | Animals, Legends and stories of |
| Discendenza reale, Famiglie di | Royal descent, Families of |

It is not clear why the word *families* in the last example should be considered to represent "a vague and indistinct concept." Nor do these rules provide clear-cut guidance in determining the form of a heading such as **Directors of corporations**.

Conceding that "uninverted phrase headings are to be preferred since they represent the normal order of words and it can be reasonably assumed that most readers would not look under the inverted form," Haykin offers this criterion for inverting headings: "Phrase headings in inverted form are used when the first element in effect qualifies the second and the second is used in the catalog as an independent heading. The inversion is then equivalent to subdivision, but is used in place of subdivisions to preserve the integrity of the commonly used phrase."[24] In practice, Haykin's statement has failed to provide a clear-cut guideline that ensures a reasonable degree of consistency in form. Compare, for example, **Knowledge, Theory of** with **Profession of faith** [in spite of the fact that **Faith** is an independent heading in the list].

Marie Louise Prevost[25] proposes a "noun rule" that reduces all phrase headings to the **[Noun] — [Subdivision]** form:

Libraries — Branches
    — Centralization
    — Chemical
    — History
    — Librarians — Interchange of
    — Loans — Interlibrary
    — Medical
    — (relations with) School
    — Science (of) — Schools

However, critics usually wince at this proposal when they see the heading **International relations** reduced to Nations — Interrelations.

Granting that inverted headings are necessary, E. J. Coates[26] proposes a criterion for choosing the most significant term as the entry element based on "the word which evokes the clearest mental image." He concludes that "images of things are simpler, more readily formed, more accessible to memory than images of actions." However, he immediately recognizes the difficulty in applying this criterion to headings containing two or more equally concrete things, as in the case of double noun phrases such as *conveyor belt*.

Jessica Lee Harris proposes the criterion of word frequency, suggesting that in an adjective-noun combination, "the less common of the two words might be regarded as best specifying the subject."[27] Unfortunately, it has not been demonstrated how this criterion is to be applied in establishing new subject headings.

All these efforts at justifying the inverted heading are perhaps attempts at solving the problem of distributed relatives, meaning the scattering of related headings. Listing the subject Ancient Egypt in the natural word order scatters materials about Egypt, and putting it under Egypt scatters material about ancient history. As Jean M. Perreault points out:

> The whole discussion of direct *vs.* inverted word order in phrases ... is really only a symptom of the syndrome 'distributed relatives'.... What must be remembered is that both direct and inverted phrases result in distributed relatives, and we must ask ourselves, before we attempt to solve the obvious and serious problem therein implied, whether we want a solution that can apply to all cases (which means that our solution will have to be in terms of broad linguistic or logical categories), or want to deal with each phrase on its own merits (which means that our solution will have to be in terms of narrow bibliographical characteristics).[28]

With the advent of the online catalog, the question of direct versus inverted headings may become less significant. While a manual catalog provides linear access to a phrase (i.e., each phrase can be accessed only through the beginning word), an online catalog can provide multiple access to the phrase. In some of the more sophisticated online systems, a phrase may be accessed through any of the component words or any combination of these words in any word order. This capability will no doubt be refined even further as time goes on and may eventually render the debate over direct versus inverted headings in the online environment a purely academic exercise.

FUNCTIONS OF HEADINGS

In terms of functions of headings—what they indicate about the works they are applied to—the headings in an alphabetical subject catalog may be divided into the following three categories: topical, bibliographic form, and artistic and literary form.

Topical Headings

A topical heading represents the subject content of a work. The overwhelming majority of subject headings assigned to works fall into this category. For example, a work about clinical chemistry is assigned the heading **Chemistry, Clinical**; a work on the process of arriving at decisions for action is assigned the heading **Decision-making**.

·Bibliographic Form Headings

Some headings indicate the bibliographic form of a work rather than its subject content. Most of these are assigned to works not limited to any particular subject or to works on very broad subjects, e.g., **Encyclopedias and dictionaries; Almanacs; Yearbooks; Devotional calendars**. There are relatively few of these headings. The same headings are often assigned to works discussing the particular forms, e.g., a work about compiling almanacs. In these cases, no attempt is made to distinguish works *in* the forms from works *about* the forms.

Some headings representing bibliographic forms are used only as topical headings and are not assigned to individual specimens of the form. For example, the heading **American periodicals** is assigned to a work *about* American periodicals, but not a publication such as *Atlantic Monthly*.

Artistic and Literary Form Headings

Many headings indicate the artistic or literary genre of the work. They are used extensively in three fields in particular: literature, art, and music. In these fields, the forms of the works are considered of greater importance than their subject content. Examples of this type of heading are:

Painting, Dutch
Short stories
Suites (Wind ensemble)

In some cases, a distinction is made between works in a particular genre and works about it, e.g., **Short story** [as a literary form]; **Short stories** [a collection]. Detailed discussions on headings for literature and music will be presented in later chapters.

REFERENCES

[1]Charles A. Cutter, *Rules for a Dictionary Catalog*, 4th ed. (Washington, D.C.: Government Printing Office, 1904), 71-72.

[2]David Judson Haykin, *Subject Headings: A Practical Guide* (Washington, D.C.: Government Printing Office, 1951), 21-25.

[3]Richard S. Angell, "Library of Congress Subject Headings—Review and Forecast," in *Subject Retrieval in the Seventies: New Directions: Proceedings of an International Symposium*, ed. Hans (Hanan) Wellisch and Thomas D. Wilson (Westport, Conn.: Greenwood Publishing, 1972), 144.

[4]Jay E. Daily, "The Grammar of Subject Headings: A Formulation of Rules for Subject Headings Based on a Syntactical and Morphological Analysis of the Library of Congress List" (Ph.D. diss., Columbia University, 1957).

[5]Cutter, *Rules for a Dictionary Catalog*, 72.

[6]Ibid., 74.

[7]Ibid.

[8]Many of these guidelines have been published in *Cataloging Service* and *Cataloging Service Bulletin* in the past, and recently in Library of Congress, Subject Cataloging Division, *Subject Cataloging Manual: Subject Headings*, prelim. ed. (Washington, D.C.: Library of Congress, 1984).

[9]Daily, "The Grammar of Subject Headings," 56.

[10]"Animal and Plant Names," *Cataloging Service Bulletin* 20:42 (Spring 1983); Library of Congress, *Subject Cataloging Manual*, H1332.

[11]"Art Headings," *Cataloging Service* 121:13-14 (Spring 1977).

[12]Haykin, *Subject Headings*, 21.

[13]Library of Congress, *Subject Cataloging Manual*, H310.

[14]" 'As' Headings," *Cataloging Service* 125:21-22 (Spring 1978); Library of Congress, *Subject Cataloging Manual*, H360.

[15]"Parenthetical Qualifiers in Subject Headings," *Cataloging Service Bulletin* 1:15-16 (Summer 1978); Library of Congress, *Subject Cataloging Manual*, H357.

[16]Lois Mai Chan, " 'American Poetry' but 'Satire, American': The Direct and Inverted Forms of Subject Headings Containing National Adjectives," *Library Resources & Technical Services* 17:330-339 (Summer 1973).

[17]Haykin, *Subject Headings*, 22.

[18]Margaret Mann, *Introduction to Cataloging and Classification of Books*, 2nd ed. (Chicago: American Library Association, 1943), 144.

[19]Wyllis E. Wright, "The Subject Approach to Knowledge: Historical Aspects and Purposes," in *The Subject Analysis of Library Materials*, ed. Maurice F. Tauber (New York: School of Library Service, Columbia University, 1953), 10-11.

[20]Cutter, *Rules for a Dictionary Catalog*, 72-74.

[21]Francis Miksa, *The Subject in the Dictionary Catalog from Cutter to the Present* (Chicago: American Library Association, 1983), 139-142.

[22]Vatican Library, *Rules for the Catalog of Printed Books*, trans. from the second Italian edition by Thomas J. Shanahan, Victor A. Schaefer, and Constantin T. Vesselowsky, and ed. Wyllis E. Wright (Chicago: American Library Association, 1948), 257.

[23]Ibid., 260.

[24]Haykin, *Subject Headings*, 23-24.

[25]Marie Louise Prevost, "An Approach to Theory and Method in General Subject Heading," *Library Quarterly* 16:140-151 (April 1946).

[26]E. J. Coates, *Subject Catalogues: Headings and Structure* (London: Library Association, 1960), 50.

[27]Jessica Lee Harris, *Subject Analysis: Computer Implications of Rigorous Definition* (Metuchen, N.J.: Scarecrow Press, 1970), 67.

[28]Jean M. Perreault, "Library of Congress Subject Headings: A New Manual," *International Classification* 6:161 (1979).

4

SUBDIVISIONS

INTRODUCTION

Subdivisions are used extensively in the Library of Congress subject headings system. The rationale for subdividing a heading, according to David Judson Haykin, is that subdivision serves as a device for subarranging a large number of works that share the same main heading: "Subdivision is distinguished from qualification in that it is ordinarily used not to limit the scope of the subject matter as such, but to provide for its arrangement in the catalog by the form which the subject matter of the book takes, or the limits of time and place set for the subject matter."[1] Margaret Mann states: "The tendency to group under one subject heading all books in a given field is desirable up to a certain point, but such a procedure will lead to a day of reckoning when the entries under that caption become so numerous that it is difficult to differentiate between titles. When this happens the subject must be subdivided."[2]

E. J. Coates disagrees with this reasoning. He calls Haykin's argument of subdivision as a device for subarrangement "a mere play upon words." Coates explains: "In the alphabetical subject catalogue the degree of subject specification and the mechanics of arrangement are simply two aspects of a single operation. One decides upon a particular heading and by the same token determines the position of the entry in the catalogue."[3] The question is, then, whether subdivisions are used as a means of subject specification, i.e., to limit the scope of the main subject, or as a means of subarranging a large number of entries under a particular subject.

The decision whether to subdivide a subject depends to a large extent on one's perception of the purpose of subdivision. If subdivision is used solely as a means of subarrangement, it is called for only if there is a substantial amount of material on a subject. But if subdivision is used for the purpose of rendering a subject more specific, which is by and large the current philosophy of the Library of Congress, a heading is subdivided when there are documents that focus on a specific aspect of the subject. The subdivided heading thus serves to maintain coextensivity between the heading and the document.

In *Library of Congress Subject Headings* there are four types of subdivisions: topical, geographic, period, and form. Topical subdivisions have always been used to achieve specificity as well as to provide for subarrangement. On the other hand, period subdivisions have been used mainly as a device for subarrangement of large files. Many subjects that lend themselves to chronological treatment are not subdivided by period, e.g., **English essays.** Likewise, the histories of many small countries are not divided chronologically. In the past, form and geographic subdivisions were also used mainly as a means of subarrangement. This is why many headings have not been subdivided by place even though some of the library materials on the subject are limited to a certain locality. Current policy requires the use of form subdivisions when applicable and appropriate. Newly established headings indicate a trend toward greater use of geographic subdivision even where the size of the file would not require it; the criterion followed now is suitability of geographic qualification to the literature of the subject.[4]

TOPICAL SUBDIVISION

A main subject heading subdivided by a topical subdivision resembles an entry in an alphabetico-classed catalog. Both Charles A. Cutter and Haykin believed that classed entries should be avoided in a dictionary catalog. Cutter's rules do not treat subdivision. Haykin's opinions about subdivision are expressed in the following statement:

> The use of topics comprehended within a subject as subdivisions under it is to be avoided. It is contrary to the principle of specific entry, since it would, in practice, result in an alphabetico-classed catalog.
>
> That subject catalogs, as a matter of fact, contained headings subdivided by topics is evidence of a lack of a clear understanding of the purpose of the alphabetical subject catalog and of the distinction between a specific heading of the direct type and an alphabetico-classed heading.[5]

A subdivision that represents a kind or a part of the main subject (thus forming a hierarchical relationship, such as a genus-species, thing-part, or class-inclusion relationship) is characteristic of an entry in a classed catalog. A classed heading usually consists of a string of terms beginning with the broadest term, with each term subordinate to the one preceding it and containing the one following it. The heading represents a hierarchy based on the genus-species or thing-part relationship that indicates a class-inclusion unit. Haykin writes that this type of heading should not be introduced into a dictionary catalog:

> If alphabetico-classed headings are to be avoided, limitations must be set on methods of subdivision. In the case of alphabetico-classed headings, by definition, subdivision is by areas, elements, and phases of the main subject. In other words, subordination is by topic. In subject headings proper; that is, headings which name the

topic directly, without subordination, subdivision can only serve as a convenient shorthand for long phrases and a means of desirable, logical grouping of material recorded under the heading. In other words, subdivision should usually be limited to the form organization and bibliographic character of the material (for instance such subdivisions as HISTORY, DICTIONARIES, YEARBOOKS), the geographic area covered by it, and the time of publication or period covered. In effect these subdivisions are extensions or modifications of the subject heading, and not more specific subject areas within those covered by the main heading.[6]

However, there are different types of topical subdivisions, some of which are not of the genus-species or class-inclusion type; these resemble alphabetico-classed entries in their outward form only. For example, the relationship between the main heading and the topical subdivision in headings such as **Heart — Diseases**; **Agriculture — Taxation** is not that of genus-species or thing-part type. Haykin writes: "CONSTRUCTION INDUSTRY — TAXATION is another way of saying 'taxation of the construction industry', and obviously not 'taxation as a division of the subject CONSTRUCTION INDUSTRY'."[7] He states that the topical subdivision is used "only where the broad subject forms part of the name of the topic and a convenient phrase form sanctioned by usage is lacking, or, for the purpose of the catalog, where it is desirable to conform to an existing pattern."[8] For example, *legal research* is a commonly accepted phrase, while *physical research* is not. Therefore, the headings used for these subjects are **Legal research**; **Physics — Research**. Thus, aspects of a subject may be represented in several different ways: by topical subdivisions, by phrase headings, or, in some cases, by headings with qualifiers. In order to ensure greater uniformity among newly established headings, current policy requires the use of the form **[Topic] — Research**.

In *Library of Congress Subject Headings*, topical subdivisions are most often used to bring out aspects or facets of the main subject, rather than to indicate its kinds or parts. Nonetheless, a small number of headings characteristic of the classed entries (i.e., hierarchically divided headings) have been introduced into the list.

The following examples are of the genus-species type: **Shakespeare, William, 1564-1616 — Characters — Children**; **Shakespeare, William, 1564-1616 — Characters — Fathers**; **Wages — Minimum wage**. In the first two examples, the genus-species relationship is most obvious between the subdivision and the sub-subdivision, e.g., **— Characters — Children**. While these headings bring together all types of characterization in Shakespeare's works — an advantage of the classed catalog — the practice results in inconsistency, because this form is not used regularly with similar or related headings, e.g., **Children in literature** [not Literature — Characters — Children]; **Retirement income** [not Income — Retirement income]. In these examples, the principle of specific entry is observed.

Some headings are of the thing-part type, e.g., **Airplanes — Motors — Carburetors**; **Airplanes — Motors — Mufflers**; **Airplanes — Wings**. The purpose of this form is subject collocation, i.e., to group different parts of the airplane together. Again, there is the problem of maintaining consistency and predicta-bility in similar headings. Although **Motors** and **Wings** are entered as subdivisions under **Airplanes**, other parts of the airplane are entered in the direct form: **Ailerons; Flaps (Airplanes); Tabs (Airplanes)**. Fortunately, *see* references are made from the forms not used and the user is guided to the forms used:

> Aircraft carburetors
> > *See* **Airplanes — Motors — Carburetors**
>
> Airplanes — Flaps
> > *See* **Flaps (Airplanes)**

GEOGRAPHIC SUBDIVISION

Many subjects lend themselves to geographic treatment. When the geographic aspect of the subject is of significance, geographic (also called place or local) subdivisions are provided. Principles concerning geographic subdivision are stated by Haykin: "When the data of the subject treated are limited to a geographic or political area, the heading may be subdivided by the name of the place. This method of subdivision is variously called place, local, or geographic. It is applicable to such subjects as possess a geographic connotation."[9]

The policies regarding geographic subdivision have varied over the years. Until 1981, a heading that was limited to a geographic area might appear in one of two forms:

o [Topic] — [Place]

> **Churches, Catholic — Italy**
> **Education — Japan**

o [Topic] in [Place]

> **Church and education in Connecticut, [Italy, United States, etc.]**
> **Germans in Poland**

Beginning in 1981, the type of heading [Topic] in [Place] was discontinued and replaced by the **[Topic] — [Place]** type of heading.[10]

In the Library of Congress subject headings system, not all headings may be subdivided geographically. When a heading is subdivided by a place within a country, the name of the relevant country (with certain exceptions to be discussed below) is interposed between the subject heading and the name of any subordinate political, administrative, or geographical division. With the exception of Antarctic regions and the names of certain island groups, no geographical name higher than the level of a country is to be used as an interposing element, and none below the level of a city or town is used as a geographic subdivision. Furthermore, no geographic subdivision may contain more than two levels of geographic elements:

Music — Europe
Music — Germany (West)
   [not Music — Europe — Germany (West)]

Music — Germany (West) — Bavaria
Music — Germany (West) — Munich
   [not Music — Germany (West) — Bavaria — Munich]

The designation *(Indirect)* following a heading is used to indicate that the heading may be subdivided by place. The reason for this apparently strange way of marking headings that can be divided geographically is that until November 1976 some headings could be divided geographically by using local place names directly, without the interposition of the name of a higher jurisdiction (e.g., **Art — Paris**), while others had to have the indirect form (e.g., **Music — France — Paris**). When it was decided that, with a few exceptions, all geographical subdivisions involving subordinate jurisdictions or localities should be in the indirect form in order to achieve consistency and lessen confusion, there was no further need for the notation *(Direct)* in the list. Nevertheless, it was decided to keep the term *(Indirect)* instead of using a more expressive term for the instruction, such as "May be subdivided by place."

Although the interposition of the name of the larger geographic entity renders the heading a blatantly classed entry, the benefit of collocating materials relating to the larger area has been considered important enough by the Library of Congress to suspend the principle of specific and direct entry.

The procedures listed below represent the current Library of Congress policy regarding geographic subdivision.[11]

1) *General procedure.* A heading coded *(Indirect)* is subdivided locally by interposing the name of the country between the heading and the name of any geographic entity contained wholly within the country. These geographic entities include:

   subordinate political jurisdictions, such as provinces, districts, counties, cities, etc.

   historic kingdoms, principalities, etc.

   geographic features and regions, such as mountain ranges, bodies of water, lake regions, watersheds, metropolitan areas, etc.

   islands situated within the territorial limits of the country in question

Examples:

   Agriculture and state — Brazil — Para (State)
   Architecture — Italy — Venice
   Taxation — Spain — Leon (Kingdom)
   Elephants — Tunisia — Carthage (Ancient city)
   Guerrillas — Bulgaria — Razlog Region
   Geology — Romania — Apuseni Mountains
   Excavations (Archaeology) — Japan — Nemuro Peninsula
   Architecture — Belgium — West Flanders
   Architecture — Finland — Mariehamn (Åland Islands)

No level lower than that of a city or town is to be used in an indirect subdivision. When the topic treated is limited to a locality within a city or town, two headings are assigned:

1. **Tourist trade — California — San Francisco.**
2. **Chinatown (San Francisco, Calif.)**
    [not 1.   Tourist trade — California — Chinatown
             (San Francisco)]

Metropolitan areas and city regions are assigned as subdivisions indirectly through the jurisdiction in which the city proper is located, even if the metropolitan area spreads over more than the jurisdiction in question, e.g., **Minorities — Missouri — Saint Louis Metropolitan Area.** The local place name used in an indirect subdivision is not qualified by the name of a larger geographic entity if the qualifier* (abbreviated or spelled out) is the same as the interposing element:

    Art — France — Paris
       [not Art — France — Paris (France)]
    Tourist trade — Germany (West) — Vogelsberg Region
       [not Tourist trade — Germany (West) — Vogelsberg
          Region (Germany)]
    Eutrophication — Iowa — Clear Lake (Lake)
       [not Eutrophication — Iowa — Clear Lake (Iowa : Lake)]

Note these forms, however: **Geology — Italy — Etna, Mount (Sicily); Architecture — Australia — Sydney (N.S.W.).**

2)   *Latest name.* When the name of the place in question has changed during the course of its existence, the latest name is always used in the heading, regardless of the form of the name or period covered in the work being cataloged:

    Title: *The Banks of Leopoldville, Belgian Congo.* 1950
       1.   Banks and banking — Zaire — Kinshasa.

3)   *Use of present territorial sovereignties.* If a region or jurisdiction has existed under various sovereignties in its history, the name of the country currently in possession of the place is interposed, regardless of past territorial arrangements described in the work cataloged, as long as the region or jurisdiction is now wholly contained in that country:

    Title: *Alsace: Bas-Rhin, Haut-Rhin, Territoire-de-Belfort*
       1.   Castles — France — Alsace.
       2.   Alsace (France) — Description and travel.

---

*For a discussion of qualifiers for geographic names, see chapter 6.

4) *Exceptions.* To the above general pattern, there are a number of exceptions to indirect subdivision.

a) The first-order political divisions of the following four countries are always subdivided directly (i.e., without interposing the name of the country):

Country	*First-order divisions*	*Examples**
Canada	provinces	**Ontario; Alberta**
Great Britain	constituent countries	**England; Scotland**
Soviet Union	republics	**Ukraine; Russian S.F.S.R.**
United States	states	**Alaska; Montana**

Examples of headings include **Animal industry — Alberta; Energy policy — Scotland; Historic buildings — Georgian S.S.R.; Coastal ecology — Alaska.** For local places within these four exceptional countries, the names of the first-order political divisions instead of the names of the countries are used as interposing elements:

Excavations (Archaeology) — England — Merseyside
Excavations (Archaeology) — Georgia — Sapelo Island
Art, American — Illinois — Chicago
Architecture — Russian S.F.S.R. — Leningrad Metropolitan Area

It should be noted that, for Canada, the Soviet Union, and the United States, the first-order political divisions used in indirect subdivision are the same as the qualifiers used in establishing geographic headings according to the current *Anglo-American Cataloguing Rules* (*AACR2*). It may therefore appear that *AACR2* governs subject cataloging policies for indirect subdivision. This is not the case; the coincidence is limited to the three countries just mentioned. This fact should be borne in mind particularly in dealing with places in Great Britain.

b) If the name of the local place is in the form of the name of the country (or the name of a first-order political division in Canada, Great Britain, the Soviet Union, or the United States) followed by an adjectival qualifier, no interposing element is required:

Nutrition surveys — Italy, Southern
  [not Nutrition surveys — Italy — Italy, Southern]
Baths, Hot — California, Southern
  [not Baths, Hot — California — California, Southern]

---

*For a complete list of the first-order political divisions of these countries, see appendix J.

c)   When the place in question does not lie wholly within a single country (or first-order political division of the four exceptional countries listed above), no interposing element is used. Places of this nature include

places in the four exceptional countries noted above, e.g., **Southern States**

historical kingdoms, empires, etc., e.g., **Holy Roman Empire**

geographic features and regions, such as continents and other major regions, bodies of water, mountain ranges, etc., e.g., **Europe; Great Lakes; West (U.S.); Mexico, Gulf of; Rocky Mountains; Nile River Valley**

Examples of headings include **Earth movements—Sierra Nevada Mountains (Calif. and Nev.); Oceanography—Baltic Sea; Art—Mediterranean Region**. In such cases, any geographic qualifier* normally accompanying the name is retained.

d)   The following cities are not used with interposing elements: **Berlin (Germany)**[12]; **Jerusalem; New York (N.Y.); Washington (D.C.)**[13]:

Education—Berlin (Germany)
Commuting—Berlin Metropolitan Area (Germany)
Aquatic sports—Berlin Region (Germany)
Art—Washington (D.C.)
Armenians—Jerusalem

Hong Kong and **Vatican City** are also used without interposing elements,[14] e.g., **Export marketing—Hong Kong; Christian art and symbolism—Vatican City**.

e)   *Islands in* (Indirect) *subdivision practice.*[15] The procedures described above are followed when subdividing a heading by the name of an island or island group. There are, however, the following exceptions: If the island or island group is located some distance away from the controlling jurisdiction, the name of the island or island group is assigned directly after the heading; in the case of a single island that is part of a group located some distance away from its controlling jurisdiction, the name of the island group of which it is a part is interposed, e.g., **Crabs—Easter Island; Meteorology—Falkland Islands; Mollusks—Galapagos Islands; Water-supply—Canary Islands—Teneriffe**. If the island or island group is autonomous or comprises more than one autonomous jurisdiction, the name is assigned directly, e.g., **Natural history—Borneo; Reptiles—Hispaniola; Labor and laboring classes—Philippines; Botany—Islands of the Pacific**. Names of individual Caribbean islands south of the Virgin Islands are assigned directly after the heading regardless of their present political status, the reason being that most of these islands have achieved independence or are likely to do so relatively soon. Examples of headings include:

---

*For an explanation of geographic qualifiers, see chapter 6.

Ethnology—Grenada
[not Ethnology—West Indies—Grenada]
Marine algae—Bonaire
[not Marine algae—Netherlands Antilles—Bonaire]

5) *City flip*. Previously, for a number of subjects, subdivision by city was not used even though the subject heading is coded *(Indirect)*. Instead, a heading in the form of [City]—[Topic] [e.g., **Boston (Mass.)—Buildings**] was used. This practice, called "city flip," was discontinued in 1985.*

Summarized Rules for Indirect Subdivision

Because of the complexity of geographic subdivision, the Library of Congress has prepared a summary outlining the details discussed above.[16] It is reproduced below in slightly altered form.

1. Basic rule for indirect subdivision
    a. Country or not wholly within a country, direct
        —France; —Europe; —Andes Mountains; —Bering Sea; —Pacific Ocean
    b. Inside two countries, direct
        —Severn River (Wales and England); —Gobi Desert (Mongolia and China)
    c. Inside one country, indirect; only two levels permitted
        —France—Paris; —Argentina—Buenos Aires; —Italy—Rome

2. Four exceptional countries: United States, Soviet Union, Canada, Great Britain
    Do not divide through them to get to anything smaller; divide through states, provinces, etc., to get to smaller; if larger than a state, divide to it directly
    —Illinois, —Illinois—Chicago; —Ukraine, —Ukraine—Kiev; —British Columbia, —British Columbia—Vancouver; —Scotland, —Scotland—Edinburgh (Lothian); —Rocky Mountains; —Azov, Sea of (Ukraine and R.S.F.S.R.)

3. Inverted terms with name of the country, etc., first, direct
    —California, Southern; —Italy, Northern; —Tennessee, Eastern

4. Four exceptional cities: New York; Berlin; Washington, D.C.; Jerusalem
    Divide direct to all, and also to Hong Kong and Vatican City, which are treated as countries

---

*This change of policy is not reflected in the tenth edition of *Library of Congress Subject Headings*, which contains headings effective as of December 1984.

5. Metropolitan areas
   If in several states, divide through the state the city is in

6. City sections
   Do not divide down to city sections; stop at the city

7. Islands
   If at a distance from "owning" land mass, direct

   If an island in a group distant from "owners," indirect through the island group

   If close to land mass and political subdivision of same, indirect

8. Name changes
   Divide through and to the latest form of name, whether changed for cataloging purposes (**Argentina, Czechoslovakia, Soviet Union, Russian S.F.S.R.**) or because of real name changes (**Ghana, Benin, Sri Lanka, Vanuatu**)

9. Territorial changes
   Divide through present territory

10. Alteration of the entry during indirect subdivision
    Alter only if what one divides through makes the qualifier redundant

11. Order of precedence of local subdivision
    If subdivision is divided, geographical subdivision is placed after subdivision

    If subdivision is not divided, geographical subdivision is interposed

12. Impact of *AACR2* on indirect subdivision
    The fact that Malaysia, Yugoslavia, and Australia are not used as qualifiers and that their constituent states or provinces are used as qualifiers does not affect indirect subdivision. One continues to divide through these countries, since the countries are not among the exceptions named in rule 2 above.

PERIOD SUBDIVISION

A period subdivision under a heading denotes a certain point in time or a span of time. Period subdivisions are most frequently used with headings in the fields of history (particularly the history of specific countries or places), literature, and the arts to show chronological sequences of events or development. Not all headings in these fields are subdivided by period, however; the general criterion is the amount of material on the subject in the Library of Congress collection. Also, there are a few headings for which period subdivisions (in the form of date spans) are used to show when the material cataloged under those headings was published rather than the historical period the material treats.

Previously, many of the period subdivisions assigned to cataloging records did not appear in the printed list. This policy was changed in 1975. Now all period subdivisions that have been established appear in the printed list.

General Principles of Period Subdivision

The division of chronological periods varies from place to place and from subject to subject. The general rule stated by Haykin is: "The period subdivisions used should either correspond to generally recognized epochs in the history of the place or should represent spans of time frequently treated in books whether they possess historic unity or not.[17] In other words, scholarly consensus is the general guide.

Period subdivisions under the history of a given country are not always mutually exclusive. As Haykin points out, "the presence in the catalog of broad subdivisions does not preclude the use of subdivisions covering events or lesser epochs falling within the broad period.[18] In application, a broad period subdivision and a more specific period subdivision falling within it are not usually used together for the same work. Prior to the eighth edition of *Library of Congress Subject Headings*, when period subdivisions began with the same date greater periods were placed before lesser periods:

> **France — History — 1789-1900**
> **— 1789-1815**
> **— Revolution**
> **— Revolution, 1789-1793**
> **— Revolution, 1789**

This, of course, is a logical arrangement reflecting the principle of general before specific. However, since the eighth edition, in order to facilitate computer filing, a strictly numerical arrangement has been adopted, resulting in shorter periods being filed before broad periods:

> **France — History — Revolution, 1789**
> **— Revolution, 1789-1793**
> **— Revolution, 1789-1799**
> **— 1789-1815**
> **— 1789-1900**

In period subdivisions under the name of a country that has undergone one or more name changes, the latest name of the country is used as the main heading; occasionally, this practice produces anachronistic headings, e.g., **Soviet Union — History — 1689-1800; United States — History — Colonial period, ca. 1600-1775**. The advantage of collocating the history of a particular country under the same heading has outweighed logical considerations.

Period subdivisions under subjects other than countries are usually mutually exclusive:

English literature — Middle English, 1100-1500
— Early modern, 1500-1700
— 18th century
— 19th century
— 20th century

Corporate headings for chiefs of state, which are used as main or added entries [e.g., **Great Britain. Sovereign (1558-1603 : Elizabeth)**], are not used as subject headings except in cases of name-title subject entries. For a work about the reign or administration of a chief of state, a counterpart in the form of [**Name of jurisdiction**] — **History** — [**Period subdivision**] is used:

Title: *An Humble Supplication to Her Maiestie*
1. **Great Britain. Sovereign (1558-1603 : Elizabeth). Declaration of great troubles pretended against the realme.**

Title: *Elizabethan Backgrounds: Historical Documents of the Age of Elizabeth I.*
1. **Great Britain — History — Elizabeth, 1558-1603 — Sources.**

One peculiarity in the treatment of wars and battles has been pointed out by Haykin.[19] Wars, other than civil wars, are entered under their own names with references from the names of participating countries followed by the appropriate periods of their history and from variant names that have been applied to the wars:

Austro-Prussian War, 1866
 *x** Austria — History — Austro-Prussian War, 1866
  Austro-German War, 1866
  Prussia (Germany) — History — Austro-Prussian War, 1866
  Seven Weeks' War

Spain — History — Civil War, 1936-1939

Exceptions are made for wars, other than those of worldwide scope, in which the United States (or the American colonies) participated; these are entered under **United States**:

United States — History — King George's War, 1744-1748
 x Governor Shirley's War
  King George's War, 1744-1748

United States — History — War of 1898
 x American Spanish War, 1898
  Hispano-American War, 1898
  Spain — History — War of 1898
  Spanish American War, 1898
  War of 1898

---

*For an explanation of the cross-references represented by *x* and *xx*, see chapter 5.

World War, 1914-1918
   x European War, 1914-1918
      First World War
      World War I

Battles, on the other hand, are entered under their own names rather than under the war headings, with *see also* references from the latter:

Berlin, Battle of, 1945
   x Berlin (Germany) — Siege, 1945
   xx **World War, 1939-1945 — Campaigns — Germany (East)**

Lenino, Battle of, 1943
   xx **World War, 1939-1945 — Campaigns — Byelorussian S.S.R.**

Forms of Period Subdivisions

This section describes the various forms of period subdivisions. First, however, it is important to note that period subdivision is not the only device in the Library of Congress system for representing the chronological aspects of a topic. Some main headings include both period and topical elements, the most common form for such headings being an inverted adjectival phrase:

Art, Ancient
Art, Baroque
Art, Gothic
Art, Medieval
Art, Renaissance
Art, Rococo
Art, Romanesque

Because such headings denote both subject and period characteristics, in the Library of Congress system they are interfiled alphabetically with other inverted headings.

There are several different forms for actual period subdivisions. Different forms may appear under the same heading, depending on which form is most appropriate for representing a particular period.

1) A main heading may be followed by a subdivision containing the beginning and ending dates or the beginning date alone (also called an open-ended date):

English language — Grammar — 1800-1869
English language — Grammar — 1950-

Egypt — Economic conditions — 332 B.C.-640 A.D.
France — Politics and government — 1589-1610

2) A main heading may be followed by a subdivision containing the name of a monarch, a historical period, or an event, followed by dates:

English drama — Restoration, 1660-1700
German poetry — Middle High German, 1050-1500

China — History — Ming dynasty, 1368-1644
Germany — History — Ferdinand I, 1556-1564
Japan — History — Meiji period, 1868-1912
United States — History — Colonial period, ca. 1600-1775
United States — History — Revolution, 1775-1783

This form is mostly used with the subdivision —**History** under names of places. The same periods, when applied under other topical subdivisions such as —**Foreign relations;** —**Politics and government**, usually appear without the descriptive terms or phrases:

Great Britain — History — Puritan Revolution, 1642-1660
Great Britain — Politics and government — 1642-1660

Great Britain — History — Victoria, 1837-1901
Great Britain — Foreign relations — 1837-1901

3) A main heading may be followed by the name of the century as a subdivision, e.g., **Italian poetry — 15th century; Netherlands — Church history — 17th century**. This form of period subdivision is usually adopted when there is no distinctive name for the period or event, when a longer period of time than a single event or movement has to be covered, or when only very broad period subdivisions are required. The designation for a century may also take the form of the beginning and ending years of the century, e.g., **Great Britain — Description and travel — 1701-1800**. This form is used most frequently with the subdivision —**Description and travel**. In fact, the designation —**18th century** is filed as if written —**1701-1800**.

4) A main heading may be followed by a period subdivision constructed with the preposition *to* followed by a date, e.g., **Great Britain — Civilization — To 1066; Rome — History — To 510 B.C.** This type of period subdivision usually appears as the first of the period subdivisions under a subject or place. It is used when the beginning date is uncertain or cannot be determined.

5) A main heading may be followed by a subdivision in the form of —**Early works to [date]**. While period subdivisions usually indicate the periods covered in works, this type of period subdivision represents the date of publication, e.g., **Aeronautics — Early works to 1900; Geometry — Early works to 1800**. This type of period subdivision is used most frequently with headings in the scientific or technical fields in which the scholars often want to separate recent works from earlier literature.

FORM SUBDIVISION

Haykin defines the term *form subdivision* and explains its nature and function in the following terms: "Form subdivision may be defined as the extension of a subject heading based on the form or arrangement of the subject matter in the book. In other words, it represents what the book is, rather than what it is about, the subject matter being expressed by the main heading."[20] Form subdivisions include those indicating the physical or bibliographical forms of works, such as **— Bibliography; — Collected works; — Dictionaries; — Maps; — Periodicals; — Pictorial works**. Traditionally, certain subdivisions that indicate authors' approaches to their subjects are also considered to be form subdivisions, occasionally referred to as inner forms, e.g., **— History; — Juvenile literature; — Study and teaching**. In some cases, a form subdivision may be further subdivided by one or more additional form subdivisions:

> **China — Presidents — Biography — Addresses, essays, lectures**
> **Chinese classics — 20th century — History and criticism — Addresses, essays, lectures**
> **Great Plains — History — Sources — Bibliography — Catalogs**
> **France — Industries — Statistics — Periodicals**

Form subdivisions appear under all types of headings, including topical, geographic, corporate, and personal name headings. Previously, use of form subdivisions under corporate and name headings was restricted. This policy has been changed. Now form subdivisions are used under these headings where appropriate.[21] One area still not fully developed in regard to form subdivisions is nonprint media. In the treatment of subject content, there should not be any difference between book and nonbook materials. Since the main difference between them is the physical format or media, it would appear that using form subdivisions indicating the media to bring out the differences would be appropriate. In practice, only a few subdivisions representing nonprint media have appeared in *Library of Congress Subject Headings*, e.g., **— Juvenile films; — Juvenile sound recordings**. There are no parallel subdivisions for adult nonbook materials. This is perhaps a reflection of the nature of the Library of Congress collection, which is still basically book oriented.

FREE-FLOATING SUBDIVISIONS[22]

Definition and Application

At the Library of Congress, each time a subdivision is used under a heading for the first time, its usage must be established editorially in the same manner that a new heading is established. (This procedure is described in chapter 7.) There are certain exceptions to this pattern of practice. A number of subdivisions, generally of wide application, have been designated as "free-floating" subdivisions. The term refers to certain form and topical subject subdivisions that Library of Congress subject catalogers are authorized to use, whenever appropriate, under a subject heading without establishing a new usage editorially. The various combinations of free-floating subdivisions with subject headings, therefore, appear in the subject tracings on Library of Congress cataloging records but are not necessarily so listed in the printed list.

Although the official designation of a large number of subdivisions as free-floating did not take place until 1974, limited use of such subdivisions dated back to the second edition (1919) of *Subject Headings Used in the Dictionary Catalogues of the Library of Congress*, in which certain form subdivisions were omitted from the printed list but used in cataloging. In the fourth edition, the concept of model headings (also called pattern headings) — meaning the use of certain headings as the models for subdivisions for headings in the same subject category — was introduced by the inclusion of four persons (Lincoln, Napoleon, Shakespeare, and Washington) as models for personal name headings. In subsequent editions, the common form subdivisions and model headings continued to expand until 1974, when a large number of commonly used subdivisions* were declared free-floating.

The extended use of free-floating subdivisions and pattern or model headings has contributed toward the transformation of the Library of Congress subject headings system from a basically enumerative system into an increasingly analytico-synthetic one. In a way, these subdivisions are analogous to the standard subdivisions in the Dewey Decimal Classification, which reflect the principle of facet analysis and provide for freedom of synthesis. The use of free-floating subdivisions has also resulted in a significant increase in productivity among subject catalogers at the Library of Congress, and it has reduced both the cost of editorial processing and the size of the printed list.

In application, although the free-floating subdivisions may be assigned freely by catalogers, they should not be used indiscriminately without regard for appropriateness or established principles governing the use of a particular subdivision. In determining the appropriateness of using a free-floating subdivision for the first time under a subject heading, the following considerations should be borne in mind.

1) *Correct usage.* The cataloger should consider the compatibility of the subdivision with the subject heading to which it is being attached. Any limitations in scope and application stated in scope notes accompanying the free-floating subdivisions should be observed.

2) *Conflict.* Before assigning a free-floating subdivision, the cataloger should first determine whether the use under consideration conflicts with previously established headings. If there is a conflict, the subdivision should not be assigned. Frequently, there may already exist a phrase heading carrying the same meaning as the heading with subdivision being considered. For example, since the heading **Library administration** already exists as a valid

---

*A list of most commonly used subdivisions, with scope notes, appeared in the introduction to the eighth edition of *Library of Congress Subject Headings* and was reprinted in *Library of Congress Subject Headings: A Guide to Subdivision Practice* (Washington, D.C.: Library of Congress, 1981).

heading, the subdivision — **Administration** should not be used under **Libraries**. Further examples are **Electronic apparatus and appliances** instead of Electronics — Equipment and supplies; **Christmas music** instead of Christmas — Songs and music.

3) *Reconciling entries in the catalog.* When using a combination for the first time, the cataloger should check existing entries in the catalog in order to reconcile any inconsistencies or conflicts resulting from the use of the new combination.

Categories of Free-Floating Subdivisions

Free-floating subdivisions appear in the six categories listed in the following pages.

1) *Free-floating form and topical subdivisions of general application.* A list of common subdivisions that have been designated free-floating appears in appendix C. These are form and topical subdivisions of a common nature. Some of them are further subdivided by other form, topical, or, in a few cases, period sub-subdivisions. Usage of these subdivisions is explained in the scope notes that appear in the *Subject Cataloging Manual* as well as in the introduction to the tenth edition of *Library of Congress Subject Headings* and under individual headings in the list.

Many of the **[Heading] – [Free-floating subdivision]** combinations that were established and numerated in the printed list are being gradually removed. The removal is indicated in *Supplement to LC Subject Headings* in the following form:

Physical geography
CANCEL:
— Field work
>   This is still a valid heading, but is no longer printed in
>   LCSH because it uses a free-floating subdivision.

2) *Free-floating form and topical subdivisions controlled by pattern headings.*[23] For headings in a particular subject category, there are often subdivisions of common application. In order to avoid repeating these subdivisions under each heading in that category, they are listed under one or occasionally several representative headings, which then serve as "patterns" or "models" for subdivision. These subdivisions then become free-floating among headings within that category and can be used with all headings of that category if appropriate and when there is no conflict. For example, the heading **German language — Grammar, Historical** is a valid heading, even though it does not appear in the printed list, because the subdivision — **Grammar, Historical** appears under the pattern heading **English language**. Likewise, the heading **Milton, John, 1608-1674 — Political and social views** is a valid heading patterned after the heading for Shakespeare.

Table 4.1 shows the pattern headings designated by the Library of Congress as of 1984. Lists of free-floating subdivisions under many of the pattern headings listed in Table 4.1 appear in *Subject Cataloging Manual: Subject Headings*. Lists for some of the more common pattern headings are included in appendix D of this book. Where there is a discrepancy or conflict between the subdivisions appearing in one of these lists and those listed under the pattern heading in *Library of Congress Subject Headings*, the source that bears a later date has precedence since it represents more recent revisions.

Table 4.1. Pattern Headings Established by the Library of Congress
as of 1984

Subject Field	Category	Pattern Heading
Philosophy and religion	Religious and monastic orders	**Jesuits**
	Religions	**Buddhism**
	Christian denominations	**Catholic Church**
	Sacred works (including parts)	**Bible**
	Theological topics	**Salvation**
History and geography	Colonies of individual countries	**Great Britain – Colonies**
	Legislative bodies (including chambers)	**United States. Congress**
	Military services (including armies, navies, marines, etc.)	**United States – Armed Forces; United States. Air Force; United States. Army; United States. Marine Corps; United States. Navy**
	Wars	**World War, 1939-1945; United States – History – Civil War, 1861-1865**
	Indians (including individual tribes)	**Indians of North America**
Recreation	Sports	**Soccer**
Social sciences	Industries	**Construction industry; Retail trade**
	Types of educational institutions	**Universities and colleges**
	Individual educational institutions	**Harvard University**
	Legal topics	**Labor laws and legislation**

(Table 4.1 continues on page 82.)

Table 4.1. *Continued*

Subject Field	Category	Pattern Heading
The Arts	Groups of literary authors (including authors, poets, dramatists, etc.)	**Authors, English**
	Individual literary authors	**Shakespeare, William, 1564-1616**
	Literary works entered under author	**Shakespeare, William, 1564-1616. Hamlet**
	Literary works entered under title	**Beowulf**
	Languages and groups of languages	**English language; French language; Romance languages**
	Literatures (including individual genres)	**English literature**
	Newspapers	**Newspapers**
	Music compositions	**Operas**
	Musical instruments	**Piano**
Science and technology	Land vehicles	**Automobiles**
	Materials	**Concrete; Metals**
	Chemicals	**Copper**
	Organs and regions of the body	**Heart; Foot**
	Diseases	**Cancer; Tuberculosis**
	Plants and crops	**Corn**
	Animals (General)	**Fishes**
	Domestic animals	**Cattle**

Many of the free-floating subdivisions listed under pattern headings may be further subdivided by place, as instructed by the designation *(Indirect)* after the subdivision,* or by common free-floating form subdivisions when appropriate:

> **English language — Rhetoric — Study and teaching — United States — Directories**
> **French language — Semantics — Addresses, essays, lectures**
> **Indians of North America — Aged — Congresses**

It should also be noted that free-floating subdivisions that may be used with headings controlled by pattern headings are not limited to those appearing in the model lists. The general free-floating subdivisions (discussed in category 1 above), although not printed under pattern headings, may also be applied to headings in these categories:

---

*A list of subdivisions to be further subdivided by place appears in appendix E of this book.

Birds—Poetry
> [**—Poetry** is a general free-floating subdivision, although it is not listed under either the heading **Birds** or the pattern heading for animals, **Fishes**]

German language—Periodicals
Shakespeare, William, 1564-1616—Criticism and interpretation—
> **History**

When there is a conflict in wording between a common free-floating subdivision and one listed under a pattern heading, the latter takes precedence.

3) *Free-floating subdivisions under personal headings.* Previously, a number of personal headings were designated as pattern headings for subdivisions in several broad categories of persons: rulers and statesmen, musicians, philosophers, founders of religions, and literary authors. Free-floating subdivisions were established and printed in *Library of Congress Subject Headings* under these pattern name headings. In 1985 the Subject Cataloging Division consolidated the separate lists of free-floating subdivisions used under personal names into one list for all personal headings except those of literary authors, for which the heading **Shakespeare, William, 1564-1616** continues to serve as the pattern heading.

The list of free-floating subdivisions used under names of persons appears in appendix F of this book. Among the subdivisions listed, four relate the person to specific disciplines, fields, or topics:

> —**Career in [specific field or discipline]**
> —**Contributions in [specific field or topic]**
> —**Knowledge—[specific topic]***
> —**Views on [specific topic]**

These subdivisions are to be completed on a free-floating basis, with a running phrase or subdivision representing the specific field or topic:

> **Washington, George, 1732-1799—Career in surveying**
> **Jefferson, Thomas, 1743-1826—Contributions in architecture**
> **Debussy, Claude, 1862-1918—Knowledge—Literature**
> **John Paul II, Pope, 1920-   —Views on church and state**

4) *Free-floating subdivisions under geographic headings.* The following lists of free-floating subdivisions have been prepared for different types of geographic headings:

---

*Represents the person's knowledge of a particular topic as well as the person's educational background in a specific topic.

a) *Subdivisions used under names of places.* Until 1985 two separate lists of subdivisions were used under headings for places—one for cities and one for regions, countries, etc. When the policy of "city flip" (see discussion on p. 72) was discontinued, the two lists were consolidated. (For a complete listing of these subdivisions, see appendix G.) The subdivisions may be used, within the limitations stated in the notes accompanying the list, under the following types of geographic name headings that have been established as valid *AACR2* name headings or subject headings: continents; regions; islands; countries; states, provinces, and equivalent jurisdictions; counties and other local jurisdictions larger than cities; metropolitan areas, suburban areas, and regions based on names of cities; cities; ancient or early cities; city sections, districts, or quarters. Examples of headings include:

Asia – Foreign relations – United States
Antarctic regions – Description and travel
Bermuda Islands – History – Sources
China – Diplomatic and consular service
Hong Kong – Description and travel
Dover Region (N.H.) – Biography
Boston (Mass.) – Officials and employees – Salaries, allowances, etc.
Washington Suburban Area – Intellectual life – Addresses, essays, lectures
Left Bank (Paris, France) – Description – Views

Appropriate subdivisions from this list may also be used under headings for geographic features or regions based on geographic features, e.g., **Indian Ocean Region – Emigration and immigration – History – Congresses.**

b) *Subdivisions used with names of bodies of water, streams, etc.*[24] (For a complete listing of these subdivisions, see appendix G.) These subdivisions may be used under names of individual bodies of water, including manmade lakes, reservoirs, and canals,* for example,

California, Gulf of (Mexico) – Shorelines
Colorado River (Colo.-Mexico) – Navigation
Glacier Bay (Alaska) – Water level
Suez Canal (Egypt) – Water-rights
Superior, Lake – Climate
Tug Fork – Name
Wolfgangsee (Austria) – Poetry

5) *Free-floating period subdivisions.* The following period subdivisions are used under the free-floating subdivision **– History: – 16th century; – 17th century; – 18th century; – 19th century; – 20th century.** Their use is restricted to topical headings to which the free-floating subdivision **– History** can be

---

*The list does not apply to generic headings for types of bodies of water such as **Lakes; Saline waters; Sounds (Geomorphology).**

assigned appropriately. However, they are not used with headings that begin with the name of a region, country, etc. For example, America—History—19th century is not a valid heading. Period subdivisions under place name headings are enumerated in *Library of Congress Subject Headings*.

6) *Subjects or topics as free-floating subdivisions.* According to Library of Congress practice, under certain headings names of subjects may be assigned as subdivisions whenever appropriate without establishing the usage editorially. These headings are indicated in the printed list either with an instructional scope note:*

Bibliography
   —Bibliography
      Subdivided by subject, *e.g.* Bibliography—Bibliography—Botany, and by country, *e.g.* Bibliography—Bibliography—America

Bibliography—Best books
      Subdivided by subject, *e.g.,* Bibliography—Best books—Economics

or by means of a "multiple" subdivision:

Baptism—Anglican Communion, [Catholic Church, etc.]
Mysticism—Brahmanism, [Judaism, Nestorian Church, etc.]
English language—Dictionaries—French, [Italian, etc.]

The following headings may be generated from the headings with multiple subdivisions above:

Baptism—Judaism
Mysticism—Hinduism
French language—Dictionaries—Sango
      [the multiple subdivision **—Dictionaries—French, [Italian, etc.]** appears under the pattern heading for languages, **English language**]

(For further details concerning multiple subdivisions, see chapter 8.)
   In addition to free-floating subdivisions as discussed above, there are also free-floating phrases in the Library of Congress subject headings system. These include free-floating combinations of certain words or phrases with geographic names and with headings used in literature and art. (For discussions of these headings, see chapters 6 and 10.)

---

*These instructional scope notes should not be confused with general *see also* references, which do not necessarily indicate free-floating status of a subdivision.

ORDER OF SUBDIVISIONS

The practice of subdividing a subject in the Library of Congress subject headings system comes closest to manifesting the modern theory of facet analysis and synthesis. In general, the subdivisions bring out various aspects or facets of the main subject.

In the earlier stages of development, subdivisions were relatively simple. Usually, a subject was divided by a form, period, place, or topical aspect. Gradually, more and more subdivisions were introduced and various kinds of subdivisions were allowed to be combined and applied to the same heading, forming a string of terms. In many cases, more than one subdivision of the same kind may now be used under a particular heading. The combination in some cases can be quite elaborate, for example, **United States — History — Civil War, 1861-1865 — Secret service — Juvenile literature; Mathematics — Study and teaching (Secondary) — Illinois — Chicago — Addresses, essays, lectures.**

In the formation of headings with numerous subdivisions, the order of the subdivisions in the string is important. Interestingly, there have been few stated instructions concerning the arrangement of elements in the string, similar to the citation formulae that are part of modern classification schemes. In most cases, one follows the arrangement already established in the subject headings list: new headings are generally established according to existing patterns. Because there are no guidelines for citation order, however, one often finds patterns that are inconsistent and even incompatible with other patterns under the same heading. The following discussion treats major questions regarding the order of subdivisions.

Order of Main Heading and Subdivision

When a heading contains a topical element and a form, place, period, or another topical aspect, a decision must be made on which is to be the main heading and which the subdivision, in other words, on which should be the entry element.

Topic versus topic

In the Library of Congress system, the term representing a concrete subject generally serves as the main heading, and the term indicating an action is used in the subdivision; the usage is similar to the key system/action arrangement in PRECIS. This concrete/action citation order is in line with the modern theory of facet analysis and synthesis, which has been expounded by Julius O. Kaiser (concrete/process),[25] Marie Louise Prevost (noun rule),[26] S. R. Ranganathan (personality/energy),[27] Coates (thing/action),[28] Brian C. Vickery (substance/action),[29] and Derek Austin (key system/action).[30] In the Library of Congress system, this citation pattern is generally observed, e.g., **Kidneys — Surgery; Kidneys — Diseases — Diagnosis; Automobiles — Taxation.** However, there are exceptions, e.g., **Advertising — Cigarettes; Classification — Books.**

Topic versus form

On the whole, the topic serves as the main heading, with the form as a subdivision, e.g., **Chemistry — Bibliography; Library science — Periodicals.** There are a few exceptions to this pattern, e.g., **Reference books — Chemistry.**

Topic versus period

Like the form subdivision, the period division does not usually stand alone without first conceding the subject. Rather, topics are divided by time periods, e.g., **Drama — 18th century.** There is, however, an exception to this pattern: widely used names of historical periods may appear as main headings. In such cases, they are not usually subdivided by topic, although they are often subdivided by form of material, e.g., **Renaissance — Juvenile literature; Middle Ages — Bibliography.**

Topic versus place

Place names are often used as subdivisions under a topic to indicate the geographical aspect from which a subject is treated, just as period and form subdivisions show time and literary approach. In contrast with period or form, place may be the main subject of a work, particularly in the fields of history and geography. In many areas of the social sciences, in fact, place may be considered of more significance than topic even when it is not featured as such. In such cases, a place name may be used as the main heading, with subdivisions for topical and/or other elements as appropriate, e.g., **United States — History; United States — Social life and customs.** In some cases, the distinction or emphasis is not so obvious, as in works on geology.

Because of the principle of uniform heading, catalogers do not have the option of using reciprocal place/topic and topic/place headings for the same concept. What principles can they then follow in reaching a decision on whether to favor place or topic?

Cutter's rules do not cover subdivision practice. His rules with regard to topic versus place concern mainly the choice between the subject and the place as the heading:

164.   The only satisfactory method is double entry under the local and the scientific subject — to put, for instance, a work on the geology of California under both **California** and **Geology**.... But as this profusion of entry would make the catalog very long, we are generally obliged to choose between country and scientific subject.

165.   A work treating of a general subject with special reference to a place is to be entered under the place, with merely a reference from the subject.[31]

In his attempt to solve the topic/place problem, Coates proposes ranking the main areas of knowledge according to the extent to which they appear to be significantly conditioned by locality:

1. Geography & biological phenomena
2. History & social phenomena
3. Language & literature
4. Fine arts
5. Philosophy & religion
6. Technology
7. Phenomena of physical sciences.[32]

Coates suggests that subjects near the top of this list be entered under the place subdivided by the subject and those at the bottom be treated in reverse. He recognizes, however, that the "problem is at what point in the middle of the list should the change be made."

Library of Congress practice in this respect reflects these difficulties. Some headings are in the form of topics subdivided by place, while others have place names subdivided by topics. There are no clear-cut criteria for determination, and as a result, it is difficult for the user to predict which form is used in each case.

To remedy this inconsistency, the following devices are used:

1) The list of free-floating subdivisions under place names (see appendix G) indicates which topics are used as subdivisions under place names. Furthermore, for each topic used as a subdivision under place names, a cross-reference is given under the name of the topic in the printed list:

Frontiers
See subdivisions Boundaries *and* Frontier troubles *under names of countries, states, etc.*

Industry
sa subdivision Industries *under names of regions, countries, cities, etc.*

2) In those instances in which users may approach the catalog through either the topic or the place, a modified form of duplicate entry is used. For example, in cataloging materials of interest to genealogists and historians dealing with a particular place, a heading in the form of **[Place] — [Broader topic]** is assigned in addition to the **[Topic] — [Place]** heading normally assigned:

Title: *Wills and Their Whereabouts*
1. **Wills — Great Britain.**
2. **Great Britain — Genealogy.**

This practice does not violate the principle of uniform heading because the second heading consists of a topic broader than the one contained in the first. This type of **[Place] — [Topic]** is called a generic heading.

As was seen to be the case for other entry element questions, the choice of the order of elements in a subdivided heading is not as important in most online systems as it is for card catalogs or printed indexes. In online systems where main heading and subdivision are equally accessible, one may assign headings of either form, **[Topic]** — **[Place]** or **[Place]** — **[Topic]**, as long as the citation order does not affect the meaning of the heading.

Order of Subdivisions under the Same Main Heading

When two or more subdivisions appear under the same main heading, the order of the string becomes an important issue, because it provides the context and often determines the meaning of the heading. One of the superior features of the PRECIS system is the very rigorous formulae that dictate the order of the elements of a string.[33] In the Library of Congress system, guidelines for ordering subdivisions under the same main heading are gradually being developed. Among these are the following:[34]

1) When combining subdivisions, one should follow a logical thought process.

2) The form subdivision is usually the last element in a string.

3) When a heading contains a geographic subdivision and one or more of the other subdivisions, the geographic subdivision is normally placed between the main heading and the other subdivision(s):

Education *(Indirect)*
  — **Finance**

Education — Florida — Finance
Education — New Jersey — Finance — Statistics

However, a number of subdivisions are themselves further subdivided by place. In such cases, the designation *(Indirect)* appears after the subdivision in the printed list and the various free-floating subdivision lists:

Education *(Indirect)*
  — **Economic aspects** *(Indirect)*

Education — Economic aspects — Finland
Education — Economic aspects — United States
  — **Addresses, essays, lectures**

A list of these subdivisions, called "Subdivisions to Be Further Subdivided by Place," appears in appendix E.

In some cases, different ordering of the same elements in a heading may result in different meanings. For example, the following headings contain the same elements but have different meanings:

Labor supply — Research — United States
Labor supply — United States — Research

The first implies research conducted in the United States on labor supply in general, and the second means research on labor supply in the United States. In the Library of Congress subject headings system, the distinction is not always made. For instance, a heading in the form of **[Name of discipline]** — **[Place]** — **History**, e.g., **Agriculture — United States — History**, denotes both the history of the discipline in a place and the history of conditions in a place.

On the other hand, in a number of cases the distinction is made. In the case of the subdivisions listed below, the geographic aspect of a work may be brought out either by interposition of a geographic subdivision, by further subdividing the topical or form subdivision by place, or by both methods, as appropriate:

- **Archival resources**
- **Catalogs and collections**
- **Collectors and collecting**
- **Conservation and restoration**
- **Documentation**
- **Forgeries**
- **Information services**
- **Library resources**
- **Mutilation, defacement, etc.**
- **Private collections**
- **Research**
- **Study and teaching**
     [and all parenthetically qualified forms of this
     subdivision]
- **Teacher training**
- **Vocational guidance**

Examples include:

Postage-stamps — United States — Collectors and collecting
[the collecting of U.S. postage stamps without regard to where the collecting is done]
Postage-stamps — Collectors and collecting — United States
[the collecting of any postage stamps that is done in the United States]
Postage-stamps — France — Collectors and collecting — United States
[the collecting of French postage stamps done in the United States]
Blacks — Latin America — Study and teaching — United States
[the study and teaching in the United States about blacks in Latin America]

In a few special cases, the history of a discipline in a place and condition in a place are represented by different headings, e.g., **Economics — United States — History** [history of the discipline of economics in the United States]; **United States — Economic conditions** [economic conditions in the United States]. In such instances, scope notes are provided in the printed list:

Economics *(Indirect)*
Here and with local subdivision are entered works on the discipline of economics. Works on the economic conditions of particular countries, regions, cities, etc., are entered under the name of the place subdivided by Economic conditions.

Economics – United States
Here are entered works on the discipline of economics in the United States. Works on the economic history or conditions of the United States are entered under the heading United States – Economic conditions.

Economics – History
Here are entered works on the history of economics as a discipline. Works on economic history or conditions are entered under the heading Economic history or the subdivision Economic conditions under names of countries, regions, cities, etc.

REFERENCES

[1]David Judson Haykin, *Subject Headings: A Practical Guide* (Washington, D.C.: Government Printing Office, 1951), 27.

[2]Margaret Mann, *Introduction to Cataloging and the Classification of Books*, 2nd ed. (Chicago: American Library Association, 1943), 146.

[3]E. J. Coates, *Subject Catalogues: Headings and Structure* (London: Library Association, 1960), 75.

[4]Richard S. Angell, "Library of Congress Subject Headings – Review and Forecast," in *Subject Retrieval in the Seventies: New Directions: Proceedings of an International Symposium*, ed. Hans (Hanan) Wellisch and Thomas D. Wilson (Westport, Conn.: Greenwood Publishing, 1972), 151.

[5]Haykin, *Subject Headings*, 35-36.

[6]David Judson Haykin, "Subject Headings: Principles and Development," in *The Subject Analysis of Library Materials*, ed. Maurice F. Tauber (New York: School of Library Service, Columbia University, 1953), 51.

[7]Ibid.

[8]Haykin, *Subject Headings*, 36.

[9]Ibid., 29.

[10]Library of Congress, Subject Cataloging Division, *Subject Cataloging Manual: Subject Headings*, prelim. ed. (Washington, D.C.: Library of Congress, 1984), H900.

[11]Ibid., H830.

[12]Ibid., H915.

[13]Ibid., H1050.

[14]Ibid., H1045.

[15]Ibid., H807.

[16]Material distributed at Regional Institutes on Library of Congress Subject Headings, sponsored by ALA Resources and Technical Services Division, Library of Congress, and ALA/RTSD Council of Regional Groups, 1982-1984.

[17]Haykin, *Subject Headings*, 33.

[18]Ibid., 34.

[19]Ibid., 34-35.

[20]Ibid., 27.

[21]"Form Subdivisions," *Cataloging Service Bulletin* 3:13-14 (Winter 1979).

[22]Library of Congress, *Subject Cataloging Manual*, H1095.

[23]Ibid., H1146-1200.

[24]Ibid., H1145.5.

[25]Julius O. Kaiser, *Systematic Indexing*, The Card System Series, vol. 2 (London: Pitman, 1911), 300-303.

[26]Marie Louise Prevost, "An Approach to Theory and Method in General Subject Headings," *Library Quarterly* 16:140-151 (1946).

[27]S. R. Ranganathan, *Elements of Library Classification*, 3rd ed. (Bombay: Asia Publishing House, 1962), 82-89.

[28]Coates, *Subject Catalogues*, 50-58.

[29]Brian C. Vickery, "Systematic Subject Indexing," *Journal of Documentation* 9(1):48-57 (1953).

[30]Derek Austin, *PRECIS: A Manual of Concept Analysis and Subject Indexing*, 2nd ed., with assistance from Mary Dykstra (London: The British Library, Bibliographic Services Division, 1984), 107-121.

[31]Charles A. Cutter, *Rules for a Dictionary Catalog*, 4th ed. (Washington, D.C.: Government Printing Office, 1904), 68.

[32]Coates, *Subject Catalogues*, 61.

[33]Phyllis A. Richmond, *Introduction to PRECIS for North American Usage* (Littleton, Colo.: Libraries Unlimited, 1981).

[34]Material distributed at Regional Institutes on Library of Congress Subject Headings.

5

CROSS-REFERENCES

INTRODUCTION

In the alphabetical subject catalog, cross-references carry a great deal of the burden of leading users to wanted material. Under the principle of uniform heading, a given subject is represented by only one term; users, however, cannot always be expected to know which of several synonyms or near-synonymous terms, or which of several possible forms, has been used as the heading. Furthermore, under the principle of specific and direct entry, material will be listed under a specific term even though many users may look for it under a more general term. Finally, the principle of alphabetical arrangement has the effect of dispersing headings for related subjects.

It is considered to be in the interest of users to lead them from terms that are not used in the catalog to those that are and, in addition, to lead them to terms used for related subjects. Both objectives are achieved by means of cross-references.

Four types of cross-references* are used in *Library of Congress Subject Headings*: *see* references, *see also* references, general references, and subject-to-name references. These are discussed below.

SEE REFERENCES[1]

A *see* reference guides the user from a term that is not used as a heading to the term that is. Synonymous terms, variant spellings, alternative forms, different entry elements, opposite terms, and "overly" narrow terms make such references necessary.

---

*Patterns and examples of cross-references for various types of headings in the Library of Congress system are given in appendix H of this book.

See references are important in that they provide an entry vocabulary in addition to the valid subject headings. A term in a subject heading provides only one access point, while a subject heading with, for example, four *see* references provides five access points; in other words, the user is able to access the subject through any of five possible synonymous or variant terms instead of one. In an effort to improve *Library of Congress Subject Headings* particularly for use in online catalogs, a recent project conducted by Pauline A. Cochrane[2] and sponsored by the Council on Library Resources studied this aspect of the syndetic structure of the Library of Congress system and explored means by which the entry vocabulary may be enriched.

See references from synonymous terms and variant spellings are generally made in most indexing systems. The other types of *see* references in the Library of Congress system are provided because of the principle of uniform heading and the unique features of specific and direct entry discussed earlier.

Synonymous Terms

When a heading has been chosen from two or more synonymous terms, *see* references are made from the unused terms to the heading. Charles A. Cutter's rule states: "Of two exactly synonymous names choose one and make a reference from the other."[3] In practice, this kind of reference is extended to near-synonymous terms when it is considered impractical to distinguish between them. David Judson Haykin notes that the basic significance of such references is that "the subject matter is entered not under the heading which occurred to the reader, but under the one chosen by the cataloger even when the terms are not completely synonymous."[4] Examples of *see* references from synonymous and near-synonymous terms are:*

Appetite depressants
   x Diet pills

Archaeology
   x Prehistory
       Ruins

Big bang theory
   x Superdense theory

Color vision
   x Color perception
       Color sense

Dogma
   x Doctrines

---

*The symbol *x* means a *see* reference is to be made *from* the term or terms that follow. For example, the list would include
   Ruins
      see **Archaeology**
   Prehistory
      see **Archaeology**

Genealogy
> *x* Genealogical research

Government lending
> *x* Government loans

Greenhouses
> *x* Hothouses

Liberty
> *x* Freedom

Stuffed foods (Cookery)
> *x* Filled foods (Cookery)

Variant Spellings

See references are made from different spellings and different grammatical structures of the same term:

Aeolian harp
> *x* Eolian harp

Airplanes
> *x* Aeroplanes

Archaeology
> *x* Archeology

Dialing
> *x* Dialling

Dogs
> *x* Dog

Fishing nets
> *x* Fish nets
>   Fishnets

Geoduck
> *x* Goeduck
>   Gooeyduck

Microcrystalline polymers
> *x* Microcrystal polymers
>   Polymer microcrystals

Seafood
> *x* Sea food

Abbreviations, Acronyms, Initials, Etc.

If the heading has been established in the spelled-out form, *see* references from abbreviated forms are not generally made unless such forms are well-known to the general public:

Adenylic acid
   x AMP

Ammonium nitrate fuel oil
   x AN-FO
      ANFO

If the heading has been established in the form of an abbreviation, an acronym, or initials, a *see* reference is made from the spelled-out form:

MARC System
   x Machine-readable Catalog System

ADEPT (Computer program)
   x A Distinctly Empirical Prover of Theorems

Different Language Terms

As a general rule, if the heading has been established in a foreign language because the foreign term is the more widely used term, *see* references are made from equivalent terms in English:

Laissez-faire
   x Free enterprise

On the other hand, *see* references are generally not made from equivalent terms in foreign languages *to* topical headings that are well established in English. However, they are regularly made to headings representing named entities:

Cubagua Island (Venezuela)
   x Isla Cubagua (Venezuela)

Texcal Cave (Mexico)
   x Cueva del Texcal (Mexico)

Popular and Scientific Terms

See references are made from popular terms to the scientific term chosen as the heading, and from scientific terms to the popular term if the latter has been chosen as the heading:

Prosencephalon
Forebrain

Cockroaches
    x   Blattariae

Medusahead wildrye
    x   Elymus caput-medusae
         Taeniatherum caput-medusae

Alternative Forms

Because of the principle of uniform heading, which requires that a heading appear in the catalog in only one form, other forms of the same heading likely to be consulted by users are referred to the form chosen as the heading. It should be pointed out, however, that in *Library of Congress Subject Headings* this is true in principle but not always consistent in practice, particularly among headings established earlier. Newly established headings show greater consistency.

Cataloging of manuscripts
    x   Manuscripts—Cataloging

Glass research
    x   Glass—Research

Education of the aged
    x   Aged—Education

Deaf—Education
    x   Education of the deaf

Foreign exchange—Accounting
    x   Foreign exchange accounting

Galaxies—Evolution
    x   Galactic evolution

Schools—Accounting
    x   School accounting

Cataloging of rare books
[No *see* references]

Hospitals — Accounting
[No *see* references]

Different Entry Elements

When a heading is inverted, a *see* reference is generally provided from the direct form:

Chemistry, Inorganic
    x   Inorganic chemistry

Exclusion, Right of
    x   Right of exclusion

In cases in which the first word in the direct form is nondistinctive and therefore not likely to be consulted by users, the reference is often omitted or made in a different form:

Plants, Effect of water levels on
    x   Water level effect on plants

Plants, Effect of hydrogen fluoride on
[No *see* references]

See references are made from inverted forms to direct headings when they are considered to provide useful access points:

Cataloging of anonymous classics
    x   Anonymous classics (Cataloging)

Cataloging of special collections in libraries
    x   Special collections in libraries, Cataloging of

Catalyst poisoning
    x   Poisoning of catalysts

Choice by lot
    x   Lot, Choice by

Electronics in biology
    x   Biology, Electronics in

Christian education
    x   Education, Christian

Mexican American arts
    x   Arts, Mexican American

When a compound heading expresses a relationship between two objects or concepts, a *see* reference is made from the form with the terms in reverse order:

Computers and civilization
    x Civilization and computers

Education and state
    x State and education

In the case of previously established compound headings that connect two parallel or opposite objects or concepts that are often treated in the same work but not necessarily in relationship to each other,* a *see* reference is made from the second term in the heading:

Encyclopedias and dictionaries
    x Dictionaries

Cities and towns
    x Towns

Emigration and immigration
    x Immigration

Opposite Terms Not Used as Headings

In the past, when a choice was made between two opposite terms as the heading, a *see* reference was made from the one not chosen:

Literacy
    x Illiteracy

Militarism
    x Antimilitarism

Temperance
    x Intemperance

This practice is now rare. Current policy is to establish both terms as separate headings when required.

Narrow Terms Not Used as Headings

When a term is considered too narrow to be established as a separate heading, a *see* reference, also called an upward reference, is sometimes made from the narrow term to a broader one which is used as a heading:

---

*Compound headings of this type are no longer being established. Separate headings are made instead.

Children as authors
> *x* Children as poets

Church management
> *x* Parish management

Pollution
> *x* Pollution — Control
> Pollution — Prevention

Schools — Accounting
> *x* High schools — Accounting
> Public schools — Accounting

Occasionally a *see* reference is made from a narrow term not used as a heading to a broader heading and to other related headings at the same time:

> Christmas books
> > *See* **Christmas**
> > **Christmas plays**
> > **Christmas stories**
> > **Gift-books (Annuals, etc.)**

In recent years fewer and fewer upward-pointing references have been added to the list. Recent policies prefer establishing the narrow terms as separate headings.

SEE ALSO REFERENCES[5]

The primary objective of the dictionary catalog is direct access, at the expense of subject collocation. In terms of subject relationship, the entries in a dictionary catalog appear in what Cutter calls a "most absurd proximity."[6] Yet the advantages of the classed catalog are not to be abandoned. As Cutter observes: "The dictionary catalog sets out with another object and a different method, but having attained that object — facility of reference — is at liberty to try to secure some of the advantages of classification and system in its own way."[7] Cutter seeks to combine the advantages of the dictionary catalog with those of an alphabetico-classed catalog by means of *see also* references: "By a well-devised network of cross-references, the mob becomes an army, of which each part is capable of assisting many other parts."[8] It is the *see also* references that impose a logical structure on the alphabetical subject catalog.

A *see also* reference connects two or more terms that are both (or all) used as subject headings. It usually expresses certain kinds of subject relationships. Cutter's rule states: "Make references from general subjects to their various subordinate subjects and also to coordinate and illustrative subjects."[9] Haykin rephrases the rule in these terms:

> In binding related headings together the basic rule is that a "see also" reference be made from a given subject: 1) to more specific subjects or topics comprehended within it, or to an application of

the subject; and 2) to coordinate subjects which suggest themselves as likely to be of interest to the user seeking material under the given heading, because they represent other aspects of the subject, or are closely related to it.[10]

Broad to Narrow

In modern indexing terms, a *see also* reference is made from a broader term (BT) to a narrower term (NT). In a hierarchy of subjects, each level is led to the one immediately subordinate to it, thus forming what Cutter calls a "pyramid of references."

In the Library of Congress system, each term in a chain of subjects from a hierarchical structure is usually connected to the one immediately below it by means of the *see also* reference.* This type of *see also* reference is called hierarchical reference. Examples include:

Chordata
    sa **Vertebrates**

Vertebrates
    sa **Mammals**

Mammals
    sa **Primates**

Primates
    sa **Monkeys**

Monkeys
    sa **Baboons**

Baboons
    sa **Hamadryas baboon**

Using the subject Cats as an example, Phyllis Allen Richmond[11] demonstrates the "hidden classification" in the cross-reference structure. Even though the structure is imperfect and could be improved, the potential is there.

Figure 5.1 illustrates part of a classificatory structure based on the *see also* references in *Library of Congress Subject Headings*. The hierarchical structure is embodied in the references, with only occasional irregularities. For instance, for the chain **Monkeys – Macaques – Japanese macaque**, the following references have been made:

Monkeys
    sa **Japanese macaque**
          Macaques

Macaques
    sa **Japanese macaque**

---

*The symbol *sa* means a *see also* reference is to be made *to* the term that follows.

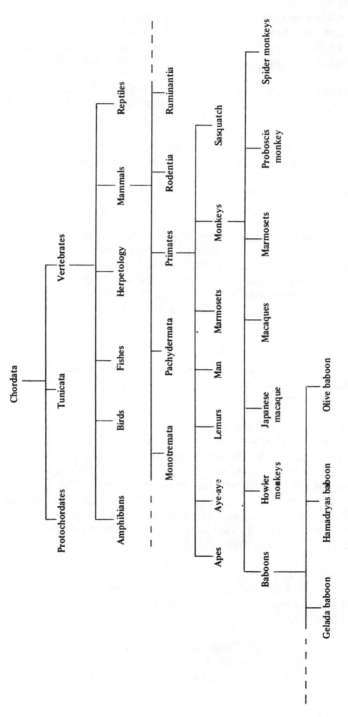

Figure 5.1. Part of a classificatory structure based on the *see also* references in *Library of Congress Subject Headings*.

In this case, a *see also* reference that circumvents a level in the hierarchy was made: **Japanese macaque**, which is a subordinate subject to **Macaques**, appears also on the same level of the hierarchy with the latter. Furthermore, the subject **Chordata** is not connected to any subject superordinate to it, e.g., **Animals.**

Theoretically, an alphabetical subject catalog with a thorough, systematically constructed network of cross-references can provide the best of both worlds by combining the advantages of the alphabetical and classified approaches. In practice, it has been questioned whether the labor required for the construction of such a system of reference is justified. Cutter experimented with "a synoptical table of subjects" for the Catalogue of the Library of the Boston Athenaeum. However, the Library's committee voted not to include the table, and Cutter conceded that the "immense labor" required was probably not justified after all:

> My experience then disposes me to adhere to the phrase "immense labor" and my observation since of the way in which catalogs are used makes me think that little practical utility was lost to the catalog by the Committee's vote. Such a table would be infrequently consulted, and it would be incomplete, as new headings are continually added to the catalog of a growing library.[12]

He was content to leave it to the tables and indexes of the Decimal and Expansive classification systems to satisfy the rare reader who wishes "to push his investigations into every ramification of his subject."

Haykin also expresses his thoughts on this topic:

> Subject references have been described in the literature of subject headings as a kind of substitute for the systematic arrangement of the classed catalog, in the sense that they make it possible for a reader to find in the alphabetical catalog the material on a subject and all of its ramifications. However, this claim for the alphabetical subject catalog is worth little since the reader could find all the material only with the great effort involved in following up all the references. In any case, the need for a comprehensive approach, whether through the classed catalog or syndetic features of the alphabetical subject catalog, has been overplayed: it is very rarely that a catalog can supply a sufficiently complete record of the literature of a subject, and the user who wants a comprehensive view of the literature of a subject would be better advised to resort to a bibliography.[13]

In 1984 the Library of Congress formalized its policy with regard to hierarchical references. Currently, hierarchical references are made between headings having the relationships delineated in items 1 through 5 below.

1) *Genus/species (or class/class member).* Examples include:

> **Sheep dogs**
> > *sa* **Belgian sheepdog**
>
> **Ecology**
> > *sa* **Sublittoral ecology**
>
> **Apes**
> > *sa* **Gorillas**
>
> **Airplanes**
> > *sa* **Biplanes**
>
> **German fiction**
> > *sa* **Science fiction, German**

The *see also* reference is *not* made, however, in cases of inverted headings qualified by names of languages, nationalities, or ethnic groups when the broader term is identical to the narrower heading without the qualifier. *See also* references such as

> **Art**
> > *sa* **Art, German**

are not made.

2) *Whole/part.* Examples include:

> **Fingers**
> > *sa* **Fingernails**
>
> **Coats**
> > *sa* **Lapels**

In some cases, a heading may belong to more than one hierarchy. A *see also* reference is made from the next-broader heading in each hierarchy:

> **Bridges**
> > *sa* **Arches**
>
> **Building**
> > *sa* **Arches**

3) *Instance (or generic topic/proper name heading).** Examples include:

> **World War, 1939-1945 — Campaigns — Italy**
> > *sa* **Cassino (Italy), Battle of, 1944**

---

*Forms of name headings and their qualifiers are discussed in detail in chapter 6.

> **Botanical gardens — California**
> *sa*   Huntington Herb Garden (San Marino, Calif.)
>
> **Mountains — France**
> *sa*   Vanoise Mountains (France)
>
> **Rivers — Colorado**
> *sa*   Gunnison River (Colo.)
>   North Platte River
>   Piedra River (Colo.)
>
> **Streets — France**
> *sa*   Boulevard du Temple (Paris, France)
>
> **Palaces — England**
> *sa*   Blenheim Palace (Blenheim, Oxfordshire)
>   Hampton Court (Hampton, Middlesex)
>
> **Buildings — Texas**
> *sa*   Old Stone Fort (Nacogdoches, Tex.)

The geographic subdivision in the generic heading is at the level of the country or first-order political division in the case of the United States, Great Britain, Canada, and the Soviet Union. This level is often broader than that represented by the qualifier of the individual name heading.

4)   *Subject-to-name references.* A special category of hierarchical references representing the instance relationship is called subject-to-name references. At the Library of Congress, the term (previously also called red-to-black references because of the once-common practice of typing subject headings in red) refers only to those *see also* references from topical headings to name headings, established according to *Anglo-American Cataloguing Rules*, second edition, that are to be used also as main or added entries in descriptive cataloging. These references, with a few exceptions, appear in the records in the name authority file but are not included in the printed list of *Library of Congress Subject Headings*.

The reason for making such references, as Haykin points out, is that "It avoids the multiplication of subject entries in instances where the author, or inevitable added entries, are sufficient to bring the material to the attention of the reader."[14]

a)   *Subject to personal names.* Previously, according to Haykin,[15] references to personal name headings from subject headings representing occupations were generally made:

> **Architects, British**
> *sa*   Wren, Sir Christopher, 1632-1723

However, this practice has been discontinued by the Library of Congress. The only types of personal name headings for which subject-to-name references are still made are those for biblical figures:

Bible — Biography
    sa Judas Iscariot
        Noah (Biblical figure)

(Forms of headings and references for legendary, mythological, and fictitious characters are discussed in chapter 6.)

    b) *Subject to corporate names.*[16] References from subject headings to corporate bodies associated with the particular subjects are very useful because of the numerous corporate publications that deal with their activities or their special fields of interest. Current practice at the Library of Congress is to provide such references to the following kinds of corporate headings: individual societies, institutions, firms, government agencies, and named exhibitions. The references are made from subject headings that most closely characterize the general nature and overall activities of the corporate body in question. In general, the subject heading is a generic heading subdivided by place (at the level of the country or, in the case of Canada, Great Britain, the Soviet Union, or the United States, at the level of a first-order political division or the country, as appropriate):

Engineering — United States — Societies, etc.
    sa American Institute of Mining, Metallurgical, and Petroleum Engineers

Hospitals, Voluntary — New York (State)
    sa Peekskill Community Hospital

Medical libraries — Maryland
    sa William H. Welch Medical Library

Art museums — Washington (State)
    sa Seattle Art Museum

Soft drink industry — Great Britain*
    sa Schweppes (Firm)

Cookie industry — United States*
    sa Famous Amos Chocolate Chip Cookie Corporation

United States — Diplomatic and consular service — France
    sa United States. Embassy (France)

Urban transportation — United States
    sa United States. Urban Mass Transportation Administration

---

*The generic heading for an industry or trade is subdivided at the level of the country in all cases.

Art — Exhibitions
    sa   Biennale di Venezia

Agricultural colleges — Michigan
    sa   Michigan State University.   College of Agriculture

Airports — New York (State)
    sa   La Guardia Airport

International airports — New York (State)
    sa   John F. Kennedy International Airport

German literature — Societies, etc.
    sa   Verband Deutscher Schriftsteller

    c) *Subject to uniform titles.* Subject-to-name references are made for the uniform titles of sacred books and of radio and television programs. Examples include:

Buddhism — Sacred books
    sa   Tantras.   Guhyasamājatantra

Confucianism — Sacred books
    sa   Shih san ching

Radio programs — United States
    sa   Voice of America (Radio program)

Television programs — Canada
    sa   Connections (Television program)

    5) *References to compound and complex headings.* For headings containing multiple topics or concepts, *see also* references are made from those topics or concepts not used as the entry element. Such topics, which often represent generic concepts with regard to the compound or complex headings, are presented in their established heading form:

Anthropology
    sa   Communism and anthropology

Crime and criminals
    sa   Education and crime

Fuel
    sa   Hydrogen as fuel

City planning
    sa   Aerial photography in city planning

Photography, Aerial
    sa   Aerial photography in city planning

Moving-pictures
 sa **Surrealism in motion pictures**

Roman law
 sa **Domestic relations (Roman law)**

Contracting out
 sa **Municipal services — Contracting out**

Narrow to Broad

The question is often raised as to why *see also* references are not made from narrow headings to broad ones. Paul S. Dunkin sees the advantage of references going both up and down. He feels that upward *see also* references will help the subject catalog to fulfill a third objective: "To show what books the library has on broader subjects which include the narrow topic the user specifically wants."[17]

Wyllis E. Wright also feels that the lack of such upward references represents a loss to the user: "The practice of referring from the general to the particular but not vice versa means that a large segment of the available material on any subject may be lost, since it is generally true that more useful material on a topic is usually to be found in sections of works on larger subjects than in any of the books on more specific subjects."[18]

In fact, Cutter has a rule dealing with this aspect: "Make references occasionally from specific to general subjects." While recognizing that "much information about limited topics is to be found in more general works; the very best description of a single plant or of a family of plants may perhaps be contained in a botanical encyclopaedia,"[19] Cutter concedes that it is out of the question to make all possible references of the ascending kind. He explains the reason with an example:

> From **Cathedrals**, for example, one would naturally refer to **Christian art** and to **Ecclesiastical architecture**, because works on those subjects will contain more or less on cathedrals. But so will histories of architecture and histories of English, French, German, Italian, or Spanish architecture; so will travels in England, France, Germany, Italy, Spain. And anyone who desired to take an absolutely complete survey of the subject, or who was willing to spend unlimited time in getting information on some detail, would have to consult such books. Yet the cataloger may very excusably not think of referring to those subjects, or if he thinks of it may deem the connection too remote to justify reference, and that he should be overloading the catalog with what would be generally useless.[20]

Dunkin appears to accept Cutter's argument: "Perhaps it is just as well. If the system of 'see also' references were complete both going up and coming down, it is likely that the user would never bother to follow the directions hither and yon. Even if he did bother, he would soon grow weary."[21] Haykin also agrees: "References from the specific to the broader heading would have the effect of sending the reader on a wild goose chase.... Furthermore, if references from all topics comprehended within a given subject were to be made, on the assumption that the reader would find in treatises on that subject material on these topics, the catalog would be cluttered up with a plethora of references."[22] In practice, upward *see also* references are seldom ever made in *Library of Congress Subject Headings.*

Coordinate Subjects (Related-Term References)

See also references are made between terms that are related other than hierarchically, i.e., related terms which do not constitute a genus/species or whole/part relationship. In this case, since neither term is broader than the other, the *see also* references are made both ways:*

Religion
    sa **Theology**
    xx **Theology**

Theology
    sa **Religion**
    xx **Religion**

Comprehension
    sa **Memory**
    xx **Memory**

Memory
    sa **Comprehension**
    xx **Comprehension**

In most indexing systems, the symbols BT (broader term), NT (narrower term), and RT (related term) are used to indicate the relationships between subjects connected by the references. In *Library of Congress Subject Headings, sa* and *xx* are used for both types of *see also* references. Although there has been a long-standing policy to make *see also* references from broad to narrow terms between hierarchically related concepts and to make them both ways if they are coordinate concepts, unfortunately the policy has not been strictly adhered to in the past, making the automatic conversion of *sa* and *xx* to BT, NT, RT and the automatic construction of hierarchical trees practically impossible.

Beginning in 1984, when the Library of Congress formalized its policy with regard to *see also* references, two-way related-term references are now required in the following cases:

---

*The symbol *xx* means that a *see also* reference is to be made *from* the heading that follows.

o To link two terms with overlapping meanings

Ships
    sa **Boats and boating**
    xx **Boats and boating**

o To link a discipline and the object studied

Epithelial cells
    sa **Exfoliative cytology**
    xx **Exfoliative cytology**

Entomology
    sa **Insects**
    xx **Insects**

o To link persons and their fields or endeavor

Physicians
    sa **Medicine**
    xx **Medicine**

o To link products and industries

Airplanes
    sa **Aircraft industry**
    xx **Aircraft industry**

o To link other closely related terms

Drugs — Overdosage
    sa **Medication errors**
    xx **Medication errors**

Clinical sociology
    sa **Social psychiatry**
    xx **Social psychiatry**

Longevity
    sa **Old age**
    xx **Old age**

Purchasing power
    sa **Income**
    xx **Income**

Earthquakes
    sa **Seismetry**
    xx **Seismetry**

GENERAL REFERENCES

See and *see also* references made to individual headings are called specific references. Frequently, a *see also* reference is made to an entire group or category of headings instead of individual members of the group or category. This is called a general reference. Such references represent an open-ended approach, in that no exhaustive list of headings referred to is given, and the user is left to formulate the terms to be searched. In the past, a frequently used type of general *see also* reference was one made from the generic heading to its members named collectively, with one or more specific examples given:

Tools
    sa specific tools, e.g. Files and rasps, Saws

The policy of making this type of general *see also* reference has now been largely abandoned by the Library of Congress[23] in favor of making specific references. Nonetheless, many such references that were established in the past remain in the printed list. Attempts are being made to replace these gradually with specific references.

Still, there are situations under which it is impractical or redundant to make specific references. In such cases, general *see also* references are used. Currently there are two types of such references:

1) *General* see also *references to headings beginning with synonymous terms*:

Kidneys
    sa headings beginning with the word Renal

Strictly speaking, these references are not open-ended, in that the headings referred to are enumerated in the printed list. Because they can be readily identified and located, it would be redundant to list them in the reference.

2) *General* see also *references to subdivisions.* Under topical or form headings, general *see also* references are given to indicate the use of the concept as a topical or form subdivision under other headings:

o   References to subdivisions under name headings

    Cults
        sa subdivision Cult *under names of individual deities, saints, etc., e.g.* Mary, Blessed Virgin, Saint — Cult

    Exhibitions
       — Awards
              sa subdivision Awards *under names of individual exhibitions*

o   References to subdivisions under place names

Census
   sa   subdivision Census *or* Census, [date] *under names of countries, cities, etc.*

o   References to subdivisions under topical headings

Rare books *(Indirect)*
   sa   subdivision Bibliography—First editions *under names of literature, e.g.,* English literature—Bibliography—First editions

Most of these references are made to free-floating subdivisions. However, a number of them are made to non-free-floating subdivisions. Therefore, the presence of such a reference does not indicate the free-floating status of a particular subdivision.[24]

CONCLUSION

The cross-references in the alphabetical subject catalog provide a useful structure of subject relationships. In practice, however, it has not been demonstrated whether the effectiveness and usefulness of these references have been realized in actual use. In many libraries, it is a question whether all appropriate references have been provided in the catalog. To ensure that all the suggested references are made and placed in a catalog requires a great deal of effort and time. At a time when fast cataloging is of first priority and online cataloging is often performed by technicians at the terminal, one wonders how many libraries are actually able to follow up on all the references each time a new heading is introduced into the catalog or a new reference has been suggested by the Library of Congress. On the other hand, both the principle of specific entry and the principle of uniform heading rely heavily on cross-references for subject collocation. Omission or negligence in the provision of cross-references reduces access points and greatly lessens the effectiveness of the alphabetical subject catalog as a tool for subject retrieval.

REFERENCES

[1]Library of Congress, Subject Cataloging Division, *Subject Cataloging Manual: Subject Headings*, prelim. ed. (Washington, D.C.: Library of Congress, 1984), H373.

[2]Pauline A. Cochrane, "LCSH Entry Vocabulary Project: Final Report to the Council on Library Resources and to the Library of Congress," March 1983.

[3]Charles A. Cutter, *Rules for a Dictionary Catalog*, 4th ed. (Washington, D.C.: Government Printing Office, 1904), 70.

[4]David Judson Haykin, *Subject Headings: A Practical Guide* (Washington, D.C.: Government Printing Office, 1951), 14.

[5]Library of Congress, *Subject Cataloging Manual*, H371, H375.

[6]Cutter, *Rules for a Dictionary Catalog*, 79.

[7]Ibid.

[8]Ibid.

[9]Ibid.

[10]Haykin, *Subject Headings*, 14.

[11]Phyllis Allen Richmond, "Cats: An Example of Concealed Classification in Subject Headings," *Library Resources & Technical Services* 3:102-112 (Spring 1959).

[12]Cutter, *Rules for a Dictionary Catalog*, 80.

[13]David Judson Haykin, "Subject Headings: Principles and Development," in *The Subject Analysis of Library Materials*, ed. Maurice F. Tauber (New York: School of Library Service, Columbia University, 1953), 52.

[14]Haykin, *Subject Headings*, 16.

[15]Ibid.

[16]Library of Congress, *Subject Cataloging Manual*, H392.

[17]Paul S. Dunkin, *Cataloging U.S.A.* (Chicago: American Library Association, 1969), 81.

[18]Wyllis E. Wright, "Standards for Subject Headings: Problems and Opportunities," *Journal of Cataloging and Classification* 10:175-176 (October 1954).

[19]Cutter, *Rules for a Dictionary Catalog*, 80.

[20]Ibid.

[21]Dunkin, *Cataloging U.S.A.*, 81.

[22]Haykin, "Subject Headings: Principles and Development," 51.

[23]"General See Also References," *Cataloging Service Bulletin* 19:15 (Winter 1982).

[24]Ibid., 16.

6
PROPER NAMES IN SUBJECT HEADINGS

INTRODUCTION

Proper names are frequently used as subject headings, as parts of subject headings, or as subdivisions. These names include personal names, names of corporate bodies, geographic names, names of works established as uniform titles, and names of individual entities. In the past, most of these headings were not printed in *Library of Congress Subject Headings*, but this policy has been changed. The tenth edition reflects the policy change made in 1976 to include the name headings established by the Subject Cataloging Division. At the Library of Congress, headings for proper names that have been or are likely to be used in descriptive cataloging are established by the Descriptive Cataloging Division according to *Anglo-American Cataloguing Rules*, second edition (*AACR2*).[1] These include headings for persons, corporate bodies, jurisdictions, and uniform titles. These headings are not printed* in *Library of Congress Subject Headings* except for the few that are included for the purpose of displaying special subdivisions or unique references, or of serving as pattern headings. Also omitted from the printed list are free-floating phrase headings such as regions of geographic features, regions of cities, and metropolitan areas. For headings not included in the printed list, one should consult name authority files or publications issued by the Library of Congress, such as the automated name authorities database or *Name Authorities: Cumulative Microform Edition*.[2]

This chapter discusses and presents numerous examples of the types of proper name headings used in subject headings. Appendix H shows the patterns of cross-references for such headings.

---

*For a more detailed discussion of unprinted headings, see chapter 8.

AACR2 AND SUBJECT HEADINGS[3]

In 1981, with the implementation of *AACR2*, many of the name headings previously established under earlier codes became obsolete. By far the greatest impact of *AACR2* is seen in headings containing jurisdictional names. For example, virtually all headings containing names of cities have had to be revised in order to be compatible with *AACR2* provisions. Many personal and corporate name headings, as well as other types of geographic name headings, are also affected. The Library of Congress Subject Cataloging Division made the decision to cancel all such existing headings and reinstate in *AACR2* form those headings required for new cataloging or for the purpose of displaying subdivisions, examples, notes, or references. Such changes are regularly published in *LC Subject Headings Weekly Lists* and incorporated into the cumulated quarterly microfiche editions of *Library of Congress Subject Headings*.

PERSONAL NAMES

Names of Individual Persons

Names of individual persons are used as subject headings for biographies, eulogies, festschriften, criticisms, bibliographies, and literary works in which the persons figure. At the Library of Congress, to ensure that the same form of a personal name is used for both author and subject entries, headings consisting of names of persons are established by the Descriptive Cataloging Division according to *AACR2*. Following are some examples of personal name headings:

> **Adams, James, d. 1794**
> **Adams, G. J. (George Jones), 1813-1880**
> **Adrian VI, Pope, 1459-1523**
> **Andrews, C. S., 1901-**
> **Alexander, the Great, 356-323 B.C.**
> **Beatrix, Queen of the Netherlands, 1938-**
> **Adam, of Orlton, Bishop of Winchester, d. 1345**
> **Catherine II, Empress of Russia, 1729-1790**
> **Charlemagne, Emperor, 742-814**
> **Thomas, Aquinas, Saint, 1225?-1274**

Personal name headings for literary authors may be subdivided according to the pattern heading Shakespeare.* Name headings for other persons may be subdivided by the subdivisions appearing in the list of free-floating subdivisions used under names of persons.* Examples include:

---

*For complete lists of these subdivisions, see appendixes D and F.

> Eliot, T. S. (Thomas Stearns), 1888-1965 — Criticism and interpretation
> Dickens, Charles, 1812-1870 — Technique
> Alexander, the Great, 356-323 B.C. — Friends and associates
> Mozart, Wolfgang Amadeus, 1756-1791 — Iconography
> Kennedy, John F. (John Fitzgerald), 1917-1963 — Assassination

A number of subdivisions appear under the heading for Shakespeare that are not applicable to works about him. Because the heading for Shakespeare serves as the pattern for subdivisions, such subdivisions are included for use with headings for other literary authors; for example: **Shakespeare, William, 1564-1616 — Political career**.

Names of Families, Dynasties, Royal Houses, Etc.[4]

The heading for a family name appears in the form of **[Proper name] family**, e.g., **Rockefeller family**. The older form with qualifier, e.g., Smith family (William Smith, 1669-1743), has been discontinued. No effort is made to distinguish between families with the same surname. The heading **Kennedy family**, for example, is used for works about any family with the surname Kennedy.

See references are made from each known variant of the family name:

> **Adams family**
>   *x* Adamson family
>   Addam family
>   Addams family
>
> **Goodenough family**
>   *x* Goodenow family
>   Goodnough family

Variants are usually determined from the work being cataloged and from standard reference works. Individual entries in the catalog often serve as a source for name variants based on surnames found there.

Similar family names from different ethnic backgrounds and family names that have been changed as the result of emigration are established as separate headings, connected by *see also* references:

> **Koch family**
>   *sa* **Cook family**
>
> **Cook family**
>   *sa* **Koch family**
>
> **McGregor family**
>   *sa* **Gregory family**
>
> **Gregory family**
>   *sa* **McGregor family**

Topical *see also* references are not made for family names.

Names of dynasties and royal houses are established in the following forms: [**Name**] **dynasty** [for non-European royal houses]; [**Name**], **House of** [for European royal houses]. Dates indicating the span of years of a particular dynasty are added to the heading whenever possible. *See* references are made from variant forms of the name, and *see also* references are made from appropriate history headings for dynasties and from [**Country (or region)**] — **Kings and rulers** for royal houses. Examples include:

Hoysala dynasty, ca. 1006-ca. 1346
    xx **India — History — 1000-1526**

Habsburg, House of
    x Austria, House of
        Hapsburg, House of
    xx **Austria — Kings and rulers**

Saxe-Coburg-Gotha, House of
    x Coburg, House of
    xx **Bavaria (Germany) — Kings and rulers**

Savoy, House of
    xx **Italy — Kings and rulers**

Orange-Nassau, House of
    xx **Netherlands — Kings and rulers**

Headings for individually named houses of dukes, counts, or earls are established in the form of [**Name**], [**Title of rank in English**] **of**. For such names, *see also* references are made from [**Country**] — **Nobility**. Examples include:

Leinster, Dukes of
    xx **Ireland — Nobility**

Celje, Counts of
    xx **Slovenia — Nobility**

Derby, Earls of
    xx **England — Nobility**

Names of Mythological, Legendary, or Fictitious Characters

Names of mythological, legendary, or fictitious characters are not covered by *AACR2*. However, they are often required as subject headings. As David Judson Haykin comments,

Beings whose existence belongs in the realm of myth or pure literary invention may achieve identity to a point where books are written about them. Names of such beings may be used as subject headings exactly as those of real persons. The same rules apply with respect to the choice of form of name and references. The best-known English form should be given preference and references made from other, including vernacular, forms.[5]

Headings for mythological characters that are not gods or goddesses are established in the form of [Name of character] ([Ethnic adjective] mythology), e.g., Draupadī (Hindu mythology); Lilith (Semitic mythology). The qualifier (Legendary character) is used with headings for legendary characters:

> Pregnant man (Legendary character)
> Anansi (Legendary character)
> Bunyan, Paul (Legendary character)
> Pecos Bill (Legendary character)

However, the qualifiers ([Ethnic adjective] mythology) and (Legendary character) are not used with pre-1501 European legendary or mythological characters:

> Arthur, King
> Robin Hood
> Aeneas

The qualifier (Fictitious character) is used with names of characters of literary or artistic invention, as opposed to legendary characters originating from legends, myths, or folklore. Examples of headings for fictitious characters include:

> Tarzan (Fictitious character)
> Octobriana (Fictitious character)
> Bond, James (Fictitious character)
> Holmes, Sherlock (Fictitious character)

Literary characters associated with a particular author's work or works are also represented by headings of the type [Author] — Characters — [Name of character], e.g., Shakespeare, William, 1564-1616 — Characters — Falstaff. This results in duplicate entries:

> 1. Holmes, Sherlock (Fictitious character)
> 2. Doyle, Arthur Conan, Sir, 1859-1930 — Characters
>   — Sherlock Holmes.

Names of comic characters are also established in the form of [Name of character] (Fictitious character),* e.g., Snoopy (Fictitious character); Felix the Cat (Fictitious character).

---

*Headings for comic characters were established formerly with the qualifier (Cartoon character). These headings will continue to be used, but newly established headings will carry the qualifier (Fictitious character).

Names of Gods and Goddesses

Names of gods and goddesses are established in the form of [**Name of god** *or* **goddess**] ([**Ethnic adjective**] **deity**), e.g., **Krishna (Hindu deity); Sekmet (Egyptian deity); Apollo (Greek deity)**. Previously, names of gods and goddesses of classical mythology were usually established only in the Latin form, with *see* references from the names of their Greek counterparts. Charles A. Cutter defends the use of the Latin form for the reasons "(1) that the Latin names are at present more familiar to the majority of readers; (2) that it would be difficult to divide the literature, or if it were done, many books must be put both under **Zeus** and **Jupiter, Poseidon** and **Neptune**, etc., filling considerable room with no practical advantage."[6] This policy has been changed. The current policy[7] requires that the heading be established in the form used in the work being cataloged, e.g., **Hermes (Greek deity); Cacus (Roman deity)**.

When equivalencies can be determined between Greek and Roman gods and goddesses, reciprocal *see also* references are made between them:

Jupiter (Roman deity)
    sa **Zeus (Greek deity)**

Zeus (Greek deity)
    sa **Jupiter (Roman deity)**

NAMES OF CORPORATE BODIES

Works related to the origin, development, activities, and functions of corporate bodies are assigned subject entries under their names. Headings for corporate bodies, like personal name headings, are established according to *AACR2* by the Descriptive Cataloging Division at the Library of Congress.

Corporate bodies include public and private organizations, societies, associations, institutions, government agencies, commercial firms, churches, and other groups identified by a name, such as conferences and exploring expeditions. Examples of corporate names used as subject headings are given below. Some of the headings are qualified by generic terms or names of places,* as required according to *AACR2* and Library of Congress descriptive cataloging policies.

Alexandria Archaeological Research Museum
Austin High School (Austin, Tex.)
Bahamas. Dept. of Agriculture
Błyskawica (Destroyer)
Board of Governors of the Federal Reserve System (U.S.)
California. Dept. of Parks and Recreation
Canada. Royal Canadian Navy

---

*For the forms of geographic names used as qualifiers, see pages 134-139.

Carnegie Institution of Washington.   Desert Botanical Laboratory
Catholic Church.   Diocese of Sansepolcro (Italy)
China.   Chung-kuo jen min chieh fang chun
Church of Jesus Christ of the Latter-Day Saints
Clairvaux (Abbey).   Bibliothèque
Cleveland Museum of Art
Community Church (East Williston, N.Y.)
Conferencia General del Episcopado Latinoamericano
      (3rd : 1979 : Puebla, Mexico)
Council of Economic Advisers (U.S.)
Freemasons.   Henrico Union Lodge, No. 130 (Richmond, Va.)
Freie Deutsche Jugend
League of Women Voters (U.S.)
New York Yankees (Baseball team)
Ohio State University.   Marching Band
Olympic Games (1980 : Moscow, R.S.F.S.R.)
Royal Oak (Battleship)
Synanon (Foundation)
Teens (Musical group)

Certain categories of corporate headings, particularly headings for religions and religious orders, may be subdivided geographically to bring out the actual physical presence of a corporate body or its individual members in a particular location. Examples include: **Benedictines—Europe; Church of England—New England; Peace Corps (U.S.)—Ghana**. Through 1982, the indication that a corporate heading may be subdivided geographically was given in *Library of Congress Subject Headings* by listing the corporate heading with the designation *(Indirect)*. Beginning in 1983, the indication that a corporate heading may be subdivided geographically is given in the record for the heading in the name authority file. Newly established corporate headings appear in *Library of Congress Subject Headings* only if unique subdivisions are required or if the heading serves as a model heading.[8] The previous practice of using the type of heading **[Corporate body name] in [Place]** to bring out the geographic aspect has been discontinued. Current practice requires the form **[Corporate body name]** *(Indirect)*, e.g., **Catholic Church—Belgium**.

Name Changes in Corporate Bodies

When the name of a corporate body is changed, successive entries are established according to *AACR2*. However, for subject cataloging purposes, successive entries for the same corporate body are not assigned to the same work even if it covers the history of the body under different names;* instead, *see also* references are provided under the various headings established.

---

*For the assignment of subject headings to works about a corporate body, see chapter 9.

Information References

Previously, when a corporate body or jurisdiction had undergone complicated name changes, an information reference (also called a history card or information card) was made. The information reference consisted of the heading, an explanatory text that included a brief history of the changes (date of founding, name changes, connection with other bodies, date of dissolution, etc.), a list of headings in catalog entry form, and a subject entry statement. Examples are shown in Figure 6.1.

Kensington and Chelsea Public Libraries.

After the London boroughs of Kensington and Chelsea joined to form the Royal Borough of Kensington and Chelsea, the Kensington Public Library and its branches, and the Chelsea Public Library became part of the Kensington and Chelsea Public Libraries.
Works by these bodies are found under the following headings according to the name used at the time of publication:

Kensington, Eng. Public Libraries.
Chelsea, Eng. Public Libraries and Museums.
Kensington and Chelsea Public Libraries.

SUBJECT ENTRY: Works about these bodies are entered under the name resulting from the merger. Works limited in subject coverage to the pre-merger period are entered under the name of one or more of the original bodies.

74-236474

Library of Congress   75 [2]

Catholic Church. Congregatio Sacrorum Rituum.

The Congregatio Sacrorum Rituum (established in 1588) was divided in 1969 to form the Sacra Congregatio pro Cultu Divino and the Sacra Congregatio pro Causis Sanctorum.
Works by these bodies are found under the following headings according to the name used at the time of publication:

Catholic Church. Congregatio Sacrorum Rituum.
Catholic Church. Congregatio pro Cultu Divino.
Catholic Church. Congregatio pro Causis Sanctorum.

SUBJECT ENTRY: Works about these bodies are entered under one or more of the names resulting from the separation. Works limited in coverage to the pre-separation period are entered under the name of the original body.

73-210400

Library of Congress   73 [2]

Figure 6.1. Information references. Card at top illustrates merger; card at bottom illustrates separation.

In the spring of 1981 the Library of Congress discontinued making this type of reference because the workload at the Descriptive Cataloging Division was such that the staff was unable to cope with the tremendous amount of maintenance required to keep such references current. Information about changes is still recorded in the name authority records. However, the references now appear in the catalog in the form of simple successive *see also* references. In the Library of Congress name authority file, the phrase *search also under* is used instead of *see also*. Examples include:

> **Orange County State College**
> Search also under the later heading:
> **Orange State College**

> **Orange State College**
> Search also under the earlier heading:
> **Orange County State College**

> **Orange State College**
> Search also under the later heading:
> **California State College at Fullerton**

> **California State College at Fullerton**
> Search also under the earlier heading:
> **Orange State College**

> **California State College at Fullerton**
> Search also under the later heading:
> **California State University, Fullerton**

> **California State University, Fullerton**
> Search also under the earlier heading:
> **California State College at Fullerton**

> **American Library Association.   Information Science and Automation Division**
> Search also under the later heading:
> **Library and Information Technology Association (U.S.)**

> **Library and Information Technology Association (U.S.)**
> Search also under the earlier heading:
> **American Library Association.   Information Science and Automation Division**

OTHER INDIVIDUAL ENTITIES BEARING PROPER NAMES

In addition to the proper names discussed above, many other individual entities that bear proper names also serve as subject headings. Some of the categories are given below with examples.

Historical Events

Historical events identified by specific names are entered under their names, usually accompanied by dates. They may appear as main headings or as period subdivisions:

World War, 1939-1945
King Philip's War, 1675-1676
United States—History—King William's War, 1689-1697
Waterloo, Battle of, 1815
Canadian Invasion, 1775-1776
Northwestern Conspiracy, 1864
Canadian Spy Trials, 1946
Pacific Coast Indians, Wars with, 1847-1865
Chrysler Corporation Slowdown Strike, 1939*
Anthracite Coal Strike, 1887-1888*
Garment Workers' Strike, New York, N.Y., 1912-1913*
Bookbinders' Strike, London, England, 1901*
American Revolution Bicentennial, 1776-1976
American Revolution Bicentennial, 1776-1976—Pennsylvania—
    Philadelphia
Louisiana Purchase

Names of other events may also be used as headings, e.g., **Brighton Run (Antique car race)**; **National Library Week**.

Named Projects

The word *project* is defined in a generic sense to refer to all named undertakings or plans for action toward a desired goal, including "projects," "operations," "programs," "plans," etc. The Library of Congress usually adopts the form of the name found in the work cataloged or in other sources. If there is a choice, the form in which the generic word appears first is used. In either case, the first letter of the generic word is capitalized. Examples of headings for named projects are:

---

*For instruction concerning the forms of headings for strikes, consult the note under the heading **Strikes and Lockouts** in the printed list.

Appalachian Oral History Project
Operation Menace
Project Neptune
MARC System
Right to Read Program
Pacific Ocean Biological Survey Program
National Program for Acquisitions and Cataloging

Animals[9]

Subject headings are sometimes required for works about famous animals:

Morris (Cat)
   xx Cats

Dancer's Image (Race Horse)
   xx Race horses

Prizes, Awards, Scholarships, Etc.

Individual prizes, awards, scholarships, etc., are represented by specific headings:

Geroĭ Sovetskogo Soĭuza
   x Hero of the Soviet Union

Evening Standard Drama Awards

Hadiah Adinegoro
   x Adinegoro prize

Music Festivals

Music festivals are entered under their names in direct order, e.g., **Internationales Heinrich-Schutz-Fest; Latvian Song Festival; Mount Pilot Festival.**

Holidays, Festivals, Etc.

Examples of headings for holidays, festivals, etc., are:

Ascension Day
Christmas
Fools, Feast of
Halloween
Memorial Day
Thanksgiving Day
Yom Kippur

Ethnic Groups, Nationalities, Tribes, Etc.[10]

Previously, many headings for individual nationalities were established in the form of **[National group] in [Place]**, e.g., **Poles in Austria; Russians in France**. All such headings have been converted to the form of **[National group] — [Place]**, e.g., **Poles — Austria; Russians — France**.

Headings for groups of individual nationalities living in the United States as permanent residents or naturalized citizens are established in the composite form **[Qualifier designating country of origin] Americans**, e.g., **Japanese Americans**. These headings may be further subdivided by locality. Headings such as **Japanese — United States** and **Germans — United States** are used for aliens living in the United States, students from abroad, etc. For groups of Americans already identified with ethnic groups whose names are in composite form, e.g., Russian Germans in the United States, headings such as **Russian Germans — United States** are used instead of Russian German Americans.

For a specific nationality in a foreign country, headings of the type **[Nationality] — [Place]** are used whether these people reside in the country permanently or temporarily.

Examples of headings for ethnic groups, etc., are:

North Africans
North Africans — Belgium
Saracens
Arabs
Italians
Italians — Foreign countries*
Italians — United States [for aliens]
Italian Americans [for natives]
Japanese — California [for aliens]
Japanese Americans — California — San Francisco [for natives]
Indians of North America
Nzakara (African people)

Religions, Philosophical Systems, Etc.

Examples of headings for individual religions, philosophical systems, etc., are **Buddhism; Christianity; Confucianism; Islam; Neoplatonism**.

Objects Bearing Proper Names

Specific name headings are also established for objects bearing proper names, e.g., **Bury Saint Edmunds Cross; Conquistadora (Statue); Rubik's Cube**.

---

*This is a free-floating subdivision under headings for nationalities.

GEOGRAPHIC NAMES[11]

Geographic names are widely used in both subject and descriptive cataloging. In subject headings, they may be the main heading or part of a heading phrase, they may be used as a subdivision, or they may figure as a qualifier. Examples are **Jamaica — Description and travel; Paris (France) in literature; Library finance — United States; Building permits — Belgium; Church of God (Cleveland, Tenn.).**

Names of countries and divisions of countries such as provinces, states, cities, and towns, are referred to as jurisdictional names. Such names are used very heavily in descriptive cataloging as entries in themselves, as parts of corporate names, or as additional designations or qualifiers. At the Library of Congress, therefore, the establishment of such names is the responsibility of the Descriptive Cataloging Division, which follows the provisions of *AACR2* for geographic names. Other geographic names, such as those for natural features and man-made structures associated with places, are referred to as nonjurisdictional names. With few exceptions, nonjurisdictional headings are established and maintained by the Subject Cataloging Division, which attempts to ensure compatibility with *AACR2* whenever possible.

It is for geographic names that the implementation of *AACR2* has had the most significant impact. Because of the new rules themselves and the Library of Congress's decisions on various options in the rules, many pre-1981 geographic headings are obsolete and must be updated before they can be used in new cataloging. Obsolete headings are being canceled and removed from *Library of Congress Subject Headings*, and those required for cataloging new works or needed for displaying unique subdivisions or references are being reestablished in *AACR2* form.[12]

The following sections discuss general aspects of geographic heading formation and usage. Because the distinction between jurisdictional and non-jurisdictional names comes into the discussion at many points, the first two sections extend and give examples for the brief definitions presented above. Later sections treat language, choice of entry element, qualifiers, free-floating phrase headings, changes of name, and cross-references. A final section deals with categories of geographic headings that require special treatment.

Jurisdictional Headings

Entities that can be called jurisdictions include countries, principalities, territories, states, provinces, counties, administrative districts, cities, archdioceses, and dioceses. When names for these entities figure in subject cataloging, it is the *AACR2* forms established by the Descriptive Cataloging Division that are used. Examples of jurisdictional names are:

Great Britain
Sardinia (Kingdom)
Ontario
Pennsylvania
Brittany (France)

Dorset
Berks County (Pa.)
Alexandria (Egypt)
Alexandria (Va.)
Anglesey (Gwynedd)
London (England)
Bavaria (Germany)
Hanover Township (Ill.)
Berlin (Germany)*

Nonjurisdictional Headings

There are many headings for geographic areas or entities that are not jurisdictional units. As noted above, these headings are established by the Subject Cataloging Division. They are printed in *Library of Congress Subject Headings*, with the exception of those formed by using free-floating terms (a matter that is covered on pages 140-142 of this chapter). Types of places with nonjurisdictional names include:

archaeological sites, ancient cities, kingdoms
areas and regions
canals
city sections
dams
forests, grasslands, etc.
geographic features (e.g., caves, deserts, islands, lakes, mountains,
    plains, ocean currents, rivers, seas, steppes, valleys)
geologic basins
parks, reserves, refuges, etc.
reservoirs
roads
trails
tunnels

Examples of headings for nonjurisdictional place names are:

Arroyo Hondo Site (N.M.)
Knossos (Ancient city)
Africa, Southern
Gulf Region (Tex.)**
Lehigh Canal (Pa.)
South Philadelphia (Philadelphia, Pa.)
North End (Boston, Mass.)
Missouri River
Grand Canyon (Ariz.)

---

*The formations **Berlin (Germany : East)** and **Berlin (Germany : West)** are used only as parts of headings for corporate bodies located in East or West Berlin, e.g., **Berlin (Germany : West). Abgeordnetenhaus; Berlin (Germany : West). Senat.**
**A discussion of geographic qualifiers appears on pages 134-139.

Glacier Bay (Alaska)
Himalaya Mountains
Tahoe, Lake (Calif. and Nev.)
Gateway National Recreational Area (N.J. and N.Y.)
Black Hills National Forest (S.D. and Wyo.)
Big Sur Coast National Scenic Area (Calif.)
Big Cypress National Preserve (Fla.)
Big Bend National Park (Tex.)
Santa Fe Trail

Language

In determining the language of a geographic name to be used in a heading, the Library of Congress usually gives priority to the decisions of the U.S. Board on Geographic Names (BGN) as a favored authority. The decisions made by the BGN are evaluated in connection with the other reference sources used as authorities for establishing geographic names (see appendix I for a list of these authorities) to determine if there are any conflicts with existing headings and to aid in the preparation of cross-references.

Naturally, for places in English-speaking regions, English names are used. For foreign places, on the other hand, a choice must often be made between English names and vernacular names. In some cases, the BGN may approve both an English and a vernacular form of the name; in such cases, in accordance with *AACR2*, if there is an English form of the name in general use, it is chosen as the heading.[13] This policy is in general agreement with Haykin's comments:

> The language of the heading is fundamentally an aspect of usage and should respond to it. Of the several forms of a place name found in works of reference or monographs, that one is to be preferred which is found in English-language works, representing, therefore, the usage in English-speaking countries.... Smaller, remote, or little-known geographic entities are likely to possess names only in the vernacular, or, to lack English forms. No choice remains in this case but to use the vernacular form and, in the instance where the vernacular employs a non-Roman alphabet, the transliterated form which is most often found in English-language publications.[14]

Based on these policies, the following forms are used in cataloging entries:

South America
    [not Sudamerica; America del sur]
Soviet Union
    [not Soîuz Sovetskikh Sotsialisticheskikh Respublik]
Spain
    [not España]

Bavaria (Germany)*
  [not Bayern]
Vienna (Austria)
  [not Wien]
Rhine River
  [not Rhein]
Japanese Alps (Japan)
  [not Nihon arupusu]
West Lake (China)
  [not Hsi-hu]

The vernacular form is chosen when there is no English form in general use or when the vernacular form is widely accepted in English-language works, e.g., **Rio de Janeiro (Brazil)**. When the vernacular name is chosen as the heading for a nonjurisdictional entity, the generic term in the name is translated into English, unless the vernacular form is better known in the English-speaking world or is part of the conventional name:

Steinhuder Lake (Germany)
  x   Steinhuder Meer (Germany)

Fontainebleau, Forest of (France)
  x   Forêt de Fontainebleau (France)

Rio de la Plata (Argentina and Uruguay)
  x   Plate River (Argentina and Uruguay)

Tien Shan
  x   Tien Mountains

Vernacular names in non-Roman scripts are transliterated according to Library of Congress transliteration tables. Occasionally these forms may not agree with the transliterated forms approved by the BGN. For example, for names in the Chinese script, the Library of Congress uses the Wade-Giles romanization rather than the pinyin system followed by the BGN:[15]

Yangtze River (China)
  [not Yangzi River (China)]
Peking (China)
  [not Beijing (China)]

Entry Element

When a geographic name contains more than one word, there is also the problem of choice of entry element. With few exceptions, names of political jurisdictions generally appear in their natural word order, without inversion; this holds even for foreign names beginning with an article, e.g., **South Africa; North Carolina; Lake Forest (Ill.); El Salvador.**

---

*A discussion of geographic qualifiers appears on pages 134-139.

Initial articles in nonjurisdictional geographic names for places located in English-speaking countries are retained. The heading is inverted if the initial article is *the*.[16] Examples include:

El Rancho Gumbo (Mont.)
   x Rancho Gumbo (Mont.)

Geysers, The (Calif.)
   x The Geysers (Calif.)

Initial articles in nonjurisdictional geographic names for places located in non-English-speaking countries are omitted unless the initial article is *the* and forms an integral part of the name:

Bierzo (Spain)
   x El Bierzo (Spain)

Sound, The (Denmark and Sweden)

The inverted form is used when the name of a natural feature begins with a generic term with a proper name in a later position. The proper name is used as the entry word:

Berkeley, Vale of (England)
Blanc, Mont (France and Italy)
Dover, Strait of
Hood, Mount (Or.)
Mexico, Gulf of
Michigan, Lake

In a small number of cases in which a foreign-language generic term has little generic significance for most English-speaking users and when the vernacular form is well known, the direct form is retained:

Costa del Sol (Spain)
   x Sol, Costa del (Spain)

Geographic names that contain adjectives indicating directions or parts and that are not considered proper names are generally inverted:

Africa, East
Africa, Central
Africa, North
Africa, Southern
Asia, Southeastern
Asia, Central
Alps, Eastern
California, Southern
Tennessee, East

Compare, however, **Central America; East End (Long Island, N.Y.); South China Sea; West Indies.**

For a given place, when the inverted form is used in a main heading, the same form is used when the same place appears as a subdivision under another heading:

Asia, Southeastern — Economic conditions
Social service — Asia, Southeastern

Africa, Northeast — Strategic aspects
United States — Relations — Africa, Northeast

Qualifiers[17]

A qualifier is frequently added to a geographic name to identify it more clearly or to distinguish it from another place or places with the same name. Haykin[18] identifies three types of qualifiers: generic (e.g., **Dover, Strait of; Faroe Islands**), geographic (e.g., **Saint-Dizier, France; Athens, Ga.**), and political or jurisdictional (e.g., **New York (State); Mexico (Viceroyalty)**).

In current practice, the qualifier is placed within a single set of parentheses after the name. If two or more types of qualifier are required for a heading, they are enclosed in the same set of parentheses and separated by the sequence space-colon-space. Examples include **Naples (Italy); Naples (Kingdom); Cape of Good Hope (South Africa : Cape); Dolores River (Colo. and Utah).** The name of a city used as a qualifier takes the form of the established heading for the city reformulated by (a) placing it within a single set of parentheses, (b) separating the city name from the name of its own larger qualifying jurisdiction with a comma, and (c) omitting any additional information that is part of the established heading for the city unless there is a conflict. Examples include:

Florence (Italy) [form of heading for city]
(Florence, Italy) [form when used as qualifier]

Richmondville (N.Y. : Village) [form of heading for city]
(Richmondville, N.Y.) [form when used as qualifier]

The following discussion treats current Library of Congress policies regarding different types of qualifiers for geographic headings. These include generic qualifiers, geographic qualifiers, and political or type-of-jurisdiction qualifiers.

Generic qualifiers

The names of many natural features contain generic terms as an integral part, e.g., **Mississippi River Valley; Rocky Mountains.** When there are two or more geographic entities with the same name and the conflict cannot be resolved by the geographic qualifiers, a generic qualifier is added in parentheses, even if it repeats a generic term in the place name, e.g., **Grand Island (N.Y. : Island); Cold Lake (Alta. : Lake).**

Geographic qualifiers

Geographic qualifiers are used when it is appropriate to add the name of a place to a heading. Qualifiers for jurisdictional headings are formulated according to *AACR2*. As noted before, it is in this particular use of geographic names that the implementation of *AACR2* in 1981 has had the most significant impact on subject headings because, as a result of rule changes, desuperimposition, and Library of Congress adoptions of various options in *AACR2* rules, a large number of pre-1981 geographic headings have become obsolete.

Names used as geographic qualifiers include those of countries, regions, provinces, states, islands, counties, and cities. Names of continents are not used as qualifiers; nor are names of sections within cities (e.g., Brooklyn, Georgetown, etc.), except in cases of conflict.

The following discussion of geographic qualifiers for jurisdictional headings is based on *AACR2* and on Library of Congress policies regarding options; the discussion of geographic qualifiers for nonjurisdictional headings follows policies established by the Subject Cataloging Division.

1) *Geographic qualifiers for jurisdictional headings.* Rule 23.4 in *AACR2* specifies that if it is necessary to distinguish between two or more places of the same name, the name of a larger place should be added to each name. This rule contains an option to add the name of the larger place even if there is no need to distinguish between places. The Library of Congress[19] has decided to apply this option to the names of all cities, towns, etc., and also to the names of all larger places below the national level, with the following exceptions to which *no* geographic qualifier is added:*

states, provinces, territories of Australia, Canada, and the United States

counties, regions, and island areas in the British Isles (other than the counties of Northern Ireland)

constituent states of Malaysia, the Soviet Union, and Yugoslavia

islands that are jurisdictions

the city of Jerusalem

Hong Kong and Vatican City

---

*In indirect geographic subdivision, the geographic qualifier is omitted when it is identical to the name of the larger geographic entity that already appears as the broader subdivision:

Vienna (Austria)
Music — Austria — Vienna

Long Island (N.Y.)
Housing — New York (State) — Long Island

Clear Lake (Iowa : Lake)
Eutrophication — Iowa — Clear Lake (Lake)

Note, however, instances such as **Sydney (N.S.W.); Architecture — Australia — Sydney (N.S.W.).** For a discussion of indirect geographic subdivision, see pages 67-73.

Examples include:

Vermont
Ontario
New South Wales
Cambridgeshire
Strathclyde
Pinang
Ukraine
Croatia
Jerusalem
Hong Kong
Vatican City

In order to understand the extent of the application of the option and the forms of the qualifier, it may be useful to become familiar with the types of geographic names used as qualifiers. Normally, the qualifier is the name of a country, e.g., **Paris (France); Tokyo (Japan); Rome (Italy); Bavaria (Germany);* Hamburg (Germany);* Leipzig (Germany).*** However, there are a number of notable exceptions. For places in the United States, Canada, Australia, Great Britain, Malaysia, the Soviet Union, Yugoslavia, and certain places on islands, the primary qualifiers are the first-order political divisions or the island or island group.** Table 6.1 lists the types of qualifiers used with jurisdictional headings. Examples of such headings include:

San Francisco (Calif.)
Bourbon County (Ky.)
Toronto (Ont.)
Newcastle (N.S.W.)
[not Newcastle (Australia)]
Belfast (Northern Ireland)
Tarbert (Strathclyde)
[not Tarbert (Scotland)]

---

*Note that the qualifier **(Germany)** is used for places in both East and West Germany. This is different from the practice in indirect subdivision where — **Germany (East)** and — **Germany (West)** are used.

**The seven countries that receive exceptional treatment overlap but do not coincide with the countries that receive exceptional treatment in indirect subdivision. Only four of the seven countries listed above receive special treatment in indirect subdivisions — Canada, Great Britain, the Soviet Union, and the United States:

Toronto (Ont.) — Buildings, structures, etc.
Architecture — Ontario — Toronto

Sheffield (Yorkshire) — Social conditions
Social classes — England — Sheffield (Yorkshire)

Sydney (N.S.W.) — Buildings, structures, etc.
Architecture — Australia — Sydney (N.S.W.)

For a discussion of indirect subdivision, see pages 67-73.

Table 6.1. Qualifiers for Jurisdictional Headings

Heading Being Established	Qualifier*
Cities, counties, etc.	
in United States	Name of state
in Canada	Name of province
in Australia	Name of state
in Northern Ireland	Northern Ireland
in Malaysia, the Soviet Union, and Yugoslavia	Name of the constituent state or republic
Cities in the British Isles (except Northern Ireland)	Name of county, region, or island area
All places below the national level on an island or island group**	Name of island or island group
in countries other than those listed above	Name of country

*For a list of qualifiers for exceptional countries, see appendix J.

**Qualifiers for nonjurisdictional islands or island groups are discussed on page 138 of this book.

George Town (Pinang)
Kiev (Ukraine)
Split (Croatia)
Edinburgh (Lothian)
Oxford (Oxfordshire)
Palma (Majorca)
Ramsey (Isle of Man)
Cairo (Egypt)
Nagasaki-ken (Japan)
North Holland (Netherlands)

The names of many of the first-order political jurisdictions and some of the countries are abbreviated when used as primary qualifiers but are spelled out in full when used as main headings:

Minnesota [the state]
Alberta (Minn.)

Alberta [the province]
Edmonton (Alta.)

A list of first-order political divisions and their appropriate abbreviations appears in appendix J.

If the name of a larger place used as a qualifier has changed, the current name is used:

Kinshasa (Zaire)
   x Kinshasa (Congo)

2) *Geographic qualifiers for nonjurisdictional headings.* In general, the Subject Cataloging Division of the Library of Congress also follows *AACR2* in establishing nonjurisdictional headings. However, there are a number of variations because of the different nature of nonjurisdictional headings. The variations and situations not covered by *AACR2* are discussed below.

a) *Entities located wholly within a single country or first-order political division.* The qualifier used is the same as that used for jurisdictional headings except for places in Great Britain and Ireland, for which the qualifiers used are: **(England), (Northern Ireland), (Scotland), (Wales),** and **(Ireland):**

Assunpink Creek (N.J.)
Great Barrier Reef (Qld.)
Hayachine Mountain (Japan)

Lake District (England)
Shannon River (Ireland)
Cairngorms (Scotland)

b) *Entities located in two countries or two first-order political divisions.* For an entity located in two countries or two first-order political divisions, the names of both are added as qualifiers. The names are added in alphabetical order unless the entity is located principally in one of the jurisdictions, which then will be the one listed first. For a river, however, the place of origin is always listed first:

Everest, Mount (China and Nepal)
Rudolf, Lake (Kenya and Ethiopia)
Wye, River (Wales and England)
Antietam Creek (Pa. and Md.)

This policy, however, does not apply to international bodies of water, which are not qualified unless there is a conflict: **Bering Strait; English Channel**.

c) *Entities located in more than two jurisdictions.* For an entity that spreads over three or more jurisdictions, no qualifier is added unless there is a conflict or the name is ambiguous, e.g., **Appalachian Region; Gaza Strip; Caribbean Sea; Amazon River; West (U.S.).**

d) *Conflicts between geographic entities.* In cases of conflicts between headings representing the same type of geographic entity, one or more narrower jurisdictions are added, followed by a comma, before the regular qualifier within the same set of parentheses.

Pelican Lake (Otter Tail County, Minn.)
Pelican Lake (Saint Louis County, Minn.)

Kailua Bay (Oahu, Hawaii)
Kailua Bay (Hawaii Island, Hawaii)

Blackwater River (Essex, England)
Blackwater River (Hampshire and Berkshire, England)

If the conflict involves a river located in more than two jurisdictions, a qualifier containing the name of the jurisdiction in which the river originates and the name of the jurisdiction where the mouth is located is added. In this case, the two names are joined with a hyphen instead of with *and*: **Red River (Tex.-La.); Coon Creek (Monroe County-Vernon County, Wis.).**

If the conflict exists between headings representing different types of geographic entities, a generic qualifier is added after the regular qualifier in the same set of parentheses and separated by the sequence space-colon-space:

Mecklenburg (Germany : Region)
Mecklenburg (Germany : Castle)

Cape of Good Hope (South Africa) [the city]
Cape of Good Hope (South Africa : Cape)

e) *Individual nonjurisdictional islands or island groups.* Individual nonjurisdictional islands or island groups that lie near a land mass and are under its jurisdiction, as well as individual islands that form part of a jurisdictional island cluster, are qualified by the name of the country or first-order political division:*

Aegina Island (Greece)
Hawaii Island (Hawaii)
Santa Catalina Island (Calilf.)
[not Santa Catalina Island (Channel Islands, Calif.)]
Izu Islands (Japan)
Elizabeth Islands (Mass.)

Qualifiers are not used with isolated islands or island groups that are not associated with a mainland country, or with islands that comprise more than one autonomous jurisdiction: **Borneo; Islands of the Pacific; Midway Islands.**

f) *Natural features within cities.* Lakes, hills, etc., located within cities are qualified by the name of the larger jurisdiction rather than by the name of the city, except in cases of conflict, e.g., **Corpus Christi, Lake (Tex.).**

---

*The name of the city is used as the qualifier if the island is a city section or if the city name is needed to resolve a conflict, e.g., **Ile de la Cité (Paris, France).**

g) *Other entities within cities.* Headings for city districts, quarters, sections, and other entities located within a city (such as buildings, streets, plazas, bridges, monuments, etc.) are qualified by the name of the city in the established form. The name of a borough, city section, or city district is used as a qualifier only if it is necessary to resolve a conflict between entities with identical names located in the same city. Examples include:

Bronx (New York, N.Y.)
Quartier des Halles (Paris, France)
Times Square (New York, N.Y.)
Flushing (New York, N.Y.)
Sunset Boulevard (Los Angeles, Calif.)
Hôtel de Ville (Lausanne, Switzerland)
Roman Forum (Rome, Italy)
Golden Gate Bridge (San Francisco, Calif.)

Seventh Avenue (Manhattan, New York, N.Y.)
Seventh Avenue (Brooklyn, New York, N.Y.)

h) *Entities on islands.* Headings for entities on islands are qualified by the name of the island established either as a jurisdictional or nonjurisdictional heading:

Lincoln Downs Brook (R.I.)
Etna, Mount (Sicily)
Storm, Cape (Ellesmere Island, N.W.T.)

Headings for entities on islands in Hawaii, Japan, or New Zealand are qualified by **(Hawaii)**, **(Japan)**, or **(N.Z.)**, instead of the names of the individual islands, which are used only in cases of conflict. Examples include:

Kaneohe Bay (Hawaii)
Fuji, Mount (Japan)
Taupo, Lake (N.Z.)

Kailua Bay (Oahu, Hawaii)
Kailua Bay (Hawaii Island, Hawaii)

i) *Other qualifiers.* Places in Antarctica are qualified by **(Antarctic regions)**, and places on the moon are qualified by **(Moon)**, e.g., **Transantarctic Mountains (Antarctic regions); Victoria Land (Antarctic regions); Mare Crisium (Moon)**.

Political or type-of-jurisdiction qualifiers

When two or more places belonging to different types of jurisdictions bear the same name, a qualifier indicating the type of jurisdiction is added, in accordance with *AACR2*. The political qualifier follows the geographic qualifier if there is one. Since headings for all modern cities now carry geographic qualifiers, the qualifier **(City)** used with some of the pre-1981 headings, e.g., **New York (City); Rome (City)**, is no longer used except with medieval cities that no longer exist. The political qualifier is usually an English term, if available. The vernacular term is used when there is no equivalent in English. Examples include:

Québec (Province)
Québec (Québec : County)
Québec (Québec)

Naples (Italy : Province)
Naples (Italy)
Naples (Kingdom)

Sardinia (Kingdom)
Sardinia

Poznan (Poland : Voivodeship)
Poznan (Poland)

The political qualifier indicating a type of jurisdiction is omitted when the name of the jurisdiction is used as a qualifier:

New York (State) [form of heading]
(N.Y.) [form when used as qualifier]

Micronesia (Federated States) [form of heading]
(Micronesia) [form when used as qualifier]

Arequipa (Peru : Dept.) [form of heading]
(Arequipa, Peru) [form when used as qualifier]

Free-Floating Phrase Headings Involving Names of Places[20]

There are a number of free-floating phrases that may be combined with certain types of geographic names to form valid headings. As free-floating combinations, these headings are not printed in *Library of Congress Subject Headings*.

1) *Geographic regions.* The word *region* may be added to a valid heading for a geographic feature (including parks, but not islands, river valleys, or watersheds) to form a subject heading:

Geographic heading	*Heading for region*
Caspian Sea	Caspian Sea Region
Danube River	Danube River Region*
Death Valley (Calif. and Nev.)	Death Valley Region (Calif. and Nev.)**
Rocky Mountain National Park (Colo.)	Rocky Mountain National Park Region (Colo.)
Saint Helens, Mount (Wash.)	Saint Helens, Mount, Region (Wash.)
Sandia Mountains (N.M.)	Sandia Mountains Region (N.M.)
Sierra Nevada Mountains (Calif. and Nev.)	Sierra Nevada Mountains Region (Calif. and Nev.)

Regions that are well known by alternative name forms and those having unique names are entered under those names instead of names constructed as above:

Caribbean Area
    x Caribbean Sea Region

Mediterranean Region
    x Mediterranean Sea Region

Black Country (England)

Midlands (England)

Innviertel (Austria)

Texas Hill Country (Tex.)

2)   *Watersheds.* The word *watershed*, which designates river basins† and drainage basins as well as watersheds, may be combined with valid headings for bodies of water, streams, etc., to form subject headings:

Geographic heading	*Heading for watershed*
Baiting Brook (Mass.)	Baiting Brook Watershed (Mass.)
Champlain, Lake	Champlain, Lake, Watershed
Nile River	Nile River Watershed
Seneca Creek (Montgomery County, Md.)	Seneca Creek Watershed (Montgomery County, Md.)

---

*A river region differs from a river in that the region includes the drainage basin and other adjacent territories beyond the basin.

**For valley regions associated with a river, see page 142.

†The term *basin* is used to designate geological basins, e.g., **Diamond Basin (Nev.)**.

3) *Estuaries.* The word *estuary*, which designates the broad and partly enclosed mouth of a river where its current meets the sea tide, may be combined with the valid heading for a river to form a subject heading:

Heading for river	*Heading for estuary*
Potomac River	Potomac River Estuary
Fraser River (B.C.)	Fraser River Estuary (B.C.)
Delaware River (N.Y.-Del. and N.J.)	Delaware River Estuary (N.Y.-Del. and N.J.)

4) *Valleys.* The word *valley*, which designates the flatlands extending along the course of a river and its tributaries, may be added to the valid heading for a river to form a subject heading.

Heading for river	*Heading for valley*
Po River (Italy)	Po River Valley (Italy)
Connecticut River	Connecticut River Valley

Headings for valley or watershed regions are formed by adding the word *region* to the river name, rather than the name of the valley or watershed, e.g., **Potomac River Region** [not Potomac River Valley Region; Potomac River Watershed Region].

5) *Metropolitan areas and city regions.* See discussion on page 147.

6) *Places "in art" and places "in literature."* The phrase *in art* or *in literature* may be added to an established geographic heading to form a phrase heading:

Rocky Mountains Region in art
London (England) in art
Pompeii (Ancient city) in art
Harlem (New York, N.Y.) in art
San Francisco (Calif.) in literature
Carthage (Ancient city) in literature
Greenwich Village (New York, N.Y.) in literature
Spain in literature

Since these are free-floating combinations, they are normally not printed in *Library of Congress Subject Headings* except when unique cross-references are required or when they are being used as examples.

Changes of Name[21]

Names of places change frequently. In such cases a decision must be made on which name or names to use as headings. There are two types of changes, linear name changes and mergers and/or splits. Following is a discussion of Library of Congress policies regarding these changes.

Linear name change

When the change of the name of a country, state, city, etc., does not affect its territorial identity, all new subject entries are made under the new name — with *see* reference(s) from the earlier name(s) — regardless of the period covered by the works being cataloged, and all subject entries under the old name are changed to the new name. Such a change may be the result of an official government decision or of a change in political situation, or it may be the result of changes in cataloging rules.

1) *Changes resulting from official government decision or change in political situation.* Examples include:

Old name(s)*	Latest name**
Congo, Belgian	
Congo Free State	**Zaire**
Congo (Democratic Republic)	
Gold Coast	**Ghana**
British Honduras	**Belize**
Ceylon	**Sri Lanka**

Both the earlier and later names are used as valid headings in descriptive cataloging, while only the latest name is used in subject entries. Information concerning such subject cataloging usage is carried in Library of Congress's automated name authority records in field 667. For examples see Figure 7.1 in chapter 7.

2) *Changes because of cataloging rule changes or cataloging decisions.* Examples include:

Old heading	Current heading
Argentine Republic	**Argentina**
Czechoslovak Republic	**Czechoslovakia**
Greece, Modern [used only as a subject]	**Greece**
Germany, West [used only as a subject]	**Germany (West)**
Russia (1923- U.S.S.R.) [This heading was not used as a subject; Russia was used instead]	**Soviet Union**

The practice of using a uniform heading as the subject entry for a place regardless of name changes results in a number of anachronistic headings, such as **Soviet Union — History — Period of consolidation, 1462-1605.** However, it has the advantage of collocating material about a particular place.

---

*Old name(s) may be used as author entries, but not as subject entries.

The latest name is also used as a geographic qualifier, e.g., **(Zimbabwe) instead of (Rhodesia, Southern).

The policy is, however, at variance with descriptive cataloging practice, as *AACR2* specifies successive entries rather than a uniform heading for works issued under different names of a government.

Merger and/or split

When the change of name involves substantial changes affecting territorial identity, the latest form of name is used except when the following conditions *all* apply:

the work cataloged deals with the time period prior to the merger or split

the work is limited to historical, political, or cultural matters pertaining to the earlier jurisdiction(s)

the name is to be applied in the initial part of the subject heading and not in a subdivision

In these cases, an earlier name may be used as the subject entry instead of the latest form.

An example of a merger is the joining of the Territory of Papua and the Territory of New Guinea in 1945 to form the administrative unit of the Territory of Papua-New Guinea, which became self-governing in 1973 as Papua-New Guinea. The following headings are used in cataloging works about this place as appropriate: **Papua; New Guinea (Territory); Papua New Guinea**.

Examples of a split are the two Germanies and the two Koreas:

Germany
Germany (East)
Germany (West)

Korea
Korea (North)
Korea (South)

Cross-References

See references are made from variant (including former) names or forms of names for geographic headings:

Aizu Region (Japan)
    x Aizu-bonchi (Japan)

Gallipoli Peninsula (Turkey)
    x Gelibolu Peninsula (Turkey)

Mohave Desert (Calif.)
    x Mojave Desert (Calif.)

Godeanu Mountains (Romania)
  x Munţii Godeanu (Romania)

Texas Panhandle (Tex.)
  x Panhandle (Tex.)

Berkeley, Vale of (England)
  x Vale of Berkeley (England)

Soviet Union
  x Russia

See also references are made from generic headings subdivided by country or first-order political division to specific nonjurisdictional geographic headings:

Mohave Desert (Calif.)
  xx Deserts—California

Berkeley, Vale of (England)
  xx Valleys—England

Drysdale Creek (Vic.)
  xx Rivers—Australia

Wheeling Creek (Pa. and W. Va.)
  xx Rivers—Pennsylvania
       Rivers—West Virginia

Dnieper River
  xx Rivers—Byelorussian S.S.R.
       Rivers—Russian S.F.S.R.
       Rivers—Ukraine

These references are not made if the place is located in more than three countries or political divisions.

It should be noted that the level of geographic subdivision in these *see also* references is often broader than that used in formulating a heading to be assigned to a specific work. For patterns of the complete structure of cross-references for different types of headings, see appendix H.

In the case of name changes from mergers or splits in which different names of the same place are used as headings for works covering different periods, *see also* references are made between the successive entries. These references are traced in the name authority records but do not necessarily appear in *Library of Congress Subject Headings*. The previous practice of making history or information references for these changes has been discontinued.

Geographic Headings Requiring
Special Treatment

Some types of geographic headings are given special treatment because of their unique nature. These include names of ancient or early cities and archaeological sites; areas associated with cities; entities within cities; railroads; parks, reserves, etc.; and other man-made structures associated with places.

Ancient or early cities and archaeological sites[22]

Names of ancient or early cities and archaeological sites were previously unprinted headings. Since 1976 newly established headings in this category have been printed in *Library of Congress Subject Headings*. Because cities that went out of existence before the creation of modern states (ca. A.D. 1500) are rarely required for descriptive cataloging, these headings are generally established by the Subject Cataloging Division. If there is evidence that the exact original site of the ancient or early city has been continuously or recurrently occupied until modern times, the heading established for the modern city is used, e.g., **London (England)** instead of Londinium; **Vienna (Austria)** instead of Vindobona.

The general guidelines for establishing ancient or early cities that no longer exist are described below.

1) Use the form of the name most commonly found in standard reference sources (encyclopedias, gazetteers, etc.).

2) Add the qualifier **(Ancient city)** to a city in Europe, Africa, or Asia if it existed only before medieval times.* Add the qualifier **(City)** to a city if it existed during medieval times. Examples include **Pompeii (Ancient city); Coba (City)**. The previous practice of adding a qualifier in the form of the name of the current larger jurisdiction in which the city would be located today has been discontinued.

3) When the name of an ancient or early city is used as a qualifier for another heading, **(Ancient city)** or **(City)** is omitted. Except for those dealing with archaeological aspects (e.g., **—Antiquities**), the free-floating subdivisions under names of places may be used with headings for ancient or early cities if appropriate, e.g., **Carthage (Ancient city)—Social life and customs**. Established names of ancient or early cities may also be used as geographic subdivisions under topical headings, e.g., **Elephants—Tunisia—Carthage (Ancient city)**.

4) For an archaeological site, the heading is established on the basis of the work being cataloged. The term **Site** and the appropriate geographic qualifier are added to the name. Examples include **Fourth of July Valley Site (Colo.); Copán Site (Honduras); Walter F. George Dam Mound Site (Ga.)**.

---

*Cities of the Americas that ceased to exist by 1500 are treated as archaeological sites.

If the site is located in a modern city, the name of the city is used as the qualifier, e.g., **Lewis-Weber Site (Tucson, Ariz.); Uryudo Site (Osaka, Japan).** If the site is a cave and the cave has been named, the cave name is used as the site name, e.g., **Texcal Cave (Mexico); Shanidar Cave (Iraq).**

Areas associated with cities[23]

There are four kinds of headings that designate the various areas associated with an individual city, as shown in these examples based on Boston: **Boston (Mass.); Boston Metropolitan Area (Mass.); Boston Suburban Area (Mass.); Boston Region (Mass.).*** In terms of territory, these four types of headings have been defined as follows:

1) **[City name]:** the city jurisdiction itself.

2) **[City] Metropolitan Area:** an area consisting of the city itself and those densely populated territories immediately surrounding it that are socially and economically integrated with it.

3) **[City] Suburban Area:** the territory associated with the city, including neighboring residential areas lying outside the city, as well as nearby smaller satellite jurisdictions, but not the city itself.

4) **[City] Region:** an area including the city itself and its surrounding territory, the exact size and boundaries of which are not defined and may vary according to the work being cataloged.

Headings for metropolitan and suburban areas and city regions are qualified in the same manner as cities, e.g., **Atlanta Suburban Area (Ga.); Pensacola Metropolitan Area (Fla.); Montréal Metropolitan Area (Québec); Binghamton Metropolitan Area (N.Y.)** [not Binghamton Metropolitan Area (N.Y. and Pa.)]. Metropolitan and suburban areas and regions associated with the cities of Jerusalem, Washington, and New York are not qualified, e.g., **Jerusalem Region; New York Metropolitan Area; Washington Suburban Area.** A metropolitan or suburban area or a region involving two cities is represented by two separate headings, e.g., **Dallas Metropolitan Area (Tex.); Fort Worth Metropolitan Area (Tex.)** [not Dallas-Fort Worth Metropolitan Area (Tex.)]. Names of metropolitan and suburban areas and city regions may be used as main headings or subdivisions. When used as main headings, they may be subdivided according to the free-floating list of subdivisions used under names of places (see appendix G). When they are used as local subdivisions, they are assigned indirectly (with the exceptions noted below) through the jurisdiction in which the city proper is located, even if the area or region spreads over more than one jurisdiction, e.g., **Minorities—Missouri—Saint Louis Metropolitan Area.** By way of exception, areas and regions associated with New York City, Berlin, Washington, and Jerusalem are used as direct subdivisions, e.g., **Minorities—New York Metropolitan Area; Minorities—Berlin Metropolitan Area (Germany); Minorities—Washington Suburban Area; Minorities—Jerusalem Region.**

---

*The phrases **Metropolitan Area; Suburban Area;** and **Region** are free-floating; they may be combined with the name of a city and its qualifier to form valid headings.

Entities within cities[24]

Headings for districts, quarters, sections, and other entities located within a city, such as buildings, streets, plazas, parks, bridges, monuments, etc., consist of the name of the entity qualified by the name of the city.* The name of the entity is normally in the vernacular form of the country in which it is located, except for pre-1500 buildings and structures that have well-established English names. Examples include:

> **Brooklyn (New York, N.Y.)**
> **Federal Hill (Baltimore, Md.)**
> **North End (Boston, Mass.)**
> **Library of Congress Thomas Jefferson Building (Washington, D.C.)**
> **Blenheim Palace (Blenheim, Oxfordshire)**
> **Hôtel de Ville (Aix-en-Provence, France)**
> **Boulevard du Temple (Paris, France)**
> **Promenade du Peyrou (Montpellier, France)**
> **Gateway Arch (Saint Louis, Mo.)**
> **Pont-Neuf (Paris, France)**
> **Fontana di Trevi (Rome, Italy)**
> **Balboa Park (San Diego, Calif.)**
> **Western Wall (Jerusalem)**
> **Richmond Bridge (London, England)**
> **2040 Union Street (San Francisco, Calif.)**
> **Mount Clare (Baltimore, Md. : Building)**
> **Hauptbahnhof (Hamburg, Germany)**
> **Cleveland Municipal Stadium (Cleveland, Ohio)**
> **Great Pyramid (Jizah, Egypt)**

Details of buildings that bear proper names are represented by headings of the type [Name of structure] ([Geographic qualifier]) — [Name of detail]. Examples include **Yakushiji (Nara-shi, Japan) — Saitō; South African National Gallery — Hyman Liberman Memorial Door.**

Railroads

Individual railroads are represented by their names without geographic qualifiers, except in cases of conflict between two or more railroads with the same name. *See also* references are made from the generic *heading* **Railroads — [Country]**. Examples include:

> **Burlington Northern Railroad**
>   *xx* **Railroads — United States**
>
> **London and North-Western Railway**
>   *xx* **Railroads — Great Britain**

---

*Note that the names of city sections and districts may be used as main headings, but are not used as geographic subdivisions. They are used as qualifiers only if necessary to resolve a conflict between entities with identical names located in the same city (see discussion on page 139).

Hankyū Dentetsu
    xx   Railroads — Japan
        Street-railroads — Japan

Canadian Pacific Railway
    xx   Railroads — Canada
        Railroads — United States

Great Northern Railway (U.S.)
    xx   Railroads — United States

Glacier Express (Express train)
    xx   Railroads — Switzerland — Express-trains

Parks, reserves, etc.[25]

At the Library of Congress, names of individual parks, reserves, etc., to be used as subject headings are established by the Subject Cataloging Division. The following types of entities fall into this category and are treated in a similar manner:

public and private parks of all kinds

nature conservation areas, natural areas, natural history reservations, nature reserves

wild areas, wilderness areas, roadless areas

forests, forest reserves and preserves

seashores, marine parks and reserves, wild and scenic rivers

wildlife refuges, bird reservations and sanctuaries, game ranges and preserves, wildlife management areas

historic sites, national monuments, etc.

trails

Headings for individual parks, reserves, etc., including those located within cities, consist of the names of the parks with appropriate geographic qualifiers. The previous practice of entering the name of a park located within a city under the name of the city has been discontinued.

See references are made from variant names and their variant forms. *See also* references are made from generic headings with appropriate geographic subdivisions. For patterns of cross-references and examples, see appendix H.

Examples of headings for individual parks, reserves, etc., include:

North York Moors National Park (England)
Parque Nacional de Ubajara (Brazil)
Hiawatha National Forest (Mich.)

Mount Saint Helens National Volcanic Area (Wash.)
Spruce Knob-Seneca Rocks National Recreation Area (W. Va.)
Naturpark Pfälzerwald (Germany)
Bandelier National Monument (N.M.)
Ice Age National Scientific Reserve (Wis.)
Rock River Canyon Wilderness (Mich.)
Palos Forest Reserve (Ill.)
Fortress of Louisbourg National Historic Park (Cape Breton Island, N.S.)
City Park (New Orleans, La.)
Vestvolden (Copenhagen, Denmark)

Other man-made structures associated with places[26]

Other man-made structures include physical plants, roads, bridges, monuments, etc., not located within a particular city. They are normally entered directly under their own names, with the addition of geographic and/or generic qualifiers as appropriate (see discussion of geographic qualifiers on pages 137-139). Examples include:

Jarrell Plantation (Ga.)
EPCOT (Fla.)
Harry S. Truman Dam (Mo.)
Three Mile Island Nuclear Power Plant (Pa.)
Battle Road (Mass.)
Bering Land Bridge
Hearst-San Simeon State Historical Monument (Calif.)
Great Wall of China (China)
Overland Telegraph Line (N.T. and S. Aust.)
Grini (Norway : Concentration camp)
Stalag 12 D (Trier, Germany : Concentration camp)
Balmoral Castle (Grampian)
Mount Vernon (Va. : Estate)
Silver Bluff (S.C.)
Sturgeon Fork (Sask.)

REFERENCES

[1]*Anglo-American Cataloguing Rules*, 2nd ed., prepared by the American Library Association, the British Library, the Canadian Committee on Cataloguing, the Library Association, and the Library of Congress, ed. Michael Gorman and Paul W. Winkler (Chicago: American Library Association, 1978).

[2]Library of Congress, *Name Authorities: Cumulative Microform Edition* (Washington, D.C.: Library of Congress, 1983-), issued quarterly.

[3]"AACR2 Changes," *Supplement to LC Subject Headings* (Washington, D.C.: Library of Congress, 1981).

[4]Library of Congress, Subject Cataloging Division, *Subject Cataloging Manual: Subject Headings*, prelim. ed. (Washington, D.C.: Library of Congress, 1984), H1574, H1597.

[5]David Judson Haykin, *Subject Headings: A Practical Guide* (Washington, D.C.: Government Printing Office, 1951), 41.

[6]Charles A. Cutter, *Rules for a Dictionary Catalog*, 4th ed. (Washington, D.C.: Government Printing Office, 1904), 69.

[7]Library of Congress, *Subject Cataloging Manual*, H1636.

[8]"Dividing Corporate Body Headings by Place," *Cataloging Service Bulletin* 22:57-58 (Fall 1983).

[9]"Animal and Plant Names," *Cataloging Service Bulletin* 20:44 (Spring 1983); Library of Congress, *Subject Cataloging Manual*, H1332.

[10]"Headings for Individual Nationalities," *Cataloging Service Bulletin* 16:57-59 (Spring 1982).

[11]Library of Congress, *Subject Cataloging Manual*, H690-H1050.

[12]"AACR2 Changes," *Supplement to LC Subject Headings*, 1981.

[13]"English Form," *Cataloging Service Bulletin* 16:40-43 (Spring 1982); Library of Congress, *Subject Cataloging Manual*, H690.

[14]Haykin, *Subject Headings*, 46.

[15]Library of Congress, *Subject Cataloging Manual*, H690.

[16]"Geographic Features," *Cataloging Service Bulletin* 12:56 (Spring 1981); Library of Congress, *Subject Cataloging Manual*, H690.

[17]Library of Congress, *Subject Cataloging Manual*, H810.

[18]Haykin, *Subject Headings*, 49-53.

[19]"Apply the First Option in Rule 23.4B to the Names of Cities, Towns, etc. ...," *Cataloging Service Bulletin* 13:31-32 (Summer 1981).

[20]Library of Congress, *Subject Cataloging Manual*, H760, H800, H1145.5.

[21]Material distributed at the Regional Institutes on Library of Congress Subject Headings, sponsored by ALA Resources and Technical Services Division, Library of Congress, and ALA/RTSD Council of Regional Groups, 1982-1984.

[22]Library of Congress, *Subject Cataloging Manual*, H715, H1225.

[23]Ibid., H790.

[24]Ibid., H720, H1334; "Streets and Roads," *Cataloging Service Bulletin* 28:36-38 (Spring 1985).

[25]"Parks, Reserves, National Monuments, etc.," *Cataloging Service Bulletin* 28:32-36 (Spring 1985).

[26]Library of Congress, *Subject Cataloging Manual*, H1334.

7

SUBJECT HEADINGS CONTROL AND MAINTENANCE

INTRODUCTION

The vocabulary of the Library of Congress subject headings system is controlled: only terms authorized as subject headings are used as entries in the catalog. Assignment of terms from the controlled list is governed by the principle of specificity, which requires that a heading assigned to a work being cataloged represent its content exactly. Any topic encountered in cataloging but not yet represented in *Library of Congress Subject Headings* is established as a subject heading so long as it represents a "discrete, identifiable concept."[1]

Developing and maintaining a list of controlled vocabulary is often referred to as thesaurus construction and maintenance. The vehicle for thesaurus construction and maintenance at the Library of Congress is an editorial group within the Subject Cataloging Division. This group is composed of the chief and the assistant chief of the Subject Cataloging Division, the editor of subject headings, representatives from the office of the principal subject cataloger, and the cataloger who serves as the secretary. This group meets weekly to consider all proposals of changes in *Library of Congress Subject Headings:* additions, alterations, or deletions of headings, heading/subdivision combinations, cross-references, free-floating subdivisions, etc. For new headings, the group deliberates on terminology (wording, form [phrase or subdivision], language, entry element), conformity to existing patterns and broad policies of the system, compatibility with descriptive headings (if applicable), cross-references, and notes. Changes that are approved by this group are said to be editorially established. The lack of specific rules for forming subject headings is compensated for, to a large degree, by the expertise of the subject catalogers and the editorial group's knowledge of and familiarity with the system.

ESTABLISHING NEW HEADINGS[2]

New headings proposed and examined at the editorial meeting are generally of four types: headings representing new objects or concepts, combinations (coordinations) of existing headings, new subdivisions under existing headings, and cross-references. Even headings proposed for revision and updating are handled in the same way—they must be reviewed by the editorial group before they are formally established in their new form.

As a means of controlling subject headings, the Library of Congress maintains an authority record for each heading. A subject authority record contains information regarding the following aspects of the subject represented:

the exact form of the approved subject heading

instruction for geographic subdivision and Library of Congress classification number(s), if any

the references from related subject headings and from synonyms or alternative forms of the heading

the authorities consulted in determining the choice of the heading

Until 1986 authority records for subject headings established and maintained by the Subject Cataloging Division were kept in a card file. These headings include topical headings, nonjurisdictional headings, headings for named objects and entities (with a few exceptions), headings for families, and headings for fictitious or legendary persons. In 1986 the Library of Congress implemented the automated subject authority file (see discussion on pages 165-166).

Authority records for name headings established by the Descriptive Cataloging Division are kept in the automated name authority file, a file that is structured according to the MARC format for authorities. Many of these records contain information regarding subject cataloging usage in a field tagged 667. Examples of such records are shown in Figure 7.1.

In proposing a new subject heading, the first step is the identification of the concept in the work being cataloged. This concept is then verified in reference sources. If the proposed heading is analogous to an existing heading or a pattern, the existing heading or pattern may be cited as one of the authorities on which the proposed heading is based.

(Text continues on page 157.)

```
  n80-61038
03/22/84          [AUTH]            [PCRD]                PAGE 1 OF   1
0*FAC* DISPLAYED RECORD HAS BEEN VERIFIED.                          112

VERIFIED                                  EVAL     RETRO  M/AE

THIS RECORD IS FOR USE BY LC STAFF.  IT IS NOT A BIBLIOGRAPHIC RECORD.

  001  n  80-61038
  040  DLC DLC
  151  Ceylon. [AACR 2]
  667  SUBJECT USAGE: This heading is not valid for use as a subject. Works
       about this place are entered under Sri Lanka.
  451  Cejlon
  451  Taprobane
  451  Serendib
  451  Sirinduil
  451  Zeylon
```

Linear name change in political jurisdictions.

```
  n79-79314
03/22/84          [AUTH]            [PCRD]                PAGE 1 OF   1
0*FAC* DISPLAYED RECORD HAS BEEN VERIFIED.                          112

VERIFIED                                  EVAL     RETRO  M/AE

THIS RECORD IS FOR USE BY LC STAFF.  IT IS NOT A BIBLIOGRAPHIC RECORD.

  001  n  80-82472
  040  DLC DLC
  151  Aran Islands. [AACR 2]
  667  SUBJECT USAGE: As a geographic subdivision, this heading is used
       indirectly through Ireland.
  451  Arran Islands
  960  AOC AMC NUC AGM
  985  KEY/EKI
```

```
  n79-18774
03/22/84          [AUTH]            [PCRD]                PAGE 1 OF   1
0*FAC* DISPLAYED RECORD HAS BEEN VERIFIED.                          112

VERIFIED                                  EVAL     RETRO  M/AE SU

THIS RECORD IS FOR USE BY LC STAFF.  IT IS NOT A BIBLIOGRAPHIC RECORD.

  001  n  79-18774
  040  DLC DLC
  151  Washington (D.C.) [AACR 2]
  667  SUBJECT USAGE: As a geographic subdivision, this heading is used
       directly.
  451  Bellevue (D.C.)
  451  Washington, D.C. [old catalog heading] [do not make]
  965  IEN
  960  AOC NUC MCL
```

Decisions regarding direct/indirect usage.

Figure 7.1. Name authority records with information regarding subject usage.

```
    n80-20283
   03/22/84          [AUTH]            [PCRD]                    PAGE 1 OF   1
   0*FAC* DISPLAYED RECORD HAS BEEN VERIFIED.                                112

   VERIFIED                                EVAL     RETRO  M/AE SU

   THIS RECORD IS FOR USE BY LC STAFF.   IT IS NOT A BIBLIOGRAPHIC RECORD.

    001  n  80-20283
    040  DLC DLC
    110  Mus'ee du Louvre. [AACR 2]
    667  SUBJECT USAGE:  This heading is used for works on the museum housed
         within the Louvre palace.  Works on the building are entered under the
         subject heading Louvre (Paris, France).
    410  Mus'ee national du Louvre
```

Scope note for subject usage.

```
    n79-53176
   03/22/84          [AUTH]            [PCRD]                    PAGE 1 OF   1
   0*FAC* DISPLAYED RECORD HAS BEEN VERIFIED.                                112

   VERIFIED                                EVAL     RETRO  M/AE SU

   THIS RECORD IS FOR USE BY LC STAFF.   IT IS NOT A BIBLIOGRAPHIC RECORD.

    001  n  79-53176
    040  DLC DLC
    110  Philippines. Armed Forces. [AACR 2]
    667  SUBJECT USAGE: This heading is not valid for use as a subject. Works
         about this body are entered under Philippines—Armed Forces.
    410  AFP
    410  Philippines (Republic). Armed Forces of the Philippines.
         [old catalog heading] [do not make]
```

Information regarding a name heading not valid
for subject usage.

Figure 7.1. *Continued*

```
  n79-41716
03/22/84            [AUTH]              [PCRD]                    PAGE 1 OF   1
0*UPD* DISPLAYED RECORD HAS BEEN VERIFIED.                                 112

VERIFIED                                  EVAL      RETRO   M/AE SU
                                                    INDIRECT

THIS RECORD IS FOR USE BY LC STAFF.  IT IS NOT A BIBLIOGRAPHIC RECORD.

  001  n  79-41716
  010  n80-4086
  040  DLC DLC
  110  Catholic Church.   [AACR 2]
  410  Church of Rome
  410  Roman Catholic Church
  670  Derrick, C. C.S. Lewis and the Church of Rome, c1981: t.p. (Church of
       Rome)
  960  AOC
```

Indirect subdivision under corporate bodies.

All sources consulted as authorities are recorded on the proposed authority record, regardless of whether the term sought appears in them or not. The most frequently consulted sources* include the following:[3]

general dictionaries, especially *Webster's Third New International Dictionary* (Web. 3), which is always cited when applicable

general encyclopedias, e.g., *Americana, Britannica, Collier's*, etc.

general indexes and thesauri, e.g., *New York Times (NYT) Index, Hennepin County Authority List, Legislative Indexing Vocabulary (LIV), Readers' Guide*, and other periodical indexes, etc.

titles in the MARC database

work being cataloged, and the bibliography in the work being cataloged

topical reference sources and other authoritative works in the field in question, if the topic is peculiar to a particular discipline

Following are examples of authority record notations, showing the types of authorities that are consulted for typical headings being proposed in various subject fields:

---

*For certain categories of headings, the subject catalogers have been instructed to use specific reference sources. For a list of these sources, see appendix I.

o   Topic currently in the news

   Heading proposed: **Abscam Bribery Scandal, 1980-**

   Sources found:
      LC pattern: Watergate Affair, 1972-74
      NYT Index (Abscam; Abscam scandal; indexed under "Abscam, Operation")
      Washington Post (terminology used in recent articles: Abscam scandal; Abscam affair; Abscam investigation)
      LIV (Abscam Bribery Scandal)
      Work cat. (Abscam; Arab scam; Abdul scam [from name of phony company offering bribes, "Abdul Enterprises"])

   Sources not found:
      MARC database

o   Historical event

   Heading proposed: **Soviet Union—History—Streltsy Revolt, 1698**

   Sources found:
      Britannica Micropaedia, v. 9, p. 610 (streltsy: "Russian military corps established in the middle of the 16th century ... at the end of the 17th century, exercised political influence by revolting against certain factions")
      Americana, v. 25, p. 791 (Streltsy: "... in 1698, the Streltsy rose in revolt, deposed their officers, and marched against Moscow")
      Work cat.

   Sources not found:
      Web. 3
      MARC database

o   Named entity in a city

   Heading proposed: **Promenade du Peyrou (Montpellier, France)**

   Sources found:
      Britannica Micropaedia, v. 7, p. 1
      Americana, v. 19, p. 417 ("promenade called Le Peyrou")
      Oizon, René. Dictionnaire géographique de la France.
      Guide des capitales regionales.
      Work cat. (Peyrou)

   Sources not found:
      MARC database

o   Contemporary public affairs issue

Heading proposed: **Right to die**

Sources found:
   Index Medicus   Terms "Right to die" and "Death
   NYT Index   with dignity" used in titles indexed
   Readers' Guide   under "Death" and "Terminal
   MARC database   care"
   Work cat. (Natural death)

Sources not found:
   Web. 3
   Random House dictionary

o   Literary topic

Heading proposed: **Questione della lingua**

Sources found:
   Cudden, J. A., Dict. lit. terms, p. 547 ("a controversy or debate
      about the suitability of the vernacular as opposed to the
      language of literature")
   Britannica, 15th ed., vol. 10, p. 1099
   Work cat.

Sources not found:
   Web. 3
   Americana

o   Topic in technology

Heading proposed: **Tailings dams**

Sources found:
   Dict. of mining, mineral, and related terms
   McGraw-Hill encyc. of S & T
   SME Mining engineering handbook
   Work cat.

Sources not found:
   Web. 3
   TEST
   ASTI

   In formulating cross-references, subject catalogers are instructed to
ensure that the terms used in the proposed *see* references do not conflict with
existing headings or existing *see* references, and that *see also* references
connect valid headings and conform to established patterns for cross-
references, if any. On the proposed authority record, *see* references are

recorded with the label x (UF),* and *see also* references are recorded with the label *xx* (BT)* for hierarchical references and *xx* (RT)* for related-term references.

When a new heading being established consists in part of an existing heading that is obsolete in spelling or form but that has not yet been updated, the policy[4] is to retain the obsolete term in the new heading if it appears in the initial position. This practice keeps the original heading and the new heading together in the alphabetical file. An example is:

Original heading	*Current heading based on the old*
Moving-pictures	**Moving-picture locations**

However, if the obsolete portion of the heading does not appear in the initial position, the current or preferred form is used:

Original heading	*Current heading based on the old*
Moving-pictures	**Violence in motion pictures**
	World War, 1939-1945 — Motion pictures and the war

This policy occasionally results in a mixture of obsolete and current forms in the same heading, e.g., **Moving-picture industry in motion pictures**.

REVISING AND UPDATING HEADINGS

A catalog entry standing by itself fulfills the finding function of the catalog, but only in the way it stands as part of a larger whole in relation to other entries can it fulfill the catalog's collocation function. For this latter function, there are two requirements: the entry must be compatible with analogous entries, and there must be cross-references to related entries.

A major requirement in ensuring a logically structured subject catalog is to reconcile the conflicts that result from heading changes. Each change of heading affects not only the actual entries in the catalog under the old heading but also all cross-references that involve that heading. The magnitude of the work involved can be enormous. When resources are limited, large-scale revision and updating can only be performed gradually.

Changes in subject headings generally fall into the following five categories:

1) *Simple one-to-one changes for the purpose of updating terminology or spelling.* Examples include:

---

*The abbreviations UF, BT, and RT stand for *used for, broader term*, and *related term*, respectively.

Old heading	*Current heading*
Friends	**Quakers**
Nurserymen	**Nursery growers**
Community antenna television	**Cable television**
Folk-lore	**Folklore**
Sea food	**Seafood**
Xosa	**Xhosa**
European War, 1914-1918	**World War, 1914-1918**

2) *Changes in headings containing proper names in order to conform to* AACR2. Examples include:

Old heading	*Current heading*
Fuji	**Fuji, Mount (Japan)**
Jerusalem, Temple	**Temple of Jerusalem (Jerusalem)**
Russia	**Soviet Union**
Vienna	**Vienna (Austria)**

3) *Changes in form or entry element.* Examples include:

Old heading	*Current heading*
Animals, Food habits of	**Animals — Food habits**
Chronology, Maya	**Mayas — Chronology**
Secrecy (Psychology)	**Secrecy — Psychological aspects**

4) *Changes resulting from splitting a compound heading or a heading containing two or more concepts into separate headings.* Examples include:

Old heading	*Current heading*
Negroes	{ **Afro-Americans** **Blacks**
Amateur theatricals	{ **Amateur theater** **Amateur plays**
Programming languages (Electronic computers) — Business Programming languages (Electronic computers) — Computer graphics	{ **Business — Data processing** **Computer graphics** **Programming languages (Electronic computers)**

5) *Changes involving subdivisions or cross-references.* Examples include:

Old heading	Current heading
America — Description and travel — 1951-	**America — Description and travel — 1951-1980**

Coins as an investment
    xx **Capital investments**
	Coins as an investment
	    xx **Investments**

When a subject heading containing an obsolete term is updated, all existing entries bearing the obsolete term in *Library of Congress Subject Headings* are revised to reflect the current term. All cross-references related to the obsolete heading are also revised. In addition, a *see* reference is made from the obsolete term to the new heading.

The ideal way to effect a change in the catalog is to revise all cataloging records that contain the subject entry affected by the change as well as all references to, from, or about the changed heading. At the Library of Congress, changes involving updated headings are generally carried out in this manner. However, this method is prohibitively time-consuming and costly in cases where large files of records are affected. In 1975 the Library of Congress adopted the "split files" method to cope with major subject heading changes in the card catalog. The new heading was applied to newly cataloged works, but older records carrying the obsolete heading were left unchanged; the obsolete heading and the new heading were then linked by *see also* references.[5] The split files method was used by the Library of Congress for only a brief period of time before it was abandoned. It was not used in the MARC database.

In the MARC database, each time a change in a subject heading takes place, all records bearing the heading are revised. The split files device described above was adopted by the Library of Congress on the assumption that in the near future most subject heading changes could be made to the records in the MARC database with a simple instruction.[6] However, such a method of changing MARC records has not yet been implemented. As a result, subject heading changes must be performed on a record-by-record basis, and changes involving large files of records can be effected only gradually. Following are examples of some of the recent changes that affected large numbers of records:

Former heading	Current heading
Aeroplanes	**Airplanes**
Ceylon	**Sri Lanka**
Hygiene, Public	**Public health**
Insurance, Social	**Social security**
Phonorecords	**Sound recordings**

Reords carrying these headings are being changed gradually in the MARC database as special projects.

After editorial approval, all new and revised headings are published in the *Weekly List* and the *Supplement to LC Subject Headings* (issued quarterly with annual cumulations) and incorporated into the microfiche edition of *Library of Congress Subject Headings*, which is fully cumulated at each quarterly issue. The *Supplement* carries notices of changes and cancellations; a new regular edition of *Library of Congress Subject Headings* does not. Cancellation and change notices appear in the *Supplement* as follows:

> **Exiles**
> CHANGE:
> > *sa* subdivision Exiles *under names of regions, countries, etc.*

> CANCEL:
> **Hungarian language in foreign countries**
> > This heading has been replaced by the heading Hungarian language—Foreign countries, a heading not printed in LCSH because it uses a freefloating subdivision controlled by a pattern heading.

> CANCEL:
> **Plasma membranes**

The last heading was replaced by

> **Cell membranes**
> > *x* Plasma membranes

In addition to obsolete headings, many other kinds of headings have been or are being removed from the printed list for various reasons. These are also indicated as canceled headings in the *Supplement*; they include the types listed below.

1) *Free-floating subdivisions and free-floating phrase headings.* An effort is under way to remove free-floating subdivisions under existing headings, free-floating subdivisions controlled by pattern headings, and free-floating phrase headings, unless they contain unique cross-references or subdivisions. These subdivisions and phrase headings are still valid and can be used in subject cataloging even though they are no longer printed. The reason for cancellation is usually stated. Examples include:

> **Extremities, Lower**
> CANCEL:
> > —Muscles (*Comparative anatomy, QL831; Human anatomy, QM165*)
> > > This is still a valid heading, but is no longer printed in LCSH because it uses a freefloating subdivision controlled by a pattern heading.

France.   Armée
CANCEL:
— Military life
> This is still a valid heading but will no longer be printed in
> LCSH because it uses a freefloating subdivision.

2) *Nonjurisdictional headings not compatible with* Anglo-American
Cataloguing Rules, second edition *(AACR2)*. Previously established
nonjursidictional headings that are incompatible with *AACR2* are being
removed from the printed list. Those required for cataloging new works are
reinstated in the *AACR2*-compatible form and printed in *Library of Congress
Subject Headings* unless they involve a free-floating phrase form:

CANCEL:
Naturpark Nassau, Ger.

CANCEL:
Triadelphia Reservoir, Md.

CANCEL:
Dirty Devil River, Utah

The last heading has been replaced by

Dirty Devil River (Utah)

The heading **Dirty Devil River Watershed, Utah** was canceled but not
reinstated because the combination of a river heading with the term **Watershed**
is a free-floating phrase.

3) *Name headings*

*a) Non-*AACR2 *name headings.* Personal, corporate, and jurisdictional name headings established by descriptive catalogers are normally not
printed in *Library of Congress Subject Headings* unless they serve as examples
or pattern headings or involve unique cross-references or subdivisions. All
such headings that do not conform to *AACR2* are being canceled from *Library
of Congress Subject Headings*, and those required in cataloging new works are
replaced by headings in *AACR2* form. Examples include:

CANCEL:
Lincoln, Abraham, Pres. U.S., 1809-1865

CANCEL:
Tyrol

CANCEL:
Mexico (City)

These headings have been replaced by

Lincoln, Abraham, 1809-1865
Tyrol (Austria)
Mexico City (Mexico)

b) *Other name headings*. Other previously printed name headings, even though still valid under *AACR2*, are also being removed if they do not serve as patterns or do not involve unique subdivisions or cross-references. An example is:

United States. Federal Bureau of Investigation
This name heading will no longer be printed in *LCSH*.

The systematic removal of headings in the unprinted headings categories and of free-floating subdivisions and phrases is being carried out in order to make the listing of subject headings in *Library of Congress Subject Headings* consistent with policies regarding unprinted headings and free-floating subdivisions and phrases. It has the added advantage of reducing the bulk of the printed list.

SUBJECT AUTHORITY FILE

For many years, *Library of Congress Subject Headings* represented the Library's subject authority file. Various supplementary lists (see appendix B) were published, and a number of card files have been created and maintained for internal use by the Subject Cataloging Division. For other libraries using the system, *Library of Congress Subject Headings* may be the sole subject authority file. There have been recent efforts to automate the subject headings list. Following is a summary and discussion of current developments and some of the future plans.

The first application of automation was the conversion of the subject headings list into machine-readable form to enable the Government Printing Office to print the seventh edition of *Library of Congress Subject Headings* by photocomposition. The system used until 1985 was developed and implemented by the Library of Congress between 1969 and 1972, that is, while *Subject Headings Used in the Dictionary Catalogs of the Library of Congress* was in its seventh edition, and soon after the Library began inputing its new English-language cataloging into the MARC database. It was thus one of the oldest of the Library's automation efforts.

In recent years, considerable effort has been devoted to the development of an automated subject authority system to be implemented in 1986. The format of the subject authority records is similar to, or compatible with, that of name authority records as specified in *Authorities: A MARC Format*.[7] Initially the subject authority records will be maintained in a separate file from the name authority records, but it is anticipated that eventually the two files will be merged to form one automated authority file. As in the case of the name authority system, there is no plan to link the authority records to the bibliographic records.

REFERENCES

[1]Library of Congress, Subject Cataloging Division, *Subject Cataloging Manual: Subject Headings*, prelim. ed. (Washington, D.C.: Library of Congress, 1984), H187.

[2]Ibid., H200, H475.

[3]Ibid., H202.

[4]Ibid., H318.

[5]"Subject Heading Changes and the Catalogs," *Cataloging Service* 119:22 (Fall 1976).

[6]Material distributed at Regional Institutes on Library of Congress Subject Headings, sponsored by ALA Resources and Technical Services Division, Library of Congress, ALA/RTSD Council of Regional Groups, 1982-1984.

[7]*Authorities: A MARC Format* (Washington, D.C.: Library of Congress, 1981).

Part 2
APPLICATION

8

SUBJECT CATALOGING

INTRODUCTION

Part 1 of this book contains a discussion of the principles, form, and structure of *Library of Congress Subject Headings*, all of which are preliminary to the ultimate purpose of subject headings, i.e., their application to subject analysis and representation in library catalogs. This chapter and the ones that follow in Part 2 deal with this practical aspect. The discussions are based largely on consultation with the staff of the Library of Congress Subject Cataloging Division, examination of Library of Congress cataloging records, information published in *Cataloging Service Bulletin* and *Subject Cataloging Manual: Subject Headings*, and materials prepared by the Library of Congress for use at the Library of Congress Subject Headings institutes held in 1982-1984 (sponsored by the Resources and Technical Services Division of the American Library Association, the Library of Congress, and the Council of Regional Groups).

Among the factors contributing to effective subject cataloging are the cataloger's familiarity and understanding of the nature and structure of subject headings, the proper interpretation of the work being cataloged, and the ability to coordinate the heading(s) with the work. Were all these factors optimum, for all works cataloged, the resulting cataloging would show a high degree of uniformity and consistency—except, of course, for the dissonances that spring from changing approaches to a subject over time. But the optimum is rarely achieved, and no subject catalog is as internally consistent as one might wish. Over the years, many theorists in the field have speculated that consistency would be greater if there were a code to govern subject heading work. However, it is extremely difficult to codify the procedures for assigning subject headings to specific works because of the inevitable subjective element that is a factor in subject cataloging. There are differences from cataloger to cataloger in interpretation of content. Different people may read the same book and acquire different ideas about it. Sometimes even the same individual reading the same work at two different times may have two different interpretations of the content.

Another complicating factor is introduced by different assumptions about the appropriate depth of analysis and representation. Such depth varies from summarization, with the aim to express only the overall subject content of a document (i.e., to assign a heading coextensive with what is regarded as *the* subject of the document), to exhaustive indexing or in-depth indexing, with the aim of enumerating all significant concepts or aspects and, frequently, component parts of a document. The examples shown in Figures 8.1 and 8.2 demonstrate the extremes of these approaches to the same work. In Figure 8.1, the nine subject headings bring out individual topics covered by the schedule for Class C of the *Library of Congress Classification*. The record shown in Figure 8.2, a revision of the record shown in Figure 8.1, represents more closely the current general policy of the Library of Congress; a heading representing the overall content of the schedule (i.e., Auxiliary sciences of history) is used instead. The difference between the two examples lies in the depth of analysis.

United States. Library of Congress. Subject Cataloging Division.
    Classification. Class C, Auxiliary sciences of history / Subject Cataloging Division, Processing Department, Library of Congress. — 3d ed. — Washington : The Library, 1975
vi, 126 leaves ; 26 cm.
First published in 1915 by the Classification Division.
Includes index.
ISBN 0-8444-0053-X
1. Classification—Books—Archaeology. 2. Classification—Books—Diplomatics. 3. Classification—Books—Archives. 4. Classification—Books—Chronology. 5. Classification—Books—Numismatics. 6. Classification—Books—Heraldry. 7. Classification—Books—Genealogy. 8. Classification—Books—Biography. 9. Classification—Books—Inscriptions. I. United States. Library of Congress. Classification Division. Classification. Class C, Auxiliary sciences of history. II. Title: Auxiliary sciences of history.

Z696.U5C 1975	025.4'6'9	75-619090
_____ _____Copy 3.	Z663.78.C5C 1975	MARC

Figure 8.1. Exhaustive or in-depth analysis and representation.

United States. Library of Congress. Subject Cataloging Division.
    Classification. Class C, Auxiliary sciences of history / Subject Cataloging Division, Processing Department, Library of Congress. — 3d ed. — Washington : The Library, 1975.
    vi, 126 leaves ; 26 cm.

    First published in 1915 by the Classification Division.
    Kept up to date by the Division's L.C. classification—additions and changes, and by an irregular cumulative publication issued by Gale Research Company, entitled Library of Congress classification schedules: a cumulation of additions and changes, Class C.
    Includes index.

(Continued on next card)

75-619090
MARC

75ᵣ76ᵣrev

United States. Library of Congress. Subject Cataloging Division. — Classification. Class C, Auxiliary sciences of history . . . 1975. (Card 2)
    ISBN 0-8444-0053-X

    1. Classification—Books—Auxiliary sciences of history. 2. Classification, Library of Congress. I. United States. Library of Congress. Classification Division. Classification. Class C, Auxiliary sciences of history. II. Gale Research Company.

Z696.U5C 1975   025.4'6'9   75-619090
————— Copy 3.   Z663.78.C5C 1975   MARC

Library of Congress   75ᵣ76ᵣrev

Figure 8.2. The record shown in figure 8.1, revised according to the summarization approach.

It is the cataloging policy of a given library or information agency that primarily governs depth of analysis, though individual judgments may vary considerably even under a given policy. Library of Congress policy leans heavily toward summarization. In libraries where the summarization approach is felt to be insufficient and a more in-depth analysis is desired, additional subject access points taken either from *Library of Congress Subject Headings* or from the work itself may be assigned to bring out individual topics or aspects of the work. One approach, tested in the Syracuse Subject Access Project,[1] augmented MARC records by additional subject access points based on words and phrases found within the index and/or table of contents of the work being analyzed. This device increases the number of subject access points and allows a measure of free text access to terms used in the document cataloged. Another attempt to augment subject access points is reflected in the Hennepin County Library's *Cataloging Bulletin*,[2] each issue of which contains a list of subject headings that may be used in place of or in addition to Library of Congress subject headings assigned to cataloging records.

GENERAL CONSIDERATIONS

General Policy

The general policy of assigning subject headings has been stated in the following words: "Summarize the contents of the work. Do not make 'chapter analytics' or 'page analytics.' Do not bring out part of the book, unless it is more than approximately 20% of the work or is not considered to be covered by the heading assigned."[3]

Format of *Library of Congress Subject Headings*

In order to be able to apply Library of Congress subject headings properly and effectively, an understanding of the physical format and characteristics of the Library of Congress subject headings list is important. Over the years, certain conventions have been assumed or understood. The following discussion is intended to help the user understand some of these conventions and characteristics.

Unprinted headings

As discussed in chapter 6, a large number of name headings are used in subject entries but do not appear in the printed list. These are often referred to as unprinted or nonprint headings. Formerly, unprinted headings also included many common names, such as names of chemical compounds and systematic names of families, genera, and species in botany and zoology. In recent editions of the subject headings list, the categories of unprinted headings have been narrowed down to the following:

o Name headings established by descriptive catalogers according to *AACR2*:

   Headings for persons
   Headings for corporate bodies
   Headings for jurisdictions
   Uniform titles

o Headings resulting from combinations of valid main headings with free-floating subdivisions or phrases

o Music headings belonging to the following categories:*

   Headings for instrumental chamber music not entered under musical form
   Headings for musical forms that take qualifiers for instrumental medium

However, many of the headings in the categories listed above are printed when they serve as examples or when unique cross-references or subdivisions are required. Furthermore, many of the music headings and headings with free-floating subdivisions established earlier still remain in the list, because deletions can only be carried out gradually.

Reading *Library of Congress Subject Headings*

Because of normal updating and the many recent changes that resulted from the implementation of *AACR2*, users must be able to recognize the headings in the tenth edition of *Library of Congress Subject Headings* that are no longer valid. The latest microfiche edition and weekly lists must be consulted in order to ascertain cancelled and changed headings. At the same time, users may need to remind themselves that cancellation does not necessarily imply that a heading is no longer valid—a particular cancellation may simply be part of the effort to remove unprinted headings from the list.[4]

Multiple headings[5]

"Multiple" subject headings and headings with "multiple" subdivisions were introduced in the fifth edition of *Library of Congress Subject Headings* as a device to save space in the printed list. A multiple subject heading appears in the form of a heading followed by a bracketed series of terms ending with *etc.* The most common type of multiple heading is an inverted adjectival heading with a series of illustrative adjectival qualifiers representing languages, nationalities, ethnic groups, or religions, e.g., **Authors, American, [English, French, etc.]; Coins, Arab, [Austrian, French, etc.]; Theological seminaries, Catholic, [Lutheran, Presbyterian, etc.].** Until 1979 these multiple headings were treated in essence like free-floating phrases, in that headings

---

*For a more detailed list of these headings, see pages 272-274.

such as **Authors, Spanish; Coins, Italian** were used as subject entries even though they were not printed in *Library of Congress Subject Headings*. Beginning in 1979 the establishment of new multiple headings was discontinued; all newly created headings of this type, including those covered by an existing multiple heading, are printed individually. Previously established multiple headings are kept in the printed list to illustrate how a heading may be qualified and to show that the individually printed headings do not necessarily constitute an exhaustive list of valid forms of the heading that were assigned to works cataloged before 1979.[6] However, multiple headings are no longer treated as free-floating phrases. In other words, each time the main heading is to be combined with an adjectival qualifier never printed before, the combination must be proposed as a new heading to be printed in the list. For example, although covered by the multiple heading **Authors, American, [English, French, etc.]**, the following heading was established and printed in the 1985 *Supplement:* **Authors, Urdu.**

Headings with multiple subdivisions[7]

The device of multiples is also used in subdivisions, e.g., **Birth control — Religious aspects — Baptists, [Catholic Church, etc.]**. The policies governing multiple subdivisions are quite different from those regarding multiple headings. While multiple headings are no longer being established or treated as free-floating, multiple subdivisions are. Currently, there are four types of multiple subdivisions in *Library of Congress Subject Headings*, all of which are considered free-floating:

1) *Multiple subdivisions under established headings*, e.g., **Subject headings — Aeronautics, [Education, Law, etc.]; Names, Personal — Scottish, [Spanish, Welsh, etc.]**. These headings are printed in *Library of Congress Subject Headings* as multiples, and any topic or qualifier falling into the categories indicated in the brackets may be combined with the main heading, e.g., **Subject headings — Psychology; Names, Personal — Hungarian**.

2) *Multiple subdivisions under pattern headings:*

**World War, 1939-1945 — Personal narratives, American,
    [French, German, etc.]
English language — Dictionaries — French, [Italian, etc.]
Shakespeare, William, 1564-1616 — Contemporary England,
    [Contemporary America, Contemporary France, etc.]**

Because the multiple subdivisions are free-floating, the following headings, though not listed in *Library of Congress Subject Headings*, are valid:

**Korean War, 1950-1953 — Personal narratives, Korean
Chinese language — Dictionaries — Latin
Goethe, Johann Wolfgang von, 1749-1832 — Contemporary
    Germany**

3) *Multiple free-floating subdivisions under place names*, e.g., **[Region, country, etc.] — Foreign opinion, British, [French, Italian, etc.]**. The following headings are valid as a result: **France — Foreign opinion, American; United States — Foreign opinion, Latin American**.

4) *Multiple subdivisions displayed by means of instructional scope notes:*

Ocean currents
Subdivided by body of water, *e.g.* Ocean currents — Atlantic Ocean.

Eclipses, Solar
Subdivided by date, *e.g.* Eclipses, Solar — 1854.

The scope notes, which allow for free-floating subdivision as described, should not be confused with general *see also* references, which do *not* necessarily authorize free-floating usage of a subdivision:

Pamphlets
sa subdivision Pamphlets *under 16th, 17th and 18th century period subdivisions of European and American history, e.g.* Germany — History — 1517-1648 — Pamphlets; *and under individual wars, e.g.* United States — History — Civil War, 1861-1865 — Pamphlets

In this case, the subdivision **— Pamphlets** is *not* free-floating under period subdivisions. However, it is a free-floating subdivision under names of individual wars, because it is listed under the pattern heading for wars.

Scope notes[8]

Scope notes are provided under many headings in *Library of Congress Subject Headings* for the purpose of helping users to determine the scope of the material covered by the heading and enabling catalogers to maintain consistency in assigning the heading to works being cataloged. Scope notes in the subject headings list generally provide information concerning one or more of the following aspects of the headings: definition, relation to other headings, and application. Examples are given below.

1) *Definition.* This type of note is particularly helpful in situations in which the heading represents a new concept for which the name has not yet been firmly established in usage and for which there is no dictionary definition, or situations in which reference sources fail to agree completely on the meaning of the term used. Examples include:

Absentee mothers *(Indirect)*
    Here are entered works on mothers who have voluntarily or involuntarily relinquished custody of their natural born children after having kept them for a period of time after birth.

Creationism
    Here are entered works on the doctrine that the universe was created by God out of nothing in the initial seven days of time and that all biological aspects were created rather than evolving from preexisting types through modification in successive generations.

No first use (Nuclear strategy)
    Here are entered works on the principle that a military power, in the event of war, would not be the first to resort to the tactical or strategic use of nuclear weapons.

Western and Northern Territories (Poland)
    Here are entered works which discuss the former German areas of Poland that lie east of the Oder-Neisse Line.

2) *Relation to other headings.* This type of note is used to indicate the scope of the heading in question and to call attention to overlapping or more specific headings. Examples include:

Amateur plays *(Indirect)*
    Here are entered collections of plays, skits, recitations, etc. for production by nonprofessionals. Works about, including history and criticism of, such plays are entered under Amateur theater.

Amateur theater *(Indirect)*
    Here are entered works about, including history and criticism of, productions of plays, skits, recitations, etc. for production by nonprofessionals. Collections of such plays are entered under Amateur plays.

Animal food
    Here are entered works on human food of animal origin. Works on the food and food habits of animals are entered under Animals — Food.

World War, 1939-1945
    — Occupied territories
    Here are entered works on enemy occupied territories discussed collectively. Works on the occupation of an individual country are entered under the name of the country with appropriate period subdivision, e.g., Belgium — History — German occupation, 1940-1945; Norway — History — German occupation, 1940-1945.

3) *Instructions, explanations, referrals, etc.* This type of note provides information about making additional entries, about subdivisions used under the heading, or about general references to other headings. Examples include:

Material culture *(Indirect)*
>When this heading is divided by place an additional subject entry is made under the name of the place with an appropriate subdivision such as Industries, Social life and customs, Civilization, etc.

Ocean waves
>This heading may be subdivided by bodies of water, *e.g.* Ocean waves — Atlantic Ocean.

School prose
>For works limited to one school, the heading is qualified by nationality and subdivided by place, and an additional subject entry is made under the name of the school.

Developing countries
>Here are entered comprehensive works on those countries having relatively low per capita incomes in comparison with North American and Western European countries.
>This heading may be subdivided by those topical subdivisions used under names of regions, countries, etc., *e.g.* Developing countries — Economic conditions, and may be used as a geographic subdivision under those topics authorized for local subdivision, *e.g.* Technology — Developing countries.

Subject Tracings[9]

On a cataloging record prepared for a manual card catalog or book catalog, the tracings for subject and added entries are recorded in a paragraph following the notes. The subject headings are listed first, each preceded by an arabic numeral. If two or more subject headings have been assigned to the work, they are arranged according to their closeness to the overall content of the work. The heading that represents the overall content, normally the one corresponding to the class number assigned to the work, is usually listed first, followed by those headings that designate secondary topics or a special approach to the major topic. In the case of individual biography, for instance, the first subject heading assigned is the name heading for the biographee. Those headings assigned to elaborate subsidiary aspects or local interest, such as biographical headings, extra local history headings, etc., are given last. Examples are shown in Figure 8.3.

Kaufman, Herb.
　　Calligraphy in the copperplate style / Herb Kaufman and Geri
Homelsky. — New York : Dover, 1980.
　　31 p. : ill. ; 28 cm.
　　ISBN 0-486-24037-1 (pbk.) : $1.75

　　1. Calligraphy.　2. Plate-printing.　3. Lettering.　I. Homelsky, Geri.　II.
Title.

Z43.K215　　　　　　　　　　745.6′1—dc19　　　　　80-66324
　　　　　　　　　　　　　　　　　　　　　　　　AACR 2　MARC

Library of Congress

Ewing, Raymond P., 1925-
　　Mark Twain's steamboat years : the years of command / by
Raymond P. Ewing. — Hannibal, Mo. (Cave Hollow Steamboat
Landing) : R.P. Ewing, c1981.
　　xiv, 66 p. : ill. ; 23 cm.
　　Bibliography: p. 66.

　　1. Twain, Mark, 1835-1910—Careers.　2. Authors, American—19th century
—Biography.　3. Pilots and pilotage—United States—Biography.　4. Steam-
boats—United S　　-History.　5. Mississippi River—Navigation—History.
I. Title.

PS1334.E9　　　　　　　　　818′.409—dc19　　　　81-68856
　　　　　　　　　　　　　　　[B]　　　　　　　AACR 2　MARC

Library of Congress

Figure 8.3. Subject tracings on catalog cards.

On a MARC record, the subject headings are tagged according to types of headings as follows:

600 Subject added entry - Personal name
610 Subject added entry - Corporate name
611 Subject added entry - Conference or meeting
630 Subject added entry - Uniform title heading
650 Subject added entry - Topical heading
651 Subject added entry - Geographic name

When any of these fields is repeated, as they are when there is more than one subject-added entry in a given category, listings for a given field follow the order noted above for manual records. For more details see appendix K.

Assigning Subject Headings

General versus specific

The principle of specific entry requires that a work be assigned the most specific heading that ideally represents exactly the contents of the work. In Charles A. Cutter's words, assign the heading **Cats** to a work about cats.[10] At the Library of Congress, subject catalogers are instructed to propose a new heading for each new topic encountered in cataloging but not yet represented in the subject headings list. In practice, however, there are occasions when it is considered impossible or impractical for various reasons to establish a new concept or topic as a heading. In such cases, the subject content of the work is brought out either through a general heading or through several related headings.

A question related to the policy of specific entry is whether, after assigning a specific heading such as **Cats** to a work about cats, one should also assign one or more general headings, such as **Domestic animals** and **Pets**. On the whole, a general heading and a specific one comprehended within it, e.g., **Mathematics** and **Algebra**, are not assigned to a work dealing with the specific subject (e.g., Algebra). A work about book classification is assigned the heading **Classification—Books**, but not **Library science** as well. In other words, when a heading that is coextensive with the overall content of a work is assigned, neither more specific headings subsumed under the given heading nor more general headings that comprehend the given heading are assigned in addition. This means neither in-depth indexing nor generic posting is done as a matter of general policy.

In a number of cases, the Library of Congress has relaxed its general policies of not assigning a generic heading in addition to the specific heading coextensive with the content of the work and of not assigning a specific heading to a part of a work. This is evident in its treatment of individual biographies, analytical entries, and doubling.

1) *Individual biographies.* For individual biographies, a generic heading representing the class of persons to which the individual belongs is assigned in addition to the personal name heading. (For a more detailed discussion, see chapter 9.)

2) *Analytical entries.* Although in-depth indexing is not a general policy in preparing cataloging records at the Library of Congress, when a work on a general topic devotes 20 percent or more of its space to a specific topic, two headings are assigned, one to cover the overall content of the work and the other to represent the specific topic. Heading 1 in the example below is assigned to represent a part of the content:

Title: *Small Gardens Are More Fun*
1. **Landscape gardening.**
2. **Gardening.**

The two headings are assigned even though there is a *see also* reference from **Gardening** to **Landscape gardening**. It is the policy of the Library of Congress that the presence of a *see also* reference between two headings should not preclude the use of both headings for the same work as long as the two headings represent the actual content of the work.

3) *Doubling in specific cases.* The term *doubling* refers to the practice of assigning bilevel (generic and specific) headings to the same work. Bilevel headings are assigned in the cases described below.[11]

a) If the work being cataloged deals with a topic in general as well as applies to a particular locality, two headings are assigned as follows:

Title: *Economics for East Africa: An Introductory Course*
1. **Economics.**
2. **Africa, East — Economic conditions.**

Title: *Southern Living Garden Guide: Houseplants, Vegetables, Trees, Shrubs and More*
1. **Gardening — Southern states.**
2. **Gardening.**

b) If the heading appropriate for the work being cataloged contains a geographic subdivision and the subdivision **— Early works to 1800** (or a similar subdivision), two headings are assigned:

1. **Quacks and quackery — Early works to 1800.**
2. **Quacks and quackery — England — Early works to 1800.**

The reason for doing this is to keep all early works on a topic together in the catalog.

c) Bilevel headings are assigned by tradition to certain subjects, such as **World War, 1939-1945; Paleontology**.

d) Works of interest to local historians and genealogists are assigned headings of the type **[City] — [Topic]** in addition to other appropriate heading(s).

e)   Works discussing buildings or structures within a city are assigned additional headings in the form of **[City] — Buildings, structures, etc.**

f)   Frequently, when a heading assigned to a work contains a free-floating subdivision named in a multiple subdivision (see discussion on pages 174-175), an additional heading representing the topic named in the subdivision is also assigned:[12]

Title: *The Best Name Book in the Whole Wide World*
    1.   Names, Personal — English.
    [Authorized by : **Names, Personal — Scottish, [Spanish, Welsh, etc.]]**
    2.   English language — Etymology — Names.

Title: *Ordination of Priests in the Roman Catholic Church*
    1.   Ordination — Catholic Church.
    [Authorized by : **Ordination — Baptists, [Catholic Church, etc.]]**
    2.   Catholic Church — Clergy.

Duplicate entries

As discussed in chapter 2, exceptions are sometimes made to the principle of uniform heading in cases in which two concepts in a heading are of equal significance and it is therefore desirable to provide access points to both. In such cases, specific instructions are given in the printed list to assign both headings to the same work, even though they consist of the same elements and have identical meanings:

United States
    — Foreign relations
    — — Canada, [France, Japan, etc.]
            Duplicate entry is made under Canada [France, Japan, etc.] — Foreign relations — United States.

English poetry
    — Translations from French, [German, etc.]
            Duplicate entry is made under French, [German, etc.] poetry — Translations into English.

Cataloging examples include:

Title: *United States Foreign Policy and South Africa*
    1.   United States — Foreign relations — South Africa.
    2.   South Africa — Foreign relations — United States.

Title: *Old Friend from Far Away: 150 Chinese Poems from the Great Dynasties*
    1.   Chinese poetry — Translations into English.
    2.   English poetry — Translations from Chinese.

SPECIAL CONSIDERATIONS

It is difficult, and perhaps not practical, to regulate the number of subject headings to be assigned to each work. In general, such a decision is based on the requirement of the work and the general policy of summarization. It has been estimated that the average number of subject headings assigned to a Library of Congress cataloging record is less than two.[13] Many consider this to be an indication of insufficiency in the Library of Congress's practice. The low average may have been affected by the fact that a large number of works, i.e., literary works by individual authors, especially fiction and collected works, are not assigned any subject headings. The average number of headings assigned to works exclusive of literary works by individual authors is much higher.

On the basis of the policy of summarization, the ideal situation is to be able to assign to each work a heading that is coextensive with its content. However, in most instances it is not possible to do this. Many works deal with multiple topics or complex subjects and so require more than one heading. Even works dealing with a single subject may occasionally require more than one heading.

In determining the number of headings to be assigned, the following guidelines are followed by the subject catalogers at the Library of Congress:

o   Assign a specific heading that represents precisely the content of the work, if one is available; or establish such a heading, if it is feasible.

o   Assign separate headings to a work covering two or three topics when there is no single heading that precisely represents its content.

o   Assign a broad or generic heading that encompasses all the topics treated in a work covering four or more topics, even if the generic heading covers other topics not included in the work.

These guidelines are discussed and illustrated in the following sections.

Works on a Single Topic

The heading that exactly represents the content is assigned to a work on a single topic:

Title: *A Practical Introduction to Business*
   1.   **Business.**

Title: *Datsun Car Care Guide*
   1.   **Datsun automobile.**

Title: *General Chemistry: Principles and Structure*
   1.   **Chemistry.**

Form subdivisions, most of which are free-floating (see chapter 4), are used when appropriate. They may be assigned under all types of headings — personal names, corporate names, meetings and conferences, uniform titles, geographic headings, and topical headings:

Title: *Baseball Rules Illustrated*
  1. **Baseball — Rules.**

Title: *The Condensed Chemical Dictionary*
  1. **Chemistry — Dictionaries.**

Title: *To Advance the Gospel: New Testament Studies*
  1. **Bible.   N.T. — Addresses, essays, lectures.**

On the rare occasions when the topic of the work being cataloged is not represented in *Library of Congress Subject Headings* and for various reasons it is impossible or impractical to establish the concept as a new heading, a more general heading or several related headings, whichever designates most closely the topic of the work, are assigned:

Title: *Knowledge, Ideology, and Politics of Schooling: Towards a Marxist Analysis of Education*
  1. **Educational sociology.**

Title: *Managing Human Resources: The Art of Full Employment*
  1. **Job enrichment.**
  2. **Work environment.**
  3. **Personnel management.**

Multielement Works

Many works treat a single topic with regard to one or more aspects, such as time, place, or subject. In most cases, these aspects are represented by subdivisions. In other cases, they are represented by a complex heading (a phrase heading or a heading with a qualifier) that combines the aspect(s) with the main topic. In these cases, all the elements are precoordinated. Examples include:

Title: *The Elementary Teacher's Art Handbook*
  1. **Art — Study and teaching (Elementary) — United States — Handbooks, manuals, etc.**

Title: *K-Mart Special Emissions Manual*
  1. **Automobiles — Pollution control devices — Maintenance and repair.**

Title: *Philosophy of Education since Mid-Century*
  1. **Education — Philosophy — History — 20th Century — Addresses, essays, lectures.**

Title: *A Practical Approach to Adapted Physical Education*
  1. **Physical education for handicapped children.**

Title: *The Great Potato Cookbook*
  1. **Cookery (Potatoes)**

In some cases, the various elements in a complex subject are brought out by means of two or more headings:

Title: *Using Microcomputers in Business*
    1.   **Business — Data processing.**
    2.   **Microcomputers.**

Title: *Advances in the Social Psychology of Language*
    1.   **Sociolinguistics.**
    2.   **Psycholinguistics.**

Title: *Protective Groups in Organic Synthesis*
    1.   **Chemistry, Organic — Synthesis.**
    2.   **Protective groups (Chemistry)**

In these cases, each of the headings assigned is broader than the subject treated in the work. Specificity is achieved only through postcoordination (i.e., combining the heading being consulted with other headings during the process of searching). This is a more powerful device in automated information retrieval systems than in manual ones, but it is effective in both. This approach is taken most frequently when a large number of concepts are involved:

Title: *Methods of Conducting a Wind Tunnel Investigation of*
            Lift in Roll at Supersonic Speeds of Sweptback Wings
    1.   **Airplanes — Wings, Swept-back — Testing.**
    2.   **Lift (Aerodynamics)**
    3.   **Rolling (Aerodynamics)**
    4.   **Aerodynamics, Supersonic.**
    5.   **Wind tunnels.**

Title: *A Method of Setting up the Eigenvalue Problem for the*
            Linear, Shallow-Water Wave Equation for Irregular
            Bodies of Water with Variable Water Depth and
            Application to Bays and Harbors in Hawaii
    1.   **Ocean waves.**
    2.   **Wave equation.**
    3.   **Eigenvalues.**
    4.   **Oceanography — Data processing.**
    5.   **Bays — Hawaii.**
    6.   **Harbors — Hawaii.**

Geographic aspect

The geographic aspect of a work is normally brought out by means of a geographic subdivision or a geographic heading:

Title: *The History of Education in Cherokee County, Alabama*
    1.   **Education — Alabama — Cherokee County — History.**

Title: *Uniforms of the French Revolutionary Wars, 1789-1802*
1. **Uniforms, Military — History — 18th century.**
2. **France — History, Military — 1789-1815.**

Since geographic subdivisions are generally not provided under names of species, breeds of animals, and specific musical instruments, the geographic aspect is brought out by assigning, in addition to the specific heading, a broader heading under which geographic subdivisions are provided:

Title: *Spanish Arabians in America*
1. **Arabian horse.**
2. **Horses — United States — Stud-books.**

Title: *The Spanish Baroque Guitar*
1. **Guitar.**
2. **Musical instruments — Spain.**
3. **Guitar music.**

Time aspect

The time, or chronological, aspect of a subject is usually brought out by means of period subdivisions:

Title: *Masters of Twentieth Century Art*
1. **Art, Modern — 20th century.**

Title: *Guide to Canada*
1. **Canada — Description and travel — 1951-   — Guide-books.**

If the specific heading assigned to the work treating the subject with respect to a period does not provide for period subdivisions, an additional, broader heading that allows for period subdivision is sometimes assigned to bring out the chronological aspect:

Title: *The Comic in Renaissance Comedy*
1. **English drama — 17th century — History and criticism.**
2. **English drama (Comedy) — History and criticism.**
3. **Comic, The.**

In many cases, the time aspect of a work is ignored in cataloging if it is considered insignificant.

Multitopical Works

Works with two or three topics

For a work covering two or three topics treated separately, a specific heading is assigned to each of the topics unless there is a broader or generic heading that represents precisely the two or three topics involved. In the latter case, the generic heading is used instead of the separate headings:

Title: *Glossary of Astronomy and Astrophysics*
1. **Astronomy — Dictionaries.**
2. **Astrophysics — Dictionaries.**

Title: *Let's Reach for the Sun: 30 Original Solar and Earth
            Sheltered Home Designs*
1. **Solar houses — Designs and plans.**
2. **Earth sheltered houses — Designs and plans.**

Title: *The History of the Norristown Area (East Norriton,
            Norristown, and West Norriton)*
1. **East Norriton (Pa.) — History.**
2. **Norristown (Pa.) — History.**
3. **West Norriton (Pa.) — History.**

Title: *The Characters, Plots and Settings of Calderón's Comedias*
1. **Calderón de la Barca, Pedro, 1600-1681 — Characters.**
2. **Calderón de la Barca, Pedro, 1600-1681 — Plots.**
3. **Calderón de la Barca, Pedro, 1600-1681 — Settings.**

Title: *The Distinctive Excellences of Greek and Latin*
1. **Classical literature — Addresses, essays, lectures.**
        [instead of separate headings for Greek literature and
            Latin literature]

In some cases, additional headings (headings 3, 4, and 5 in the following
example) may be used to bring out other aspects of the work:

Title: *Technology Transfer, Productivity and Economic Policy*
1. **Industrial productivity — United States.**
2. **Technology transfer — Economic aspects — United States.**
3. **Technical assistance, American — Costs.**
4. **Research, Industrial — United States — Costs.**
5. **United States — Foreign economic relations.**
6. **United States — Economic policy.**

When a form subdivision is used under a heading for a work with more than
one heading, the same form subdivision should be used with all the headings if
it is applicable. Exceptions are naturally made for cases in which different
parts of the work are in different forms. Examples include:

Title: *A Search for Structure: Selected Essays on Science, Art
            and History*
1. **Science — Addresses, essays, lectures.**
2. **Art — Addresses, essays, lectures.**
3. **History — Addresses, essays, lectures.**

Title: *Montana Comprehensive Plan for Alcohol and Drug Abuse Prevention, Treatment and Rehabilitation*
1. **Alcoholism — Montana — Prevention — Planning — Periodicals.**
2. **Drug abuse — Montana — Prevention — Planning — Periodicals.**
3. **Alcoholism — Treatment — Montana — Planning — Periodicals.**
4. **Drug abuse — Treatment — Montana — Planning — Periodicals.**
5. **Alcoholics — Rehabilitation — Montana — Planning — Periodicals.**
6. **Narcotic addicts — Rehabilitation — Montana — Planning — Periodicals.**

Title: *Food Aid and Policy for Economic Development: An Annotated Bibliography and Directory*
1. **Underdeveloped areas — Food relief — Bibliography.**
2. **Underdeveloped areas — Food relief — Directories.**
3. **Economic assistance — Bibliography.**
4. **Economic assistance — Directories.**

Works with four or more topics

For a work treating four or more related topics, a single generic heading that encompasses all the topics treated is used if one exists or can be established, even if the generic heading includes other topics not present in the work being cataloged:

Title: *How to Collect: A Complete Guide: The Art of Buying, Displaying, Preserving, Protecting and Selling Your Antiques*
1. **Art — Collectors and collecting — Handbooks, manuals, etc.**

Title: *A Survey of Selected Projects in the Gulf States (Bahrain, Kuwait, Oman, Qatar, U.A.E.) Awarded in 1979 and 1980*
1. **Economic development projects — Persian Gulf States — Directories.**

Title: *Acts of Implication: Suggestion and Covert Meaning in the Works of Dryden, Swift, Pope and Austen*
1. **English literature — 18th century — History and criticism — Addresses, essays, lectures.**

If such a generic heading does not exist or cannot be established, a separate heading for each topic is assigned, if there are no more than four. If more than four headings would be required, either several very broad headings or a single heading for form only (e.g., **American essays**) is used. Examples include:

Title: *Essays*
1. **College readers.**
2. **Essays.**

Title: *The McGraw-Hill Reader*
1. **College readers.**

Phase relations

For works treating subjects in relation to each other, i.e., in cases of phase relations (including influence, tool or application, comparison, and bias), headings representing such relationships, if available, are assigned, e.g., **Fungi in agriculture; Plants, Effects of electricity on; Shakespeare, William, 1564-1616 — Influence — Scott; Television and children.** If such headings do not exist, subject catalogers at the Library of Congress may propose new headings if the relationship is considered significant, or they may use separate headings for each topic involved:

Title: *The Econometric Analysis of Time Series*
   1. **Econometrics.**
   2. **Time series analysis.**

Title: *Educational Technology in Engineering*
   1. **Engineering — Study and teaching.**
   2. **Educational technology.**

The author's or publisher's viewpoint is often brought out in the subject heading, particularly concerning the intention regarding readership (juvenile or adult) and the approach (fact or fiction, etc.):

Title: *From Egg to Butterfly*
   1. **Butterfly — Metamorphosis — Juvenile literature.**
   2. **Insects — Metamorphosis — Juvenile literature.**

Title: *The Shield Ring*
   1. **Great Britain — History — Norman period, 1066-1154 — Juvenile fiction.**

In the case of general textbooks intended for special groups of persons, a heading indicating the special interest and/or application is often assigned in addition to the heading(s) for the topic(s):

[textbook of psychology for nurses]
   1. **Psychology.**
   2. **Nursing — Psychological aspects.**

Title: *Computer Basics for Librarians and Information Scientists*
   1. **Computers.**
   2. **Electronic data processing.**
   3. **Libraries — Automation.**

In other cases, the aspect of special audience or readership may be ignored:

Title: *Statistics for Engineers*
   1. **Statistics.**
   2. **Probabilities.**

Title: *Basic Economics for Conservative Democrats*
    1. Economics.

The cataloger is advised to use good judgment and apply common sense in such cases.

Topics without Representation in the Subject Headings List

If the topic of the work being cataloged is not represented in the list and, because of various factors such as uncertain terminology, it is impossible to establish it as a valid subject heading, it is the practice of the Library of Congress to assign a more general heading or several related headings, whatever designates most accurately the topic of the work in view of the various headings available. It is recognized that this is not a satisfactory approach, and this procedure is followed only when a more precise or more specific heading is not available.

Title Cataloging

Because titles of works usually state the subject matter of the work in the words of the author or publisher, they are extremely important and often helpful in subject cataloging, in spite of the fact that they are sometimes misleading. In scientific and technical fields particularly, a term or expression used in a title is likely to be what the user consults. At the Library of Congress, subject catalogers make use of titles that explicitly state the subject matter of works in the ways described below.

1) *By assigning a subject heading corresponding to the title*. If there is a subject heading corresponding directly to the topic designated in the title, it is assigned. In cases in which an approximate heading must be assigned instead of the topic named in the title because of the special scope or twist of the work, a second heading is assigned to correspond as closely as possible with the topic named in the title:

Title: *Computers and the Union*
    1. Electronic data processing and industrial relations.
    2. Trade-unions—Great Britain—Data processing.

2) *By a* see *reference*. In some cases, the term or expression used in the title may be made into a *see* reference to the heading actually assigned.

3) *By title-added entry*. If no other means are available, the title-added entry may be used to bring out the exact topic of the work. Seymour Lubetzky[14] criticizes this practice, and it is recognized at the Library of Congress that it is not a fully satisfactory approach; it is therefore used only as a last resort.

4) *By partial-title-added entry.*[15] When the above-listed devices fail, a partial-title-added entry may be made. Such added entries provide topical access through natural language. They also allow the cataloger to locate and retrieve the records when a new heading is finally establilshed for the concept. This practice is discussed below.

a) A partial-title-added entry is used when the subject heading assigned does not precisely represent the concept of the work and the concept is named in the title proper but does not occur in the initial position. The added entry is not used, however, if the concept is represented by a *see* reference to the heading assigned.

b) The partial-title-added entry is not assigned unless all possibilities of establishing the concept as a subject heading have been exhausted.

c) The practice applies to titles in all languages. However, it is not followed if the concept has an acceptable subject heading equivalent when it is translated into English.

d) A partial-title-added entry is traced as "Title:" before any series-added entries. Examples include:

Title: *Keys to Enhancing System Development Productivity*
    1. Electronic data processing departments — Labor productivity.
    I. Title.
    II. Title: System development productivity.

Title: *Essentials of Advertising Strategy*
    1. Advertising.
    I. Title.
    II. Title: Advertising strategy.

Subject Headings Identical to Descriptive Access Points[16]

Previously, the Library of Congress had a policy of not assigning to a work a subject heading that matched exactly an author heading (main or added entry). This policy was discontinued in 1972. Currently, an appropriate subject heading is assigned to a work even though the heading may duplicate a main or added entry assigned in descriptive cataloging. This is often the case in works entered under corporate bodies, autobiographical works, nontopical compilations of general laws, and artistic reproductions with commentary.* It also occurs when the valid heading is identical with the title of the work. These duplicate access points may be considered unnecessary in a manual dictionary catalog. They are, however, necessary in a divided catalog in which subject

---

*A discussion and examples of specific types of materials and special subject areas appear in the two chapters that follow.

entries are maintained in an alphabetical file separate from the author and title entries. In an online catalog, duplicate access points are also considered necessary because subject searches may be limited to the subject fields only; a user wanting material *about* a given corporate body, for instance, would probably not make an author search for it. Author and title entries are not retrieved in subject searches, only in searches for author or title.

The following examples illustrate duplicate access points:

Title: *The Association of Consulting Engineers Directory*
         [main entry: Association of Consulting Engineers (Malaysia)]
    1. **Association of Consulting Engineers (Malaysia)—Directories.**

Title: *Through the Narrow Gate* / by Karen Armstrong
    1. **Armstrong, Karen.**
    2. **Ex-nuns—Biography.**

Title: *Economics*
    1. **Economics.**
    I. Title.

Title: *Chemistry, Experiment and Theory*
    1. **Chemistry.**
    I. Title.

The discussion above concerns subject cataloging in general. In the Library of Congress subject headings system, several types of materials and special subject areas receive special or unique treatment. These are discussed in the following two chapters.

REFERENCES

[1]Pauline Atherton and Karen Markey, *Subject Access Project: Books Are for Use: Final Report to the Council on Library Resources* (Syracuse, N.Y.: Syracuse University, School of Information Studies, 1978).

[2]Hennepin County Library, Cataloging Section, *Cataloging Bulletin*, nos. 1- (Edina, Minn.: Hennepin County Library, 1973-).

[3]Material distributed at Regional Institutes on Library of Congress Subject Headings, sponsored by ALA Resources and Technical Services Division, Library of Congress, ALA/RTSD Council of Regional Groups, 1982-1984.

[4]Ibid.

[5]"Multiples in LCSH," *Cataloging Service Bulletin* 4:13-14 (Spring 1979); Library of Congress, Subject Cataloging Division, *Subject Cataloging Manual: Subject Headings*, prelim. ed. (Washington, D.C.: Library of Congress, 1984), H330.

[6]"Multiple Subdivision," *Cataloging Service Bulletin* 19:19 (Winter 1982).

[7]Ibid., 19-21; Library of Congress, *Subject Cataloging Manual*, H1090.

[8]"Scope Notes," *Cataloging Service Bulletin* 16:55-57 (Spring 1982); Library of Congress, *Subject Cataloging Manual*, H400.

[9]"Order of Subject Tracings," *Cataloging Service Bulletin* 1:15 (Summer 1978); Library of Congress, *Subject Cataloging Manual*, H80.

[10]Charles A. Cutter, *Rules for a Dictionary Catalog*, 4th ed. (Washington, D.C.: Government Printing Office, 1904), 66.

[11]Library of Congress, *Subject Cataloging Manual*, H870.

[12]Ibid., H1090.

[13]Edward T. O'Neill and Rao Aluri, *Research Report on Subject Heading Patterns in OCLC Monographic Records* (Columbus, Ohio: OCLC, Inc., Research and Development Division, 1979), 7.

[14]Seymour Lubetzky, "Titles: Fifth Column of the Catalog," *Library Quarterly* 11:412-430 (1941).

[15]Library of Congress, *Subject Cataloging Manual*, H150, H187.

[16]Ibid., H184.

9

SUBJECT CATALOGING OF SPECIAL TYPES OF MATERIALS

SERIALS

For serial publications in general, and for periodicals and journals in particular, the subject range of a publication over its expected life is cataloged, not the subjects in individual issues. Topical and/or geographical headings are assigned as appropriate, with a form subdivision used to show the material's bibliographical form. The following list shows the form subdivisions most frequently used for serials:

- —Abstracts—Periodicals
- —Collected works
- —Congresses
- —Directories
- —Indexes
- —Periodicals
- —Societies, etc.
- —Yearbooks

Of these, as might be expected, the one in widest use is —**Periodicals**.[1] It is used as a form subdivision under topical, corporate, or geographical headings or other subdivisions assigned to regularly issued serial publications. There are, however, some restrictions on this subdivision. It is *not* used in the following cases:

under headings for publications issued regularly in revised form, such as *J.K. Lasser's Your Income Tax*; such publications are not considered true serials

under headings for annual publications that summarize the years they cover; such publications take the subdivision – **Yearbooks***

as a further subdivision under the following form subdivisions:

– **Addresses, essays, lectures**	– **Juvenile sound recordings**
– **Amateurs' manuals**	– **Laboratory manuals**
– **Atlases**	– **Maps**
– **Catalogs**	– **Observers' manuals**
– **Catalogs and collections**	– **Outlines, syllabi, etc.**
– **Collected works**	– **Phonotape catalogs**
– **Congresses**	– **Photo maps**
– **Directories**	– **Registers**
– **Discography**	– **Road maps**
– **Film catalogs**	– **Social registers**
– **Gazetteers**	– **Thematic catalogs**
– **Guide-books**	– **Union lists**
– **Handbooks, manuals, etc.**	– **Voting registers**
– **Juvenile films**	– **Yearbooks**
– **Juvenile literature**	– **Zoning maps**

As a result, headings such as **[Topic] – Congresses – Periodicals** are not used by the Library of Congress. However, the subdivision – **Periodicals** may be used as a further form subdivision under most of the other free-floating form subdivisions, e.g., **Tuberculosis – Statistics – Periodicals**. In some cases, the subdivision – **Periodicals** may be further subdivided by another form subdivision or a combination of form subdivisions. The following combinations are listed among the free-floating subdivisions: – **Periodicals – Bibliography**; – **Periodicals – Bibliography – Catalogs**; – **Periodicals – Bibliography – Union lists**; – **Periodicals – Indexes**.

In choosing a form subdivision, the cataloger should be guided by both the nature of the publication in question (not just what is suggested by the wording of the title) and the scope notes accompanying the form subdivisions in *Library of Congress Subject Headings: A Guide to Subdivision Practice* (1981) and *Subject Cataloging Manual: Subject Headings* (1984).

The following examples reflect current Library of Congress subject cataloging practice for various types of serial publications. (When discussion of a given publication type is better suited to a different section of this book, a cross-reference to the relevant pages is given.)

Abstracts

See discussion on pages 201-202.

---

*As an aid in determining whether an annual publication does or does not summarize the year, Jean M. Perreault offers the following suggestions: "Two helpful diagnostics are (a) the sort of bibliography each article includes: is it largely confined to references from one recent year, or is it broadly retrospective? and (b) is the table of contents for each volume of the same title largely repetitive?"[2]

Almanacs

Title: *Poor Joe's Pennsylvania Farm Almanack*
1. Almanacs, American.

Title: *Almanak Yogyakarta*
1. Almanacs, Indonesian.

Annual Reports

See discussion on pages 199-200.

Bibliographies

See discussion on pages 203-204.

Biographical Reference Works

Title: *American Artists of Renown, 1981/1982-*
1. Artists – United States – Biography – Periodicals.
2. Art, Modern – 20th century – United States – Periodicals.

Title: *Who's Who in Finance*
1. Capitalists and financiers – Great Britain – Registers.

Title: *Contemporary Authors: New Revision Series, 1981-*
1. United States – Bio-bibliography – Periodicals.
2. Authors, American – Biography – Periodicals.

Book and Media Reviews

Title: *The Library Journal Book Review*
1. Books – Reviews – Periodicals.

Title: *Book Review Digest*
1. Books – Reviews – Periodicals.
2. Bibliography – Periodicals.

Title: *Litteris: An International Critical Review of the Humanities*
1. Humanities – Bibliography – Periodicals.
2. Books – Reviews – Periodicals.

Title: *Filmfacts*
1. Moving-pictures – Reviews – Periodicals.

Title: *The Washington Book Review, 1981-*
1. Books – Reviews – United States – Periodicals.
2. Book reviewing – Periodicals.

Title: *Harrison's Reports*
1. **Moving-pictures — Reviews — Periodicals.**

Title: *Jazz Rag*
1. **Jazz music — Periodicals.**
2. **Jazz music — Discography.**
3. **Sound recordings — Reviews — Periodicals.**

Catalogs

See discussion on pages 204-207 and 211.

Conference (Congress, Symposium, Etc.) Publications

Publications emanating from conferences, congresses, symposia, etc., are assigned topical headings with the subdivision **— Congresses.** Except for the subdivision **— Juvenile literature,** such headings are not further subdivided by form, even when the publication in question consists of collected papers issued in condensed form; in other words, the form [Topic] — Congresses — Abstracts is not used. When one or more lectures originally given at a conference are later published under separate cover and no longer strictly identified with the original conference, the subdivision **— Addresses, essays, lectures** is used instead of **— Congresses.** Examples include:

Title: *Proceedings of the Annual Meeting of Biochemistry*
1. **Biological chemistry — Congresses.**

Title: *Proceedings of the ... International Physicochemical Hydrodynamics Conference*
1. **Chemistry, Physical and theoretical — Congresses.**
2. **Hydrodynamics — Congresses.**

Title: *Religion and Public Education*
    [A revision of papers presented at the Conference on the Role of Religion in Public Education]
1. **Religion in the public schools — United States — Addresses, essays, lectures.**

Directories

See discussion on pages 214-216.

Government Publications

Serially issued government publications are assigned subject headings appropriate to their subject content and form. In other words, a form subdivision is not used to bring out the fact that a publication is issued by a government.*

Handbooks

See discussion on pages 216-217.

Indexes

See discussion on pages 207-208.

Irregular Serial Publications, Each Issue of Which Consists of Papers Written by Various Authors[3]

A topical heading subdivided by —Collected works is assigned:

Title: *Microbiologia*
    1. Microbiology—Collected works.

Title: *Studia Geobotanica*
    1. Botany—Alps, Eastern—Collected works.
    2. Botany—Adriatic Sea Region—Collected works.

Title: *Guide to Research in Air Pollution*
    1. Air—Pollution—Research—Collected works.

Lists and Abstracts of Dissertations and Theses

See discussion on page 209.

Monographic Series[4]

When a monographic series is cataloged as a whole, a topical heading or headings (subdivided by —Collected works) representing the overall subject of the entire series is assigned:

Title: *Stagflation*
    1. Unemployment—Effect of inflation on—Collected works.
    2. Wage-price policy—Collected works.

Title: *Smithsonian Contributions to Zoology*
    1. Zoology—Collected works.

---

*The subdivision —**Government publications** is a topical subdivision used in cataloging *lists* of government publications.

Title: *Studies in Pre-Columbian Art and Archaeology*
  1. **America — Antiquities — Collected works.**
  2. **Indians — Antiquities — Collected works.**
  3. **Indians — Art — Collected works.**

Periodicals and Journals

Periodicals that cover very broad or general subjects are not assigned subject headings. Headings such as **American periodicals** indicate topic, not form; in other words, the heading **American periodicals** is assigned to a work *about* American periodicals, but is not used with periodicals such as *Saturday Evening Post* or *Atlantic Monthly*. Examples include:

Title: *The Smith*
          [no subject heading]

Title: *Dialogo*
          [no subject heading]

Title: *Advances in Data Processing Management*
  1. **Electronic data processing — Management — Periodicals.**

Title: *Journal of Adolescent Health Care*
  1. **Adolescent medicine — Periodicals.**
  2. **Adolescence — Periodicals.**

Title: *Nelson Survey of Industrial Research*
  1. **Corporations — United States — Finance — Research — Periodicals.**
  2. **Investment analysis — Periodicals.**
  3. **Investment advisers — United States — Periodicals.**

Title: *Journal of Electronic Defense*
  1. **Electronics in military engineering — Periodicals.**

Title: *I.N.I., The Early Interurban Newsletters*
  1. **Street-railroads — United States — Periodicals.**

Title: *Traction Yearbook*
  1. **Street-railroads — Periodicals.**
  2. **Subways — Periodicals.**

Title: *Man at Arms, 1979-*
  1. **Firearms — Collectors and collecting — Periodicals.**

Title: *The Data Resources Banking Review*
  1. **Banks and banking — United States — Periodicals.**

Title: *Review of Higher Education*
  1. **Education, Higher — United States — Periodicals.**

Title: *Demonstrated Reserve Base of Coal in the United States*
          on January 1
          [issued by U.S. Dept. of Energy, Office of Coal
          and Electric Power Statistics]
    1. **Coal — United States — Reserves — Periodicals.**

Reports

For serially issued reports by government agencies or other corporate
bodies that contain substantive information, one or more topical headings are
assigned, with the subdivision — **Periodicals** (or — **Yearbooks** if appropriate):

Title: *Annual Report, Campaign Contributions and Expenditures*
          Pursuant to Acts 1976, Public Law 6 / issued under the
          authority of the [Indiana] *State Election Board*
    1. **Elections — Indiana — Campaign funds — Statistics —**
        Periodicals.

Title: *Report of the Director of Audit on the Accounts of*
          Montserrat for the Year Ended 31st Dec....
    1. **Finance, Public — Montserrat — Accounting — Periodicals.**

Title: *Report of the Comptroller and Auditor General of India*
          for the Year ..., Government of Sikkim
    1. **Finance, Public — India — Sikkim — Accounting — Yearbooks.**

Title: *Interim Report to the ... Legislature / South Dakota*
    1. **Law — South Dakota — Periodicals.**
    2. **Legislation — South Dakota — Periodicals.**
    3. **South Dakota — Politics and government — Periodicals.**

If the publication contains information about the corporate body as well
as substantive information, an additional heading under the name of the
corporate body is assigned:

Title: *Biennial Report /* ARC Food Research Institute
    1. **Food Research Institute (Great Britain) — Periodicals.**
    2. **Food research — Great Britain — Periodicals.**

Title: *Annual Report of the Department of Agriculture in the*
          Ministry of Agriculture, Fisheries and Local Government
          [Bahamas]
    1. **Bahamas.   Dept. of Agriculture — Periodicals.**
    2. **Agriculture — Bahamas — Periodicals.**

If the publication contains only information about the corporate body,
only the heading under the name of the body is assigned.

Title: *Annual Report /* General Insurance Corporation of India
    1. **General Insurance Corporation of India — Yearbooks.**

Title: *Annual Report* / Marine Environmental Data Service
   1.   **Canada.   Marine Environmental Data Service—Yearbooks.**

Serial Publications Devoted to One Person

For a serial publication devoted to one person, a heading in the form of
[Name of person]—Periodicals is assigned.

Title: *The London Collector*
   1.   **London, Jack, 1876-1916—Periodicals.**

Title: *James Joyce Quarterly*
   1.   **Joyce, James, 1882-1941—Periodicals.**

Society Publications

Publications issued serially by societies are assigned subject headings
appropriate to their subject content and form. For reports *of* societies, see
discussion above. For works *about* societies, see discussion on pages 244-245.

Statistics

Title: *Export of Major Commodities and Their Principal Markets,*
   Australia / Australia Bureau of Statistics
   1.   **Australia—Commerce—Statistics—Periodicals.**
   2.   **Commercial products—Australia—Statistics—Periodicals.**
   3.   **Commercial products—Australia—Classification—Periodicals.**

Title: *Annual Report for the Year ...* / South Pacific Epidemiologi-
   cal and Health Information Service
   1.   **Communicable diseases—Oceania—Statistics—Periodicals.**
   2.   **Poisonous fishes—Toxicology—Oceania—Statistics—**
   Periodicals.
   3.   **Oceania—Statistics, Medical—Periodicals.**

Title: *Michigan Agricultural Statistics*
   1.   **Agriculture—Michigan—Statistics—Periodicals.**

Title: *Alaska Vital Statistics*
   1.   **Alaska—Statistics, Vital—Periodicals.**

Title: *Budget Manual for Consideration of the ... General*
   Assembly / State of Arkansas
   1.   **Budget—Arkansas—Statistics—Periodicals.**

Union Lists

See discussion on pages 205-206.

Yearbooks*

Title: *Hockey Guide.* 1981-
   1. **Hockey—United States—Yearbooks.**
   2. **Hockey—Canada—Yearbooks.**

Title: *Year Book of Adult Continuing Education*
   1. **Adult education—Yearbooks.**

Title: *School Library Media Manual.*   1983-
   1. **School libraries—Yearbooks.**
   2. **Instructional materials centers—Yearbooks.**
   3. **Media programs (Education)—Yearbooks.**
   4. **Audio-visual library service—Yearbooks.**

Title: *Annual Review* / Emergency Planning Canada
   1. **Emergency Planning Canada—Yearbooks.**

LISTS OF PUBLICATIONS

Lists of publications appear in various forms, such as abstracts, bibliographies, and catalogs. These are normally brought out by form subdivisions such as:

—Abstracts
—Bibliography
—Catalogs
—Imprints
—Indexes
—Union lists

The following discussion and examples illuminate Library of Congress guidelines for the treatment of various types of lists and the proper use of the relevant form subdivisions.

Abstracts[5]

Both —**Abstracts** and —**Bibliography** are free-floating form subdivisions that may be used under topical, geographical, corporate, or personal headings to bring out the form of a publication. However, some publications, such as lists of publications with annotations, may not clearly fall into one of the two categories. To assist the cataloger in making the distinction, the Library of

---

*See page 194 for a discussion of the appropriate use of the subdivision —**Yearbooks**.

Congress has provided the following guidelines. The subdivision — **Abstracts** is used when a work lists publications and provides full bibliographical information together with *substantive* summaries or condensations of the facts, ideas, or opinions for each publication listed. The nature of the annotations or summaries is the criterion. The following characteristics are considered to be typical of abstracts:

They present in brief form all of the essential points made in the original publication, usually including the conclusion, if any, drawn by its author.

They provide enough detail to enable the user to decide whether or not to refer to the original publication.

They evaluate or criticize the publication.

Examples include:

Title: *Resources in Education. Annual Cumulation: RIE*
1. **Education — Abstracts — Periodicals.**
2. **Government publications — Abstracts — Periodicals.**

Title: *Physics Briefs*
1. **Physics — Abstracts — Periodicals.**

Title: *Journal of Chemical Research: Synopsis*
1. **Chemistry — Research — Abstracts — Periodicals.**
2. **Chemistry — Abstracts — Periodicals.**

Title: *Abstracts Strengthening Research Library Resources Program*
1. **Library science — United States — Research — Abstracts — Periodicals.**
2. **Federal aid to libraries — United States — Abstracts — Periodicals.**
3. **Research libraries — United States — Finance — Abstracts — Periodicals.**

Title: *The Best of Health*
1. **Nutrition — Abstracts.**
2. **Diet — Abstracts.**
3. **Exercise — Abstracts.**
4. **Health — Abstracts.**

Title: *Criminal Investigation: A Guide to Techniques and Solutions*
1. **Criminal investigation — Abstracts.**
2. **Evidence, Criminal — Abstracts.**
3. **Crime and criminals — Abstracts.**

Bibliographies

The free-floating subdivision — **Bibliography** is used for unannotated or annotated lists of publications. The annotations are distinguished from abstracts in that the former give an indication of the general nature of each publication listed but are seldom critical in nature.

For the distinction between the subdivisions — **Indexes** and — **Bibliography**, the Library of Congress offers the following criteria:

> — **Indexes** is used as a form subdivision under subject headings for works that provide a comprehensive subject approach to printed materials published in a specific field of knowledge.... The subdivision — **Bibliography** is used for works that merely list publications. Many bibliographies, however, are themselves indexed by subject. When a subject-indexed bibliography is judged to be sufficiently comprehensive in scope as to be usable as a general index to the publications in the field in question, the subdivision — **Indexes** is used instead of — **Bibliography**.[6]

The combination — **Bibliography** — **Indexes** is not authorized for use.

Examples of bibliographies include:*

Title: *Truck Escape Ramps: Annotated Bibliography on the State-of-the-Art*
    1. **Roads — Design — Bibliography.**
    2. **Roads — Safety measures — Bibliography.**
    3. **Motor-trucks — Bibliography.**

Title: *Electric Vehicle Batteries: Selected Citations*
    1. **Electric vehicles — Batteries — Bibliography.**

Title: *A Bibliography of Works on Canadian Foreign Relations, 1976-1980*
    1. **Canada — Foreign relations — 1945-   — Bibliography.**
    2. **Canada — Military policy — Bibliography.**

Title: *Business and Economics Books and Serials in Print.*   1981-
    1. **Business — Bibliography — Periodicals.**
    2. **Business — Periodicals — Bibliography — Periodicals.**
    3. **Economics — Bibliography — Periodicals.**
    4. **Economics — Periodicals — Bibliography — Periodicals.**

Library of Congress policies[7] require that whenever one of the following types of headings is assigned to a work, a duplicate entry must be made under **[Topic] — Bibliography:**

---

*Examples of different types of indexes are given on pages 207-208.

       Bibliography — Bibliography — [Topic]
       Bibliography — Best books — [Topic]
       Reference books — [Topic] — Bibliography*

Examples include:

    Title: *A Bibliography of Bibliographies on Malaysia*
       1. **Malaysia — Bibliography.**
       2. **Bibliography — Bibliography — Malaysia.**

    Title: *A Guide to Serial Bibliographies for Modern Literature*
       1. **Literature, Modern — Bibliography — Periodicals — Bibliography.**
       2. **Bibliography — Bibliography — Literature, Modern.**
       3. **Bibliography — Bibliography — Periodicals.**

    Title: *A Guide to Historical Literature*
       1. **History — Bibliography.**
       2. **Bibliography — Best books — History.**

For a bibliography that lists works by or about an individual, a personal name heading subdivided by **—Bibliography** is used.[8] If the work has a topical orientation, an additional heading in the form of **[Topic] — Bibliography** is also assigned:

    Title: *Martin Buber: A Bibliography of His Writings, 1897-1978*
       1. **Buber, Martin, 1878-1965 — Bibliography.**
       2. **Jews — Bibliography.**

For a work that contains biographical information about authors active in a particular field or associated with a particular place as well as lists of their works, a heading in the form of **[Topic or place] — Bio-bibliography** is used:

    Title: *Blues Who's Who: A Biographical Dictionary of Blues Singers*
       1. **Blues (Songs, etc.) — United States — Bio-bibliography.**

Catalogs of Publications**

Catalogs of library materials[9]

The following types of headings are assigned to catalogs of library materials:

    [Topic of works listed] — [Form of works listed] — Catalogs
    [Name of institution, if any] — Catalogs
    [Name of the collection, if any] — Catalogs

---

*For examples of bibliographies of reference books, see pages 210-211.
**For catalogs of objects, see discussion on page 211.

The most commonly used subdivisions for the forms of works are:

- — Bibliography — Catalogs
  [for printed works]
- — Periodicals — Bibliography — Catalogs
  [for serials]
- — Audio-visual aids — Catalogs
- — Discography
  [for sound recordings]
- — Film catalogs
- — Phonotape catalogs
- — Video tape catalogs
- — Microform catalogs
- — Manuscripts — Catalogs

Examples include:

Title: *A Collection of Abraham Lincoln Pamphlets & American Civil War* / Tokyo Lincoln Center
1. Lincoln, Abraham, 1809-1865 — Bibliography — Catalogs.
2. Tokyo Lincoln Center — Catalogs.
3. United States — History — Civil War, 1861-1865 — Bibliography — Catalogs.

Title: *Accessions* / Federal Archives Division [Canada]
1. Public Archives Canada. Federal Archives Division — Catalogs.
2. Public records — Canada — Bibliography — Catalogs.
3. Canada — History — Sources — Bibliography — Catalogs.

Title: *Who's Who in Rock Music*
1. Rock music — Bio-bibliography.
2. Rock music — Discography.

Title: *Seeing Canada: Films for Canadian Studies*
1. Canada — Film catalogs.
2. National Film Board of Canada — Film catalogs.

Title: *American Sunday School Union Papers, 1817-1915: A Guide to the Microfilm Edition*
1. American Sunday School Union — Archives — Microform catalogs.

Union lists

For union lists or catalogs, a heading in the form of **Catalogs, Union — [Place]** is assigned in addition to other appropriate headings subdivided by **— Union lists:**

Title: *A Checklist and Union Catalog of Holdings of Major*
         Published Library Catalogs in METRO Libraries
   1. **Library catalogs — Bibliography — Union lists.**
   2. **Libraries — New York (State) — Union lists.**
   3. **Catalogs, Union — New York (State).**

Title: *A Union List of Selected Microforms in Libraries in the New*
         York Metropolitan Area
   1. **Microforms — Union lists.**
   2. **Catalogs, Union — New York Metropolitan Area.**

Title: *Union List of Periodicals of the Southeastern Pennsylvania*
         Theological Library Association
   1. **Theology — Periodicals — Bibliography — Union lists.**
   2. **Catalogs, Union — Pennsylvania.**

Title: *Union List of Periodicals Held in the Libraries of*
         Scottish Colleges of Education
   1. **Periodicals — Bibliography — Union lists.**
   2. **Catalogs, Union — Scotland.**

Publishers' catalogs[10]

The following types of headings are assigned to catalogs of individual publishing houses:

   [Name of publishing house] — Catalogs
   Catalogs, Publishers' — [Country]

and one of the following three:

   [Country] — Imprints — Catalogs
   [Country] — Government publications — Bibliography — Catalogs
   [Topic] — Bibliography — Catalogs

If the publications listed are in a specific form, headings similar to the following are assigned in addition:

   Microforms — Catalogs
   Pamphlets in microform — Catalogs
   Books on microfilm — Catalogs
   Periodicals on microfiche — Catalogs

Examples include:

Title: *A Full Howes: A Catalogue of Books and Pamphlets*
         Listed in Wright Howes' U.S.iana
   1. **United States — Bibliography — Catalogs.**
   2. **Jenkins Company — Catalogs.**
   3. **Catalogs, Publishers' — United States.**

Title: *Le edizioni della Voce*
1. **Voce (Firm) — Catalogs.**
2. **Italy — Imprints — Catalogs.**
3. **Catalogs, Publishers' — Italy.**

Title: *Research Abstracts* [University Microfilms International]
1. **Research — Abstracts — Periodicals.**
2. **University Microfilms International — Catalogs.**
3. **Microfilms — Catalogs.**

Imprints[11]

The following types of headings are assigned to lists of works published in a particular place and/or language:

[Place of origin] — Imprints
[Language] imprints — [Place]
    [not assigned if the language is predominant in the place of question]
[Name of library] — Catalogs
    [for a listing of a library's special collection of imprints]

If the work lists imprints existing at a specific locality or available from a specified source, the subdivision **— Catalogs** is added to the headings above. These headings are not further subdivided by **— Bibliography**, since the term *imprints* already implies lists of publications. The headings may be further subdivided by other appropriate form subdivisions. Examples include:

Title: *Brinkman's Cumulatieve Catalogus van Boeken*
1. **Netherlands — Imprints — Periodicals.**
2. **Flanders — Imprints — Periodicals.**

Title: *Bibliografía argentina: catálogo de materiales argentinos en las bibliotecas de la Universidad de Buenos Aires*
1. **Argentina — Imprints — Catalogs.**
2. **Universidad de Buenos Aires — Libraries — Catalogs.**

Title: *Classified Catalog and Subject Index of the Chinese and Japanese Collections: First Supplement* [Far Eastern Library, University of Chicago]
1. **Chinese imprints — Catalogs.**
2. **Japanese imprints — Catalogs.**
3. **University of Chicago. Far Eastern Library — Catalogs.**

Indexes[12]

The free-floating form subdivision **— Indexes** is used under subject headings for "works that provide a comprehensive subject approach to printed materials published in a specific field of knowledge." The treatment of various kinds of indexes is illustrated below.

1) *General indexes and indexes limited to books*:

Title: *QRIS, Quick Reference to IEEE Standards*
  1. **Electric engineering — Standards — United States — Indexes.**

Title: *A Bibliography of Business and Economic Forecasting*
  1. **Business forecasting — Indexes.**
  2. **Economic forecasting — Indexes.**

Title: *Speech Index: An Index to Collections of World Famous
         Orations and Speeches for Various Occasions*
  1. **Speeches, addresses, etc. — Indexes.**
  2. **Orations — Indexes.**
  3. **American orations — Indexes.**

2) *Indexes limited to specific forms of materials other than books.* A
subdivision representing the specific form of material (except for indexes to
films on a topic)* is interposed between the topical heading and the
subdivision — **Indexes**:

Title: *Index of English Literary Manuscripts*
  1. **English literature — Manuscripts — Indexes.**
  2. **Manuscripts, English — Indexes.**

Title: *Index to Hard-to-Find Information in Genealogical
         Periodicals*
  1. **Genealogy — Periodicals — Indexes.**

Title: *Africa Index to Continental Periodical Literature*
         [1977-   ]
  1. **Africa — Periodicals — Indexes.**
  2. **African periodicals — Indexes.**

3) *Indexes to works of an individual author.* A heading in the form of
[Name of author] — Dictionaries, indexes, etc. is assigned:

Title: *Companion to Charles Lamb: A Guide to People and
         Places, 1760-1847*
  1. **Lamb, Charles, 1775-1834 — Dictionaries, indexes, etc.**
  2. **Lamb, Charles, 1775-1834 — Friends and associates.**
  3. **Lamb, Charles, 1775-1834 — Homes and haunts.**
  4. **Great Britain — Biography.**
  5. **Great Britain — Gazetteers.**

4) *Indexes to individual monographic works or individual serials.* See
discussion on page 251.

---

*The subdivision — **Film catalogs** is used for indexes to films on a topic.

Lists and Abstracts of Dissertations and Theses[13]

The following types of headings are assigned to lists and abstracts of dissertations and theses:

[Topic] — Bibliography [or **Abstracts**]
[Institution] — Dissertations — Bibliography [or **Abstracts**]
Dissertations, Academic — [Country] — Bibliography [or **Abstracts**]

An example is:

Title: *Doctoral Dissertations on South Asia at the University of Pennsylvania, 1898-1981*
1. **South Asia — Abstracts.**
2. **Dissertations, Academic — Pennsylvania — Abstracts.**
3. **University of Pennsylvania — Dissertations — Abstracts.**

The third type of heading listed above is assigned to all lists of dissertations and theses. If the list is not limited to a specific institution, the first and third types are used:

Title: *Research in Black Child Development: Doctoral Dissertation Abstracts, 1927-1979*
1. **Afro-American children — Abstracts.**
2. **Dissertations, Academic — Abstracts.**

Title: *Women's Education: A World View*
1. **Education of women — Bibliography.**
2. **Dissertations, Academic — Canada — Bibliography.**
3. **Dissertations, Academic — United States — Bibliography.**

Title: *Index to Doctoral Dissertations in Business Education*
1. **Business — Bibliography.**
2. **Business education — Bibliography.**
3. **Dissertations, Academic — United States — Bibliography.**

If the list is not limited to a specific topic, the second and third heading types are used:

Title: *Catalogue of Theses and Dissertations Accepted at the University of Port Elizabeth, 1966-1979*
1. **University of Port Elizabeth — Dissertations — Bibliography — Catalogs.**
2. **Dissertations, Academic — South Africa — Bibliography — Catalogs.**

REFERENCE MATERIALS

Works about Reference Books[14]

Works *about* reference books are assigned the heading **Reference books**. This is a topical heading; it is not used for reference books per se, which are simply assigned topical headings as appropriate. The heading **Reference books** is used without subdivision when the work being cataloged is not limited by topic; it may, however, be qualified by language, e.g., **Reference books, German**. Examples include:

Title: *Introduction to Reference Work*
1. **Reference services (Libraries)**
2. **Reference books.**

Title: *Refarensu Bukku*
1. **Reference books, Japanese.**

To a work *about* reference works in a particular field, a heading of the type **Reference books—[Topic]** is assigned. The —**[Topic]** subdivision is free-floating, provided that the topic is a valid heading. Examples include **Reference books—Chemistry; Reference books—Canada; Reference books—Shakespeare, William, 1564-1616.**

Bibliographies of Reference Books

Nontopical bibliographies

The heading **Reference books—Bibliography** is assigned to nontopical bibliographies:

Title: *Guide to Reference Books*
1. **Reference books—Bibliography.**

Topical bibliographies

To a bibliography of the reference sources in a particular field, two headings are assigned:

[Topic]—Bibliography.
Reference books—[Topic]—Bibliography.

Examples include:

Title: *The Philosopher's Guide to Sources, Research Tools, Professional Life, and Related Fields*
1. **Philosophy—Bibliography.**
2. **Reference books—Philosophy—Bibliography.**

Title: *American Literature and Language: A Guide to Information Sources*
    1. **American literature — Bibliography.**
    2. **Reference books — American literature — Bibliography.**
    3. **English language — Bibliography.**
    4. **Reference books — English language — Bibliography.**

If the reference sources listed in the bibliography are limited to a specific language other than English, an additional heading in the form of **Reference books, [Language] — Bibliography** is also assigned. If the reference sources listed in the bibliography have been published in a particular place, an additional heading in the form of **[Place] — Imprints** is assigned.

Reference Books

In the Library of Congress subject headings system, several categories of reference books are given special treatment or represented by special subdivisions. These include catalogs of objects, dictionaries, directories, and handbooks and manuals.

Catalogs of objects[15]

The subdivision **— Catalogs** is used under headings for listings of different types of objects, including merchandise, art objects, products, publications,* collectors' items, technical equipment, etc., that are available or are located at particular places or are offered on a particular market, often systematically arranged with descriptive details, prices, etc., e.g., **Automobiles — Catalogs; Postage-stamps — Great Britain — Catalogs; Food service — Equipment and supplies — Catalogs; Flags — United States — Catalogs.**
For catalogs of natural objects and musical items, the subdivision **— Catalogs and collections** instead of **— Catalogs** is used:

Title: *Directory of Coleoptera Collections*
    1. **Beetles — Catalogs and collections.**

Title: *Univers du pianoforte*
    1. **Pianos — Catalogs and collections.**

Dictionaries[16]

The subdivision **— Dictionaries** is the most frequently used subdivision for both language and subject dictionaries. However, many different kinds of dictionaries and dictionary-like publications exist. There is, therefore, a considerable list of free-floating subdivisions that may be appropriate to a

---

*Catalogs of publications are discussed on pages 204-207. Art catalogs are discussed on pages 292-294.

particular dictionary or dictionary-like publication. These are listed below; full information on their use may be found in *Library of Congress Subject Headings: A Guide to Subdivision Practice* and *Subject Cataloging Manual.*

— **Abbreviations**
— **Acronyms**
— **Concordances**
— **Dictionaries, Juvenile**
— **Dictionaries and encyclopedias**
— **Dictionaries, indexes, etc.**
— **Directories**
— **Gazetteers**

— **Glossaries, vocabularies, etc.**
— **Language – Glossaries, etc.**
— **Language (New words, slang, etc.)**
— **Nomenclature**
— **Registers**
— **Slang**
— **Terminology**
— **Terms and phrases**

Library of Congress guidelines for the major categories of dictionary-like materials are briefly summarized below.

1) *Language dictionaries.* For a comprehensive dictionary in one language, a heading of the type [**Name of language**] – **Dictionaries** is used:

Title: *Webster's New Collegiate Dictionary*
   1.   **English language – Dictionaries.**

For a bilingual dictionary that gives the terms of one language in terms of the other, a heading of the type [**Name of first language**] – **Dictionaries** – [**Name of second language** (adjective only)] is used:

Title: *Dictionnaire de l'anglais contemporain*
   1.   **English language – Dictionaries – French.**

If the second language is also given in terms of the first, a duplicate heading with the languages reversed is also assigned:

Title: *Spanish-English, English-Spanish Dictionary*
   1.   **Spanish language – Dictionaries – English.**
   2.   **English language – Dictionaries – Spanish.**

For a polyglot dictionary, if one language is given in terms of more than one other language, a heading of the type [**Name of language**] – **Dictionaries** – **Polyglot** is assigned. When each language in a polyglot dictionary is given in terms of the others, the general heading **Dictionaries, Polyglot** is assigned.

The subdivision – **Glossaries, vocabularies, etc.** is used for a dictionary containing a subset of individual words in a language, with or without definitions, arranged alphabetically or otherwise:

Title: *Penguin Dictionary of Confusibles*
   1.   **English language – Glossaries, vocabularies, etc.**

The subdivision – **Terms and phrases** is used if the work contains a list of expressions, phrases, etc., found in a particular language:

Title: *Dictionnaire du gai parler: 4500 expressions tradi-*
           tionnelles et populaires
       1. **French language — Terms and phrases.**

2) *Subject dictionaries.* If the dictionary is limited to a subject field, a heading of the type **[Topic] — Dictionaries — [Name of language** (other than English)] is assigned.* For a subject dictionary in the English language, the subdivision by language is omitted. Examples include:

Title: *Kemi*
       1. **Chemistry — Dictionaries — Danish.**

Title: *The Condensed Chemical Dictionary*
       1. **Chemistry — Dictionaries.**

The subdivision **— Terminology** instead of **— Dictionaries** is used if the work contains a noncomprehensive list of terms on the topic, or if the comprehensive list is not arranged alphabetically:

Title: *Economie générale: lexi-guide des mécanismes de l'économie*
       1. **Economics — Terminology.**

For a bilingual or polyglot subject dictionary, language headings are assigned in addition to the topical headings:

Title: *Juristisches Wörterbuch, Englisch-Deutsch*
       1. **Law — Dictionaries.**
       2. **English language — Dictionaries — German.**
       3. **Law — Dictionaries — German.**
       4. **German language — Dictionaries — English.**

Title: *Glossary of Social Security Terms, English-French*
       1. **Social security — Dictionaries.**
       2. **English language — Dictionaries — French.**

Title: *Fachwörterbuch für das Edelmetallgewerbe:*
           dt.-engl.-franz
       1. **Jewelry — Dictionaries — Polyglot.**
       2. **Precious metals — Dictionaries — Polyglot.**
       3. **German language — Dictionaries — Polyglot.**

---

*Note that under the following types of headings, the subdivision for dictionaries takes a different form:
    [Geographic name] — Dictionaries and encyclopedias
    [Ethnic group] — Dictionaries and encyclopedias
    [Personal name] — Dictionaries, indexes, etc.
    [Literary author] — Language — Glossaries, etc.

Title: *Wörterbuch der Werkstoffprüfung*
     [each language is given in terms of several others]
    1. Materials — Testing — Dictionaries — Polyglot.
    2. Dictionaries, Polyglot.

3) *Biographical dictionaries.* A heading in the form of [**Class of persons, organizations, place, etc.**] — **Biography** — **Dictionaries** is assigned to biographical dictionaries. The previous practice of *not* further subdividing — **Biography** by — **Dictionaries** has been discontinued. Examples include:

Title: *Canada's Playwrights: A Biographical Guide*
    1. Dramatists, Canadian — 20th century — Biography — Dictionaries.

Title: *Biographical Dictionary of Modern Peace Leaders*
    1. Pacifists — Biography — Dictionaries.

Title: *Performing Arts Biography Master Index*
    1. Performing arts — Biography — Dictionaries — Indexes.

Directories

The free-floating subdivision — **Directories** may be used under the following categories of headings:

names of regions, countries, cities, etc., for lists containing the names and addresses of the inhabitants or organizations of a place

topical headings, classes of persons, types of corporate bodies, or names of particular corporate bodies, for lists containing the names, addresses, and other identifying data of persons or organizations connected with the entities

headings for particular kinds of newspapers or periodicals, for alphabetical or classified lists containing names, addresses, and other identifying data.

Examples include:

Title: *Indiana Amish Directory, Ekhart and Lagrange Counties*
    1. Amish — Indiana — Ekhart County — Directories.
    2. Amish — Indiana — Lagrange County — Directories.
    3. Ekhart County (Ind.) — Directories.
    4. Lagrange County (Ind.) — Directories.

Title: *Upstate New York Directory of Manufacturers*
    1. New York (State) — Manufactures — Directories.

Title: *Youth Group Travel Directory, 1981/82-*
1. **Church work with youth — United States — Directories.**
2. **Church group work with youth — United States — Directories.**
3. **Youth hostels — United States — Directories.**

Title: *Directory of Registered Professional Architects,*
Engineers, and Land Surveyors [Virgin Islands]
1. **Architects — Virgin Islands of the United States — Directories.**
2. **Engineers — Virgin Islands of the United States — Directories.**
3. **Surveyors — Virgin Islands of the United States — Directories.**

Title: *The Top 1,500 Companies*
1. **Business enterprises — United States — Directories.**
2. **Corporations — United States — Directories.**

Title: *The Directory of Athletic Scholarships*
1. **Sports — United States — Scholarships, fellowships, etc. — Directories.**
2. **Universities and colleges — United States — Directories.**

Title: *Directory of South Dakota Libraries*
1. **Libraries — South Dakota — Directories.**

Title: *Directory of Financial Institutions* / The Monetary
Authority of Singapore
1. **Financial institutions — Singapore — Directories.**

Title: *ASTD Media Resource Directory*
1. **American Society for Training and Development. Media Division — Directories.**
2. **Employee training directors — Directories.**
3. **Instructional materials personnel — Directories.**
4. **Employees, Training of — Audio-visual aids.**

Title: *Cabell's Directory of Publishing Opportunities in Business,*
Administration, and Economics
1. **Social sciences — Periodicals — Directories.**
2. **Business — Periodicals — Directories.**
3. **American periodicals — Directories.**
4. **Publishers and publishing — United States — Directories.**

Title: *A Historical Directory of Manitoba Newspapers, 1859-1978*
1. **Canadian newspapers — Manitoba — Directories.**

If a list contains names of persons without addresses or other identifying data, the subdivision **— Registers** is used instead:

Title: *Directory of Chinese Officials: Scientific and Educational*
         Organizations: A Reference Aid
   1. **China — Officials and employees — Registers.**
   2. **Scientists — China — Registers.**
   3. **Educators — China — Registers.**

No distinction is made between serially published directories and monographs.

Handbooks and manuals[17]

The free-floating subdivision **— Handbooks, manuals, etc.** may be used under topical headings and under names of regions, countries, etc., for concise reference works in which facts and information pertaining to a subject field or place are arranged for ready reference and consultation rather than continuous reading and study. The presence of the word *handbook* or *manual* in the title does not necessarily require the use of the subdivision. For specialized manuals, the following subdivisions are used where appropriate: **— Amateurs' manuals; — Guide-books; — Laboratory manuals; — Observers' manuals; — Tables.** Examples include:

Title: *Engineers' Relay Handbook*
   1. **Electric relays — Handbooks, manuals, etc.**

Title: *The Elementary Principal's Advocate*
   1. **Elementary school principals — Handbooks, manuals, etc.**

Title: *The Campaign Manual*
   1. **Campaign management — United States — Handbooks,**
       manuals, etc.
   2. **Electioneering — United States — Handbooks, manuals,**
       etc.

Title: *Digital Counter Handbook*
   1. **Digital computers.**
   2. **Electronic instruments, Digital.**

Title: *Electronics Explained: A Handbook for the Layman*
   1. **Electronics.**
   2. **Electronic apparatus and appliances.**

Title: *25 Ski Tours in Central New York*
   1. **Cross-country skiing — New York (State)**
       — Guide-books.
   2. **New York (State) — Description and travel**
       — 1951-   — Guide-books.

Title: *Hematology Laboratory Manual*
   1. **Blood — Examination.**
   2. **Hematology — Technique.**
   3. **Hematology — Laboratory manuals.**

Title: *How to Be an Astronomer*
   1.   **Astronomy—Observers' manuals—Juvenile literature.**

Title: *Conserving Energy in Older Homes: A Do-It-Yourself*
         Manual
   1.   **Dwellings—Energy conservation—Amateurs' manuals.**

CHILDREN'S MATERIALS[18]

In 1965 the Library of Congress initiated the Annotated Card (AC) Program for children's materials. The purpose of the program was to provide more appropriate and in-depth subject cataloging of juvenile titles through more liberal application of subject headings and through the use of headings more appropriate to juvenile users. In some cases, existing Library of Congress subject headings were reinterpreted or modified; in others, new headings were created. As a result, a list of headings that represent exceptions to the master Library of Congress list has been compiled. This list was first issued as a separate publication entitled *Subject Headings for Children's Literature*. With the eighth edition of *Library of Congress Subject Headings*, the list was included in the main publication and also published separately. Since 1979 each issue of the quarterly *Supplement to LC Subject Headings* has contained a full cumulation of subject headings for children's literature, and the children's list is no longer published separately. Since the March 1983 issue, the microfiche edition of *Library of Congress Subject Headings* has included a fiche containing the complete list of subject headings for children's literature.[19]

The term *annotated card* comes from the practice of providing a summary of the content of the work in a note. In subject cataloging, two sets of headings are assigned: the regular headings with the appropriate subdivisions, such as **—Juvenile literature;* —Juvenile fiction; —Dictionaries, Juvenile**; etc., and headings for children's literature without the juvenile subdivisions.

On Library of Congress cataloging cards, works cataloged under the AC Program are identified by (a) bracketed subject headings without the juvenile subdivision, (b) the presence of the summary, and (c) the designation AC in the lower right-hand corner (see Figure 9.1). On MARC records, juvenile materials are characterized by a C or a 1 as the second indicator in the subject field, the presence of the summary, and the omission of the juvenile subdivisions.

Many juvenile works are designated as such by their publishers, through such phrases as K-3 (kindergarten through third grade), 10 up, 14+, and so on. At the Library of Congress, all materials intended primarily for children through the ninth grade (age fifteen) are treated as juvenile material and included in the AC Program. In addition, general or adult works that are also suitable for children and young adults may also be included in the program.

---

*Note that the subdivision **—Juvenile literature** is used under topical headings but *not* for juvenile belles lettres, for which juvenile headings such as **Children's stories; Nursery rhymes; Children's poetry** or headings with the subdivisions **—Juvenile drama; —Juvenile fiction; —Juvenile poetry** are used.

Berliner, Don.
　　Flying-model airplanes / Don Berliner. — Minneapolis : Lerner Publications Co., c1982.

47 p. : col. ill. ; 19 x 22 cm. — (Superwheels & thrill sports)

Summary: Discusses the history, types, and construction of flying-model airplanes. Also describes sport and contest flying of radio-controlled and control-line models.
　　ISBN (invalid) 0-8225-0449-9

1. Airplanes—Models—Juvenile literature.　2. Model airplane racing—Juvenile literature.　[1. Airplanes—Models.　2. Model airplane racing]　I. Title. II. Series.

TL770.B442　1982　　　　　629.133'134—dc19　　81-20720
　　　　　　　　　　　　　　　　　　　　　　　　　　　　　　AACR 2　MARC

Library of Congress　　　　　　　　　　　　　　　　　　　　　　　　　　AC

Martin, Mollie.
　　Pittsburgh Pirates / Mollie Martin. — [Mankato, MN] : Creative Education, [c1982]

48 p. : ill. ; 25 cm.

Summary: Presents the history of a team that has almost always been near the top of major league baseball, despite a rocky start just a decade after the Civil War.
　　ISBN 0-87191-871-4

1. Pittsburgh Pirates (Baseball team)—History—Juvenile literature.　[1. Pittsburgh Pirates (Baseball team)—History.　2. Baseball—History]　I. Title.

GV875.P5M37　1982　　　　　　　　　　　　　　　　　　82-13027
　　　　　　　　　　　　796.357'64'0974886—dc19
　　　　　　　　　　　　　　　　　　　　　　　AACR 2　MARC
Library of Congress　　　　　　　　　　　　　　　　　　AC

Figure 9.1. Examples of Library of Congress cataloging cards for children's materials.

Juvenile headings on LC cards are distinguished by the presence of brackets and the omission of the subdivision "Juvenile literature." Juvenile headings on MARC records are distinguished by the presence of a C or 1 as the second indicator in the subject field and the omission of the subdivision "Juvenile literature."

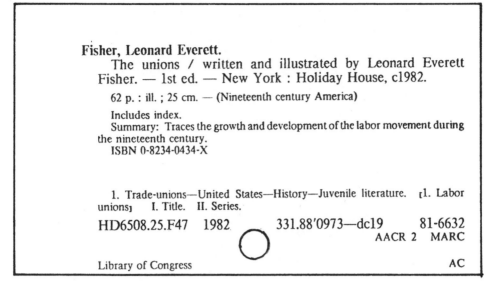

Fisher, Leonard Everett.
    The unions / written and illustrated by Leonard Everett
Fisher. — 1st ed. — New York : Holiday House, c1982.
    62 p. : ill. ; 25 cm. — (Nineteenth century America)

    Includes index.
    Summary: Traces the growth and development of the labor movement during
the nineteenth century.
    ISBN 0-8234-0434-X

    1. Trade-unions—United States—History—Juvenile literature. [1. Labor
unions] I. Title. II. Series.

HD6508.25.F47   1982   331.88'0973—dc19   81-6632
                                                AACR 2   MARC

        Library of Congress   AC

Figure 9.1. *Continued*

Fiction for high school students or young adults (often designated as "young
adult" or YA) is also included; nonfictional works intended solely or primarily
for high school age and above, on the other hand, are treated as adult
materials. For works in which the intended age is not explicitly stated,
determination of level is based on contents, format, publisher, treatment of
previous works in the same series, and so on.
    For poetry and drama or other literary works written for children,[20] by
one author or several authors, headings of the type **Children's poetry;
Children's poetry, American, [English, etc.]** are always assigned in addition to
the other required form and topical headings for literature (see discussion on
pages 260-261.
    Topical headings assigned to literature for children are subdivided by the
forms **—Juvenile poetry; —Juvenile drama; —Juvenile fiction.**
    Following are examples of subject headings for children's books:

Title: *Future Family*
    1.   **Family—Juvenile literature.**
    [1. **Family]**

Title: *Pete Rose, Baseball's Charlie Hustle*
    1.   **Rose, Pete, 1941-   —Juvenile literature.**
    2.   **Baseball players—United States—Biography—Juvenile
         literature.**
    [1. **Rose, Pete, 1941-**
    2.   **Baseball players]**

Title: *Away We Go! On Bicycles in 1898*
    1. Cycling – History – 19th century – Juvenile literature.
    2. Bicycles – History – 19th century – Juvenile literature.
    [1. Bicycles and bicycling – History]

Title: *Holidays on Stage: A Festival of Special-Occasion Plays*
    1. Holidays – Juvenile drama.
    2. Children's plays, American.
    [1. Holidays – Drama.
    2. Plays]

Title: *Birds: Poems*
    1. Birds – Juvenile poetry.
    2. Children's poetry, American.
    [1. Birds – Poetry.
    2. American poetry]

Title: *The Magic of Rhymes*
    1. Nursery rhymes.
    2. Children's poetry.
    [1. Nursery rhymes]

For fiction in particular, the use of topical headings subdivided by the subdivision – **Fiction** and headings representing the form of literature is more liberal in the AC Program than in regular subject cataloging practice:

Title: *The True Francine*
    [1. Friendship – Fiction.
    2. Honesty – Fiction.
    3. School stories.
    4. Animals – Fiction]

Title: *Pack of Wolves*
    [1. World War, 1939-1945 – Soviet Union – Fiction.
    2. Soviet Union – Fiction]

Title: *The Call of the Wild and Other Stories*
    1. Adventure stories, American.
    2. Children's stories, American.
    [1. Adventure and adventurers – Fiction.
    2. Dogs – Fiction.
    3. Short stories]

Title: *Silent Fear*
    [1. Foster home care – Fiction.
    2. Child abuse – Fiction]

Title: *Running of Magic with Houdini*
    1. **Houdini, Harry, 1874-1926 — Juvenile fiction.**
    [1. **Houdini, Harry, 1874-1926 — Fiction.**
    2. **Magic — Fiction.**
    3. **Space and time — Fiction]**

Title: *The Feathered Serpent*
    [1. **Mayas — Fiction.**
    2. **Aztecs — Fiction.**
    3. **Indians of Mexico — Fiction.**
    4. **Mexico — History — Conquest, 1519-1540 — Fiction]**

NONBOOK MATERIALS

General

In Library of Congress practice, the same types and forms of headings are assigned to works on the same subject whether they are in book form or not; in other words, except for some juvenile materials, the medium of publication of a work is not brought out in the subject headings. The exceptions are juvenile films and nonmusical juvenile sound recordings,* for which the free-floating subdivisions **—Juvenile films** and **—Juvenile sound recordings** are used. Examples include:

Title: *Music for 4's, 5's, & 6's* [sound recording]
    1. **Children's songs.**

Title: *Host Defenses, Mechanisms of Disease* [filmstrip]
    1. **Immunity.**
    2. **Immunologic diseases.**

Title: *Host Defense, Mechanisms of Disease* [slide]
    1. **Immunity.**
    2. **Immunologic diseases.**

Title: *The Manager/Supervisor as Trainer* [transparency]
    1. **Employees, Training of.**
    2. **Management.**

Title: *Management of Pain* [videorecording]
    1. **Pain.**

Title: *Pavarotti at Juilliard* [videorecording]
    1. **Singing — Interpretation (Phrasing, dynamics, etc.)**
    2. **Operas — Excerpts.**

---

*For examples of subject cataloging of musical sound recordings, see page 280.

Title: *Housewarming — The Solar Alternative* [motion picture]
1. Solar heating.
2. Dwellings — Energy conservation.
3. House construction — Northeastern states.

Title: *The House at Pooh Corner* [sound recording]
         [a musical rendition]
[1. Toys — Fiction]

Title: *The Criminal Procedure* [sound recording]
1. Criminal procedure — United States — Outlines, syllabi, etc.

Title: *The Doctor Talks to You about Losing Weight Intelligently*
         [sound recording]
         [intended for ages 16 through adult]
1. Reducing diets.
2. Nutrition.
[1. Weight control.
2. Nutrition]

Title: *Ode to the West Wind* [microform]
1. Songs (High voice) with orchestra — Scores.
2. Arnell, Richard, 1917-   — Manuscripts — Facsimiles.
3. Shelley, Percy Bysshe, 1792-1822 — Musical settings.

Title: *The Light Princess* [sound recording]
1. Children's stories, English — Juvenile sound recordings.
2. Fairy tales — England — Juvenile sound recordings.
[1. Fairy tales]

Title: *People, Animals, and Other Monsters* [sound recording]
1. Children's poetry, American — Juvenile sound recordings.
[1. American poetry]

The main difference in the subject cataloging of books and nonbook materials is probably in the more liberal use of subject headings for the latter. This is partly because users cannot browse through nonbook materials and therefore rely more heavily on the subject catalog to bring out the subject content of the materials. Analytical, or partial content, subject entries are also used more frequently with nonbook materials.

Films*

Library of Congress subject catalogers follow certain guidelines for films, which are summarized below.

---

*For the definition of a film, see appendix A.

Fiction films

Nontopical films, including feature films, are *not* assigned form headings such as **Comedy films; Horror films; Western films**; these are topical headings reserved for works *about* the kinds of films the headings denote. Nor are form headings used for special film formats (such as telefeatures, trailers, or short features) or special techniques (such as animated or silent).*

Fiction films and identifiable subjects are treated in the same way their scripts (or any drama in book form) would be handled, with the appropriate topical heading plus the subdivision — **Drama**, e.g., **Baseball — Drama; World War, 1939-1945 — Drama; Merlin — Drama**. It should be noted that the form subdivision — **Drama** is used only in connection with fiction films, with the connotation *dramatization of*; it does not apply to topical films, such as documentaries, as a means of bringing out the medium.

Topical (nonfiction) films

At least one subject heading is assigned to each topical film, and in general the rules governing the assignment of subject headings to books also apply to these types of films. However, as in the case of other nonbrowsable materials, the Library of Congress often provides fuller information on the subject content of films than it does for books. The treatment of topical or nonfiction films is described below.

1) *Each* important topic mentioned in the summary statement on the cataloging record receives a subject entry. In particular, if one specific topic is especially emphasized in the summary in order to illustrate a more general concept, both the specific topic and the general concept are assigned subject headings. Examples include:

[film on the highlights of Colombia, with much footage on
coffee production]
    1. **Colombia — Description and travel.**
    2. **Coffee — Colombia.**

[film on the industries of India, with emphasis on the steel
industry]
    1. **India — Industries.**
    2. **Steel industry and trade — India.**

[film documenting the intellectual expansion in medieval Germany,
as illustrated by the Nuremberg chronicle]
    1. **Schedel, Hartmann, 1440-1514. Liber cronicarum.**
    2. **Germany — Intellectual life — History.**

---

*Note that this restriction applies to fiction films; form headings may be used for some categories of nonfiction films (see the discussion under points 4, 5, and 6 below).

2) If a geographic region and a special topic are described, subject entries for both the region and the topic are provided. Examples include:

[film on the oases of the Sahara]
   1. Oases — Sahara.
   2. Sahara — Description and travel.

[film on a program in New York City to solve the drug abuse problem]
   1. Drug abuse — New York (N.Y.)
   2. New York (N.Y.) — Social conditions.

3) If a film uses a particular person as a representative of a particular profession in order to describe the profession, entries are made under both the name of the individual and the professional activity. (Such films will normally not be regarded as biographies.) Examples include:

[film on a day in the life of the matador Jaime Bravo]
   1. Bravo, Jaime.
   2. Bullfights.

[film on how Paul Taylor, an exponent of modern dance, functions as a performer]
   1. Taylor, Paul, 1930-
   2. Modern dance.

4) A commercial for a particular brand of product is assigned a subject heading under the generic name of the product. Subject entries are also made for particular types of commercials, such as television commercials. An example is:

[film for television advertising Bayer aspirin]
   1. Aspirin.
   2. Television advertising.

5) Experimental films are assigned the heading **Experimental films** and, if appropriate, other form headings:

Title: *Phoenix* [motion picture]
        [about a woman who, representing the legendary Egyptian bird, the phoenix, is caught in a cyclical conflict between the fate of her mystical nature and the modern world, personified by a strong-willed man]
   1. Experimental films.

Title: *Lab 17.1* [motion picture]
        [a humorous cinema verité treatment of a school class trying to dissect laboratory rats]
   1. Experimental films.
   2. Comedy films.
   [1. Schools — Fiction.
   2. Dissection — Fiction]

6) Short films on general or unidentifiable topics are assigned the heading **Short films** and, if appropriate, other form headings:

Title: *Living* [motion picture]
    1. Short films.

Title: *Yule Rules* [motion picture]
    1. Short films.
    2. Comedy films.

Juvenile films[21]

A juvenile film is defined as a film intended for persons through the age of fifteen. On MARC records, films are given a code designating their intellectual level, as follows:

A — ages 0-5   (preschool through kindergarten)
B — ages 6-8   (primary grades)
C — ages 9-15   (intermediate grades through junior high)
D — ages 16-19 (senior high)
E — adult
F — special audiences
G — general

Headings of the type **[Topic] — Juvenile films** are assigned to films with the intellectual level codes A, B, or C, and to those films coded F with evidence that they are intended for juvenile audiences.

The subdivision **— Juvenile films** instead of **— Drama** is used for juvenile fiction films on particular subjects:

Washington, George, 1732-1799 — Drama [adult film]
Washington, George, 1732-1799 — Juvenile films [juvenile film]

In addition to the normal Library of Congress subject headings indicated above, all juvenile films, both topical and nontopical, are assigned bracketed children's literature subject headings in the same manner as for juvenile books. Examples of subject headings assigned to juvenile films include:

Title: *American Indians, Yesterday and Today* [motion picture]
        [intended for primary grades through junior high]
    1. Indians of North America — Juvenile films.
    [1. Indians of North America]

Title: *Time Zero* [motion picture]
    1. Photography, Artistic.
    2. Polaroid Land camera.
    [1. Photography, Artistic.
    2. Polaroid Land camera]

Title: *Time—Vocabulary concepts* [filmstrip]
    1.   **Vocabulary—Juvenile films.**
    2.   **Time—Language—Juvenile films.**
    [1.   **Vocabulary.**
    2.   **Time—Language]**

Title: *Autumn* [videorecording]
       [intended for primary grades]
    1.   **Autumn—Juvenile films.**
    [1.   **Autumn]**

Title: *Autobahn* [motion picture]
       [an experimental, animated tale of the adventure of a
       futuristic character and his travels through a fantastic
       landscape filled with strange apparitions and dangerous
       places]
    1.   **Experimental films.**
    2.   **Moving-picture cartoons.**
    [1.   **Fantasy.**
    2.   **Animated films]**

Title: *The Cat's Meow* [motion picture]
    1.   **Children's films.**
    [1.   **Cats—Fiction.**
    2.   **Mice—Fiction]**

Special juvenile films

For folk tales, a subject entry is made, whenever possible, under names of individual heroes and figures around whom a series of tales or legends have been told, for example, Paul Bunyan, Steamboat Bill, Old Stormalong, etc. In addition, an entry is made for the form, e.g., **Tales, American—Juvenile films**, even in the case of individual tales.

For juvenile reading films, subject entry is made not only under the topic of the film, if one exists, but also for the form. The normal heading for the latter entry is **Reading** (the subject headings **Readers** or **Primers** are not used in connection with films). An example is:

[reading readiness film for primary students on the subject of rain]
    1.   **Rain and rainfall—Juvenile films.**
    2.   **Reading readiness—Juvenile films.**
    3.   **Reading (Primary)—Juvenile films.**

BIOGRAPHY[22]

Definition

For the purpose of cataloging, biography has been defined as the special genre of works consisting of life histories of individuals, including those written by the individuals themselves, i.e., autobiographies.

Individual biography refers to a work devoted solely to the life of a single individual. *Collective biography* refers to a work that consists of two or more life histories. A *complete biography* covers the entire life story of an individual, while a *partial biography* presents only certain details of the person's life.

A work is regarded as a true biography if it makes a serious attempt to present personal details* of the life of an individual. A work on other topics that contains random facts about an individual's life is not considered a true biography. In general, a work with less than 20 percent biographical details is not treated as a true biography at the Library of Congress. Nor is a work that presents primarily nonpersonal details, such as participation in a profession, dwelling places, art collections, contemporaries, contemporary events, etc.

Types of Headings Assigned to Biography

The types of headings generally used with biography are listed below.

1) *Personal name heading for the biographee.* (For forms of personal name headings, see chapter 6.)

2) *Biographical heading* i.e., a heading representing the class of persons, organization, ethnic group, place, event, gender, etc., that the biographee belongs to or is associated with. This heading often contains the subdivision **–Biography** or a more specific biographical subdivision. If the class-of-persons heading for the group involved does not exist as a valid heading and it is impossible to establish it, a heading for the corresponding discipline with the subdivision **–Biography** is used instead, e.g., **Art–Biography**. The subdivision **–Biography** is not free-floating in this instance.

3) *Topical heading, as appropriate.*

Subdivisions That Designate Biography

The subdivisions listed below are used by the Library of Congress to designate biography. These are used with main headings denoting classes of persons, disciplines, organizations, ethnic groups, places, and events. Subdivisions used under names of individuals are listed in appendix F. For

---

*Personal details include early years, education, marriage, personal habits and personality, career, travels, personal experience and tragedies, last years and death, etc.

special meanings and uses of the listed subdivisions, consult *Library of Congress Subject Headings: A Guide to Subdivision Practice* (1981) and *Subject Cataloging Manual*. All subdivisions listed in Table 9.1 are free-floating except as noted by the asterisk.

Table 9.1. Subdivisions That Designate Biography

Subdivision	Classes of persons	Disci-plines	Organi-zations	Ethnic groups	Places	Events, wars
Anecdotes					X	X
Anecdotes, facetiae, satire, etc.	X	X	X	X		
Bio-bibliography		X			X	
Biography	X	X*	X	X	X	X
Biography – Anecdotes, facetiae, satire, etc.					X	
Biography – Dictionaries	X	X*	X	X	X	X
Biography – Portraits			X		X	
Correspondence	X			X		
Diaries	X			X		
Genealogy	X			X	X	
Iconography	X					X
Interviews	X	X*		X		
Personal narratives						X
Portraits	X			X		X

*Not a free-floater. Establish each new use under a specific discipline.

The subdivision – Biography

The subdivision – **Biography** is used as the generic subdivision for the concept of biography, designating not only individual and collective biography, but also autobiography, personal reminiscences, and personal narratives. It is used under the pertinent class of persons rather than the corresponding field or discipline, if a choice is possible.

The subdivision – Correspondence[23]

The subdivision – **Correspondence** is free-floating under headings representing classes of persons or ethnic groups as well as personal name headings, e.g., **Authors, American – 20th century – Correspondence; Chinese Americans – Correspondence; Brown, Sam – Correspondence.** For correspondence carried on by types of organizations or for the correspondence of individual organizations, the subdivision – **Records and correspondence** is used.

The subdivision — Personal narratives[24]

The subdivision — **Personal narratives**, previously also used under headings for classes of persons, is now used only under names of events and wars as a form subdivision for eyewitness reports and/or autobiographical accounts of experiences in connection with these events or wars.

Collective Biography*

Collective biography of a group of persons not associated with a particular field or discipline

The form heading **Biography** is assigned to a work containing biographies of persons not limited to a particular period, place, organization, ethnic group, gender, or specific field or discipline:

> Title: *The Vital Spark: 101 Outstanding Lives*
> 1. **Biography.**

For general collective biography in special forms, form headings such as **Anecdotes; Autobiographies; Diaries; Interviews; Letters; Obituaries; Portraits** are used as appropriate:

> Title: *Anecdotes*
> 1. **Anecdotes.**

> Title: *Confessions and Self-Portraits: 4600 Years of Autobiography*
> 1. **Autobiographies.**

> Title: *A Treasury of the World's Great Diaries*
> 1. **Diaries.**

The main heading **Biography** is subdivided by period if the biographees belong to a specific period:

> Title: *Men in the News: Personality Sketches from the New York Times*
> 1. **Biography — 20th century.**

If a collective biography does not pertain to a special field or discipline but involves an organization, ethnic or national group, place, event, or war, the appropriate heading (indicating the special aspect) is followed by the subdivision — **Biography** (or a more specific subdivision such as — **Genealogy; — Interviews**):

---

*The treatment described in this section applies to collective biographies containing four or more life histories. For collective biographies containing two or three life histories, see discussion of individual biography.

> American Academy of Pediatrics — Biography
> Afro-Americans — Genealogy
> Jews — Hungary — Budapest — Biography
> Dallas (Tex.) — Biography
> Korean War, 1950-1953 — Personal narratives, Korean

If the work focuses on a particular historical period of a specific place, two headings are assigned, one for the period with the subdivision — **Biography**, and another for the place with the subdivision — **Biography**:

> Title: *Founders of Colonial Virginia*
> 1. **Virginia — History — Colonial period, ca. 1600-1775 — Biography.**
> 2. **Virginia — Biography.**

In some cases, several headings are assigned in order to cover all aspects of the work:

> Title: *They Stopped in Oberlin: Black Residents and Visitors of the Nineteenth Century*
> 1. **Afro-Americans — Ohio — Oberlin — Biography.**
> 2. **Oberlin (Ohio) — Biography.**

> Title: *Blacks Who Served with the Army in Vietnam*
> 1. **Afro-Americans — Washington (D.C.) — Biography.**
> 2. **Washington (D.C.) — Biography.**
> 3. **United States. Army — Biography.**
> 4. **Vietnamese Conflict, 1961-1975 — Afro-Americans — Biography.**
> 5. **Vietnamese Conflict, 1961-1975 — Biography.**

For a collective biography of wives who have no special career of their own, the heading **Wives — Biography** or a heading denoting a special group of wives, e.g., **Army wives; Diplomats' wives; Non-commissioned officers' wives; Teachers' wives**, etc., subdivided by — **Biography**, is used. There are also headings for various other classes of persons not limited to a field or discipline, such as **Men; Women; Children; Adolescent boys; Adolescent girls; Young men; Widows; Widowers**.

Collective biography of persons belonging to a particular field or discipline

For collective biographies of persons belonging to a particular field or discipline, a heading in the form of **[Class of persons] — Biography** is used:

> Title: *Great Economists since Keynes*
> 1. **Economists — Biography.**

Title: *El Niño que Fue*
   1.   **Authors, Chilean — Biography.**
   2.   **Children — Biography.**

The geographic subdivision, if applicable, is interposed between the main heading representing the class of persons and the biographical subdivision:

Title: *Carolina Chemists: Sketches from Chapel Hill*
   1.   **University of North Carolina at Chapel Hill.**
        Dept. of Chemistry — History.
   2.   **Chemists — North Carolina — Biography.**

Previously, a distinction was made between a class-of-persons heading with a national qualifier,[25] e.g., **Engineers, American** (designating origin), and one with a geographic subdivision, e.g., **Engineers — United States** (designating location). Because the distinction is not always clear in practice, and the titles under a heading with the geographic subdivision all too often represent contents identical with those under the same heading with the adjectival qualifier, the Library of Congress decided in 1973 to eliminate class-of-persons headings with an adjectival qualifier indicating nationality and use the headings with geographic subdivisions to mean either *currently in* or *originally from*. An exception is made for headings related to belles lettres because of the additional complication of language.

Since the class-of-persons heading normally brings out the field or discipline discussed in the biography, no additional heading under the name of the field or discipline is necessary. However, if a term representing the special class of persons is not available, the heading for the corresponding discipline with the subdivision —**Biography** is used instead. For example, a collective biography of persons in the field of art may include many people who are not actual artists — dealers, collectors, museum personnel, and so on. As there is no class-of-persons term that encompasses these individuals, the heading **Art — Biography** is used.

If appropriate for the work being cataloged, a more specific form subdivision is used instead of —**Biography**, e.g., **Entertainers — Interviews; Poets, English — Correspondence; Afro-American artists — Portraits.**

For a collective biography of women associated with a particular field or discipline, at least two headings are assigned: **[Class of persons] — Biography** and **[Feminine class of persons] — Biography**:

Title: *Contributions of Women: Medicine*
   1.   **Women physicians — United States — Biography — Juvenile literature.**
   2.   **Physicians — United States — Biography — Juvenile literature.**
   [1. **Women physicians.**
   2.   **Physicians]**

Title: *Famous American Actresses*
   1.   **Actors — United States — Biography.**
   2.   **Actresses — United States — Biography.**

If a biographical work on persons associated with a field or discipline also involves an organization, ethnic group, place, or event, headings indicating the field as well as those indicating other aspects are assigned, as indicated below.

1) *Organization.* An example is:

Title: *Chemists in the Department of Agriculture*
    1. **Chemists—United States—Biography.**
    2. **United States. Dept. of Agriculture—Biography.**

2) *Ethnic group.* At least two headings are assigned: the class of persons, and the class of persons qualified by the ethnic group. However, the heading designating only the ethnic group is not used. An example is:

Title: *Notes and Tones: Musician to Musician Interviews*
    1. **Jazz musicians—Interviews.**
    2. **Afro-American musicians—Interviews.**
       [not Afro-Americans—Biography]

3) *Place.* Normally, an additional heading under the name of the place (e.g., **Ohio—Biography**) is assigned, as long as the work is of interest to genealogists or local historians or has local significance. Such headings are not usually assigned when the place in question is a country or larger region. This type of heading is always assigned if the class-of-persons heading is not applicable. Examples include:

Title: *The Lives of Early Abilene, Tex., Cowboys*
    1. **Cowboys—Texas—Abilene—Biography.**
    2. **Frontier and pioneer life—Texas—Abilene.**
    3. **Abilene (Tex.)—Biography.**

Title: *Lancashire Literary Worthies*
    1. **English literature—England—Lancashire—Bio-bibliography.**
    2. **Authors, English—England—Lancashire—Biography.**
    3. **Lancashire—Biography.**

4) *Event or war.* An example is:

Title: *Lives of Entertainers Who Served in World War II*
    1. **Entertainers—Biography.**
    2. **World War, 1939-1945—Biography.**

5) *Other topics.* If the biographical work covers other topics not designated by the biographical heading(s), additional topical headings, generally without biographical subdivision, are assigned:

Title: *Pirates on the Gulf of Siam: Report from the Vietnamese*
        Boat People Living in the Refugee Camp in
        Songkhla-Thailand
1. **Refugees — Thailand — Biography.**
2. **Refugees — Vietnam — Biography.**
3. **Pirates — Thailand.**
4. **Atrocities — Thailand.**

Title: *The Roman Emperors*
1. **Roman emperors — Biography.**
2. **Rome — History — Empire, 30 B.C.-284.**

Family histories*

For the history of an individual family, the following headings are assigned: a heading in the form of **[Surname] family**, and a heading bringing out the place:

Title: *The Brooks Bridge of History*
1. **Brooks family.**
2. **North Carolina — Genealogy.**

Title: *A Tale of Two Families: A Biographical Genealogy of*
        the Meyers and Sparhawk Families
1. **Myers family.**
2. **Sparhawk family.**
3. **Canada — Genealogy.**

The entry under place is omitted in the case of **United States — Genealogy**.

If more than one family is named on the title page, each family is designated by a separate entry if there are no more than three:

Title: *Elliotts and Lovells of Wisconsin: 1850's Before and*
        After
1. **Elliott family.**
2. **Lovell family.**
3. **Wisconsin — Genealogy.**

Title: *Hand, Sisson, and Scott: More Yeoman Ancestors*
1. **Hand family.**
2. **Sisson family.**
3. **Scott family.**
        [a heading under the place, i.e., **United States
        — Genealogy**, is not assigned]

If more than three families are named, subject headings are assigned only for the most important three (normally the first three listed).

---

*For treatment of genealogical materials in general, see pages 318-319.

If one or more of the members of the family are given prominent treatment in the work, a heading or headings under the personal name(s) are also assigned:

Title: *The Kennedys, 1848-1983*
1. **Kennedy family.**
2. **Kennedy, John F. (John Fitzgerald), 1917-1963 – Family.**

Previously established headings in a form such as Smith family (William Smith, 1669-1743) are no longer used.

For the history of a royal or noble family,[26] an additional heading under the name of the place is always assigned:

Title: *Biographies of the Shah Kings of Nepal*
1. **Shah dynasty, 1768-**
2. **Nepal – Kings and rulers – Biography.**

Title: *The House of Medici: Its Rise and Fall*
1. **Medici, House of.**
2. **Florence (Italy) – History – 1421-1737.**
3. **Italy – Nobility – Biography.**

Title: *The Iconography of the House of Windsor*
1. **Windsor, House of – Iconography.**
2. **Great Britain – Kings and rulers – Iconography.**
3. **Great Britain – Queens – Iconography.**
4. **Great Britain – Princes and princesses – Iconography.**

Individual Biography

Personal name headings

The name of the biographee serves as the main heading for an individual biography. The form of the heading is the same as that used for main or added entries (see chapter 6 on proper names). In general, a work containing the lives of two or three* persons treated either collectively or separately is assigned an individual heading for each person, instead of being treated as a collective biography.

Subdivisions under personal names[27]

Appropriate subdivision(s) are added to the name heading if the biography deals with specific aspect(s) of the person's life. A list of free-floating subdivisions used under names of persons (other than literary authors) appears in appendix F of this book.** Those used under names of literary

---

*Occasionally a biography containing the life stories of four persons may be treated in this manner.

**This list represents a consolidation of lists of free-floating subdivisions under the model headings for philosophers, statesmen, musicians, etc.

authors are listed under the model heading **Shakespeare, William, 1564-1616** (see appendix D). Note that the subdivision —**Biography** is used under headings for literary authors, but not under headings for other persons.

When a person with a multifaceted career belongs in more than one category, the subdivisions appropriate to the catagory emphasized in the work being cataloged are used. For example, if a person who is well known as a literary author is treated as a statesman in the work, the subdivisions from the list of free-floating subdivisions used under names of persons are used. On the other hand, if another work deals with the same person as a literary author, the appropriate literary subdivisions are used. In cases in which there is a direct conflict between the two free-floating subdivision lists, the subdivisions belonging to the category in which the person is better known are used. For example, a drama about a dual-career person who is better known as a literary author is assigned a heading in the form of **[Name of person] in fiction, drama, poetry, etc.** (a pattern used for literary authors), rather than a heading of the type **[Name of person] — Drama**.

Additional headings for individual biographies

1) *Biographical headings.* In addition to the personal name heading of the biographee, the same biographical heading(s)* assigned to a collective biography on the same topic are assigned to an individual biography. In effect, the biographical heading in these cases represents generic posting, i.e., listing under a generic heading that encompasses the personal heading. Such treatment is a deliberate departure from the general policy of not assigning both a general and a specific heading to the same body of material. The policy was probably adopted in the interest of collocating biographies of persons in the same field or sharing the same characteristics. These biographical headings are particularly useful in generic search since subject-to-personal-name references are no longer being made.

The types of biographical headings assigned to individual biographies as appropriate are listed below.

a) *Biographical headings for persons associated with a field or discipline.* To a biography of a person associated with a field or discipline, headings of the following types are assigned in addition to the personal name heading:

[Class of persons] — [Place] — [Subdivision]**
[Discipline] — Biography
  [if the class-of-persons heading is not available]
[Organization, ethnic group, place, event, or gender] — [Subdivision]
  [the heading designating the ethnic group or gender is assigned only if the point of the work is personal identification with an ethnic group or personal experiences as a woman. The place heading is assigned only when the person has local significance or when the class-of-persons heading is not available.]

---

*Additional biographical headings are not assigned to lives of legendary or fictitious persons.
**For different types of biographical subdivisions, see page 228.

Examples include:

Title: *Père Claver*
   1. **Claver, Pedro, Saint, 1580-1654.**
   2. **Christian saints — Colombia — Biography.**

Title: *Isadora Duncan*
   1. **Duncan, Isadora, 1878-1927 — Pictorial works.**
   2. **Dancers — United States — Biography — Pictorial works.**

Title: *Jean-Henri Fabre*
   1. **Fabre, Jean-Henri, 1832-1915.**
   2. **Entomologists — France — Biography.**

Title: *William Whiston*
   1. **Whiston, William, 1667-1752.**
   2. **Church of England — Clergy — Biography.**
   3. **Baptists — Clergy — Biography.**
   4. **England — Biography.**

Title: *Les amours "scandaleuses" du maréchal-duc de Richelieu: 1696-1788*
   1. **Richelieu, Louis François Armand du Plessis, duc de, 1696-1788 — Relations with women.**
   2. **France — Nobility — Biography.**

For a person who is active in several fields, multiple biographical headings are used to bring out those careers described in the work in hand. No attempt is made to name every activity in which the person was engaged. It should rarely be necessary to assign more than two or three such headings. Examples include:

Title: *Five O'clock Comes Early: A Young Man's Battle with Alcoholism* / Bob Welch
   1. **Welch, Bob, 1956-   .**
   2. **Baseball players — United States — Biography.**
   3. **Alcoholics — United States — Biography.**

Title: *Sketches from Life: The Autobiography of Lewis Mumford: The Early Years*
   1. **Mumford, Lewis, 1895-   .**
   2. **Social reformers — United States — Biography.**
   3. **City planners — United States — Biography.**
   4. **Architects — United States — Biography.**

Title: *Apologies, Good Friends ... An Interim Biography of Daniel Berrigan, S.J.*
   1. **Berrigan, Daniel.**
   2. **Catholic Church — Clergy — Biography.**
   3. **Clergy — United States — Biography.**
   4. **Poets, American — 20th century — Biography.**

Title: *A Bishop's Confession* / Jim Bishop
1. **Bishop, Jim, 1907- .**
2. **Historians — United States — Biography.**
3. **Biographers — United States — Biography.**
4. **Journalists — United States — Biography.**

If the work being cataloged focuses only on one career aspect, only the heading for that one aspect is assigned:

[work about Schweitzer's experiences as a medical missionary]
1. **Schweitzer, Albert, 1875-1965.**
2. **Missionaries, Medical — Gabon — Biography.**

Catalogers are advised not to make value judgments in the selection of the class of persons to which the biographee belongs. Headings that represent career, profession, or special pursuit are selected. For example, Hitler is described as a head of state, not as a war criminal, dictator, or National Socialist.

b) *Biographical headings for persons belonging to no particular field or discipline.* If the individual biography does not pertain to a special field or discipline, a biographical heading in the form of [**Organization, ethnic group, place, event, or war**] — **Biography** is assigned, in order to bring out any and all important associations by which the person may be identified:

Title: *Ole Foley: The Story of W. G. L. Foley (1780-1874), a Texas Planter Whose Family Tree Withered and Died*
1. **Foley, W. G. L. (Washington Green Lee), 1780-1874.**
2. **Lavaca County (Tex.) — Biography.**

Title: *George Berry Washington, Black Plantation Owner*
1. **Washington, George Berry, 1864-1928.**
2. **Afro-Americans — Arkansas — Crittenden County — Biography.**
3. **Crittenden County (Ark.) — Biography.**

2) *Topical headings.* If the biographical work also contains discussions on special topics not designated by the biographical heading(s), they are brought out by standard subject headings without biographical subdivisions:

Title: *The Lion of Redstone*
1. **Osgood, John Cleveland, 1851-1926.**
2. **Coal trade — Colorado — History.**
3. **Mineral industries — Colorado — History.**
4. **Businessmen — Colorado — Biography.**

Title: *Henry Adams and the American Experiment*
1. **Adams, Henry, 1838-1918.**
2. **United States — Civilization — 1865-1918.**
3. **Historians — United States — Biography.**

Title: *Always on the Offense*
1. **Baseball — Offense.**
2. **Schmidt, Mike, 1949-** .
3. **Baseball players — United States — Biography.**

Individual biography of specific classes of persons

Biographies of certain classes of persons are given special treatment, as delineated below.

1) *Artists.* See discussion on pages 294-295.

2) *Athletes.* For a biographical work about an athlete or sports figure, a biographical heading designating the appropriate sport, e.g., **Baseball players**; **Tennis players**; **Swimmers**; etc., is assigned:

Title: *"Magic," a Biography of Earvin Johnson*
1. **Johnson, Earvin, 1959-** .
2. **Basketball players — United States — Biography.**

Headings denoting special categories of players of individual sports are not used for individual biographies, i.e., **Baseball players — Biography** is used, but not **Pitchers (Baseball) — Biography.***

3) *Founders of religion.* A biographical heading is assigned in addition to the personal heading and any other topical heading. For example, for Christ, use **Christian biography**; for Mohammed, use **Muslims — Biography**; for Buddha, use **Buddhists — Biography**.

4) *Literary authors.* See discussion on pages 267-269.

5) *Patients, handicapped, etc.* To a biographical account of a person afflicted with a specific disease, the name of the disease with subdivision **— Patients — Biography** is assigned, e.g., **Cancer — Patients — Biography**, unless a term for the class of persons exists, e.g., **Cardiacs**. The former practice of subdividing the name of a disease by **— Biography**, e.g., Cancer — Biography, is now obsolete.

6) *Pet owners.* Biographical headings are not assigned to personal accounts of life with a particular kind of pet unless the owner is professionally involved with the animal, as in the case of trainers, horsemen, keepers, psychologists, etc. In addition to or in place of the biographical heading for the owner, a heading in the form of **[Kind of animal] — Biography** or **[Kind of animal] — Anecdotes** (for anecdotal accounts) is assigned:

---

*This is contrary to the convention in collective biography, in which specific categories of players, e.g., **Guards (Basketball)**; **Pitchers (Baseball)**; etc., are used whenever appropriate.

Title: *A Snowflake in My Hand* / Samantha Mooney
1. **Mooney, Samantha.**
2. **Cats — Anecdotes.**
3. **Veterinarians — United States — Biography.**

7) *Philosophers*. Works that discuss a philosopher's contribution in a particular field are assigned headings of the type **[Name of philosopher] — Contributions in [specific field or topic]**. When headings of this type are assigned to a work, the biographical heading is omitted, unless the work contains substantial information (at least 20 percent of the text) about the philosopher's personal life.

Title: *The Origins and Significance of Hegel's Logic*
1. **Hegel, Georg Wilhelm Friedrich, 1770-1831 — Contributions in logic.**
2. **Logic, Modern — 19th century.**

8) *Statesmen or heads of state*. When the work being cataloged presents personal facts concerning the life of a politician, statesman, or ruler, two headings are assigned: the personal name with topical subdivision, if appropriate, and the biographical heading with an appropriate subdivision, e.g., **Great Britain — Kings and rulers — Biography; Presidents — United States — Biography; Roman emperors — Biography**. Examples include:

Title: *Alexander Hamilton: An Intimate Portrait*
1. **Hamilton, Alexander, 1757-1804.**
2. **Statesmen — United States — Biography.**

Title: *Prelude to Fame: An Account of the Early Life of Napolean up to the Battle of Montenotte*
1. **Napoleon I, Emperor of the French, 1769-1821 — Childhood and youth.**
2. **France — Kings and rulers — Biography.**

If, in addition to personal facts, the work also discusses political affairs or events in which the biographee participated during a period of the country's history, a heading for this special aspect is also assigned, e.g., **[Place] — History — [Period subdivision]; [Place] — Politics and government — [Period subdivision]**. Examples include:

Title: *King Charles I*
1. **Charles I, King of England, 1600-1649.**
2. **Great Britain — History — Charles I, 1625-1649.**
3. **Great Britain — Kings and rulers — Biography.**

Title: *Life and Times of D. Webster*
1. **Webster, Daniel, 1782-1852.**
2. **Statesmen — United States — Biography.**
3. **United States — Politics and government — 19th century.**

For a work that describes the times in which a politician, statesman, etc., lived and the person's relationship to those times, but that contains few or no biographical details about the person, the biographical heading is omitted:

Title: *The Elizabethan Deliverance*
    1.   **Great Britain — History — Elizabeth, 1558-1603.**
    2.   **Elizabeth I, Queen of England, 1533-1603.**

Title: *Eugen Richter: der entscheidene Liberalismus in*
            wilhelminischer Zeit 1871-1906
    1.   **Richter, Eugen, 1838-1906.**
    2.   **Germany — Politics and government — 1871-1918.**

To a work on the events of a particular reign, without biographical facts about the ruler, only the **History** heading is assigned:

Title: *The Northerners: A Study in the Reign of King John*
    1.   **Great Britain — History — John, 1199-1216.**

9) *Travelers.* Biographical headings are not assigned to personal accounts of travel unless the journey described in the work is intimately associated with the career of the traveler (as in the case of statesmen, animal collectors, or musicians who travel) or unless the traveler is a literary author:

Title: *Italian Journey, 1786-1788* / by Johann Wolfgang von Goethe
    1.   **Goethe, Johann Wolfgang von, 1749-1832 — Journeys**
       — Italy.
    2.   **Italy — Description and travel — 1501-1800.**
    3.   **Authors, German — 18th century — Biography.**

10)   *Wives.* Biographical or autobiographical works of wives who are active in a special field are treated in the normal manner. However, if a wife has no special career of her own, a biographical work that relates her personal experiences in association with her husband and his career is assigned the following types of headings: **[Name of husband]; [Biographical heading for career of husband]; [Name of wife]; [Category of wives] — [Place] — Biography.** An example is:

Title: *In the Shadow of a Saint: Lady Alice More*
    1.   **More, Thomas, Sir, Saint, 1478-1535.**
    2.   **More, Alice, Lady, 1475?-1551.**
    3.   **Statesmen — Great Britain — Biography.**
    4.   **Christian saints — England — Biography.**
    5.   **Statesmen's wives — Great Britain — Biography.**

Similar treatment is given to the biography of a woman associated with a famous man:

Title: *Eva Braun: Hitler's Mistress*
1. **Braun, Eva.**
2. **Hitler, Adolf, 1889-1945.**
3. **Heads of state – Germany – Biography.**
4. **Mistresses – Germany – Biography.**

Special Types of Biographical Works

Autobiographies and autobiographical writings

The personal name heading is assigned to an autobiography even though it duplicates the main entry or an added entry:

Title: *Not Without Dust & Heat: My Life in Theater* / Doris Fitton
1. **Fitton, Doris, 1897-**
2. **Actors – Australia – Biography.**

Title: *Flicka's Friend: The Autobiography of Mary O'Hara*
1. **O'Hara, Mary – Biography.**
2. **Authors, American – 20th century – Biography.**

Other autobiographical writings such as memoirs, journals, diaries, etc., are treated similarly:

Title: *The Diary of Adolf Hitler*
1. **Hitler, Adolf, 1889-1945 – Diaries.**
2. **Heads of state – Germany – Diaries.**

Title: *Tagebuch* / Arthur Schnitzler
1. **Schnitzler, Arthur, 1862-1931 – Diaries.**
2. **Authors, Austrian – 20th century – Diaries.**

Correspondence[28]

To a collection of personal correspondence, the following complex of headings is assigned:

[Name(s) of the letter writer(s) (if no more than three)] **– Correspondence**
[Name(s) of the addressee(s) (if no more than two)] **– Correspondence**
[Class of persons or **ethnic group] – Correspondence**
[Special topics discussed in the letters]

Examples include:

Title: *José Luis Cuevas Letters*
1. **Cuevas, José Luis, 1934-   – Correspondence.**
2. **Artists – Mexico – Correspondence.**

Title: *The Letters of Erasmus Darwin*
1. **Darwin, Erasmus, 1731-1802 — Correspondence.**
2. **Naturalists — England — Correspondence.**
3. **Physicians — England — Correspondence.**

Title: *Letters to Ottla and the Family* / Franz Kafka
1. **Kafka, Franz, 1883-1924 — Correspondence.**
2. **David, Ottilie, b. 1892 — Correspondence.**
3. **Authors, Austrian — 20th century — Correspondence.**

Title: *Letters to Allen Ginsberg, 1953-1957* / William Burroughs
1. **Burroughs, William S., 1914-   — Correspondence.**
2. **Ginsberg, Allen, 1926-   — Correspondence.**
3. **Authors, American — 20th century — Correspondence.**

Partial biography[29]

A partial biography, i.e., a work about a person's life and work, with at least 20 percent of the content devoted to personal details, is treated like an individual biography by assigning a personal heading and additional biographical heading(s). Additional subject headings are assigned to bring out the topical aspects if they have not been represented by the biographical headings. If a work about a person contains few or no personal details, the biographical headings are not assigned. The personal heading is assigned in all cases. Examples include:

Title: *The Theology of Marcus Garvey*
1. **Garvey, Marcus, 1887-1940 — Religion.**
2. **Afro-Americans — Religion.**
3. **Afro-Americans — Biography.**

Title: *The People's Pope: The Story of Karol Wojtyla of Poland*
1. **John Paul II, Pope, 1920-**
2. **Popes — Biography.**

Title: *The Economy of France in the Second Half of the Reign of Louis XIV*
1. **France — Economic conditions.**
2. **Louis XIV, King of France, 1638-1715.**

Title: *The Papal Year*
1. **John Paul II, Pope, 1920-**

Title: *Who Is Kissinger?*
1. **Kissinger, Henry, 1923-   — Addresses, essays, lectures.**
2. **United States — Foreign relations — 1969-1974 — Addresses, essays, lectures.**
3. **United States — Politics and government — 1969-1974 — Addresses, essays, lectures.**

Festschriften[30]

The following types of headings are assigned to festschriften, i.e., publications issued in honor of a person or corporate body:

[Topical heading] — Addresses, essays, lectures [or — Congresses]

and one of the following two:

[Name of honoree] — Addresses, essays, lectures [or — Congresses]
  [if publication contains discussion of the honoree]
[Name of honoree]
  [if publication does not contain discussion of the honoree]

If the work contains a substantial bibliography (at least 20 percent of the work) related to the honoree, an additional heading in the form of [Name of honoree] — Bibliography is also assigned. A biographical heading is also assigned if the work devotes at least 20 percent of its text to the honoree's personal life. Examples include:

Title: *The Scientific Ideas of G. K. Gilbert: An Assessment on the Occasion of the Centennial of the United States Geological Survey (1879-1979)*
1. Geology — United States — Addresses, essays, lectures.
2. Gilbert, Grove Karl, 1843-1918.
3. Geologists — United States — Biography.

Title: *History & Imagination: Essays in Honour of H. R. Trevor-Roper*
1. History — Addresses, essays, lectures.
2. Trevor-Roper, H. R. (Hugh Redwald), 1914-   — Addresses, essays, lectures.

Title: *Wheat Science, Today and Tomorrow: Papers Presented at a Symposium in Honor of Sir Otto Frankel's 80th Birthday*
1. Wheat — Breeding — Congresses.
2. Frankel, O. H. (Otto Herzberg), Sir, 1900-   — Congresses.

True stories about individual animals and pets[31]

To a work containing true life stories about animals, a heading in the form of [Type of animal] — [Place (if appropriate)] — Biography [or — Anecdotes] is assigned:

Title: *Tears & Laughter: A Couple of Dozen Dog Stories* / by Gene Hill
1. Dogs — Anecdotes.
2. Hunting dogs — Anecdotes.
3. Hill, Gene.

To a true life story of an animal or pet that has an established name, the name heading is also assigned. (For individual biographies of pet owners, see discussion on pages 238-239; for fictional accounts of animals, see discussion on pages 259 and 263.)

WORKS ABOUT CORPORATE BODIES

The treatment of works about corporate bodies is similar in many ways to that of biography.

Corporate Bodies Discussed Collectively

For a work about a specific type of corporate body, the generic term is assigned as the heading, e.g., **Libraries; Trade and professional associations; Trade-unions, Catholic;** etc. Many of the headings for corporate bodies are subdivided by place, e.g., **Libraries—Finland; Libraries—Alaska.** Examples include:

Title: *University Library History: An International Review*
    1. **Libraries, University and college—History.**

Title: *International Directory of Corporate Affiliations*
    1. **Corporations—Directories.**
    2. **Subsidiary corporations—Directories.**

Title: *Great New England Churches*
    1. **Churches—New England—Guide-books.**
    2. **New England—Description and travel—Guide-books.**

Works about Individual Corporate Bodies

The name of the corporate body, as established according to *Anglo-American Cataloguing Rules*, second edition (*AACR2*) (see discussion on pages 121-124), is assigned as the subject heading for a work about an individual corporate body, even if the subject entry duplicates the main entry or an added entry.[32] Generic headings representing types of corporate bodies are not assigned. Examples include:

Title: *History of Elizabeth City State University: A Story of Survival*
    1. **Elizabeth City State University—History.**

Title: *New York Freemasonry: A Bicentennial History, 1781-1981*
    1. **Freemasons.   Grand Lodge of the State of New York —History.**

Title: *Deutschlands Heere bis 1918*
    1. **Germany.   Heer—History.**

Title: *Former Members of Congress*
1. **Former Members of Congress (Organization)**

Title: *Gold Star Wives*
1. **Gold Star Wives of America.**

Title: *The Next 16 Years of the 29th Ward in Salt Lake City, 1963-1978*
1. **Church of Jesus Christ of Latter-Day Saints. Salt Lake Stake. 29th Ward — History.**

Title: *Annual Review* / British Agencies for Adoption and Fostering
1. **British Agencies for Adoption and Fostering — Yearbooks.**

Title: *Alumni Directory* / Cornell College
1. **Cornell College (Mount Vernon, Iowa) — Alumni — Directories.**

A festschrift in honor of a corporate body is treated like one in honor of a person (see discussion on page 243).

For the proceedings of a meeting or meetings of a society or institution dealing with a specific topic, a heading in the form of **[Topic] — Congresses** is assigned. However, for the annual meeting or meetings that deal with the internal affairs of the corporate body, a heading in the form of **[Name of corporate body] — Congresses** is used.

Name Changes in Corporate Bodies

When a corporate body changes its name, the present policy in accordance with *AACR2* is to provide headings for all the names and link them with *see also* references.* In assigning subject headings to corporate bodies that have changed their names, two different policies are in effect: one for corporate bodies in general, and one specifically for political jurisdictions.

For a work about a corporate body that has had a linear name change, the name current during the latest period covered by the work is assigned:

Title: *Report* / State of California, Mediation/Conciliation Service
1. **California. State Mediation/Conciliation Service — Periodicals.**
   [former name: Conciliation Service]
2. **Mediation and conciliation, Industrial — California — Periodicals.**

---

*For forms of corporate headings, see pages 121-124.

In cases of a complicated change, such as a merger or a separation, the headings chosen depend on the nature of the change and the emphasis of the work.

For a work about a political jurisdiction that has changed its name without involving territorial changes, the latest name is assigned as the subject entry regardless of the period treated in the work:

Title: *Britain and the Congo in the Nineteenth Century*
    1. **Zaire — History — To 1908.**
    2. **British — Zaire — History — 19th century.**
    3. **Zaire — Relations — Great Britain.**
    4. **Great Britain — Relations — Zaire.**

Title: *The Beginnings of Nyasaland and North-Eastern
        Rhodesia, 1859-95*
    1. **Malawi — History — To 1891.**
    2. **Malawi — History — 1891-1953.**
    3. **Zambia — History — To 1890.**
    4. **Zambia — History — 1890-1924.**

Title: *From Rhodesia to Zimbabwe: The Politics of Transition*
    1. **Zimbabwe — Politics and government — 1979-1980.**
    2. **Lancaster House Agreement (1979)**

If the change is a complicated one, for example, one involving territorial change, the latest name used during the latest period covered by the work is assigned as the subject heading, unless the main focus of the work pertains to the natural environment rather than political or cultural aspects. An example is:

Title: *People and Power in Byzantium*
    1. **Byzantine Empire — Civilization.**

WORKS ABOUT BUILDINGS AND OTHER STRUCTURES[33]

Works about Specific Types of Buildings or Structures

To a work that discusses collectively a certain type of building or structure, a topical heading, with appropriate geographic subdivision if applicable, is assigned:

Title: *English Cathedrals: The Forgotten Centuries*
    1. **Cathedrals — England — Conservation and restoration.**

Title: *Night Dancin'*
    1. **Discotheques — New York (N.Y.)**

Title: *Scenes of Prison Life in London*
1. **Prisons — England — London.**

If the work discusses a type or class of building or structure within a city from an architectural point of view or as physical entities, an additional heading in the form of **[City] — Buildings, structures, etc.** is assigned:

Title: *The Art Deco Skyscraper in New York*
1. **Skyscrapers — New York (N.Y.)**
2. **Art deco — New York (N.Y.)**
3. **Decoration and ornament, Architectural — New York (N.Y.)**
4. **New York (N.Y.) — Buildings, structures, etc.**

Title: *The Fountains of Rome*
1. **Fountains — Italy — Rome.**
2. **Rome (Italy) — Buildings, structures, etc.**

Works about Individual Buildings or Structures

For a work about an individual building, the following types of headings are used:

[Name of structure]
[Name of city] — Buildings, structures, etc.
   [if the building or structure is located within a city and the work
   discusses it from an architectural point of view]
[Name of owner, resident, etc.] — Homes and haunts — [Place]
[Special feature or topic]

Examples include:

Title: *Cleveland Municipal Stadium*
1. **Cleveland Municipal Stadium (Cleveland, Ohio) — History.**
2. **Cleveland (Ohio) — Buildings, structures, etc.**

Title: *Brooklyn's City Hall*
1. **Brooklyn Borough Hall (New York, N.Y.)**
2. **Neoclassicism (Architecture) — New York (N.Y.)**
3. **Brooklyn (New York, N.Y.) — Buildings, structures, etc.**
4. **New York (N.Y.) — Buildings, structures, etc.**

Title: *A Giant in Texas: A History of the Dallas-Fort Worth Regional Airport Controversy, 1911-1974*
1. **Dallas-Fort Worth Regional Airport — History.**
2. **Dallas (Tex.) — Buildings, structures, etc. — History.**
3. **Fort Worth (Tex.) — Buildings, structures, etc. — History.**

WORKS INVOLVING CITY DISTRICTS, SECTIONS,* AND QUARTERS[34]

When the work deals with a topic in a city section, two headings are assigned: [Name of district, section, or quarter]; [Topic] — [Larger entity] — [City]. This approach is taken because the lowest level of geographic subdivision in the Library of Congress subject headings system is the city. In other words, subjects are not subdivided by city districts, sections, or quarters.

If the topic involved corresponds to one of the concepts represented by the free-floating subdivisions under names of places, the following headings are used instead: [Name of district, etc.] — [Topical subdivision]; [City] — [Same topical subdivision]. Examples include:

Title: *Genthe's Photographs of San Francisco's Old Chinatown*
1. **Chinatown (San Francisco, Calif.) — Description — Views.**
2. **San Francisco (Calif.) — Description — Views.**

Title: *Brooklyn — And How It Got That Way*
1. **Brooklyn (New York, N.Y.) — History.**
2. **Brooklyn (New York, N.Y.) — Description.**
3. **Brooklyn (New York, N.Y.) — Social life and customs.**
4. **New York (N.Y.) — History.**
5. **New York (N.Y.) — Description.**
6. **New York (N.Y.) — Social life and customs.**

WORKS RELATED TO INDIVIDUAL WORKS

To a work related to another work — a commentary or criticism, an edition, an index, or a supplement — a heading representing the original work is generally assigned in addition to other appropriate headings.

Commentary versus Edition[35]

Commentaries are sometimes published separately as independent works and sometimes published along with the text of the original work. In the latter case, the subject headings assigned vary, depending on whether the work as a whole is treated as a commentary or as an edition. The decision on treating such a work as a commentary or an edition generally parallels the decision made in descriptive cataloging according to *AACR2*. If main entry is under the author or the uniform title of the original work, it is treated as an edition. On the other hand, if main entry is under the name of the commentator, it is treated as a commentary.

---

*Boroughs of New York (N.Y.) are treated as city sections.

Commentaries on individual works*

To a commentary on an individual work, two types of headings are assigned: (1) a name/title heading (or uniform title for a work entered under title) for the original work and (2) the same topical headings that were assigned to the original work. Examples of subject headings assigned to commentaries include:

Title: *Marx's Capital: Philosophy and Political Economy* /
      Geoffrey Pilling
1.   **Marx, Karl, 1818-1883.   Kapital.**
2.   **Capital.**
3.   **Economics.**

Title: *The Involuntary Conversion of a 727 or Crash! Some
      Ways and Means to Deflate the Inflated Style with a
      New Look at Orwell's "Politics and the English Lan-
      guage"* / by Flossie Lewis
1.   **English language — Style — Addresses, essays, lectures.**
2.   **Orwell, George, 1903-1950.   Politics and the English
      language.**

Title: *On Set: A Personal Story in Photographs and Words* /
      Arlene Alda
1.   **Four Seasons (Motion picture : 1981)**

Title: *ISBD(S), What It Is Today and How It Got There* / by
      Randall K. Barry
1.   **Cataloging of serial publications.**
2.   **International Standard Bibliographic Description for
      Serials.**

The title in the subject entry is the uniform title, and not necessarily the title as it appears in the commentary. The reason for using the uniform title is to group together all commentaries about a particular work regardless of variant titles or titles in the different languages under which the work has appeared. The topical headings used are those that have been assigned to the original work. They are used even if the commentary does not contain the original text. If, however, the commentary consists purely of textual criticism (i.e., commentary on the text as text and not the substantive matter of the original work) the topical headings assigned to the original work are not assigned. If the headings assigned to the original work are used only as form headings, they are converted to their most appropriate topical equivalents when used for commentaries:

---

*Commentaries on certain types of literary works receive special treatment. For a discussion of these, see pages 269-272. For works about sacred scriptures and liturgical works, see pages 301-302 and 304.

France — History — Fiction [Form heading]
France in literature [Topical equivalent]

Agriculture — Periodicals [Form heading]
Agriculture — Periodicals — History [Topical equivalent]

Editions of works[36]

It is the policy of the Library of Congress to assign to each new edition of a work previously cataloged the same subject headings as were assigned to the original edition, provided that the contents of the new edition do not vary significantly from the original. Different and/or additional headings are assigned if variations in content are significant.

If the edition (the term *edition* includes issues, reprints, and translations, but not adaptations) of a work contains a substantial amount (at least 20 percent of the text) of commentary, a subject entry in the form of [**Name. Title**] or [**Uniform title**] is made, even though it may duplicate the main entry or an added entry of the work:

> Title: *The Riddle of Shakespeare's Sonnets: The Text of the*
> *Sonnets, with Interpretive Essays by Edward Hubler*
> [main entry under Shakespeare]
> 1. **Shakespeare, William, 1564-1616. Sonnets — Addresses, essays, lectures.**
> 2. **Sonnets, English — History and criticism — Addresses, essays, lectures.**

Supplements to Individual Works

The same subject headings assigned to the original work are used for its separately published supplementary works. If a supplement treats other topics as well, additional headings are assigned. Examples include:

> Title: *Speech Index. Fourth Edition* / Roberta Briggs Sutton
> 1. **Speeches, addresses, etc. — Indexes.**
> 2. **Orations — Indexes.**
> 3. **American orations — Indexes.**

> Title: *Speech Index. Fourth Edition Supplement* / Charity
> Mitchell
> 1. **Speeches, addresses, etc. — Indexes.**
> 2. **Orations — Indexes.**
> 3. **American orations — Indexes.**
> I. Sutton, Roberta Briggs. Speech index. Fourth edition supplement.

Indexes to Individual Works

Two types of headings are assigned to an index of an individual work: [Name. Title] — Indexes; [Same heading assigned to original work] — Indexes. Examples include:

Title: *Index to Paolo Sioli's 1883 History of El Dorado County, California*
1. Sioli, Paolo. Historical souvenir of El Dorado County, California — Indexes.
2. El Dorado County (Calif.) — History — Indexes.
3. El Dorado County (Calif.) — Biography — Indexes.
4. El Dorado County (Calif.) — Genealogy — Indexes.

Title: *Alphabetical Index to Stud Books*
1. American Quarter Horse Association. Official stud book and registry — Indexes.
2. Quarter horse — Indexes.
3. Horses — Stud-books — Indexes.

Title: *Library Guide to Encyclopaedia Britannica, 15th Edition*
1. New Encyclopedia Britannica — Indexes.
2. Encyclopedias and dictionaries — Indexes.

Title: *American Library Resources Cumulative Index, 1870-1970*
1. Downs, Robert B. (Robert Bingham), 1903-   . American library resources — Indexes.
2. Bibliography — Bibliography — Indexes.
3. Library resources — United States — Indexes.

Title: *Agricultural Journal Titles and Abbreviations*
                [an index of titles listed in *Bibliography of Agriculture with Subject Index*]
1. Bibliography of agriculture with subject index — Indexes.
2. Agriculture — Periodicals — Indexes.
3. Periodicals — Abbreviations of titles.

REFERENCES

[1] "The Subdivision 'Periodicals,' " *Cataloging Service Bulletin* 3:14-15 (Winter 1979).

[2] Jean M. Perreault, "Library of Congress Subject Headings: A New Manual," *International Classification* 6:159 (1979).

[3] Library of Congress, Subject Cataloging Division, *Subject Cataloging Manual: Subject Headings*, prelim. ed. (Washington, D.C.: Library of Congress, 1984), H1425.

[4]Ibid.

[5]Ibid., H1205.

[6]Ibid., H1670.

[7]Ibid., H1325.

[8]Ibid., H1322.

[9]Ibid., H1361.

[10]Ibid., H1965.

[11]Ibid., H1660.

[12]Ibid., H1670.

[13]Ibid., H1570.

[14]Ibid., H1980.

[15]Ibid., H1360.

[16]Ibid., H1540.

[17]Ibid., H1646.

[18]Ibid., H1690; "Subject Cataloging of Juvenile Materials," *Cataloging Service Bulletin* 19:5-9 (Winter 1982); "Children's Literature Subject Headings," *Cataloging Service Bulletin* 20:45-46 (Spring 1983).

[19]"Library of Congress Subject Headings in Microfiche, 1983- ," *Cataloging Service Bulletin* 25:82 (Summer 1984).

[20]Library of Congress, *Subject Cataloging Manual*, H1780, H1790, H1800.

[21]"Intellectual Level of Films" and "Juvenile Films and Sound Recordings," *Cataloging Service Bulletin* 19:6, 8 (Winter 1982).

[22]"Biography in Subject Heading Practice," *Cataloging Service Bulletin* 22:59-67 (Fall 1983); Library of Congress, *Subject Cataloging Manual*, H1330.

[23]Library of Congress, *Subject Cataloging Manual*, H1480.

[24]Ibid., H1928.

[25]Ibid., H350.

[26]Ibid., H1574.

[27]Ibid., H1155.4.

[28]Ibid., H1480.

[29]Ibid., H1330; "Partial Biography," *Cataloging Service Bulletin* 22:64-65 (Fall 1983).

[30]Library of Congress, *Subject Cataloging Manual*, H1600.

[31]Ibid., H1720; "Legends and Stories about Animals," *Cataloging Service Bulletin* 16:64 (Spring 1982).

[32]Library of Congress, *Subject Cataloging Manual*, H184.

[33]Ibid., H1334, H1334.5.

[34]Material distributed at Regional Institutes on Library of Congress Subject Headings, sponsored by ALA Resources and Technical Services Division, Library of Congress, and ALA/RTSD Council of Regional Groups, 1982-1984.

[35]Library of Congress, *Subject Cataloging Manual*, H1435.

[36]Ibid., H175.

10

SUBJECT AREAS REQUIRING SPECIAL TREATMENT

LITERATURE

Types of Headings[1]

The four types of headings used for works in the field of literature (belles lettres) are listed below.

Literary form headings

1) Headings representing literary forms or genres. Examples include: **Drama; Poetry; Fiction; Romances; Satire.**

2) Headings indicating language or nationality. Examples include: **American literature; Japanese literature; French literature; Hindu literature. English literature** is the pattern heading for subdivisions (see appendix D).

When the language and the nationality of a specific body of literature are represented by two different terms, or when a body of literature within a country is written in a nonindigenous language, one must choose which term to feature in the heading, the one for the language or the one for the nationality or place. Over the years, both approaches have been taken by the Library of Congress, e.g., **French literature – Belgian authors; Algerian poetry (French).** Current policy favors stressing country or region, with the nationality term first and the name of the language appearing as a parenthetical qualifier. With such headings, a *see* reference is routinely made from the alternative approach:

Israeli poetry (English)
    x English poetry – Israeli authors

Moroccan literature (French)
    x French literature – Moroccan authors

New headings are established according to the pattern above, and many headings of the type **[Language] literature – [Nationality] authors** have been changed to the current pattern. Nevertheless, a number of headings like **English literature – Chinese authors** remain in *Library of Congress Subject Headings* and continue to be used.

An exception is made for the literatures of Arabic-speaking countries. The Arabic literature of a particular country is represented by the heading **Arabic literature** with a local subdivision, and a *see* reference is made from the alternative form:

> **Arabic literature – Algeria**
>   *x*   Algerian literature (Arabic)

The writings of authors belonging to particular nonlinguistic subgroups within a country (e.g., Jewish authors, Catholic authors, women authors) are designated by means of a subdivision under the pertinent literature, e.g., **South African literature (English) – Women authors**. Literature written in a language indigenous to a country is represented by the literature heading without qualifiers, e.g., **Urdu literature**. When the use of an indigenous language by a subgroup extends to neighboring countries or areas, local subdivisions are added, e.g., **Urdu literature – South India**.

3) Headings that combine language/nationality and form. Examples include **American poetry; English drama (Comedy); Epic poetry, Italian; Prose poems, American; French drama; African drama (English); Ghanaian poetry (English)**. The heading **English literature** serves as the pattern heading for subdivisions that may be used under headings for individual literatures and under genres of those literatures, e.g., **Swedish literature; French drama; German essays; Epic poetry, Finnish; Short stories, Chinese**; etc. A list of these free-floating subdivisions appears in appendix D. Period subdivisions listed under the pattern heading are not used under headings for minor genres (i.e., genres other than fiction, drama, poetry, essays, and prose literature) or inverted headings, and they are not free-floating under headings with qualifiers, e.g., **Nigerian fiction (English)**. Needless to say, period subdivisions that are unique to English literature (e.g., **– Restoration, 1660-1700**) are not used under headings for other literatures. Period subdivisions that are unique to a particular literature are established and listed under the appropriate heading in the printed list.

Topical headings representing themes, characters, or features in literary works

For works about literature the following types of headings are used:

[Topic or **Name (other than personal)] in literature**
[Personal name] in fiction, drama, poetry, etc.

For literary works the following types of headings are used:

> [Topic or Name*] — Drama
> [Topic or Name*] — Fiction
> [Topic or Name*] — Literary collections
> [Topic or Name*] — Poetry
> [Name of literary author] in fiction, drama, poetry, etc.

Examples include:

> **Animals in literature**
> **Characters and characteristics in literature**
> **Shakespeare, William, 1564-1616, in fiction, drama, poetry, etc.**
> **Lincoln, Abraham, 1809-1865, in fiction, drama, poetry, etc.**
>
> **Lincoln, Abraham, 1809-1865 — Drama**
> **Animals — Poetry**
> **World War, 1939-1945 — Literary collections**
> **Bangladesh — History — Revolution, 1971 — Fiction**
> **Lewis, C. S. (Clive Staples), 1898-1963, in fiction, drama, poetry, etc.**

Headings combining form and topic

Examples include:

> **Christmas plays**
> **Patriotic poetry**
> **Detective and mystery stories, English**
> **Western stories**

Other topical headings

Examples include:

> **Criticism, Textual**
> **Literary forgeries and mystifications**
> **Literature — Research**
> **Literature and medicine**
> **Literature and society**
> **Religion and literature**

Application[2]

In literature there are two categories of works requiring different treatment: (1) literary works (or specimens) and (2) works *about* literature in general and *about* individual authors and/or their works. The treatment of the two categories is described in the following pages.

---

*Includes geographic, personal (except literary authors), and corporate names.

Literary works

Collections of two or more independent works by different authors

1) *Literary form headings.* Literary form headings are assigned to collections of two or more independent works by different authors:

Title: *Leaving the Bough: 50 American Poets of the 80s*
1. **American poetry — 20th century.**

Title: *The Third Coast: Contemporary Michigan Fiction*
1. **American fiction — Michigan.**
2. **American fiction — 20th century.**

Title: *Elements of Fiction: An Anthology*
1. **Fiction — 19th century.**
2. **Fiction — 20th century.**

Title: *Center Stage: An Anthology of 21 Contemporary Black-American Plays*
1. **American drama — 20th century.**
2. **American drama — Afro-American authors.**

Title: *Poems of Sentiment & Inspiration*
1. **American poetry.**
2. **English poetry.**

When the works in a collection belong to a minor literary form and the form heading has no provision for period subdivisions, a second, broader form heading with the appropriate period subdivision is also assigned in order to represent the time aspect:

Title: *Moralités françaises*
1. **Moralities, French.**
2. **French drama — To 1500.**

Title: *Five Elizabethan Tragedies*
1. **English drama — Early modern and Elizabethan, 1500-1600.**
2. **English drama (Tragedy)**

Title: *A Reader of New American Fiction*
1. **American fiction — 20th century.**
2. **Short stories, American.**

Note that the free-floating subdivision — **Collected works** is not used with literary form headings. The qualifiers (Collections) and (Selections, Extracts, etc.) represent previous practice and are no longer used. Headings such as American poetry (Collections) and French literature (Selections, Extracts, etc.) are now obsolete. The subdivision — **Collections*** may be used under the

---

*The subdivision — **Collections** is not free-floating. The only other headings that may be subdivided by it are **Autographs; Charters; Manuscripts; Playbills; Treaties.**

following literary headings only: **Drama; Fiction; Literature; Poetry:**

Title: *Literature from the World*
    1. **Literature — Collections.**

Title: *The Norton Introduction to Poetry*
    1. **Poetry — Collections.**

2) *Topical headings.* If the collection is centered on a theme, a person, a place, or an event, a topical heading subdivided by either the subdivision — **Literary collections** (when the works in the collection are written in two or more literary forms) or one of the major literary forms (— **Drama;** — **Fiction;** — **Poetry**),* is assigned in addition to the appropriate literary form heading(s). The form subdivisions — **Drama;** — **Fiction;** — **Poetry;** are used under an identifiable topic for a collection of literary works on that topic. However, topical headings are not assigned to collections on vague and general topics such as fate, belief, malaise, mankind, etc. Examples include:

Title: *Le madri*
    1. **Mothers — Literary collections.**
    2. **Italian literature — 20th century.**

Title: *Eight Plays for Hand Puppets about George Washington*
    1. **Puppets and puppet-plays.**
    2. **Washington, George, 1732-1799 — Drama.****

Title: *Golf Story Omnibus*
    1. **Short stories, American.**
    2. **Golf — Fiction.**

Title: *The Penguin Book of Bird Poetry*
    1. **Birds — Poetry.**
    2. **English poetry.**

Title: *Enter the Heart of the Fire: A Collection of Mystical Poems*
    1. **Mysticism — Poetry.**
    2. **American poetry — 20th century.**

Title: *On the Line: New Gay Fiction*
    1. **Homosexuality — Fiction.**
    2. **Short stories, American — Men authors.**

Title: *The Poets of Prince Edward Island*
    1. **Canadian poetry — Prince Edward Island.**
    2. **Canadian poetry — 20th century.**
    3. **Prince Edward Island — Poetry.**

---

*The subdivision — Stories has been discontinued. However, there still exist a few phrase headings that are used for certain kinds of stories, e.g., **Sea stories; Detective and mystery stories.**

For literary anthologies *about* an individual literary author, the phrase heading [Name of author] in fiction, drama, poetry, etc.** is used regardless of the literary form(s).

Title: *Gestohlene Märchen*
   1. **German literature — 20th century.**
   2. **Robbery — Literary collections.**

Title: *A Book of Railway Journeys*
   1. **Railroad travel — Literary collections.**
   2. **English literature.**
   3. **American literature.**
   4. **Railroad travel — Addresses, essays, lectures.**

Some phrase headings combine topical and form aspects, e.g., **Detective and mystery stories, American; Science fiction, American; Sea stories; Christmas plays; Ghost plays; Political plays.** When such headings exist, they are used instead of separate topic and form headings:

Title: *Great Stories of Mystery and Suspense*
   1. **Detective and mystery stories, American.**
   2. **Detective and mystery stories, English.**

Title: *The Treasury of Christian Poetry*
   1. **Christian poetry.**

If, however, a heading is assigned for a very specific topic, the topic/form heading for a more general topic is not used. Instead, a literary form heading is assigned. For example, the following headings are assigned to a collection of American drama on the theme of Trinity:

   1. **American drama.**
      [not **Christian drama, American**]
   2. **Trinity — Drama.**

In the case of fiction about animals, the heading **Animals — Fiction** or **Animals — Juvenile fiction** is used.*

Works by individual authors**

Collected works

1) *Literary form headings.* In general, literary form headings are not assigned to collected works by an individual author. In other words, the heading **English drama — Early modern and Elizabethan, 1500-1600** is not used with the complete plays of Shakespeare. However, there are two exceptions to

---

*The subdivision — Legends and stories previously used under types of animals is no longer valid. The subdivision — **Folklore** is now used under the heading **Animals** or type of animal (e.g., **Dogs**) for one or more legends about them. The subdivision — **Anecdotes** is used for anecdotal accounts, and the subdivision — **Biography** is used for true accounts about animals.

**Works by joint authors, such as *The Maid's Tragedy* by Beaumont and Fletcher, are treated in the same manner as works by individual authors.

this general rule. The literary form heading is assigned if it combines form and topic in one heading, such as **Western stories; Detective and mystery plays; Sea poetry, English; Love poetry; War poetry:**

Title: *Reveillon* / Hilaire Belloc
   1. Christmas stories.

The form heading is also assigned if the form is highly specific, such as **Allegories; Fables; Fairy tales; Radio stories; Amateur theatricals; Carnival plays; Children's plays; College and school drama; Didactic drama; Radio plays; Sonnets, American; Concrete poetry:**

Title: *Children's Plays from Beatrix Potter* / dramatized by Rona
   Laurie
   1. Children's plays, English.

Headings of the following types are *not* considered to be "highly specific": **American fiction; Short stories; Tales; English drama; English drama (Comedy); Comedy; Farces; Melodrama; One-act plays; Tragedy; Tragicomedy; English diaries.**

  2) *Topical headings.* If the works in the collection are centered on an identifiable topic or based on an event or on the life of an individual, a topical heading with an appropriate literary form subdivision (— **Fiction;*** — **Drama;*** — **Poetry;*** — **Literary collections**) is assigned. A phrase heading combining form and topic is used if it is available. Topical headings are not usually assigned for vague and general topics such as fate, mankind, belief, malaise, etc. Examples include:

Title: *Night of the Broken Glass: Poems of the Holocaust* / Emily
   Borenstein
   1. Holocaust, Jewish (1939-1945) — Poetry.

Title: *Children of Lir: Stories from Ireland* / by Desmond Hogan
   1. Ireland — Fiction.

---

*The subdivisions — **Juvenile fiction;** — **Juvenile drama;** — **Juvenile poetry** are used for juvenile works of belles lettres. Note also specific juvenile headings such as **Children's stories; Nursery rhymes**; etc. For literature written for children, see discussion on pages 219-220.

Individual works

1) *Literary form headings.* Headings representing major literary forms, such as **English drama** and **American fiction,** are not assigned to individual literary works. However, form headings of the types listed below are used.

a) Form headings for children's literature, i.e., **Children's plays, American, [English, etc.]; Children's poetry, American, [English, etc.];** and **Children's stories, American, [English, etc.],*** are assigned to individual literary works for children:

Title: *The Night before Christmas* / by Clement C. Moore
    1.   Santa Claus—Juvenile poetry.
    2.   Christmas—Juvenile poetry.
    3.   Children's poetry, American.

Title: *Mean Jack and the Devils* / by William H. Hooks
    1.   Children's stories, American.

b) Form headings that include a topical aspect, such as **Detective and mystery plays, American, [English, etc.]; War poetry, American, [English, etc.],** are assigned to individual works of drama and poetry, but not to individual works of fiction:

Title: *A Christmas Carol* / dramatized by Darwin Reid Payne
    1.   Christmas plays.

c) Headings representing highly specific forms, such as **Carnival plays; Nonsense verses; Nursery rhymes, American, [English, etc.],** are assigned to individual works of drama and poetry, but not to individual works of fiction:

Title: *Mary Had a Little Lamb*
    1.   Nursery rhymes, American.
    2.   Children's poetry, American.
    3.   Lambs—Juvenile poetry.
    [1.   Nursery rhymes.
    2.   American poetry]

---

*Not assigned to fiction for young adults.

2) *Topical headings.* An individual work of drama or poetry that focuses on an identifiable topic or is based on the life of a person is assigned a topical or name heading with the subdivision —**Poetry** or —**Drama.** Such headings are not assigned for very general or vague topics such as mankind, fate, belief, malaise, etc. Examples include:

Title: *Two Strikes: A Baseball Comedy in Two Acts*
    1. **Baseball — Drama.**

Title: *The Bridge of Change* / John Logan
    1. **Paris (France) — Poetry.**

Title: *Relics Recycled on Cloud Nine* / Margaret R. Otis
    1. **Retirement — Poetry.**

Title: *Animal Sketches* / by John Winthrop
    1. **Animals — Poetry.**

Title: *December: A Christmas Poem* / by Dorothy Schuchman
    1. **Christmas — Poetry.**

Title: *The Anniversaries* / by John Donne
    1. **Drury, Elizabeth, d. 1610 — Poetry.**

Title: *Mister Lincoln: A Drama in Two Acts* / by Herbert
        Mitgang
    1. **Lincoln, Abraham, 1809-1865 — Drama.**

For an imaginary work based on a literary author's life, the phrase heading [**Author's name**] **in fiction, drama, poetry, etc.** is used. A heading such as Shakespeare, William, 1564-1616 — Poetry is not used because it may be interpreted to mean a work about Shakespeare's poetry. An example is:

Title: *Childe Byron: A Play in Two Acts* / by Romulus Linney
    1. **Byron, George Gordon Byron, Baron, 1788-1824, in fiction, drama, poetry, etc.**

For individual works of fiction, topical headings are assigned to biographical fiction, historical fiction, and animal stories only, as delineated below.

    a) For biographical fiction, examples include:

Title: *November 22* / Bryan Woolley
    1. **Kennedy, John F. (John Fitzgerald), 1917-1963 — Fiction.**

Title: *Charlie in the House of Rue* / Robert Coover
    1. **Chaplin, Charlie, 1889-1917 — Fiction.**

Title: *Jesus Tales: A Novel* / by Romulus Linney
    1. **Jesus Christ — Fiction.**

Title: *Miss Nobody* / Caroline Ross
1. **Charles, Prince of Wales, 1948-   — Fiction.**

Title: *Mermaid Tavern: Kit Marlowe's Story* / by George
        William Cronym
1. **Marlowe, Christopher, 1564-1593, in fiction, drama,
   poetry, etc.**

b) A heading representing the specific historical event or period with the subdivision **— Fiction** is assigned to a historical novel or story. The topical heading is *not* assigned when the event or period is merely the backdrop to the actual story; it is assigned only when the event or period is the principal focus of the work. Examples include:

Title: *The Texans* / David Larry Hicks, Dan Parkinson
1. **Texas — History — To 1846 — Fiction.**

Title: *Suicide Most Foul* / J.G. Jeffreys
1. **Waterloo, Battle of, 1815 — Fiction.**

Title: *War Time Romances of Sailors* / John Drew
1. **World War, 1939-1945 — Fiction.**

c) For a fictional work about a particular kind of animal or animals in general,[3] a heading in the form of **[Kind of animal] — Fiction*** or **Animals — Fiction** is assigned:

Title: *Spotty*
1. **Dogs — Fiction.**

Medieval legends and romances

The texts of pre-1501 European legends and romances and of all non-European legends and romances require topical headings consisting of the name of the historical or legendary person, object, etc., subdivided by **— Legends** or **— Romances:****

Alexius, Saint — Legends
Faust, d. ca. 1540 — Legends
Grail — Legends
Charlemagne, Emperor, 742-814 — Romances
Arthurian romances
     [an exception to the usual form, which would be Arthur,
     King — Romances]

---

*See footnote on page 259.
For a distinction between the subdivisions **— Legends and **— Romances**, see scope notes in *Library of Congress Subject Headings: A Guide to Subdivision Practice* (1981).

These headings are assigned to all works containing texts of legends or romances, regardless of whether the work in hand represents a complete cycle or a single legend or romance:

Title: *Perceval, or, The Story of the Grail*
1. **Perceval — Romances.**
2. **Grail — Legends.**

Title: *Aiquin, ou, La Conquête de la Bretagne par le roi Charlemagne*
1. **Charlemagne, Emperor, 742-814 — Romances.**

These headings are also used for modern versions of legends and romances of medieval origin in which the characters and plots remain essentially unaltered:

Title: *The Magic Cup: An Irish Legend*
1. **Grail — Legends.**

In other words, the subdivisions **— Legends** and **— Romances** take precedence over the subdivisions **— Fiction**, **— Drama**, and **— Poetry**, which would normally be used for works of this kind written after 1501. Examples include:

Title: *Tales of King Arthur* / Sir Thomas Malory
1. **Arthurian romances**
      [not Arthur, King — Poetry]

Title: *Le voyage de Charlemagne à Jérusalem et à Constantinople: traduction critiquée*
1. **Charlemagne, Emperor, 742-814 — Romances.**

For the treatment of works *about* legends and romances, see page 272.

Works about literature

Works about literature exclusive of those about individual authors and their works are assigned headings that represent their subject content:

Title: *A Critical Theory of Literature*
1. **Literature.**

Title: *Semiotics and Interpretation*
1. **Criticism.**
2. **Semiotics and literature.**

Title: *Modern Literature Theory: A Comparative Introduction*
1. **Criticism — History — 20th century.**

If the work focuses on a particular literature or form, one or more literary form headings with the subdivision **— History and criticism** are assigned:

Title: *Eros Sophistes: Ancient Novelists at Play*
1. **Classical fiction — History and criticism.**

Title: *The Interlingual Critic: Interpreting Chinese Poetry*
1. **Chinese poetry — History and criticism.**
2. **Criticism.**

Title: *African Language Literatures: An Introduction to the Literary History of Sub-Saharan Africa*
1. **African literature — History and criticism.**

The subdivision **— History and criticism** may be further subdivided:

Title: *The English Novel: Twentieth Century Criticism*
1. **English fiction — History and criticism — Bibliography.**

Title: *Vision and Refuge: Essays on the Literature of the Great Plains*
1. **American fiction — History and criticism — Addresses, essays, lectures.**
2. **Great Plains in literature — Addresses, essays, lectures.**

Title: *The Great American Poetry Bake-Off, Second Series*
1. **American poetry — 20th century — History and criticism — Collected works.**

As noted earlier, the heading **English literature** serves as the pattern heading for subdivisions that may be used under headings for individual literatures and under genres of those literatures, e.g., **Swedish literature; French drama; German essays; Epic poetry, Finnish; Short stories, Chinese.** A list of these free-floating subdivisions appears in appendix D.

Frequently, when a work deals with a minor form of a particular period but the relevant literary form heading has no provision for period subdivisions, a second, broader heading with the appropriate period subdivision is also assigned:

Title: *Tragic Drama and Modern Society*
1. **Tragedy — History and criticism.**
2. **Drama — 19th century — History and criticism.**
3. **Drama — 20th century — History and criticism.**

Title: *Realismus in mittelalterlicher Literatur*
1. **German poetry — Middle High German, 1050-1500 — History and criticism.**
2. **Epic poetry, German — History and criticism.**
3. **Realism in literature.**

For discussions about particular themes with regard to a particular literature and/or form, paired headings are assigned: literary form heading(s) (with the subdivision —**History and criticism**) and topical heading(s) (usually in combination with the phrase **in literature**):*

> Title: *Portrait of an American City: The Novelists' New York*
>   1. **American fiction — History and criticism.**
>   2. **New York (N.Y.) in literature.**

> Title: *The Theatre of the Absurd*
>   1. **Drama — 20th century — History and criticism.**
>   2. **Absurd (Philosophy) in literature.**

> Title: *Fiction and Repetition: Seven English Novels*
>   1. **English fiction — History and criticism.**
>   2. **Repetition in literature.**
>   3. **Fiction — Technique.**

> Title: *A Negative Heritage: Images of the Indian in English-*
>   *Canadian Literature*
>   1. **Canadian literature — History and criticism.**
>   2. **Indians of North America in literature.**
>   3. **Indians of North America — Canada — History.**

For discussions of the theme of wars in literature, the headings assigned are in the form of [**Name of war**] — **Literature and the war, [revolution, etc.]:**

> Title: *Heroes' Twilight: A Study of the Literature of the Great War*
>   1. **World War, 1914-1918 — Literature and the war.**
>   2. **English literature — 20th century — History and criticism.**

A heading that combines form and topic may also be subdivided by —**History and criticism**, e.g., **Detective and mystery stories, American — History and criticism; Religious drama — History and criticism.** An example is:

> Title: *The English Poets of the First World War*
>   1. **English poetry — 20th century — History and criticism.**
>   2. **World War, 1914-1918 — Literature and the war.**
>   3. **War poetry, English — History and criticism.**
>   4. **Poets, English — 20th century — Biography.**

For a work that discusses the portrayal of a person (including literary authors) in literature, a heading in the form of [**Name of person**] **in fiction, drama, poetry, etc.** is assigned in addition to one or more literary form headings:

---

*[**Topic**] **in literature** is a free-floating form, i.e., any existing heading may be used with the phrase **in literature** to form a heading.

Title: *Images of a Queen, Mary Stuart in Sixteenth Century*
          Literature / by J.E. Phillips
    1.   **Mary Stuart, Queen of the Scots, 1542-1587, in fiction,**
         drama, poetry, etc.
    2.   **Literature, Modern — 15th and 16th centuries — History**
         and criticism.

The history and criticism of medieval legends and romances* (and
indexes, concordances, etc., to them) require a topical heading subdivided by
— **History and criticism;** — **Dictionaries;** — **Indexes**, or whatever other
subdivision is appropriate:

Title: *The Grail: Quest for the Eternal*
    1.   **Grail — Legends — History and criticism.**

Title: *Doctor Faustus: From History to Legend*
    1.   **Faust, d. ca. 1540 — Legends — History and criticism.**

Title: *Charlemagne et l'épopée romance*
    1.   **Charlemagne, Emperor, 742-814 — Romances — History**
         and criticism.

Title: *An Index of Proper Names in French Arthurian Verse*
          Romances
    1.   **Arthurian romances — Indexes.**

Works about individual authors**

Works about individual authors are assigned headings in the form of the
name of the author with appropriate subdivisions. The heading **Shakespeare,**
William, 1564-1616 serves as the model heading for subdivisions; the
subdivisions listed under it may be used under any literary author, as
appropriate. This is the reason why a number of subdivisions not applicable to
Shakespeare are listed under his name, e.g., — **Biography — Exile**. The
Shakespeare list showing subdivisions for use under literary authors is
included in appendix D. Examples of works about individual authors include:

Title: *Jane Austen in a Social Context*
    1.   **Austen, Jane, 1775-1817 — Political and social views**
         — **Addresses, essays, lectures.**
    2.   **Social problems in literature — Addresses, essays, lectures.**

Title: *Dickens and Religion*
    1.   **Dickens, Charles, 1812-1870 — Religion.**
    2.   **Religion in literature.**

---

*For works about an individual legend or romance, see discussion on pages 270 and 272.
**For works about an individual literary work, see discussion on pages 269-272.

Title: *Cervantes: Bulletin of the Cervantes Society of America*
1. **Cervantes Saaverda, Miguel de, 1547-1616 — Periodicals.**

For a work of criticism and/or interpretation of an author's works,* a heading in the form of the name of the author with the subdivision — **Criticism and interpretation,** or another, more specific subdivision, is assigned:

Title: *A George Eliot Companion: Literary Achievement and Modern Significance*
1. **Eliot, George, 1819-1880 — Criticism and interpretation.**

Title: *T. S. Eliot and the Romantic Critical Tradition*
1. **Eliot, T. S. (Thomas Stearns), 1888-1965 — Knowledge — Literature.**
2. **Criticism.**
3. **Romanticism.**

If the work contains biographical information as well as criticism of the author's literary efforts, two headings are assigned: the name of the author without subdivision, and a biographical heading:[4]

Title: *The Life and Works of David Lindsay*
1. **Lindsay, David, 1876-1945.**
2. **Novelists, English — 20th century — Biography.**

Title: *Ben Jonson*
1. **Jonson, Ben, 1573?-1637.**
2. **Dramatists, English — Early modern, 1500-1700 — Biography.**

To a true biography of a literary author, two headings are assigned: the name of the author subdivided by — **Biography,** as well as the biographical heading:

Title: *K, A Biography of Kafka*
1. **Kafka, Franz, 1883-1924 — Biography.**
2. **Authors, Austrian — 20th century — Biography.**

Title: *Young Charles Lamb, 1775-1802*
1. **Lamb, Charles, 1775-1834 — Biography — Youth.**
2. **Authors, English — 19th century — Biography.**

In the case of a partial biography or a biography in a special form, the two required headings specified above with appropriate subdivisions are assigned:

---

*For works about an individual literary work, see discussion on pages 269-272.

Title: "The Theatre We Worked For": The Letters of Eugene
         O'Neill to Kenneth Macgowan
   1. O'Neill, Eugene, 1888-1953 — Correspondence.
   2. Macgowan, Kenneth, 1888-1963 — Correspondence.
   3. Dramatists, American — 20th century — Correspondence.

Title: Heimweh nach Deutschland: ein Lesebuch / Godehard
         Schramm
   1. Schramm, Godehard, 1943-   — Journeys.
   2. Authors, German — 20th century — Biography.

Title: The Heart of Boswell: Six Journals in One Volume
   1. Boswell, James, 1740-1795 — Diaries.
   2. Authors, Scottish — 18th century — Diaries.

To ensure consistency in treatment, the Library of Congress uses a general guideline for distinguishing between biography and criticism. This is diagrammed in Figure 10.1.

Assign: 1. [Author] — Criticism and interpretation	Assign: 1. [Author] 2. [Class of authors] — Biography	Assign: 1. [Author] — Biography 2. [Class of authors] — Biography
20% biography	80% biography	100% biography

Figure 10.1. Types of headings to be assigned to works
with biography-criticism mix.

Works about individual literary works

For a work about an individual literary work, a name-title subject entry is made:

Title: El gran teatro del mundo
   1. Caldéron de la Barca, Pedro, 1600-1681.   Gran teatro
       del mundo.

Title: Wilhelm Meister
   1. Goethe, Johann Wolfgang von, 1749-1836.   Wilhelm
       Meister.

For a work about an individual literary work with a special theme, an additional heading designating the theme is assigned:

Title: A Critical and Textual Study of Faulkner's A Fable
   1. Faulkner, William, 1897-1962.   Fable.
   2. World War, 1914-1918 — Literature and the war.

If appropriate, the following subdivisions may be used with the subject entry [Name. Title]:[5]

- Addresses, essays, lectures
- Bibliography
- Concordances
- Congresses
- Criticism, Textual
- Exhibitions
- Illustrations
- Indexes
- Juvenile films
- Juvenile literature
- Juvenile sound recordings
- Sources

An example is:

Title: *Essays on Camus's Exile and the Kingdom*
    1. **Camus, Albert, 1913-1960. L'exil et le royaume**
      — Addresses, essays, lectures.

If the original work is entered under title, as in the case of anonymous or multiauthored works, the subject entry consists of the uniform title:

Title: *Scheherazade in England: A Study of Nineteenth Century English Criticism of the Arabian Nights*
    1. **Arabian nights.**

Title: *The Fortunate Fall of Sir Gawain: The Typology of Sir Gawain and the Green Knight*
    1. **Gawain and the Grene Knight.**
    2. **Fall of man in literature.**
    3. **Salvation in literature.**
    4. **Typology (Theology) in literature.**

The uniform title may be subdivided by the following free-floating subdivisions when appropriate:[6]

- Addresses, essays, lectures
- Authorship
- Bibliography
- Characters
- Concordances
- Congresses
- Critical, Textual
- Dictionaries
- Dramatic production
- Exhibitions
- Illustrations
- Indexes

—Juvenile films
—Juvenile literature
—Juvenile sound recordings
—Language
—Language—Glossaries, etc.
—Manuscripts
—Parodies, travesties, etc.
—Periodicals
—Sources
—Style
—Translations
—Translations, French, [German, etc.]
—Versification

The subdivision —**Criticism and interpretation** is not used under name-title or uniform title heading for a literary work. For a work of general criticism and interpretation or a discussion combining the approaches represented by several of these subdivisions, the name-title or uniform title heading for the literary work *without* subdivision is assigned. If another aspect of the work not represented in the lists is to be brought out, a separate heading is assigned in addition to the name-title or uniform title heading:

Title: *Middlemarch from Notebook to Novel: A Story of George Eliot's Creative Method*
1.   **Eliot, George, 1819-1880.   Middlemarch.**
2.   **Eliot, George, 1819-1880—Technique.**

Title: *Faust zweiter Teil: die Allegorie des 19. Jahrhunderts*
1.   **Goethe, Johann Wolfgang von, 1749-1832.   Faust. 2. Teil.**
2.   **Goethe, Johann Wolfgang von, 1749-1832—Symbolism.**

For an index to a literary work, the following types of headings are used:

[Name.   Title]—Indexes.
[Name of author]—Dictionaries, indexes, etc.

An example is:

Title: *Index of Recurrent Elements in James Joyce's Ulysses*
1.   **Joyce, James, 1882-1941.   Ulysses—Indexes.**
2.   **Joyce, James, 1882-1941—Dictionaries, indexes, etc.**

If the original work is entered under the title, a heading in the form of **[Uniform title]—Indexes** is assigned:

Title: *Type-Index and Motif-Index of the Roman de Renard*
1.   **Roman de Renart—Indexes.**

Works about individual medieval legends and romances

To a work that discusses a single legend or romance, or a specific version of it, two headings are assigned: the catalog entry for the specific legend or romance (i.e., the uniform title or the name-title entry) and the form heading subdivided by — **History and criticism** or another appropriate subdivision:

Title: *Le pèlerinage de Charlemagne: sources et paralleles* / by
        Frances James Carmody
  1. **Charlemagne, Emperor, 742-814.   Voyage à Jerusalem et à Constantinople.**
  2. **Charlemagne, Emperor, 742-814 — Romances — History and criticism.**

Title: *Le haut livre du Graal, Perlesvaus*
  1. **Perlesvaus.**
  2. **Grail — Legends — History and criticism.**

MUSIC

Types of Headings

Various types of headings are used in the subject cataloging of music. Some represent music in general; others indicate various kinds or aspects of music, such as musical form and medium of performance.

Changes and additions in headings related to music are regularly announced in the *Music Cataloging Bulletin* of the Music Library Association and are incorporated into the *Library of Congress Subject Headings*. Current Library of Congress policies and practice regarding subject headings used for music are discussed below.

Music headings[7]

In the past, almost all music headings were printed in *Library of Congress Subject Headings*. Beginning in the mid-1970s, the Library of Congress set up standard citation patterns for music headings with qualifiers specifying instrumental or vocal parts. With these patterns, subject catalogers could formulate such headings as required. From then on, headings so constructed have been printed in *Library of Congress Subject Headings* only when unique cross-references are required for them; thus, many valid Library of Congress subject headings for music do not appear in the printed list. By category, these are:

o   Headings for instrumental chamber music not entered under musical form

      Trios; Quartets; Quintets; etc.
      Brass trios; etc.

    String trios; etc.
    Wind trios; etc.
    Woodwind trios; etc.

o Headings for musical forms that take qualifiers for instrumental medium

    Canons, fugues, etc.
    Chaconnes
    Chorale preludes
    Marches
    Minuets
    Monologues with music
    Overtures
    Passacaglias
    Polkas
    Polonaises
    Potpourris
    Rondos
    Sacred monologues with music
    Sonatas
    Suites
    Symphonic poems
    Symphonies
    Trio-sonatas
    Variations
    Waltzes

o Certain headings for vocal music

    Choruses

    Choruses, Sacred } [qualified by number of vocal parts and
    Choruses, Secular } accompanying medium]

    Songs } [qualified by voice range and accompany-
    Sacred songs } ing medium]

When the headings in the categories listed above are qualified by instruments, the specific order of instruments is

1) keyboard instruments
2) wind instruments
3) plectral instruments
4) percussion and other instruments
5) bowed stringed instruments
6) unspecified instruments
7) continuo

Instruments within each category are given in alphabetical order, with the exception of bowed string instruments, which are given in score order, i.e., **(Violin, viola, violoncello, double bass)**. The number of each instrument, if more than one, is indicated by an arabic number enclosed in parentheses following the name of the instrument.

Headings for duets do not always follow the same citation order. All headings for duets are enumerated in the printed list because *see* references from the alternative form are required. Catalogers should consult *Library of Congress Subject Headings* for these headings.

Following are examples of unprinted headings formulated according to the established citation patterns:

Trios (Piano, clarinet, violoncello)
Trios (Oboe, harp, violoncello)
Quartets (Recorder, violins (2), continuo)
Quintets (Piano, saxophone, violin, viola, violoncello)
Octets (Pianos (2), flute, piccolo, violins (2), viola, violoncello)
Nonets (Percussion, unspecified instruments (8))
Brass sextets (Trombones (2), trumpets (3), tuba)
Woodwind trios (English horn, oboes (2))
String quintets (Violins (2), violas (2), violoncello)
Overtures (Violins (2), viola, violoncello, double bass)
Suites (Horn, trombone, trumpets (2), tuba)
Symphonic poems (Piano with orchestra)
Choruses, Sacred (Mixed voices) with instrumental ensemble
Choruses, Secular (Men's voices, 4 parts), Unaccompanied
Songs (Medium voice) with unspecified instrument

Free-floating phrase headings

The phrase heading [**Medium** or **form for instrumental music**], **Arranged** is free-floating, e.g., **Viola and piano music, Arranged**; **Sonatas (Harp), Arranged**; **Organ music, Arranged**.

Free-floating subdivisions under pattern headings

Operas and **Piano** have been designated as pattern headings for subdivisions in the field of music. The heading **Operas**[8] provides the pattern for music compositions, including headings for form, medium, style, music for special seasons or occasions, musical settings of special texts, etc., e.g., **Concertos (Oboe)**; **Trios (Piano, flute, violin)**; **Rock music**; **Easter music**; **Magnificat (Music)**. **Piano**[9] provides the pattern for musical instruments, either specific instruments or groups of instruments, e.g., **Flute**; **Wind instruments**. The free-floating subdivisions listed under **Piano** are not applicable to the general heading **Musical instruments**. Lists of free-floating subdivisions used under the headings for music compositions and musical instruments mentioned above appear in appendix D of this book.

Period subdivisions[10]

The commonly used period subdivisions under music headings are:

— To 500
— 500-1400
— 15th century
— 16th century
— 17th century
— 18th century
— 19th century
— 20th century

Period subdivisions are used for textual works about music (including headings used solely for such works, e.g., **Choral music; Symphony; Concerto;** etc.) and collections of Western art music by two or more composers emphasizing a particular period. They are *not* used for: (1) a work in which a period is emphasized only in a series statement, (2) collections of compositions by only one composer, (3) separate music compositions, or (4) folk, popular, and non-Western music.

When a collection of music has been assigned multiple headings, period subdivisions are used only under those headings that refer to the works of two or more composers.

The period subdivision is placed after the geographic subdivision and before other free-floating subdivisions:

Music — France — Paris — 19th century — History and criticism
Songs — Germany — 20th century — Bibliography
Symphonies — 20th century — Scores

The period subdivision — **To 1800** (indicating the date of publication) has been replaced by the standard free-floating subdivision — **Early works to 1800** for music literature and instruction,[11] e.g., **Music — Manuals, text-books, etc. — Early works to 1800; Chants (Plain, Gregorian, etc.) — Instruction and study — Early works to 1800.**

Patterns of references[12]

The Library of Congress has established patterns of *see also* references for the categories of music headings listed below.

Pattern headings	*Categories*
Baritone music	Brass instruments (i.e., Baritone Cornet, Euphonium, Horn, Trombone, Trumpet, and Tuba music)
Bassoon music	Woodwind instruments (i.e., Bassoon, Clarinet, English-horn, Flute, Oboe d'amore, Oboe, Piccolo, Recorder, and Saxophone music)

Pattern headings *Continued*	*Categories* *Continued*
Guitar music	Plectral instruments (i.e., Guitar, Harp, Lute, and Mandolin music)
Glockenspiel music	Percussion instruments (i.e., Glockenspiel, Kettledrum, Marimba, Vibraphone, and Xylophone music)
Celesta music	Celesta, Harpsichord, and Organ music
Double-bass music	Double-bass, Viol, Viola de gamba, Viola d'amore, and Violone music
Band music	Band, Chamber-orchestra, Dance-orchestra, String-orchestra music, and String ensembles
Accordion ensembles	Accordion ensembles and Salon-orchestra music

References for music headings in other categories are listed individually under each heading.

Topical headings with subdivisions indicating music

In addition to the music headings discussed above, other topical headings with music subdivisions are also used in cataloging music. Examples of such headings are **Fasts and feasts—Judaism—Songs and music; Germans—Texas—Music; Jesus Christ—Songs and music; Hardy, Thomas, 1840-1928—Musical settings; United States. Air Force—Songs and music—Texts; Catholic Church—Hymns.**

Application

Works in the field of music may be divided into two broad categories: (1) music scores and texts and (2) works about music. As in the field of literature, specimens and works about the subject are treated differently in subject cataloging.

Music scores and texts

Works containing scores and texts, including instrumental and vocal music, are assigned form headings (i.e., headings that describe what the works *are* rather than what the works are *about*) as appropriate.

Instrumental music

For instrumental music, subject entries are usually made to bring out the following aspects: musical form (e.g., **Canons, fugues, etc.; Overtures; Sonatas; Symphonies**), medium of performance (e.g., **Guitar music; Hu ch'in** music; **Piano music**), and performing group (e.g., **Trios; Octets; String quartets; Woodwind septets; Band music; Orchestral music**). Other topical headings with music subdivisions are also assigned as appropriate. Examples include:

Stock, David, 1939- .
   [Pieces, violin, piano]
   Three Pieces for Violin and Piano
   1. **Violin and piano music — Scores and parts.**

Berger, Jean, 1909-
   Diversions: for Keyboard (for Piano or Harpsichord)
   1. **Piano music, Juvenile.**
   2. **Harpsichord music, Juvenile.**

Schubert, Franz, 1797-1828.
   [Menuett und Finale, woodwinds, horns (2), D. 72, F major]
   Minuet and Finale in F, D. 72, for 2 Oboes, 2 Clarinets,
      2 Bassoons, and 2 Horns
   1. **Wind octets (Bassoons (2), clarinets (2), horns (2),**
       oboes (2)) — Parts.

Wilder, Alec.
   [Quintets, brasses, no. 1]
   Brass Quintet no. 1
   1. **Suites (Horn, trombone, trumpets (2), tuba)**

Mozart, Wolfgang Amadeus, 1756-1791.
   [Quintets, violins (2), violas (2), violoncello, K. Anh. 79, A minor]
   Streichquintettsatz in a-Moll, für zwei Violinen, zwei Violen
      und Violoncello, KV Anhang 79 (515c)
   1. **String quintets (Violins (2), violas (2), violoncello) — Scores**
       and parts.

Whear, Paul W.
   [Band music. Selections]
   Youngstown State University Wind Ensemble
   1. **Band music.**
   2. **Overtures (Band)**
   3. **Symphonies (Band)**

Bois, Rob du, 1934-   .
   Mir träumte von einem Königskind: für Horn und
      Klavier: 1979
   1. **Horn and piano music — Scores and parts.**
   2. **Heine, Heinrich, 1797-1856 — Musical settings.**

Vocal music

For vocal music, headings that bring out the form, voice range, number of vocal parts, and accompanying medium* are used. Typical headings for vocal music are:

o   Secular vocal music

> **Ballads**
> **Cantatas, Secular (Equal voices)**
> **Chansons, Polyphonic**
> **Choruses, Secular (Men's voices) with percussion**
> **Lieder, Polyphonic**
> **Madrigals (Music)**
> **Operas**
> **Part-songs**
> **Song cycles**
> **Songs**
>> [also headings for various kinds of songs, e.g., **Children's songs; War-songs**]
>
> **Vocal trios, Unaccompanied**

o   Sacred vocal music

> **Cantatas, Sacred (Women's voices)**
> **Carols**
> **Chants**
> **Chorales**
> **Choruses, Sacred (Mixed voices, 4 parts) with organ**
> **Hymns**
> **Masses**
> **Motets**
> **Oratorios**
> **Part-songs, Sacred**
> **Psalms (Music)**
> **Requiems (Unison)**
> **Sacred songs (Medium voice) with harpsichord**
> **Vespers (Music)**

Following are examples of subject headings assigned to works containing vocal music:

> Barab, Seymour.
>> [Moments macabres. Vocal score]
>> *Moments Macabres: For Voice and Chamber Ensemble*
>> 1.   **Songs (High voice) with instrumental ensemble—Vocal scores with piano.**
>> 2.   **Song cycles.**

---

*Medium not specified for larger works, i.e., operas, oratorios, etc.

77 Rounds and Canons
    1.   **Glees, catches, rounds, etc.**

Pinkham, Daniel.
    [Passion of Judas. Happy is the man. Vocal score]
    Happy Is the Man: (from The Passion of Judas) : for
        Mixed Chorus and Organ
    1.   **Choruses, Sacred (Mixed voices, 4 parts) with organ.**
    2.   **Choruses, Sacred (Mixed voices) with instrumental**
        ensemble — Vocal scores with organ.
    3.   **Oratorios — Excerpts — Vocal scores with organ.**
    4.   **Passion-music — Excerpts — Vocal scores with organ.**
    5.   **Psalms (Music) — 1st Psalm.**

Argento, Dominick.
    [Masque of angels. Gloria. Vocal score]
    Gloria: From the Opera The Masque of Angels
    1.   **Operas — Excerpts — Vocal scores with piano.**
    2.   **Choruses, Sacred (Mixed voices, 7 parts) with piano.**
    3.   **Choruses, Sacred (Mixed voices, 7 parts) with organ.**

Britten, Benjamin, 1913-1976.
    [Folk song arrangements (1976)]
    Eight Folk Song Arrangements: (1976) For High Voice and
        Harp
    1.   **Songs (High voice) with harp.**
    2.   **Folk music.**
    3.   **Folk songs, English.**
    4.   **Folk songs, Welsh.**

Bryan, John.
    Hamelin Town
    1.   **Cantatas, Juvenile — Scores.**

Whenever appropriate, topical headings with music subdivisions are assigned in addition to the music headings discussed above.

Arne, Thomas Augustine, 1710-1778.
    Alfred
    1.   **Operas — Scores.**
    2.   **Alfred, King of England, 840-901 — Drama.**

The Australian Hymn Book with Catholic Supplement
    1.   **Hymns, English.**
    2.   **Catholic Church — Hymns.**

Warren, Harry, 1893-
    Pasadena: An American Love Song
    1.   **Music, Popular (Songs, etc.) — England.**
    2.   **Pasadena (Calif.) — Songs and music.**

The Wild Blue Yonder: Songs of the Air Force
1. United States. Air Force — Songs and music — Texts.

Billings, William, 1746-1800.
Peace: An Anthem, SATB with Chamber Ensemble or Keyboard
1. Anthems.
2. Choruses, Sacred (Mixed voices) with instrumental ensemble — Scores.
3. Choruses, Sacred (Mixed voices, 4 parts) with piano.
4. United States — History — Revolution, 1776-1783 — Songs and music.

Sound recordings

Sound recordings of music are treated in the same manner as other musical works. No special subdivisions are used to bring out the format:

Rare Blues [sound recording]
1. Blues (Songs, etc.) — Illinois — Chicago.

Brahms, Johannes, 1833-1897.
[Sonatas, clarinet, piano, op. 120]
Sonatas for Viola and Piano [sound recording]
1. Sonatas (Viola and piano)

Presley, Elvis, 1935-1977.
Elvis — In Days Gone By [sound recording]
1. Presley, Elvis, 1935-1977.
2. Singers — United States — Biography.

If a recording contains works in more than one form, separate headings are assigned to represent the forms of individual works:

Beethoven, Ludwig van, 1770-1827.
[Quintets, piano, oboe, clarinet, horn, bassoon, op. 16, E^b major]
Quintet in E-flat Major, op. 16, for Piano, Oboe, Clarinet, Horn, and Bassoon; Serenade in D Major, op. 25, for Flute, Violin, and Viola [sound recording]
1. Quintets (Piano, bassoon, clarinet, horn, oboe)
2. Trios (Flute, violin, viola)

Mozart, Wolfgang Amadeus, 1756-1791.
[Selections]
Sacred Music [sound recording]
1. Masses.
2. Requiems.
3. Choruses, Sacred (Mixed voices) with orchestra.
4. Organ with string orchestra.
5. Organ with orchestra.

Dance music

Previously, headings for dance forms were qualified with names of instruments when appropriate. Currently, headings for dance forms (with the exception of **Minuets; Polkas; Polonaises; and Waltzes**) are no longer qualified. A work containing music for a specific dance form (other than the four exceptions) is assigned a heading under the name of the dance form and an additional heading for the medium:

Ravel, Maurice, 1875-1937.
    [Bolero, orchestra]
    Bolero
    1. Boleros.
    2. Orchestral music.
    3. Overtures.

Montgomery, David.
    Piano Pieces [sound recording]
    1. Piano music.
    2. Mazurkas.

Examples of exceptions are:

Blessner, Gustav, 1808-1888.
    Home-Sick Polka
    1. Polkas (Piano)

Brahms, Johannes, 1833-1897.
    [Liebeslieder]
    Liebeslieder Walzer: op. 52; Neue Liebeslieder Walzer:
        op. 65 [sound recording]
    1. Waltzes (Vocal quartet with piano, 4 hands)

Specific *see also* references are made from **Dance music** to headings for dance forms (including the four exceptions) and from headings for the mediums to the qualified dance headings. Examples include:

Boleros
    xx Dance music

Polonaises
    xx Dance music

Polonaises (Piano)
    xx Piano music

Polkas (Instrumental ensemble)
    xx Instrumental ensembles

Music of ethnic and national groups[13]

The following types of headings are used for works that consist of or discuss* the music of ethnic groups, music with national emphasis, and non-Western art music:

[Ethnic or national group] – [Place] – Music
[Heading(s) for musical genre or style, or for ballads and songs with national emphasis]
[Heading(s) for language i.e., Ballads, Folk-songs, or Songs with language qualifier]
Musical instruments – [Place]
[Other topical headings, as applicable]

The first two types of headings are assigned to a work of music wherever possible; the others are assigned as appropriate. For works consisting of the texts of ballads, folk songs, or songs of ethnic groups, a heading in the form of [Heading with language qualifier] – Texts is used. Examples include:

Title: *Cumbrian Songs and Ballads*
  1. **Folk music – England – Cumbria.**
  2. **Folk-songs, English – England – Cumbria.**
  3. **Ballads, English – England – Cumbria.**

Title: *Flamenco Direct* [sound recording]
  1. **Gypsies – Spain – Music.**
  2. **Folk dance music – Spain.**
  3. **Flamenco music.**
  4. **Guitar music.**

Title: *Flute Songs of the Kiowa and Comanche* [sound recording]
  1. **Indians of North America – Music.**
  2. **Kiowa Indians – Music.**
  3. **Comanche Indians – Music.**
  4. **Pipe music.**

Title: *Song Games of Yorubaland, Nigeria*
  1. **Singing games – Nigeria.**
  2. **Yorubas – Nigeria – Music.**
  3. **Folk music – Nigeria.**
  4. **Folk-songs, Yoruba – Nigeria.**

Title: *Spiritual Songs from Dry Branch* [sound recording]
  1. **Gospel music – United States.**
  2. **Bluegrass music – United States.**

Title: *Concertino over een nederlands Volksliedje:*
      Violoncello en Orkest
  1. **Concertos (Violoncello) – Scores.**
  2. **Folk-songs, Dutch – Netherlands – Instrumental settings.**

---

*Examples of works about such music are given on page 285.

Title: *Les Instruments de musique populaire en Suisse* [sound recording]
    1. Musical instruments – Switzerland.
    2. Folk music – Switzerland – History and criticism.

Title: *O Canto da Terra* [sound recording]
    1. Folk songs – Brazil.
    2. Songs, Black – Brazil.
    3. Indians of South America – Brazil – Music.

Title: *Cancionero mexicano*
    1. Music, Popular (Songs, etc.) – Mexico – Texts.
    2. Songs, Spanish – Mexico – Texts.
    3. Folk-songs, Spanish – Mexico – Texts.

Works about music

Works about music are assigned topical headings that reflect the subject content of the works.* The subdivisions **– History and criticism**** and **– Instruction and study** are used with music headings instead of **– History** and **– Study and teaching**.

Following are examples of works about music:

Title: *Exploring Music through Experience*
    1. Music appreciation.

Title: *The Musical Experience*
    1. Music appreciation.
    2. Music analysis.
    3. Musical form.

Title: *Conductors on Record*
    1. Conductors (Music) – Biography.
    2. Conductors (Music) – Discography.
    3. Music – Bio-bibliography.

Title: *The Jacksons*
    1. Jackson 5 (Musical group)
   [1. Jackson 5 (Musical group)
    2. Musicians.
    3. Afro-Americans – Biography]

---

*For a discussion of subject cataloging in general, see chapter 8.
Not applicable under the heading **Musical instruments or names of musical instruments.

Title: *The Folk, Country, and Bluegrass Musician's Catalogue*
1. **Folk music — Handbooks, manuals, etc.**
2. **Country music — Handbooks, manuals, etc.**
3. **Bluegrass music — Handbooks, manuals, etc.**
4. **Musical instruments — Handbooks, manuals, etc.**

Title: *Physics, Music Theory, and the Hammered Dulcimer*
1. **Music — Acoustics and physics.**
2. **Music — Theory.**
3. **Dulcimer.**

Title: *Sing, Chorister. 1970-*
1. **Church music — Periodicals.**
2. **Anthems — Periodicals.**
3. **Choruses, Sacred — Periodicals.**

Title: *20th Century American Composers*
1. **Composers — United States — Outlines, syllabi, etc.**
2. **Music — History and criticism — 20th century — Outlines, syllabi, etc.**

Title: *The Great Violinists*
1. **Violinists, violoncellists, etc. — Biography.**

Title: *The Listener's Guide to Chamber Music*
1. **Chamber music — History and criticism.**
2. **Chamber music — Discography.**

Title: *Piano Technique*
1. **Piano — Instruction and study.**

Title: *The Well-Tun'd Word: Musical Interpretations of English Poetry, 1597-1651*
1. **Music and literature.**
2. **Songs, English — History and criticism.**
3. **Music — History and criticism — 17th century.**
4. **English poetry — Early modern, 1500-1700 — History and criticism.**

Title: *A Pictorial History of Jazz: People and Places from New Orleans to the Sixties*
1. **Jazz music — Pictorial works.**
2. **Jazz musicians — Portraits.**

Title: *Performing World of the Musician*
1. **Musicians — Juvenile literature.**
2. **Musical instruments — Juvenile literature.**
[1. **Musicians.**
2. **Musical instruments.**
3. **Occupations]**

Title: *Chanson et société*
1. **Music, Popular (Songs, etc.) — France — History and criticism.**
2. **Music, Popular (Songs, etc.) — France — Social aspects.**

Works about music of ethnic and national groups

Works about the music of ethnic and national groups, and about their musical instruments, are assigned the same headings that are used for the music itself, with the addition of subdivisions such as — **History and criticism;*** — **Bibliography;** — **Discography:**

Title: *Categories and Substance of Embu Traditional Folksongs*
1. **Embu (Bantu people) — Music — History and criticism.**
2. **Folk music — Kenya — History and criticism.**
3. **Folk-songs, Embu — History and criticism.**

Title: *MIT Folk Dance Club Israeli Catalogue*
1. **Israelis — United States — Music — Discography.**
2. **Folk dance music — United States — Discography.**
3. **Folk dance music — Israel — Discography.**

Title: *El corrido zacatecano*
1. **Folk-songs — Mexico — Zacatecas (State) — History and criticism.**
2. **Music, Popular (Songs, etc.) — Mexico — Zacatecas (State) — History and criticism.**
3. **Ballads, Spanish — Mexico — Zacatecas (State) — History and criticism.**
4. **Corridos — History and criticism.**

Title: *Über Volksmusik und Hackbrett in Bayern*
1. **Folk music — Germany (West) — Bavaria — History and criticism.**
2. **Dulcimer.**

Works about individual composers and musicians

Personal name headings and biographical (class-of-persons) headings are assigned to works about the lives, or lives and works, of individual composers or musicians, in accordance with the general guidelines for biography (see discussion on pages 234-238):

Title: *Holst*
1. **Holst, Gustav, 1874-1934.**
2. **Composers — England — Biography.**

---

*Not applicable under the heading **Musical instruments** or names of musical instruments.

Title: *Pavarotti, My Own Story*
1. **Pavarotti, Luciano.**
2. **Singers—Biography.**

Title: *A Knight at the Opera*
1. **Bing, Rudolf, Sir, 1902-**
2. **Impresarios—Biography.**

Title: *The Elton John Tapes*
1. **John, Elton—Interviews.**
2. **Rock musicians—Interviews.**

Title: *Bach, His Life and Times*
1. **Bach, Johann Sebastian, 1685-1750.**
2. **Composers—Germany—Biography.**

Headings for names of musicians and composers may be subdivided by the free-floating subdivisions used under names of persons. (A list of these free-floating subdivisions is given in appendix F.) An example is:

Title: *Hans Eisler: eine Bildbiografie*
1. **Eisler, Hans, 1898-1962.**
2. **Composers—Germany—Biography.**
3. **Eisler, Hans, 1898-1962—Iconography.**

If the work does not pertain to the personal life of the composer or musician, the biographical heading, i.e., **[Class of persons]—Biography**, is not assigned:

Title: *Benjamin Britten, His Music*
1. **Britten, Benjamin, 1913-1976—Criticism and interpretation.**
   [for a comprehensive discussion or criticism]

Title: *Bartók's Harmonic Language*
1. **Bartók, Béla, 1881-1945—Harmony.**

Title: *Chopin Playing: From the Composer to the Present Day*
1. **Chopin, Frédéric, 1810-1849—Performances.**
2. **Piano music—Interpretation (Phrasing, dynamics, etc.)**

Works about individual musical works

Name-title subject entries are made for works about individual musical compositions. Other music or topical headings are assigned as appropriate:

Title: *The Magic Flute, Masonic Opera: An Interpretation of the Libretto and the Music*
1. **Mozart, Wolfgang Amadeus, 1756-1791. Zauberflöte.**

Title: *Aida* [includes libretto and commentaries]
  1. **Verdi, Giuseppe, 1813-1901. Aida.**
  2. **Operas—History and criticism.**
  3. **Operas—Librettos.**

Title: *Beethoven's Ninth*
  1. **Beethoven, Ludwig van, 1770-1827. Symphonies, no. 9, op. 125, D minor.**

For a work about the compositions by one composer in a specific form or medium, a heading in the form of [**Name of composer. Subheading**] is used:

Title: *Brahms, Reger, Schönberg: Streichquartette: motivischthematische Prozesse und formale Gestalt*
  1. **Brahms, Johannes, 1833-1897. Quartets, strings.**
  2. **Reger, Max, 1873-1916. Quartets, strings.**
  3. **Schönberg, Arnold, 1874-1951. Quartets, strings.**
  4. **String quartets—Analysis, appreciation.**

Title: *Il manuale di Verdi*
  1. **Verdi, Giuseppe, 1813-1901. Operas.**

The subheading used after the name of the composer corresponds to the uniform title used in cataloging the music of individual composers according to *Anglo-American Cataloguing Rules*, second edition (*AACR2*). A list of authorized subheadings used in subject cataloging is given below.

o   Subheadings for general and specific mediums of performance

  Band music
  Chamber music
  Instrumental music
  Keyboard music
  Orchestra music
  Organ music
  Piano music
  String quartet music
  Vocal music

o   Subheadings for types of compositions with qualifiers for medium, as appropriate

  Ballets
  Cantatas
  Chorale preludes
  Concerti grossi
  Concertos
  Concertos, piano, orchestra
  Concertos, violin, orchestra
  Divertimenti
  Fugues

Masses
Musical comedies
Operas
Overtures
Passions
Quartets, strings
Requiems
Serenades
Sonatas
Sonatas, piano
Sonatas, violin, piano
Songs
Suites
Symphonic poems
Symphonies

ART[14]

Types of Headings

Art headings

In general, art subject headings are assigned to represent the following topics or aspects of art:

names of individual artists, individual works of art, art movements, artists' groups

art form or genre (e.g., **Drawing; Sculpture; Architecture)**

national, ethnic, and religious background of artists

style (e.g., **Art, Classical; Architecture, Victorian)**

historical period

content or theme of art

location of art

ownership of art (collection, museum, etc.)

A particular heading may represent one or more of these elements, e.g., **Painting, Modern — 17th-18th centuries**. The subject headings assigned to each work are generally arranged in the order given above, unless one or more of these elements are given greater emphasis in the work.

Free-floating subdivisions

The general free-floating subdivisions (see discussion in chapter 4) may be used with art headings with the following exceptions and qualifications:

—**Biography**
Free-floating only when used under headings for groups of people, e.g., **Painters.**

—**Catalogs**
For exhibition catalogs, the subdivision —**Exhibitions** rather than —**Catalogs** is used.

—**Collectors and collecting** *(Indirect)*
Divided indirect by the place where the collecting occurs, e.g., **Art metal-work—Collectors and collecting—Italy.** If appropriate, geographic subdivision may also be used immediately following the object collected to show the country from which it originates, e.g., **Art metal-work—Spain—Collectors and collecting—Italy.**

—**Conservation and restoration** *(Indirect)*
For topics other than architecture, the subdivision is divided by place, e.g., **Sculpture—Conservation and restoration—Italy.** For architecture headings, local subdivision is interposed, e.g., **Architecture, Domestic—Italy—Florence—Conservation and restoration.**

—**Exhibitions**
Used under topics and under names of individual artists.

—**History**
Used only for general, all-inclusive works. The subdivision —**History** is not used after headings with national qualifiers. **Drawing, French** is used, not Drawing, French—History. The subdivision —**History** is not used after art form subdivisions such as —**Art** or —**Portraits.**

—**Themes, motives**
Also used under art headings with national qualifiers.

Period subdivisions

Period subdivisions are provided under many of the art headings, e.g., **Art, Modern—20th century; Painting, Modern—19th century; Engraving—14th century.** These headings may be further subdivided by place to indicate the location of the art, e.g., **Art, Modern—20th century—France; Engraving—16th century—Italy.**

Period subdivisions are not provided under art headings with ethnic, national, or religious qualifiers indicating the origin of the art, with the exception of headings for oriental art. Examples include **Art, Jewish; Painting, American; Engraving, English; Art, Chinese—T'ang-Five dynasties, 618-960; Painting, Japanese—Meiji period, 1868-1912.** Since period subdivisions are normally not free-floating and are editorially established, catalogers are advised to consult *Library of Congress Subject Headings* when considering period subdivisions of a given art heading.

Free-Floating Phrase Headings

The phrase **in art** may be combined with the following types of headings to form valid subject headings: **[Topic] in art; [Descriptive name** (except personal name*) **heading in *AACR2* form] in art.** Examples include: **Birds in art; Cities and towns in art; Church of Scotland in art; Chicago (Ill.) in art.**

Application

Subject headings assigned to works containing examples of art, normally in the form of photographic reproductions, and those assigned to works about art (appreciation, history, and criticism) are in the same form. The subdivision **— History** is used only for very general, all-inclusive works. The subdivision **— History and criticism** is not used with art headings.

Since art headings with ethnic, national, or religious qualifiers (except oriental art) are not subdivided by period, when the work being cataloged involves a time period, two headings are assigned:

1. **Art, American.**
2. **Art, Modern — 20th century — United States.**

1. **Drawing, Spanish — Spain — Catalonia.**
2. **Drawing — 19th century — Spain — Catalonia.**

Works of art by more than one artist treated collectively

Books or other materials containing reproductions of works of art by more than one artist, and books about such art, are assigned headings representing topics such as art form and style, nationality or ethnic or religious background of the artists, place and time in which the art was created, theme or topic depicted, place where the art is currently located, and current or past owner (individuals, collections, museums, etc.):

Title: *Il disegno liberty*
1. **Drawing — 19th century.**
2. **Drawing — 20th century.**
3. **Decoration and ornament — Art nouveau.**

---

*For personal names, the form **[Person] — Art** [for persons who lived before 1400] or **[Person] — Portraits** is used. For proper uses of these subdivisions, consult *Library of Congress Subject Headings: A Guide to Subdivision Practice* and appendix F of this book.

Title: *Painting and Sculpture in Europe, 1880-1940*
1. Art, European.
2. Art, Modern — 19th century — Europe.
3. Art, Modern — 20th century — Europe.

Title: *Art in Peninsular Thailand Prior to the Fourteenth Century, A.D.*
1. Art — Thailand — Foreign influences.
2. Art, Ancient — Thailand.
3. Art, Medieval — Thailand.

Title: *Floral Patterns: 120 Full-Color Designs in the Art Nouveau Style*
1. Decoration and ornament — Plant forms.
2. Decoration and ornament — Art nouveau.

Title: *Metal Sculptures of Eastern India*
1. Bronzes, Medieval — India.
2. Bronzes — India.
3. Sculpture, Buddhist — India.

Title: *The Classical Gods and Heroes in the National Gallery of Art*
1. Mythology, Classical, in art.
2. Art — Washington (D.C.)

Title: *The Impressionists and Their Art*
1. Impressionism (Art) — France.
2. Painting, French.
3. Painting, Modern — 19th century — France.

Title: *Sculpture, des origines à nos jours*
1. Sculpture — History — Outlines, syllabi, etc.

Title: *The Architecture of India: Buddhist and Hindu*
1. Architecture, Buddhist — India.
2. Architecture, Hindu — India.

Title: *The Architectural History of Canterbury Cathedral*
1. Canterbury Cathedral.
2. Architecture, Medieval — England.

Title: *The Development of Modern Art in Northern California*
1. Art, American — California — Addresses, essays, lectures.
2. Art, Modern — 19th century — California — Addresses, essays, lectures.
3. Art, Modern — 20th century — California — Addresses, essays, lectures.

Title: *A Documentary History of Art*
1. Art — History — Sources.

Title: *The Story of Modern Art*
    1. Art, Modern — 20th century — History.

Place in art[15]

A heading in the form of **[Place] in art** is assigned to a book consisting of reproductions of art works with a specific place as a theme and to a work discussing the treatment of a specific place in art:

Title: *The White Mountains: Place and Perceptions*
    1. White Mountains (N.H. and Me.) in art — Exhibitions.
    2. Art, American — Exhibitions.
    3. Art, Modern — 19th century — United States — Exhibitions.

Title: *A Brush with the West*
    1. Rocky Mountains Region in art.
    2. Art, American — Rocky Mountains Region.
    3. Art, Canadian — Rocky Mountains Region.

However, if the book consists of artistic photographs of a place or of paintings made before the invention of photography that merely give views (normally classed in geography rather than art), a heading in the form of **[Place] — Description and travel — Views** or **[Local place] — Description — Views** is used.

Catalogs of art museums, collections, and exhibitions[16]

The catalog of an unnamed art collection that is permanently housed in an individual museum is assigned the following types of headings:

[Type of object] — Catalogs
[Type of object] — [Place] — Catalogs
[Name of museum] — Catalogs
[Type of object] — [Period subdivision] — [Place, if applicable]
    — Catalogs

Examples include:

Title: *American Art in the Newark Museum: Paintings,*
            Drawings, and Sculpture
    1. Art, American — Catalogs.
    2. Art — New Jersey — Newark — Catalogs.
    3. Newark Museum — Catalogs.

Title: *The Brücke Museum*
    1. Expressionism (Art) — Germany — Catalogs.
    2. Art, German — Catalogs.
    3. Art, Modern — 20th century — Germany — Catalogs.
    4. Brücke-Museum — Catalogs.

Title: *Twentieth-Century Drawings: Selections from the Whitney Museum of American Art*
    1. **Drawing, American — Catalogs.**
    2. **Drawing — 20th century — United States — Catalogs.**
    3. **Drawing — New York (N.Y.) — Catalogs.**
    4. **Whitney Museum of American Art — Catalogs.**

The subdivision **—Exhibitions** is used instead of **—Catalogs** for the catalog of an exhibition:

Title: *American Realism and the Industrial Age*
    [catalog of an exhibition held at the Cleveland Museum of Art]
    1. **Realism in art — United States — Exhibitions.**
    2. **Art, American — Exhibitions.**
    3. **Art, Modern — 19th century — United States — Exhibitions.**
    4. **Art and industry — United States — Exhibitions.**

Title: *Renaissance Ornament Prints and Drawings*
    [exhibition at the Metropolitan Museum of Art]
    1. **Prints, Renaissance — Exhibitions.**
    2. **Drawing, Renaissance — Exhibitions.**
    3. **Decoration and ornament, Renaissance — Exhibitions.**

Private art collections

In addition to the headings discussed above, the following three types of headings are assigned to catalogs of private art collections, including those that have been donated or sold to public institutions but are still known by their original names:

[Name of owner] — Art collections — Catalogs [or **—Exhibitions**]
[Topical or **form heading] — Private collections** [or another appropriate subdivision] **— Catalogs** [or **—Exhibitions**]
[A partial title entry under the name by which the collection is known, if the name appears in the title of the work being cataloged and does not duplicate the regular title entry. The words "Mr. & Mrs." are omitted but not the word "Mrs." when it stands alone in the title]

Examples include:

Title: *Lessing J. Rosenwald: Tribute to a Collector*
    [an exhibition]
    1. **Prints — Exhibitions.**
    2. **Drawing — Exhibitions.**
    3. **Rosenwald, Lessing J. (Lessing Julius), 1891-1979 — Art collections — Exhibitions.**

Title: *A Private Vision: Contemporary Art from the Graham
Gund Collection, Museum of Fine Arts, Boston*
1.   **Art, Modern – 20th century – Catalogs.**
2.   **Art, Modern – 20th century – United States – Catalogs.**
3.   **Art – Massachusetts – Boston – Catalogs.**
4.   **Gund, Graham – Art collections – Catalogs.**
5.   **Museum of Fine Arts, Boston – Catalogs.**
IV.   Title: Gund Collection.

Works by and about individual artists

Works containing reproductions of an artist's works (with main entry or
added entry under the artist's name) and works about an individual artist's
work (with main entry other than the artist) are assigned a subject heading
under the name of the artist regardless of the main or added entry. Additional
headings are assigned to bring out form, style, period (for discussions of an
architect's work), theme, type of art objects, and name of museum or
collection where the art works are permanently housed. Examples include:

Title: *Goya Drawings* / Enrique Lafuente Ferrari
1.   **Goya, Francisco, 1746-1828.**
I.   Goya, Francisco, 1746-1828.

Title: *Klee Drawings: 60 Works* / by Paul Klee
1.   **Klee, Paul, 1879-1940.**

Title: *Klee en Tunisie* / textes par Jean Duvignaud
1.   **Klee, Paul, 1879-1940.**
2.   **Tunisia in art.**

Title: *The Complete Illustrations from Delacroix's Faust and
Manet's The Raven*
1.   **Delacroix, Eugene, 1798-1863.**
2.   **Goethe, Johann Wolfgang von, 1749-1832.   Faust
– Illustrations.**
3.   **Manet, Edouard, 1832-1883.**
4.   **Poe, Edgar Allan, 1809-1849.   Raven – Illustrations.**

Title: *Robert A. M. Stern, 1965-1980: Toward a Modern
Architecture after Modernism*
1.   **Stern, Robert A. M.**
2.   **Architecture, Postmodern – United States.**

The artist's name may be subdivided by the free-floating subdivisions used
under names of persons (see appendix F) in order to bring out other aspects of
the work:

Title: *Gauguin, the Complete Paintings*
1.   **Gauguin, Paul, 1848-1903 – Catalogs.**

Title: *Leonardo da Vinci, Architect and Urban Planner*
1.   **Leonardo, da Vinci, 1452-1519 — Bibliography.**
2.   **Architecture, Renaissance — Italy — Bibliography.**
3.   **City planning — Italy — Bibliography.**

Title: *Picasso's Picassos: An Exhibition from the Musée
            Picasso, Paris*
1.   **Picasso, Pablo, 1881-1973 — Exhibitions.**
2.   **Musée Picasso — Exhibitions.**

A biography of an individual artist is assigned a personal name heading without subdivision and one or more additional biographical headings:

Title: *The Unspeakable Confessions of Salvador Dali*
1.   **Dali, Salvador, 1904-**
2.   **Painters — Spain — Biography.**

Title: *Edwin Lutyens: Architect Laureate*
1.   **Lutyens, Edwin Landseer, Sir, 1869-1944.**
2.   **Architects — Great Britain — Biography.**

Title: *Rembrandt, Life and Work*
1.   **Rembrandt Harmenszoon van Rijn, 1606-1669.**
2.   **Artists — Netherlands — Biography.**

Title: *Hollingsworth: The Man, the Artist, and His Work*
1.   **Hollingsworth, William R. (William Robert), 1910-1944.**
2.   **Artists — Mississippi — Biography.**

The biographical heading is not assigned to a work containing reproductions of an artist's works unless the work contains substantial information (at least 20 percent of the text) about the artist's personal life:

Title: *The Art of Leo & Diane Dillon*
1.   **Dillon, Leo.**
2.   **Dillon, Diane.**

Title: *Dinosaurs, Mammoths, and Cavemen: The Art of
            Charles R. Knight*
1.   **Knight, Charles Robert, 1874-1953.**
2.   **Artists — United States — Biography.**
3.   **Extinct animals in art.**
4.   **Cave-dwellers in art.**

Works about individual works of art

The following types of headings are assigned to works discussing individual works of art:

[Name of artist.   English title of work]*
[Vernacular title of work] ([Type of art])*
    [for a work by an unknown artist]

Examples include:

Title: *Auguste Rodin: le monument des Bourgeois de Calais (1844-1895) dans les collections du Musée des Beaux-arts de Calais*
    1.   **Rodin, Auguste, 1840-1917.   Burghers of Calais.**

Title: *Il Mosè di Michelangelo*
    1.   **Michelangelo Buonarroti, 1475-1564.   Moses.**
    2.   **Marble sculpture, Renaissance — Italy.**

Title: *Pierre-Auguste Renoir, The Luncheon of the Boating Party: The Phillips Collection*
    1.   **Renoir, Auguste, 1841-1919.   Luncheon of the boating party.**
    2.   **Phillips Collection.**

RELIGION

Types of Headings

Headings representing religious concepts or religions[17]

A large number of headings in *Library of Congress Subject Headings* represent religions or religious concepts. Some examples are:

Buddhism
Catholic Church
Christianity
Church and state
Church history
Islam
Meditation
Muslims
Mysticism

---

*For patterns of cross-references made to these headings, see appendix H.

Ordination
Religion and music
Salvation

Many of these headings may be subdivided according to the pattern headings listed below:

Category	Pattern heading
Religious and monastic orders	Jesuits
Religions	Buddhism
Christian denominations	Catholic Church
Sacred works (including parts)	Bible
Theological topics	Salvation

There are also a number of headings that may be subdivided by religion and/or denomination. These are usually indicated in *Library of Congress Subject Headings* by means of multiple subdivisions:

Baptism — Anglican Communion, [Catholic Church, etc.]
Lord's Supper — Catholic Church, [Presbyterian Church, etc.]
  [may be subdivided by name of any Christian denomination]
Mysticism — Brahmanism, [Judaism, Nestorian Church, etc.]
  [may be subdivided by any religion]
Mysticism — Catholic Church, [Orthodox Eastern Church, etc.]
  [may be subdivided by any denomination]

In the past some of the headings involving religion or denomination were established with adjectival or parenthetical qualifiers, e.g., **Converts, Anglican; Meditation (Taoism); Ordination (Buddhism)**. These headings will continue to be used. However, newly established headings follow the subdivided pattern illustrated above. Headings of the type [**Topic**] ([**Qualifier**]) are gradually being phased out.

Headings for nonreligious topics with religious subdivisions[18]

Many nonreligious topics are subdivided by the subdivision — **Religious aspects** or — **Mythology** to represent a religious or mythological point of view. These subdivisions are not free-floating and can be used only when enumerated under the heading in question. The subdivision — Moral and religious aspects and headings of the type [Topic] (in religion, folk-lore, etc.) are no longer valid and are being removed from *Library of Congress Subject Headings* and/or replaced by the following:

[Topic] — **Religious aspects** [not free-floating]
[Topic] — **Moral and ethical aspects** [free-floating]
[Topic] — **Mythology** [not free-floating]

Examples include **Marriage — Religious aspects; Falkland Islands War, 1982 — Moral and ethical aspects; Stars — Mythology**.

The subdivision —**Religious aspects** may be further subdivided by —[**Religion** or **denomination**] as a free-floating subdivision. Examples include:

> **Birth control — Religious aspects**
>   — —**Baptists, [Catholic Church, etc.]**
>   — —**Buddhism, [Christianity, etc.]**

Application

Works on religious topics

Appropriate topical headings are assigned according to the normal procedures for subject cataloging:

> Title: *Early Buddhism and Christianity*
>   **1. Buddhism — History — To ca. 100 A.D.**
>   **2. Christianity — Early church, ca. 30-600.**
>   **3. Christianity and other religions — Buddhism.**
>   **4. Buddhism — Relations — Christianity.**

> Title: *The Intelligible Universe: A Cosmological Argument*
>   **1. God — Proof, Cosmological.**

> Title: *Word into Silence*
>   **1. Meditation.**

> Title: *The Jewish Mystical Tradition*
>   **1. Mysticism — Judaism — History — Sources.**
>   **2. Cabala — History — Sources.**
>   **3. Hasidism — History — Sources.**

When a heading of the type [**Topic**] — [**Church** or **denomination**] is assigned to a work, a duplicate entry under [**Church** or **denomination**] — [**Topical subdivision**] is always assigned:

> Title: *Shaping Faith through Involvement*
>   **1. Christian education of young people.**
>   **2. Church work with youth — Church of God.**
>   **3. Church of God — Education.**

Works on nonreligious topics treated from a religious point of view

When assigning a nonreligious topical heading with the subdivision —**Religious aspects** or —**Mythology**, the following guidelines should be observed.

The subdivision — **Religious aspects** is used under nonreligious topics for works that discuss the topic from a religious standpoint, i.e., how it occurs as a theme in religious beliefs and practices, its importance in religious doctrines, the relationship in general between the topic and religion, etc.:

Title: *Religion and Dance*
1. **Dancing — Religious aspects — Addresses, essays, lectures.**

When a heading of the type **[Topic] — Religious aspects** subdivided by religion or denomination is assigned to a work, a duplicate entry in the form of **[Religion** or **denomination] — [Topical subdivision]** is also made. The subdivisions that may be used in this way, however, are restricted to those under the relevant pattern headings or under the heading for the specific religion or denomination in question. For this reason, the topic expressed in the **[Religion** or **denomination] — [Topical subdivision]** headings is often more general than the one expressed in the **[Topic] — [Religious aspects]** heading:

Title: *The Ways We Are Together: Reflections on Marriage,*
        Family, and Sexuality
1. **Catholic Church — Doctrines.**
2. **Marriage — Religious aspects — Catholic Church.**

Title: *The Abortion Question*
1. **Anglican Church of Canada — Doctrines.**
2. **Abortion — Religious aspects — Anglican Church of Canada.**

In some cases, an additional heading in the form of **[Religion** or **denomination] — [Place]** is also assigned to bring out the geographical aspect.

If the work being cataloged discusses the topic from a moral or ethical standpoint as well as a religious point of view, an additional heading with the subdivision — **Moral and ethical aspects** is assigned:

Title: *Nuclear Ethics: A Christian Moral Argument*
1. **Catholic Church — Doctrines.**
2. **Atomic warfare — Religious aspects — Catholic Church.**
3. **Atomic warfare — Moral and ethical aspects.**

The subdivision — **Mythology** is used to represent the topic as a theme in mythology. Examples include:

Title: *Mythologie des filles des eaux*
1. **Women — Mythology.**
2. **Water — Mythology.**
3. **Sirens (Mythology).**
4. **Mermaids.**
5. **Fairies.**

Title: *The Androgyne: Fusion of the Sexes*
1. **Bisexuality — Mythology.**
2. **Bisexuality — Religious aspects.**

Additional headings may be assigned to bring out types of mythology, e.g., **Mythology, Greek; Mythology, Jewish**; etc. If the work discusses the religious implications of the theme in mythology from the standpoint of a particular religion or denomination, an additional heading of the type **[Topic]** — **Religious aspects** — **[Religion** or **denomination]** is assigned. This heading is not necessary unless a particular religion or denomination is involved.

Sacred scriptures

The Bible

Biblical texts

Subject headings are not assigned to Biblical texts except in the cases listed below.

1) *Paraphrases of Biblical texts.* Because paraphrases of Biblical texts are entered under the name of the paraphraser according to *AACR2*, form headings are assigned as follows:

Bible — Paraphrases
[used for texts of paraphrases in two or more languages]
Bible — Paraphrases, English, [French, German, etc.]
[used for texts of paraphrases in a particular language]

Paraphrases of parts of the Bible follow the same pattern, e.g., **Bible. O.T. Psalms — Paraphrases, English**. Examples include:

Title: *Sometimes I Get Scared* / by Elspeth Campbell Murphy
    1.   Bible.   O.T.   Psalms XXIII — Paraphrases, English
        — Juvenile literature.
    [1.   Bible.   O.T.   Psalms XXIII — Paraphrases.
    2.   Fear]

2) *Harmonies.* The pattern for paraphrases of Biblical texts is followed for harmonies, e.g., **Bible.   N.T.   Gospels — Harmonies, English**.

3) *Translations of a version.* Because in descriptive cataloging the translation of a version of a Biblical text is entered under the uniform title containing the name of the translator but ignoring the version from which the translation is made, a form heading is assigned to bring out the version. For example, an English translation of the Targum Onkelos made by Etheridge and published in 1968 was entered under the uniform title **Bible.   O.T. Pentateuch.   English.   Etheridge.   1968**. The following subject entry is made:

    1.   Bible.   O.T.   Pentateuch.   Aramaic.   Targum Onkelos
    — Translations into English.

Works about the Bible[19]

Works about the Bible or its parts receive subject headings in the form of the uniform title used in descriptive cataloging, except that designations for the language, version, and date are omitted. Appropriate subdivisions may also be added:

Title: *Introducing the Bible*
     1. Bible — Introductions.

Title: *Biblical Semantic Logic*
     1. Bible — Language, style.

Title: *Christ Above All: The Message of Hebrews*
     1. Bible. N.T. Hebrews — Commentaries.

Title: *Hebrews Commenting from Erasmus to Bèze, 1516-1598*
     1. Bible. N.T. Hebrews — Criticism, interpretation, etc. — History — 16th century.

Title: *Believing God: Studies on Faith in Chapter 11*
     1. Bible. N.T. Hebrews XI — Criticism, interpretation, etc.

Title: *The Human Face of God: William Blake and the Book of Job*
     1. Blake, William, 1757-1827.
     2. Bible. O.T. Job — Illustrations.

Title: *Lass deine Augen offen sein: Bildmeditationen z. Vaterunser*
     1. Lord's prayer — Meditation.

However, if the work is about a particular version or translation of the Bible, it is specifically designated:

Bible — Versions
Bible. N.T. English — Versions — Rheims
Bible. O.T. Jeremiah. Greek — Versions — Septuagint
Bible. English — Versions — Coverdale

Works about paraphrases of the Bible or its parts are assigned headings such as

Bible — Paraphrases — History and criticism
Bible — Paraphrases, English — History and criticism
    [for works about English paraphrases]
Bible. O.T. Psalms — Paraphrases, English — History and criticism

Apocryphal books

The headings **Apocryphal books; Apocryphal books (New Testament); Apocryphal books (Old Testament)** are used with appropriate subdivisions as subject headings for works dealing collectively with apocryphal books. Subdivisions follow the pattern established under the Bible:

Apocryphal books — Introductions
Apocryphal books (New Testament) — Commentaries
Apocryphal books (New Testament) — Theology
Apocryphal books (Old Testament) — Criticism, interpretation, etc.
Hymn of the soul — Criticism, interpretation, etc.

Examples include:

Title: *The Pseudepigrapha and Modern Research*
   1. **Apocryphal books (Old Testament) — Criticism, interpretation, etc.**

Title: *Apocryphes slaves et roumains de l'Ancien Testament*
   1. **Apocryphal books (Old Testament) — Versions, Slavic — Addresses, essays, lectures.**
   2. **Apocryphal books (Old Testament) — Translations into Romanian — Addresses, essays, lectures.**

Other sacred scriptures

The heading **Bible** serves as the pattern for subdivisions for other sacred scriptures, e.g., **Vedas. Ṛgveda — Criticism, interpretation, etc.; Koran — Commentaries.** Examples include:

Title: *Quran's Cultural, Literary, and Philosophical Perspectives*
   1. **Koran — Theology.**

Title: *Aitareya Āranyaka: Eka Adhyayana*
   1. **Aranyakas.   Aitareyāranyaka — Criticism, interpretation, etc.**

Title: *The Priestly Gift in Mishnah: A Study of Tractate Terumot*
   1. **Mishnah.   Terumot — Commentaries.**
   2. **Tosefta.   Terumot — Commentaries.**
   3. **Terumah.**

Liturgy

Before *AACR2*, headings of the type **Catholic Church.   Liturgy and ritual** were used as main entry for liturgical* works. Since *AACR2* abandoned the "form subheading" Liturgy and ritual, the Library of Congress introduced the subdivision **— Liturgy** in subject headings in order to collocate in one file the liturgical works of a religion or denomination. As a result, headings of the following types are no longer valid:

---

*The term *liturgy* refers to prayers, rituals, acts, and ceremonies used in the official worship of a religion or denomination, public or private.

[Name of religion or denomination].   Liturgy and ritual
[Name of religion or denomination] — Rituals
Liturgics — [Name of religion or denomination]

Texts of liturgical books

To a work (a collection, an individual liturgical book, or a selection from one or more liturgical books) containing the words and instructions for carrying out official worship (public or private), one or more headings of the following types are assigned: **[Name of religion** or **denomination] — Liturgy — Texts; [Type of liturgical book] — Texts.** Examples include:

Title: *The Book of Common Prayer and Administration of the*
         Sacraments and Other Rites ... According to the Use
         of the Episcopal Church
   1.   **Episcopal Church — Liturgy — Texts.**

Title: *Bauddha Samskāra*
   1.   **Buddhism — Liturgy — Texts.**

Title: *The Roman Pontifical*
   1.   **Catholic Church — Liturgy — Texts.**
   2.   **Roman pontifical — Texts.**

Title: *Der Psalter*
   1.   **Catholic Church — Liturgy — Texts.**
   2.   **Psalters — Texts.**

Title: *Gates of Freedom: A Passover Haggadah*
   1.   **Reform Judaism — Liturgy — Texts.**
   2.   **Haggadah (Reform, Stern) — Texts.**
   3.   **Seder.**

If the work is limited to a particular ceremony, ritual, holiday, etc., an additional heading in the form of **[Type of ceremony, etc.] — Liturgy — Texts** is also assigned:

Title: *Shabbat Shiron*
   1.   **Judaism — Liturgy — Texts.**
   2.   **Jewish hymns.**
   3.   **Sabbath — Liturgy — Texts.**

If the work contains significant commentary as well as the text of a liturgical book, a subject heading consisting of the uniform title of the book is assigned in addition to the headings mentioned above:

Title: *Passover Haggadah: The Feast of Freedom*
   1.   **Conservative Judaism — Liturgy — Texts.**
   2.   **Haggadah (Conservative, Rabbinical Assembly) — Texts.**
   3.   **Haggadah (Conservative, Rabbinical Assembly)**
        — Commentaries.
   4.   **Seder.**

Works about liturgy

A heading of the type [**Name of religion** or **denomination**] — **Liturgy** is assigned to a work about the liturgy of a particular religion or denomination:

Title: *Liturgy Made Simple*
    1.   **Catholic Church — Liturgy.**

For a work discussing the liturgy of a particular ceremony, ritual, holiday, etc., headings of the following types are assigned:

[**Name of religion** or **denomination**] — **Liturgy**
[**Type of ceremony, etc.**] — [**Name of religion** or **denomination**]

Examples include:

Title: *Mass & the Sacraments*
    1.   **Catholic Church — Liturgy — Addresses, essays, lectures.**
    2.   **Sacraments — Catholic Church — Addresses, essays, lectures.**

Title: *The Sacrifice of Praise: Studies on the Theme of Thanks-*
        giving and Redemption in the Central Prayer of the
        Eucharistic and Baptismal Liturgies: In Honour of
        Arthur Hubert Couratin
    1.   **Lord's Supper — Liturgy — Addresses, essays, lectures.**
    2.   **Baptism — Liturgy — Addresses, essays, lectures.**
    3.   **Couratin, Arthur Hubert, 1902-   — Addresses, essays, lectures.**

Works about liturgical books

For a work about a type of liturgical book or an individual liturgical book, the following types of headings are used:

[**Name of religion** or **denomination**] — **Liturgy — Texts — History**
    and criticism.
[**Type of liturgical book**]
[**Type of ceremony, ritual, holiday, etc.**]
[**Uniform title of the individual book**]

Examples include:

Title: *The Making of the First American Book of Common Prayer*
    1.   **Episcopal Church.   Book of Common Prayer.**

Title: *The Liturgy of the Hours*
    1.   **Catholic Church.   Liturgy of the hours (U.S., et al.)**
    2.   **Catholic Church — Liturgy.**
    3.   **Divine Office.**

Title: *The Passover Seder* / Ruth Gruber Fredman
1. **Haggadah.**
2. **Haggadot.**
3. **Seder.**
4. **Judaism – Liturgy – Texts – History and criticism.**
5. **Seder – Liturgy – Texts – History and criticism.**
6. **Symbol and culture.**

LAW[20]

Types of Headings

Law headings

Law headings represent different forms of legal texts, systems and branches of law, and specific legal topics:

Law	Law, Slavic
Charters	Common law
Deeds	Roman law
Ordinances, Municipal	Commercial law
Constitutional amendments	Constitutional law
Treaties	Insurance law
Law, Medieval	Habeas corpus
Law, Maya	Liens

Topical headings with legal subdivisions

Legal texts and works about law are often assigned topical headings with legal subdivisions. Previously, the legal aspects of subjects were brought out by a variety of subdivisions such as – **Law**; – **Laws and legislation**; – **Laws and regulations**, resulting in a great deal of inconsistency and unpredictability.

The Library of Congress has now normalized the legal subdivisions and authorized the following subdivisions to represent legal aspects of topics:

– **Law and legislation** *(Indirect)* [not free-floating]
– **Legal status, laws, etc.** *(Indirect)* [free-floating]
– **Safety regulations** *(Indirect)* [free-floating]

These subdivisions may be further divided by the subdivisions listed under the model heading **Labor laws and legislation** (see appendix D). Since the subdivision – **Law and legislation** *(Indirect)* is not free-floating, each new usage must be established editorially.

If the topical heading represents a group of people, the subdivision – **Legal status, laws, etc.** *(Indirect)* is used, e.g., **Children – Legal status, laws, etc. – Soviet Union; Artists – Legal status, laws, etc.; Eskimos – Legal status, laws, etc.; Hawaiians – Legal status, laws, etc.**

The free-floating subdivision – **Safety regulations** *(Indirect)* is used under headings for types of objects, chemicals, materials, machines, installations, industries, or activities, or under names of disciplines for safety rules or orders that have the force of law, e.g., **Pipe lines — Safety regulations; Coal mines and mining — Safety regulations — Soviet Union; Radioactive substances — Safety regulations.**

Application

Legal texts

General laws (nontopical compilations)

A subject entry under the heading **Law** *(Indirect)* is made for a nontopical compilation of laws when main entry has been made under the name of a jurisdiction:

New Zealand. *Reprinted Statutes of New Zealand*
    1. **Law — New Zealand.**

British Columbia. *The Revised Statutes of British Columbia*
    1. **Law — British Columbia.**

Uttar Pradesh (India). *S.M. Husain's Uttar Pradesh Local Acts*
    1. **Law — India — Uttar Pradesh.**

General laws (topical compilations)

If the laws pertain to a particular topic, a topical heading subdivided by the jurisdiction is assigned:

Mexico. *Ley federal de educación*
    1. **Educational law and legislation — Mexico.**

United States. *Economic Recovery Tax Act of 1981*
    1. **Taxation — Law and legislation — United States.**
    2. **Income tax — Law and legislation — United States.**

Philippines. *Banking Laws of the Philippines*
    1. **Banking law — Philippines.**

Texas. *Agriculture Code*
    1. **Agricultural laws and legislation — Texas.**

Great Britain. *The Companies Act 1980*
    1. **Corporation law — Great Britain.**

Constitutions[21]

The heading **Constitutions** is used for a general collection of texts of constitutions. The heading is subdivided by place if the collection contains the texts of constitutions of a particular region. To a collection of texts of constitutions or an individual constitution of a particular country, state, province, etc., a heading in the form of **[Jurisdiction]—Constitution** is assigned. For a collection of texts of the constitutions of various states, a heading in the form of **Constitutions, State** *(Indirect)* is used:

Title: *Sources and Documents of United States Constitutions*
    1. **Constitutions, State—United States.**

Title: *Grundgesetz und Verfassungen der deutschen Bundesländer*
    1. **Constitutions, State—Germany (West)**

A heading in the form of **[Jurisdiction]—Constitution—Amendments** is assigned to a collection containing texts of constitutional amendments of a particular jurisdiction. Texts of particular constitutional amendments are assigned headings of the type **[Jurisdiction]—Constitution—Amendments —1st, [2nd, 3rd, etc.]**.

Ordinances

A heading of the type **Ordinances, Municipal—[Place]** is assigned to the text of a nontopical compilation of ordinances:

Honolulu (Hawaii). *The Revised Ordinances of Honolulu*
    1. **Ordinances, Municipal—Hawaii—Honolulu.**

Charters

One or more of the following types of headings are assigned to the text of a compilation of published charters: **Charters; County charters—[Place]; Municipal charters—[Place]**. Examples include:

Title: *Amendments to Municipal Charters Adopted by the Several Municipal Corporations in Maryland from June 1, 1955 to December 31, 1967*
    1. **Municipal charters—Maryland.**
    2. **County charters—Maryland.**

For the text of a single charter, the following types of headings are used:

[City]—Charters
    [for an American city]
[City]—Charters, grants, privileges
    [for a foreign city]
County charters—[Place]

Examples include:

Falls Church (Va.). *The Code of the City of Falls Church, Virginia: The Charter and the General Ordinances*
    1. **Ordinances, Municipal—Virginia—Falls Church.**
    2. **Falls Church (Va.)—Charters.**

Title: *Proposed Home Rule Charter for Baltimore County,*
            Maryland
    1. **County charters — Maryland — Baltimore County.**

Works about law

Works about law in general are assigned the heading **Law** with appropriate subdivisions:

Title: *How to Stand Up for Your Rights — and Win!*
    1. **Law — United States — Popular works.**

Title: *Law and Society in Traditional China*
    1. **Law — China — History and criticism.**

For a periodical or journal of law, a distinction is made between the place of publication and the jurisdiction covered by the publication by placing the geographic subdivision in different orders:[22]

    Law — Periodicals *(Indirect)*
    [for periodicals on law in general, subdivided by country of publication (or first-order political subdivision in the case of Canada, Great Britain, the Soviet Union, and the United States)]

    Law — [Place] — Periodicals
    [for periodicals limited in subject coverage to the law of a particular jurisdiction]

Examples include:

Title: *Guyana Law Journal*
    1. **Law — Periodicals — Guyana.**

Title: *The Federal Law Journal* [published in Florida]
    1. **Law — Periodicals — Florida.**
    2. **Law — United States — Periodicals.**

To a work that discusses constitutions or constitutional law in general, the heading **Constitutional law** is assigned. Works that discuss the constitutions or constitutional law of particular regions, countries, states, provinces, etc., are assigned headings in the form of **[Jurisdiction] — Constitutional law**. Examples include:

Title: *Report on Certain Aspects of the Canadian Constitution*
    1. **Canada — Constitutional law.**

Title: *Fajgenbaum and Hanks' Australian Constitutional Law*
    1. **Australia — Constitutional law.**

Comparative works discussing state constitutions or state constitutional law of a particular region or country are assigned headings in the form of **[Region or** country] — **Constitutional law, State**. Works discussing constitutional amendments and the amending process in general are assigned the heading **Constitutional amendments**. Works discussing constitutional amendments or state constitutional amendments of a particular country, state, province, etc., are assigned headings in the form of **[Jurisdiction] — Constitutional law — Amendments** or **[Jurisdiction] — Constitutional law, State — Amendments**:

Title: *Die Änderungen des Grundgesetzes*
    1. **Germany (West) — Constitutional law — Amendments.**

Works discussing a specific constitutional amendment are assigned a heading in the form of **[Jurisdiction] — Constitutional Amendments — 1st, [2nd, 3rd, etc.]**.

For works about specific branches of law or specific legal topics, the same headings assigned to the texts of such laws are used:

Title: *Companies Act 1980* / by Daniel D. Prentice
    1. **Corporation law — Great Britain.**

Title: *Municipal Charters: A Discussion of the Essentials of a City Charter* / Nathan Matthews
    1. **Municipal charters — United States.**

Title: *A Trader's Guide to the Oil Heaters (Safety) Requirements, 1977* / Devon County Council, Trading Standards Department
    1. **Oil burners — Safety regulations — England — Devon.**

Title: *Australian Schools and the Law: Principal, Teacher and Student* / A.E. Knott, K.E. Tronc, J.L. Middleton
    1. **Educational law and legislation — Australia.**

Title: *Tax Tactics for the Retired* / by Terry K. Schandel and Susan M. Schandel
    1. **Aged — Taxation — Law and legislation — United States.**
    2. **Income tax — Law and legislation — United States.**

Title: *Environmental Protection: The Legal Framework* / Frank F. Skillern
    1. **Environmental law — United States.**

Form subdivisions may be added when appropriate:

Title: *NEA Federal Income Tax Guide for Teachers: 1982 Handbook* / by John C. Arch
    1. **Income tax — Law and legislation — United States — Outlines, syllabi, etc.**
    2. **Teachers — Taxation — Law and legislation — United States — Outlines, syllabi, etc.**

Title: *Modern Banking Checklists: With Commentary* / Jank
        Kusnet, Justine T. Antopol
1. **Banking law — United States — Miscellanea.**

Title: *Controlling the Atom*
1. **Atomic power — Law and legislation — United States
    — History.**
2. **Radioactive substances — Safety regulations — United
    States — History.**

Title: *The New York Times Guide to Making the New Tax Law
        Work for You*
1. **Taxation — Law and legislation — United States — Popular
    works.**
2. **Income tax — Law and legislation — United States — Popular
    works.**

A work about a particular law is assigned a heading under the uniform
title of the law in addition to other appropriate topical headings assigned to the
original text:

Title: *Brainpower for the Cold War: The Sputnik Crisis and
        National Defense Education Act of 1958* / Barbara
        Barksdale Clowse
1. **United States.   National Defense Education Act of 1958.**
2. **Federal aid to education — United States.**

Title: *Legislative History of Title I of the Speedy Trial Act
        of 1974* / by Anthony Partridge
1. **United States.   Speedy Trial Act of 1974.**
2. **Speedy trial — United States.**

Treaties[23]

Texts of treaties

As a result of implementing *AACR2*, subject headings for treaties have
been revised as follows:

1) For general (nontopical) collections of treaties, general form headings
are used as appropriate, e.g., **Peace treaties; Treaties — Collections; [Place]
— Foreign relations — Treaties.** * Examples include:

Title: *Theatrum pacis, Hoc est*
1. **Peace treaties — Collections.**

---

*The subdivision **—Treaties** is used only under names of Indian tribes, names of wars, and
headings of the type **[Place] — Foreign relations.**

Title: *Current International Treaties*
  1. **Treaties — Collections.**

Title: *List of Treaty Collections*
  1. **Treaties — Collections — Bibliography.**

Title: *Tratados bilaterales de Venezuela*
  1. **Venezuela — Foreign relations — Treaties.**

2) For topical collections of treaties, the appropriate topical headings are assigned, e.g., **Environmental law, International; Civil rights (International law); Postal conventions; Commercial treaties; Sex discrimination against women — Law and legislation; Choctaw Indians — Treaties; World War, 1939-1945 — Treaties.** An example is:

Title: *Labour Law Ratified Conventions*
  1. **Labor laws and legislation, International.**

If the purpose of the collection is to present the treaties to which a particular country is a party, a general heading without local subdivision is used to bring out the international aspect. In addition, the same heading with local subdivision is assigned to bring out the country, except for collections of commercial treaties, for which the heading **[Country] — Commercial treaties** is used. An example is:

Title: *Contratos de licencia y de transferencia de tecnología en el derecho privado*
  1. **Technology transfer — Law and legislation — Argentina.**
  2. **Foreign licensing agreements.**
  3. **Technology transfer — Law and legislation.**

If the collection is limited to only two countries, the general heading is omitted, and reciprocal headings are used to bring out both parties:

Title: *U.S.-China Commercial Relations: A Compilation of Basic Documents*
  1. **United States — Commercial treaties.**
  2. **China — Commercial treaties.**
  3. **United States — Commerce — China.**
  4. **China — Commerce — United States.**

3) For individual treaties, the types of headings used for topical collections of treaties are assigned. The heading for the name of the treaty is not assigned to a work that contains only the text of the treaty:

Title: *International Coffee Agreement, 1976*
  1. **Coffee — Law and legislation.**

For individual bilateral agreements, duplicate entries are made to bring out both parties:

Title: *Treaty to Resolve Pending Boundary Differences ...*
             Between the United States and Mexico

1. **United States — Boundaries — Mexico.**
2. **Mexico — Boundaries — United States.**

Works about treaties

The types of headings assigned to texts of treaties are also used for works about them:

Title: *Prudence in Victory: The Dynamics of Post-War*
             Settlements / Nissan Oren

1. **Peace treaties.**
2. **War (International law)**
3. **World politics — 20th century.**

Title: *Agreements of the People's Republic of China: A*
             Calendar of Events, 1966-1980

1. **China — Foreign relations — Treaties.**

Title: *Environmental Law: An In-Depth Review*

1. **Environmental law, International.**

A work about a particular treaty is assigned a heading for the name of the treaty or the international convention in addition to any topical heading(s):

Title: *The Moon Treaty*

1. **Agreement Governing the Activities of States on the Moon and Other Celestial Bodies (1979)**
2. **Space law.**

Title: *Commentary on the International Convention for Safe*
             Containers

1. **International Convention for Safe Containers (1972)**
2. **Containers — Law and legislation.**

Trials[24]

The same types of headings are assigned to the proceedings of a trial or trials as those assigned to works discussing such trials.

General collections of trials

The heading **Trials** *(Indirect)* is assigned to a nontopical collection of proceedings of trials and to a work describing various trials:

Title: *Protracted Civil Trials: Views from the Bench and the*
             Bar

1. **Trials — United States.**

Collections of particular types of trials

A heading of the type **Trials ([Topic]) — [Place]** is assigned to a collection of proceedings of a particular type of civil or criminal trial or to a work describing several trials of a specific type:

Title: *The Salem Witchcraft Trials*
  1. **Trials (Witchcraft) — Massachusetts — Salem.**
  2. **Salem (Mass.) — History.**

Title: *Some Famous Rhodesian Trials*
  1. **Trials (Murder) — Zimbabwe.**
  2. **Trials — Zimbabwe.**

Individual criminal trials

The following types of headings are used for works containing the proceedings of a criminal trial and for works about such a trial:

[Name of defendant] — Trials, litigation, etc.
[Name of the trial]
   [if it has been established as a heading]
Trials ([Topic]) — [Place]
[Topical headings, as appropriate]

An example is:

Title: *Excerpts from the Transcript of the Trial Proceedings in the Case of the United States of America v. John W. Jenrette*
  1. **Jenrette, John W. — Trials, litigation, etc.**
  2. **Trials (Fraud) — Washington (D.C.)**
  3. **Trials (Bribery) — Washington (D.C.)**
  4. **Abscam Bribery Scandal, 1980-   .**

Individual civil trials

In addition to appropriate topical or legal headings, the following types of headings are used for works containing the proceedings of an individual civil trial and for works about such a trial:

[Name of party initiating civil action] — Trials, litigation, etc.
[Name of major party] — Trials, litigation, etc.
Trials ([Topic]) — [Place]
[Topical heading, as appropriate]

An example is:

Title: *Odlum v. Stratton: Verbatim Report of Proceedings in
          the High Court of Justice, King's Bench Division,
          before Mr. Justice Atkinson*
   1.   **Odlum, George Milton — Trials, litigation, etc.**
   2.   **Stratton, Richard — Trials, litigation, etc.**
   3.   **Trials (Libel) — England — London.**

War crime trials

To proceedings of and works about a war crime trial, the following types
of headings are assigned in addition to other topical headings: **[Name of
defendant or trial]; War crime trials — [Place]**. Examples include:

Title: *The Tokyo War Crimes Trial*
   1.   **Tokyo Trial, 1946-1948.**
   2.   **War crime trials — Japan — Tokyo.**

Title: *Justice at Nuremberg*
   1.   **War crime trials — Germany (West) — Nuremberg.**

Title: *Eichmann in Jerusalem*
   1.   **Eichmann, Adolf, 1906-1962.**
   2.   **War criminals — Germany — Biography.**
   3.   **War crime trials — Jerusalem.**
   4.   **Holocaust, Jewish (1939-1945)**

SOURCE MATERIALS IN THE FIELDS OF
HISTORY AND GENEALOGY[25]

In the past, many publications of interest to genealogists and historians,
especially local historians, were assigned headings of the type **[Topic] —
[Place]**. Since December 1975 such materials have been given an additional
heading of the type **[Place] — [Topic]** if the place is below the country level.
The topical subdivision in this case is chosen from the following list:

   — **Antiquities**
   — **Biography**
   — **Church history**
   — **Description and travel**
          [or — **Description**]
   — **Economic conditions**
   — **Ethnic relations**
   — **Foreign population**
   — **Genealogy**
   — **History**
          [including the various modifications of the subdivision, e.g.,
          — **History, Military**]

- Industries
- Race relations
- Religion
- Religious life and customs
- Social conditions
- Social life and customs

All these are free-floating subdivisions. The subdivision —Genealogy or —History is used when none of the others listed above seems particularly appropriate to the work in hand.

The Subdivision — History[26]

The subdivision —History is a free-floating subdivision that is widely used under a variety of topics to designate historical treatment. However, certain restrictions to its use have developed over the years. The following information supersedes the instructions provided in *Library of Congress Subject Headings: A Guide to Subdivision Practice.*

General use

The subdivision —History is used under subjects, including names of places or organizations, for descriptions and explanations of past events concerning the topic, place, or organization, e.g., **Aeronautics—History; Indians of North America—History; Washington (D.C.)—History; Catholic Church—History; General Motors Corporation—History.**

Exceptions

The subdivision —History is not used:

1) under literary, music, or film form headings or under the heading **Law** *(Indirect)*; in these cases, the subdivision —**History and criticism** is used instead, e.g., **English poetry—History and criticism; Western films—History and criticism; Law—History and criticism**

2) under subjects for which phrase headings have been provided, e.g., **Church history; Military history; Social history;** etc.

3) under historical headings or headings with an obvious historical connotation, e.g., **Migrations of nations; Reformation; Discoveries (in geography); [Names of individual events or wars]**

4) under topical subdivisions considered historical in intent. These include all subdivisions that are obviously historical in nature (e.g., —**Discovery and exploration;** —**Territorial expansion**) and subdivisions that imply history by designating special kinds of conditions (e.g., —**Economic conditions**), special customs (e.g., —**Social life and customs**), and political affairs (e.g., —**Foreign relations;** —**Politics and government**). Following is a list of the subdivisions of this type that are not further subdivided by —**History:**

- Administrative and political divisions
- Aerial exploration
- Annexation to ...
- Anniversaries, etc.
- Antiquities
- Art
- Autonomous communities
- Boundaries
- Cantons
- Centennial celebrations, etc.
- Chronology
- Church history
- Churches
- Civilization
- Constitutional history
- Constitutional law
- Court and courtiers
- Cult
- Departments
- Description
- Description and travel
- Discovery and exploration
- Economic conditions
- Economic policy
- Exhibitions
- Exiles
- Exploring expeditions
- Foreign economic relations
- Foreign relations
- Frontier troubles
- Gold discoveries
- Government relations
- Governors
- Heraldry
- Historical geography
- Historiography
- History
- Iconography
- Illustrations
- Intellectual life
- Kings and rulers
- Military policy
- Military relations
- Moral conditions
- Origin
- Politics and government
- Portraits
- Presidents
- Princes and princesses
- Prophecies
- Provinces
- Queens
- Race relations
- Relations
- Relations (Diplomatic)
- Religion
- Religious life and customs
- Republics
- Rites and ceremonies
- Rural conditions
- Sieges
- Social conditions
- Social life and customs
- Social policy
- States
- Sultans
- Territorial expansion
- Vice-Presidents

Period subdivisions

Under certain headings, especially names of places, the subdivision — History is further subdivided by period when there is sufficient material to warrant it. If one of the exceptional headings or subdivisions noted under points 3 and 4 above is to be further subdivided by period, the period subdivision follows immediately after the heading or the topical subdivision, e.g., **Social history — 19th century; Great Britain — Economic conditions — 20th century; Chicago (Ill.) — Politics and government — To 1950.**

Historical source materials

The subdivision — **Sources** follows directly after the exceptional headings and subdivisions noted in points 2, 3, and 4 above without the interposition of the subdivision — **History**, e.g., **Reconstruction — Sources; World War,**

1914-1918—Sources; China—Foreign relations—Sources; United States—Politics and government—1783-1789—Sources.

Examples include:

> Title: *Reconstruction after the American Civil War*
> 1. **Reconstruction.**
> 2. **Reconstruction—Sources.**

> Title: *Collection of Nineteenth and Twentieth Century Documents*
> 1. **World War, 1914-1918—Sources.**
> 2. **World War, 1939-1945—Sources.**
> 3. **Military history, Modern—19th century—Sources.**

Form subdivisions

In order to bring out the bibliographic or physical form of a work, the subdivision —**History** may be subdivided by an appropriate free-floating form subdivision:

> Title: *Agricultural Technology and Society in Colorado*
> 1. **Agriculture—Colorado—History—Pictorial works.**
> 2. **Farm mechanization—Colorado—History—Pictorial works.**
> 3. **Farm life—Colorado—History—Pictorial works.**

In a few instances in which it is necessary to designate the history of a form, and there are no alternatives, the subdivision —**History** is used to further subdivide a form subdivision:

> Title: *Development of Medical Periodicals*
> 1. **Medicine—Periodicals—History.**

There are two special considerations regarding form subdivisions.

1) Certain form subdivisions are not further subdivided by —**History**. In order to express the historical aspect, another subdivision is used:

Form	*History*
Medicine—Computer programs	**Medicine—Data processing—History**
Medicine—Indexes	**Medicine—Abstracting and indexing—History**

2) By tradition, art form subdivisions, including the subdivisions —**Art**; —**Portraits**; —**Iconography**; and —**Illustrations**, are not further subdivided by —**History**.

History of a Discipline in a Place[27]

Headings of the type **[Name of discipline] — [Place] — History**, e.g., **Agriculture — United States — History**, are used to designate either the history of the discipline in a place or the history of conditions in a place. Usually no attempt is made to distinguish between the two concepts. However, a few special headings provide for conditions in a particular place in an entirely different manner. For example, in the field of economics, the economic conditions of a place are brought out by the subdivision **— Economic conditions** under the name of the place. In such instances scope notes are provided to warn the user that the heading subdivided by place refers only to the discipline in the place, including its history, and that conditions and the history of conditions are found elsewhere. Examples include:

Title: *A History of Agriculture in India*
    1.   **Agriculture — India — History.**

Title: *Feeding Multitudes: A History of How Farmers Made
       America Rich*
    1.   **Agriculture — Economic aspects — United States — History.**
    2.   **Agriculture — United States — History.**

Title: *Economic Theory and Ideology*
    1.   **Economics.**
    2.   **Economics — History.**

Title: *British Economy of the Nineteenth Century*
    1.   **Great Britain — Economic conditions — 19th century.**

Genealogical Materials[28]

The heading **[Place] — Genealogy** is used for works of value in the study of the origin, descent, and relationship of named families, especially those works that assemble such information from family papers, deeds, wills, public records, parish registers, cemetery inscriptions, ship lists, etc. Such a heading is assigned even if the place involved is a country or larger region such as a continent.

When appropriate, a form heading is also assigned. Typical headings of this nature are:

Archives	**Epitaphs**
Business records	**Heraldry**
Church records and registers	**Inscriptions**
Court records	**Inventories of descendents'**
Criminal registers	**estates**
Deeds	**Land grants**

Marriage licenses	Registers of births, etc.
Mining claims	Royal descent, Families of
Names	Slave records
Obituaries	Titles of honor and nobility
Probate records	Trials
Public land records	Wills
Public records	

All these may be subdivided by place except the heading **Royal descent, Families of**. Examples include:

Title: *In Remembrance, Cemetery Readings of Walton County, Georgia*
1. Walton County (Ga.) – Genealogy.
2. Registers of births, etc. – Georgia – Walton County.
3. Cemeteries – Georgia – Walton County.
4. Inscriptions – Georgia – Walton County.

Title: *Early Waco Obituaries and Various Related Items, 1874-1908*
1. Waco (Tex.) – Genealogy.
2. Obituaries – Texas – Waco.

Title: *List of Ancient Deeds Series E (L.R. 14)*
1. England – Genealogy.
2. Land titles – England.
3. Deeds – England.

Title: *Gravestone Inscriptions and Lineages, Wilkinson County, Georgia*
1. Wilkinson County (Ga.) – Genealogy.
2. Registers of births, etc. – Georgia – Wilkinson County.
3. Inscriptions – Georgia – Wilkinson County.
4. Cemeteries – Georgia – Wilkinson County.

Title: *Abstracts of Wills in McDonough County, Illinois, 1834-1857*
1. McDonough County (Ill.) – Genealogy.
2. Wills – Illinois – McDonough County.

Other Works of Interest to Historians

The following types of materials are also considered of interest to historians:

1) *Activities.* Typical headings include:

    Cattle trade
    Country life
    Frontier and pioneer life
    Fur trade

        Mountain life
        Plantation life
        Printing — History
        Ranch life

2) *Archaeological evidence.** Typical headings include:

        Christian antiquities
        Earthworks (Archaeology)
        Excavations (Archaeology)
        Industrial archaeology
        Kitchen-middens
        Mounds

3) *Classes of persons.* Typical headings include:

        Buccaneers
        Cowboys
        Gunsmiths
        Lawyers
        Minorities
            [including individually named groups, e.g.,
                Swedish Americans — Minnesota]
        Physicians
        Pirates
        Politicians

4) *Monuments and memorials.* Typical headings include:

        Cemeteries
        Epitaphs
        Historical markers
        Inscriptions
        Memorials
        Monuments
        Sepulchral monuments
        Soldiers' monuments
        Statues
        Tombs
        War memorials

5) *Particular uses of land; historic structures.* Typical headings include:

        Bridges
        Churches
        Farms
        Fountains
        Historic sites

---

*For works on the archaeology of particular places, see the section on archaeological works beginning on page 323.

Hotels, taverns, etc.
Mines and mineral resources
Parks
Roads

6) *Historic events.* Typical headings include:

Battles
Earthquakes
Epidemics
Fires
Storms

If a work is historical in nature and requires one of the headings of the types listed above, the additional heading **[Place] – [Topic]** is usually assigned.

Title: *Early German Printers of Lancaster*
1. **Printers – Pennsylvania – Lancaster – Biography.**
2. **Lancaster (Pa.) – Biography.**

Title: *Sign Posts; Place Names in the History of Burlington County, New Jersey*
1. **Names, Geographical – New Jersey – Burlington County.**
2. **Burlington County (N.J.) – History, Local.**

Title: *Charcoal Kilns; Historic Structures Report of Santa Fe*
1. **Charcoal kilns – New Mexico – Santa Fe.**
2. **Santa Fe (N.M.) – Antiquities.**

Title: *The Chinese in New York*
1. **Chinese Americans – New York (N.Y.) – History – 20th century.**
2. **New York (N.Y.) – History – 1898-1951.**

The prescribed extra heading **[Place] – [Topic]** is assigned to works of interest to historians only when the place in question is at a lower level than a country, e.g., a city, county, state, region of a country, etc. It is not assigned when the place in question corresponds to a country or a larger region except for works classed in D, E, and F at the Library of Congress.

Examples of works to which the additional heading is not assigned include:

Title: *Words Like Freedom: A Multi-Cultural Bibliography*
1. **Minorities – United States – Bibliography.**

Title: *War in the West*
1. **World War, 1939-1945 – Campaigns – Western.**

Title: *Historic Preservation: Grants-In-Aid Catalogue*
1. **Federal aid to historic sites — United States.**
2. **Historic buildings — United States — Conservation and restoration.**

Examples of works classed in D, E, and F requiring an additional heading include:*

Title: *National Parks and Monuments*
1. **National parks and reserves — United States.**
2. **Historic sites — United States.**
3. **United States — Description and travel — 1960-1980 — Guide-books.**

Title: *Place Names of Australia*
1. **Names, Geographical — Australia.**
2. **Australia — History, Local.**

Title: *Fighting Generals*
1. **Generals — United States.**
2. **United States. Army — Biography.**
3. **United States — History, Military.**

Title: *Australia in the Great War*
1. **World War, 1914-1918 — Australia.**
2. **Australia — History — 20th century.**

Title: *Who Lived to See the Day; France in Arms, 1940-1945*
1. **World War, 1939-1945 — Underground movements — France.**
2. **France — History — German occupation, 1940-1945.**

---

*The last heading listed in each example is the prescribed extra heading.

ARCHAEOLOGICAL WORKS[29]

Types of Headings

For works on the archaeology of particular places, one or more of the following types of headings are used:

[Name of site, if the work is about a specific site]
[Country, etc.*] — Antiquities; or [Country, etc.*] — Antiquities,
    Roman, [etc.**]
[Special locality] — Antiquities; or [Special locality] — Antiquities,
    Roman, [etc.**]
[Name of people, prehistoric culture or period, etc.]†
[Other special topics, as needed]
Excavations (Archaeology) — [Place]

Application

Works not limited to a single site

The heading for the place and the heading for the people are assigned to an archaeological work if both a single area (but not a single site) and a single people are under discussion. If two peoples are involved, a separate heading for each is assigned. If more than two peoples are involved or if the name of the people(s) cannot be identified from the work being cataloged, the heading or headings for the people(s) are omitted. If the name of the jurisdiction corresponds closely to that of the people (e.g., **Egypt** and **Egyptians**), only the heading for the place is assigned.††

Examples of works not limited to a single site include:

Title: *Vasilike Ware: An Early Bronze Age Pottery Style in*
            Crete
    1. Crete — Antiquities.
    2. Pottery, Minoan — Greece — Crete.
    3. Greece — Antiquities.

---

*The main heading is at the country level or higher (a region or continent larger than a country) except in the case of Canada, Great Britain, the Soviet Union, and the United States, for which the names of the first-order political divisions rather than the countries are used, e.g., **Arizona — Antiquities**. If the area involved is a special locality within the country or first-order political division, an additional heading under the name of the locality is assigned.

The subdivision —Antiquities** is qualified by one of the following adjectives if applicable: **Buddhist; Byzantine; Celtic; Germanic; Hindu; Phoenician; Roman; Slavic; Turkish**.

†This heading is subdivided by —**Antiquities** if the people are still extant in modern times, e.g., **Mayas — Antiquities**.

††The heading **Romans** is not assigned if the work is assigned either the heading **Rome — Antiquities** or **Italy — Antiquities**.

Title: *Excavations at Ancient Meiron, Upper Galilee, Israel,*
        1971-72, 1974-75, 1977
1. **Meron (Israel) — Antiquities.**
2. **Excavations (Archaeology) — Israel — Meron.**
3. **Israel — Antiquities.**

Title: *The Pottery of Acatlán: A Changing Mexican Tradition*
1. **Indians of Mexico — Acatlán de Osorio — Pottery.**
2. **Acatlán de Osorio (Mexico) — Antiquities.**
3. **Mexico — Antiquities.**

Title: *Ancient Ruins of the Southwest: An Archaeological Guide*
1. **Indians of North America — Southwest, New — Antiquities.**
2. **Southwest, New — Antiquities.**

Title: *Maya, The Riddle and Rediscovery of a Lost Civilization*
1. **Mayas — Antiquities.**
2. **Mexico — Antiquities.**
3. **Central America — Antiquities.**

Works on individual sites

A heading in the form of [**Name of site**] is assigned to a work about an individual archaeological site:

Title: *Excavation at Fengate, Peterborough, England*
1. **Fengate Site (England)**

In addition, the following headings may be assigned when appropriate: [**Special topics**]; [**Name of modern locality in which the site is located**] — **Antiquities.** Examples include:

Title: *The Grand Village of the Natchez Revisited: Excavations*
        at the Fatherland Site, Adams County, Mississippi,
        1972
1. **Fatherland Site (Miss.)**
2. **Mississippi — Antiquities.**
3. **Adams County (Miss.) — Antiquities.**
4. **Indians of North America — Mississippi — Antiquities.**
5. **Natchez Indians — Antiquities.**
6. **Excavations (Archaeology) — Mississippi.**

Title: *The Emergence of an Iron Age Economy: The Mecklenburg*
        Grave Groups from Hallstatt and Stična
1. **Hallstatt Site (Austria)**
2. **Stična Site (Austria)**
3. **Marie, Duchess of Mecklenburg-Schwerin, 1856-**
    1929 — Archaeological collections.

Title: *Mill Creek Ceramics: The Complex from the Brewster Site*
1. **Brewster Site (Iowa)**
2. **Indians of North America — Iowa — Pottery.**

AREA STUDIES AND RESEARCH[30]

The use of "area studies" headings, e.g., **African studies,** and "ethnic studies" headings, e.g., **Indian studies,** was discontinued in 1977. Instead, headings of the type **[Name of area** or **ethnic group] — Study and teaching,** e.g., **Africa — Study and teaching; Indians — Study and teaching,** are used.

The heading **[Name of area] — Study and teaching** is used for a work on the study of an area, including facilities, personnel, funding, projects, methodology, etc. It is not assigned to a work that represents substantive information about an area or information obtained *as a result* of an area study program. For this type of work a heading is assigned under the name of the area, or, if the work focuses on a special aspect of the area (including history, language, culture, etc.), the heading is subdivided by the appropriate subdivision, e.g., **Africa; Africa — Civilization; Africa — Intellectual life.** Examples include:

Title: *Educators' Source Book on China: A Selected List of Information Resources*
1. **China — Bibliography.**
2. **China — Study and teaching — Audio-visual aids.**

Title: *China: A General Survey*
1. **China.**

Title: *Selected Papers from the Center for Far Eastern Studies*
1. **China — Collected works.**
2. **Japan — Collected works.**

Title: *China: A Country Study*
1. **China.**

The use of "research" headings is similar to area and ethnic studies headings. Research headings, e.g., **Engineering — Research; Marine biology — Research,** are assigned to works that discuss such details as the facilities, personnel, etc., for doing research in particular disciplines. Works providing the *results* of the research are assigned headings under the names of the disciplines themselves, e.g., **Engineering; Marine biology;** etc.

ZOOLOGICAL WORKS[31]

In his *Subject Headings: A Practical Guide*, David Judson Haykin discusses a kind of duplicate entry that is "frequently and consistently used,"[32] namely, a duplicate entry under the next broader heading that allows local subdivision when assigning a heading for an animal that may not be locally subdivided. Haykin points out that such provision is most often appropriate for works on a particular genus or species in the place, using the example:

1. **Gnatcatchers.**
2. **Birds – California.**

The additional subject entry is important because it enables users to carry out area surveys. Direct access to place and topic is a standard feature of cataloging for the social sciences fields, e.g., **Ohio – Economic conditions**, but it is seldom encountered for works in pure and applied sciences, where greater stress is placed on topic. Without providing direct access to place, this handicap may be overcome by gathering all zoological works with a geographic aspect under a limited number of broad topical headings with local subdivision. By consulting these headings the user is able to obtain a complete array of the works on the zoology of a specific place.

Geographic Subdivisions

When cataloging a work on an animal of a particular place, two headings are assigned: (1) the heading for the animal's name (family name, genus name, etc.), with local subdivision if the heading also provides for local subdivision, and (2) the corresponding broader heading with local subdivision. Library of Congress practice has varied over the years on the question of the most appropriate taxonomic level for the second heading, with the result that different levels may be observed in older Library of Congress cataloging records. In current practice, the phylum level is used for invertebrates, with the exception of arachnids, crustaceans, and insects of Arthropoda, for which the class level is used. For vertebrates, the class level is used.

Below are lists of phyla and classes – using the Library of Congress's present forms of the names – under which gathering entries are made.

Phyla of invertebrates

Acanthocephala
Annelida
Arthropoda
Brachiopoda
Bryozoa
Chaetognatha
Coelenterata
Ctenophora
Echinodermata
Echiuroidea
Enteropneusta
Entoprocto
Gastrotricha
Gordiacea
Kinorhyncha
Mesozoa

Mollusks	**Priapulida**
Myzostomaria	**Protochordates**
Nematoda	**Protozoa**
Nemertinea	**Pterobranchia**
Onychophora	**Rotifera**
Pentastomida	**Sipunculida**
Platyhelminthes	**Sponges**
Pogonophora	**Tardigrada**
Porifera	**Tunicata**

Examples include:

Title: *Zwei neue interstitielle Microphthalmus-Arten (Polychaeta) von den Bermudas*
1. **Microphthalmus bermudensis.**
2. **Annelida — Bermuda Islands.**

Title: *Deep-Sea Pycnogonida from the North and South Atlantic Basins*
1. **Pycnogonida — Atlantic Ocean.**
2. **Arthropoda — Atlantic Ocean.**

Classes of Arthropoda

Arachnida
Crustacea
Insects

An example is:

Title: *Research on the Mosquitoes of Angola (Diptera, Culicidae)*
1. **Mosquitoes — Angola.**
2. **Insects — Angola.**

Classes of vertebrates

Amphibians
Birds
Fishes
Mammals
Reptiles

Examples include:

Title: *The Pronghorn Antelope in Alberta*
1. **Pronghorn antelope.**
2. **Mammals — Alberta.**

Title: *Waterfowl of the Chesapeake Bay Country*
1. **Waterfowl — Chesapeake Bay (Md. and Va.)**
2. **Birds — Chesapeake Bay (Md. and Va.)**

Topical Subdivisions

In addition to providing geographical access to individual animals, the Library of Congress also uses gathering to give access to many subdisciplines of zoology as they pertain to individual animals. In the past, the Library of Congress handled these special topics by gathering under broader taxonomic headings in the same manner as above, for example:

1. **Wood-rats.**
2. **Mammals — Anatomy.**

Because these subdisciplines, including **Anatomy; Behavior; Cytology; Evolution; Genetics; Reproduction;** etc., are now represented by the topical subdivisions found under the heading **Fishes,** the model heading for animals, they are now topics that may be used under any animal as free-floating subdivisions. Accordingly, the Library of Congress will assign the topical subdivision both under the name of the specific animal (for purposes of specificity) and under the broader heading (for purposes of gathering), using the same gathering levels stated above:

1. **Wood-rats — Anatomy.**
2. **Mammals — Anatomy.**

If a topic is more specific than any of the subdisciplines represented by a subdivision under the model heading, an additional heading to bring out that topic is assigned:

1. **Wood-rats — Anatomy.**
2. **Cornea.**
3. **Mammals — Anatomy.**

REFERENCES

[1] Library of Congress, Subject Cataloging Division, *Subject Cataloging Manual: Subject Headings*, prelim. ed. (Washington, D.C.: Library of Congress, 1984), H362, H1156.

[2] Ibid., H1780, H1790, H1800.

[3] Ibid., H1720.

[4] Ibid., H1330.

[5] Ibid., H1155.6.

[6] Ibid., H1155.8.

[7]Ibid., H1160.

[8]Ibid.

[9]Ibid., H1161.

[10]Ibid., H1160.

[11]"Invalid Music Headings in LCSH," *Music Cataloging Bulletin* 11(2):1 (Feb. 1980).

[12]"Pattern References," *Music Cataloging Bulletin* 7(9):6-7 (Sept. 1976).

[13]Library of Congress, *Subject Cataloging Manual*, H1917.

[14]Material distributed at Regional Institutes on Library of Congress Subject Headings, sponsored by ALA Resources and Technical Services Division, Library of Congress, and ALA/RTSD Council of Regional Groups, 1982-1984.

[15]Library of Congress, *Subject Cataloging Manual*, H910.

[16]Ibid., H1427.

[17]Ibid., H2015.

[18]Ibid., H1998; "Combining Religion with Particular Topics in Subject Heading Practice," *Cataloging Service Bulletin* 15:33-37 (Winter 1982).

[19]Library of Congress, *Subject Cataloging Manual*, H1435.

[20]Ibid., H1154.5, H1550, H1705, H1710, H2227, H2228.

[21]"Constitutions in Subject Heading Practice," *Cataloging Service Bulletin* 24:56-57 (Spring 1984).

[22]"Subject Heading 'Law — Periodicals (Indirect)'," *Cataloging Service Bulletin* 10:31 (Fall 1980).

[23]Library of Congress, *Subject Cataloging Manual*, H2227.

[24]Ibid., H2228.

[25]Ibid., H1845.

[26]Ibid., H1647.

[27]Ibid.; "History of a Discipline in a Place," *Cataloging Service* 121:15 (Spring 1977).

[28]Library of Congress, *Subject Cataloging Manual*, H1845.

[29]Ibid., H1225.

[30]Ibid., H1240.

[31]Ibid., H1332; "Gathering Levels in Zoology," *Cataloging Service* 122:16-18 (Summer 1977); "Animal and Plant Names," *Cataloging Service Bulletin* 20:40-42 (Spring 1983).

[32]David Judson Haykin, *Subject Headings: A Practical Guide* (Washington, D.C.: Government Printing Office, 1951), 59.

Part 3

LIBRARY OF CONGRESS
SUBJECT HEADINGS
IN THE ONLINE ENVIRONMENT

11

LIBRARY OF CONGRESS SUBJECT HEADINGS AS AN ONLINE RETRIEVAL TOOL

INTRODUCTION

In recent years the Library of Congress subject headings system has taken on a new role, a role different from that for which it was designed and developed. This is because MARC records now appear in almost all the online catalogs and many of the retrieval systems that have come into being during the past decade; in some of these systems, in fact, MARC records are the biggest part of the database. *Library of Congress Subject Headings*, the major indexing language for MARC records, has thus become an online subject retrieval tool.

The MARC format for bibliographic records was first developed in the 1960s by the Library of Congress. In 1966 the Library began creating MARC records, and in 1969 the distribution of MARC records began. Initially the MARC records were used primarily for processing cataloging information; many libraries used the available MARC records to generate catalog cards or microform catalogs. MARC records were not generally available for public use until the late 1970s.

With the development of online public catalogs that contain MARC records, the information presented on those records became accessible to the public. The format of the catalog underwent a significant transformation—from manual to mechanized. The style of presenting bibliographic elements has also gone through considerable change as a result of the specifications of the MARC format. Nonetheless, the subject headings on MARC records have not changed; in principles of structure and policies of operation the Library of Congress subject headings system remains basically the same in the online age as before. There are two minor points of difference: proper name headings follow the form called for in *Anglo-American Cataloguing Rules*, second edition (*AACR2*), and in the MARC format there are different field tags for various types of subject headings and subheadings: personal name, corporate name, geographical name, topical term, and so on. (Appendix K shows the MARC specifications for tagging subject headings.)

ONLINE BIBLIOGRAPHIC SYSTEMS

During the 1970s considerable progress was made in the development of the online public catalog in American libraries. Many such catalogs are now in operation; many more are being developed. While the content of the cataloging records is standardized — bibliographic description based on *AACR2*, Library of Congress subject headings, call numbers (Library of Congress Classification and/or Dewey Decimal Classification), and other information specified by the MARC format — recent online catalog studies show that the method of access varies considerably from catalog to catalog.[1]

Library of Congress Systems

In the Library of Congress the two main online retrieval systems are SCORPIO (Subject-Content-Oriented-Retriever-for-Processing-Information-On-Line) and MUMS (Multiple Use MARC System). SCORPIO is the system that provides the public with online access to a number of files in the Library's information retrieval system. These include LCCC (Library of Congress Computerized Catalog), which contains the cataloging records for books in the Library of Congress MARC database and which can be searched by subject through Library of Congress subject headings. Because the system was designed for unassisted searches by users with little or no experience with computers, the number of commands is deliberately limited. It does not allow keyword or component word searching, but it provides certain other online features. These include browsing the author-title-subject index (but not the *Library of Congress Subject Headings* list), which shows the number of postings for each term, set combination using Boolean logic, set storage for reserving information during a search, and limiting by certain criteria such as language and date of publication.

MUMS was originally designed for the Library's processing services to build data online quickly.[2] Because of a special feature, component word or keyword search (the capability of matching the input term with individual words in various fields in the record), which is not available in SCORPIO, MUMS also serves as an effective search tool and has been made available for public use at the Library of Congress.

Other Online Public Catalogs

The late 1970s and the early 1980s represented a period of experimentation and development for online public catalogs in American libraries. The field is changing rapidly. During the development period, a considerable amount of research was done on how patrons use online catalogs, and the published studies provide evidence not only on how the catalogs are being received but ways in which they seem to be falling short. The following account summarizes significant findings. In considering it, readers should bear in mind that the catalogs used in the studies were in various stages of development and that it is perhaps futile to attempt to draw firm conclusions at this point.

Karen Markey's 1984 report notes that all the recent online studies indicate greater use of the catalog for subject searching than was reported in studies of traditional catalogs.[3]

Charles R. Hildreth, who studied ten online public access catalogs (OPACs), reports that "the principal subject vocabulary used for constructing online indexes for subject access is the Library of Congress Subject Headings."[4] However, the mechanisms of subject access and display in the catalogs vary greatly: some offer keyword or phrase searching on index terms; others allow searching only by Library of Congress subject headings in their prescribed (cataloged) form.

Pauline A. Cochrane points out many limitations to effective online subject searching by library users, in part explained by the fact that the public online catalog is so new. Problems include false drops from keyword searching over combinations of fields, inefficiency stemming from the use of too many common words in searchable fields, and low recall from insufficiency of lead-in terms. Further sources of difficulty, Cochrane says, are lack of uniformity among the online public access catalogs with regard to the fields used to build "title" keyword searches and the number and kinds of heading indexes in which the user may browse, and users' unfamiliarity with online systems and with the mechanical details of controlled vocabularies, such as punctuation, word order, abbreviations, and filing order.[5]

Neal K. Kaske and Nancy P. Sanders, who studied online catalogs in public libraries, note some of the problems experienced by users with regard to subject access:

> Analysis of focus group remarks and questionnaire responses showed that OPAC users experienced difficulty when performing subject searches. Reasons underlying this difficulty were: (1) patrons' inability to match their input term(s) with the OPAC's controlled vocabulary; (2) the burden on the OPAC user of conjuring up broader or narrower terms; and (3) problems consulting the printed volumes of LCSH during the online search.[6]

In spite of the limitations of subject access in current online public catalogs, Hildreth envisions a promising future:

> Opportunities exist for enhancing subject access not possible in earlier forms of the catalog. The prospect of combining the best subject access features [now existing] ... is exciting, indeed. These features include (1) current terminology access through title keyword searching, (2) refining results by limiting search parameters to field, word position, publication date, language, or type of material, and (3) browsing headings files (with cross-references), keywords in titles, and the shelves themselves (represented by records in the shelf list file).[7]

Online Bibliographic Networks and Retrieval Services

Currently, a number of large online bibliographic networks also provide access to MARC records. Among these are OCLC (Online Computer Library Center), WLN (Washington Library Network), and RLIN (Research Library Information Network). Their databases contain LC MARC records as well as records contributed by member libraries. OCLC's database has the largest number of MARC records. Unfortunately, although OCLC's bibliographic records contain Library of Congress subject headings, the system as yet has no subject access capability. Both the WLN and RLIN systems allow subject searching.

The inclusion of the LC MARC data file in two of the largest commercial online retrieval systems — LC/LINE in ORBIT of SDC (Systems Development Corporation) and LC MARC in DIALOG — means that Library of Congress subject headings are being used as a subject access vocabulary by a large number of searchers outside the library context.

Library of Congress subject headings are also used to a limited extent in the CATLINE database of the National Library of Medicine: records for material in medicine and medical sciences are given subject headings from *Medical Subject Headings (MeSH)*, while Library of Congress subject headings are used for material in other subject fields.

CHARACTERISTICS OF ONLINE SUBJECT RETRIEVAL

There are a number of basic differences between a manual system and an online system for information retrieval. Certain online features or capabilities enable the user to manipulate subject headings and other parts of machine records to achieve the desired results in ways not possible in a manual system. The features and capabilities that have the most bearing on Library of Congress subject headings are discussed below.

The discussion is predicated on the availability of quite sophisticated searching and user interface features. At the present time relatively few online systems are highly sophisticated. The commercial retrieval services and some bibliographic utilities (such as RLIN and WLN) lie near the top of the range in this respect, probably because of their relatively greater access to resources for hardware and for software development. On the other hand, few online library catalogs, including those in the Library of Congress, can offer all of the features to be discussed, and relatively few of the features are present in all the systems. Nonetheless, the availability of each of the features in at least a number of systems indicates what is possible and/or feasible in online subject access.

Subject searching is a process of extracting from a large set of records a subset relevant to one's need. Certain basic requirements contribute to effective retrieval: the capability to identify relevant documents and exclude irrelevant ones, and the capability to broaden the resulting set of documents if it is too small or to limit it if it is too large. In modern information retrieval terminology, these capabilities are referred to as precision and recall. In online systems, a number of features not available in manual systems contribute to the precision and/or recall of subject searching. These features include keyword or component word search, truncation, Boolean operations, word adjacency, limiting, synonym operations, and online thesaurus display.

Keyword or Component Word Search

In online subject searching, the first step in identifying relevant records is term matching. One of the major differences between a card catalog and an online system is the capability of the latter for allowing multiple access points to a heading. A card catalog is linear; each subject entry contains one access point—the initial word—only. In an online system with keyword searching and/or searching by subfields, a heading may have as many access points as it has words. This is true of headings with subdivisions or qualifiers as well as phrase headings. In other words, individual words or subdivisions are searchable by themselves. Some online systems allow phrase searching; linked strings of words within subject headings, such as *processing machinery* or *machinery industry*, may be input as wholes.

In the manual catalog the matching process moves in only one direction—from left to right; in an online system with keyword searching, the matching process may begin with any of the words in the heading. For lack of an established term, this process will be referred to as "multidirectional access" in the following discussion. For example, a heading such as **Beverage processing machinery industry** is accessible only through the entry word *beverage* in a manual catalog; in an online system, it can be accessed through any of the four words constituting the heading. Another example is **Automobiles—Motors—Carburetors—Maintenance and repair.** (See Fig. 11.1.)

CARD CATALOG
    USER ⟶ Beverage processing machinery industry

    Beverage processing machinery industry
    ONLINE USER

CARD CATALOG
    USER
    Automobiles—Motors—Carburetors—Maintenance and repair

    Automobiles—Motors—Carburetors—Maintenance and repair
    ONLINE USER

Figure 11.1. Access points available to users in
manual catalogs and online systems.

Truncation

Truncation is another feature of online searching that improves the rate of term matching. When the root of a wanted term is known, but not the precise form used in indexing, a searcher can input the known part plus a truncation symbol. Implementation of the truncation feature varies from system to system: some include middle and initial truncation as well as the more common terminal truncation. For example, with # as the truncation symbol, M#GOWAN will obviate the need for knowing whether a name is spelled Magowan, MacGowan, McGowan, or M'Gowan; LIBRAR# will retrieve *librarian, librarianship, libraries,* and *library* but probably nothing else; WOM#N will retrieve *woman* and *women*, while WOM# will retrieve *womb* and *wombat* as well as the host of words in the family *womanhood* through *womenfolk*. (As helpful as truncation can be, obviously it must be used with caution.)

Boolean Operations

The capability of applying the Boolean operations AND, OR, and NOT is one of the most distinctive features of online information retrieval. In a manual catalog, only through a laborious scanning of individual records can one combine or exclude terms or sets in a search. In an online system, this can be done with simple commands, applied to one or more fields at a time, depending on the attributes of a given system. For example, one could give the command, "Find subject LIBRARIES *AND* BOOK SELECTION *AND NOT* CENSORSHIP." It is this feature that makes the postcoordinate approach in information retrieval feasible and effective.

Word Adjacency or Proximity

It often happens with unmodified Boolean requests that recall from a given search statement is quite different from what was expected: NORTHERN *AND* LIGHTS, for instance, could deliver a lot of material that has nothing to do with the aurora borealis. In a number of systems, MUMS and DIALOG among them, the drawback of uncontrolled Boolean operation is remedied by the feature of word adjacency or proximity. With such a capability a searcher can specify phrases, or ask for a term if it occurs within so many words of another term—before, after, or either way. A search statement asking for ROCK within four words to the left of MUSIC would retrieve titles with the phrases *rock music* and *rock and roll music* but would not retrieve a title like "Music in the desert; the song of wind against rock"— which could have appeared as a response to the request ROCK *AND* MUSIC.

Limiting

The limiting feature is a means of avoiding the retrieval of too much material by circumscribing searches in one or more of several predefined ways: to a given language, for instance, or type of publication, or span of time, or even geographic area. Too-high recall is a significant problem, noted in recent online catalog studies[8] and by theoreticians. Gerald Salton and Michael J. McGill comment on the "need to reduce to a manageable size the number of items that are to be examined.... Even in specialized, relatively narrow topic areas, one tends to become overloaded with information very rapidly."[9]

When recall is too high, it can of course be reduced by various means. One is using subdivisions; the subdivisions in *Library of Congress Subject Headings*, in fact, exist for this purpose as well as for achieving coextensivity of heading and content. Many subdivisions, particularly those relating to form, place, and time of publication, give information that is also carried in MARC fixed fields. Limiting by fixed fields is advisable whenever it is appropriate. For one thing, the device is machine-efficient: much less central processing unit capacity is needed for sorting on fixed fields than on elements in variable fields. For another, it is more effective because of its completeness of coverage. Most MARC records are fully coded; any applicable category of information for which there is fixed-field provision is included. On the other hand, subdivisions for language and period (by date of publication) are permissible only under some headings, free-floating form subdivisions may not be applied universally, and not all headings are open for geographical division even though such division might be relevant.

Synonym Operation

In some systems, the function of *see* references is taken over by automatic links that are hidden from the user. Synonyms are identified within the system, and the output when any one of them is used is the same as if the user had input the "right" or authorized term. This operation requires that the bibliographic records be linked to the thesaurus or authority file.

Online Vocabulary Display

Almost all recent online catalog studies have indicated the desirability of online vocabulary display to help users choose appropriate and properly formulated search terms.[10] These studies found that although libraries usually place the printed volumes of *Library of Congress Subject Headings* near their online terminals, and some make the microfiche edition available as well, catalog users hardly ever consult these aids even when they have great difficulty matching search terms with subject headings.[11] There is apparently a great need for guides to indexing language vocabulary and structure that are easier to use than the printed or microfiche versions of *Library of Congress Subject Headings*.

Although to date few online systems offer vocabulary display of *Library of Congress Subject Headings*, such a service is well within the bounds of system capabilities. As noted earlier, the SCORPIO system allows browsing on index terms (subject headings) and title words. DIALOG and ORBIT display alphabetical listings of the subject headings used in records in their MARC files, though without cross-references. MELVYL, the online catalog of the University of California, provides keyword-in-context display of assigned subject headings; in other words, it lists each heading under all of its terms no matter where they occur in the heading.[12]

Currently, the cross-references that are part of the Library of Congress subject headings system are the most neglected aspect of online catalogs and reference systems.[13] Few bibliographic utilities or commercial online retrieval systems provide online display of *Library of Congress Subject Headings* in the first place, and cross-references are not always incorporated even among those that do. Nevertheless, the potential for online help with indexing language vocabulary and structure is enormous. Some online systems, such as ERIC and Medline, display the indexing vocabulary with hierarchical clusters of given terms grouped with their broader and narrower terms. Some also show coordinate clusters of terms related in other ways. Recent online catalog studies identified cross-references as one of the features of the card catalog that users most wanted to be carried over to online catalogs. The deficiency in this area led Hildreth to observe that "online catalogs that do not provide 'see' and 'see also' references for term selection deprive the users of aids that they may have grown accustomed to (and benefitted from) when searching the card catalog."[14] With the development of ever more sophisticated online systems, it is reasonable to hope that *see* and *see also* references will become a standard feature in the near future.

IMPLICATIONS FOR LIBRARY OF CONGRESS SUBJECT HEADINGS

When *Library of Congress Subject Headings* is used as the indexing language for systems with the capabilities just described, many aspects of its basic features appear in a different light. Vocabulary, structure, and rules of application are all affected, structure most of all. Below, the following structural features of *Library of Congress Subject Headings* will be examined: uniform heading, entry element in main headings, citation order in subdivided headings, indirect versus direct geographic subdivision, qualified terms in headings, precoordination, and nontopical subdivision.

Uniform Heading

The principle of uniform heading, described in detail in chapter 2, ensures that material on a given topic will not be listed under more than one name for that topic: two synonymous terms will not both be used, nor two multiterm headings with the words in different orders. If there is a heading **History, Ancient**, for instance, there will not also be a heading Ancient history. Controlling synonymy is as important for online catalogs as for manual ones; hidden *see* references may make the control less obvious to users, but the control is still there in most systems. Uniformity in word order, however, becomes much less important in the online environment. In manual catalogs, with only linear access to multiterm headings, the principle of uniformity in headings greatly limits accessibility; such curtailment is an unavoidable but unfortunate effect of the principle. But with the multidirectional access capabilities of online systems, there are as many access points to a heading as there are indexed words in it. Thus the constraint of the single-entry approach imposed by the principle of uniform heading is eliminated to a large extent in an online system. There have been pressures to move the Library of Congress subject headings system in the direction of a multiple-entry system. Multidirectional access to the headings in a single-entry system makes the question moot.

Entry Element in Main Headings

In a manual system the order of words in a heading is important, because it is the first word that provides access to the heading. Generous *see* references from alternate forms go some way toward expanding access but require a two-stage lookup by those who follow through on them. For user convenience, therefore, from the inception of the Library of Congress subject headings system, inverted headings have been used in many cases to bring the "significant" word forward — **Chemistry, Organic,** for example, and **Plants, Effect of light on.** With multidirectional access, however, there is no longer a question of relative significance, for all words in a string are accessible. Of course, the "significant" word is still significant in any system that limits subject heading searches to full forms of headings or that allows only alphabetical browsing in an online thesaurus. But with increasing system power and with growth in the public availability of online systems, the question of optimal entry element will decrease in importance.

Citation Order in Subdivided Headings

The situation with subdivided headings is similar to that with main headings. There are two questions here: (1) Of two or more elements of a concept, which should be the main heading and which the subordinate? (2) What is the optimal order of subdivisions for headings with more than one subdivision? Deciding on the answers to these questions is a not insignificant part of the operation of establishing a new heading, in particular because (with some exceptions) there are no clearly defined rules or principles to follow. The second question must also be answered by indexers putting together strings with more than one subdivision from one of the lists of free-floating subdivisions.

With only linear access to a file, the answers to the first of these questions is crucial, and the answers to the second are also important because so few searchers pursue a topic through all the subdivisions of its main heading. With multidirectional access, however, both questions are moot with respect to access itself; it may be, however, that consistency in application, allowing analogous topics to be represented in parallel ways, enables greater searching efficiency for those who search over a wide range of topics. Also — and this is very important — the order of elements in a string often determines meaning. **[Topic] — [Place]** and **[Place] — [Topic]** may be interchangeable, but **History —Philosophy** and **Philosophy—History** are not. Thus the availability of multidirectional access in online retrieval decreases the significance of citation order in terms of access, but not in terms of semantics.

Geographic Subdivision:
Direct versus Indirect

A special case of citation order merits attention here: whether geographic subdivision should be direct, that is, with the name of the place in question as the first element of the subdivision as in — **Paris (France)**, or indirect, with the name of the larger geographic entity intervening as in — **France – Paris)**. Until a decade ago there was a mixture of both in *Library of Congress Subject Headings*, but in 1976 direct subdivision was abandoned so that all headings that allow geographic subdivision would be subdivided in the same way. The indirect subdivision method was chosen because, in a manual catalog, it provides the capability of gathering material on a broader geographic area. The advantage of direct subdivision, i.e., ease in application and in use, was outweighed by the desire for collocation. As previously noted, collocation is much less important in online searching than in manual searching. As the need for collocation is the main argument for indirect subdivision, therefore, it seems that the advantages of both indirect and direct subdivision may be realized by using direct subdivision in all cases. Since *AACR2* and Library of Congress policy specify that local place names be qualified by the names of larger areas, e.g., **Tokyo (Japan); San Francisco (Calif.)**; the qualifiers may be used for the purpose of gathering in much the same way the interposing elements in indirect subdivision are used. Currently (with a number of exceptions) the interposing geographic names and qualifiers coincide, as shown in the following examples:

> **Paris (France) – Intellectual life**
> **Music – France – Paris**
>
> **San Francisco (Calif.) – Social conditions**
> **Coffee houses – California – San Francisco**

In online systems, gathering of material on a larger geographic area can be achieved whether the name of the larger area precedes or follows the local place name.

Qualified Terms in Headings

The capability of searching individual words in a heading provides an interesting dimension to headings with parenthetical qualifiers. Generic qualifiers are added to headings for the purpose of distinguishing homographs and identifying obscure or highly technical terms. Examples include:

> **Sequences (Liturgy)**
> **Sequences (Music)**
> **Cold (Disease)**
> **Crowns (Dentistry)**
> **Shape theory (Topology)**
> **Rheology (Biology)**
> **Fasciae (Anatomy)**
> **Finite fields (Algebra)**

Generic qualifiers are also added to certain categories of name headings, such as names of legendary, fictitious, or mythological characters and names of gods and goddesses, e.g., **Draupadi (Hindu mythology); Snoopy (Fictitious character); Pregnant man (Legendary character); Apollo (Greek deity).** For geographic and corporate headings, three types of qualifiers are used — generic, type of jurisdiction, and geographic:

Schweppes (Firm)
Pompeii (Ancient city)
Naples (Kingdom)
Rome (Italy)
Des Moines (Iowa)
Left Bank (Paris, France)
Church of God (Cleveland, Tenn.)
Rhodes (Greece : Island)
Auschwitz (Poland : Concentration camp)
Misti (Peru : Volcano)
Québec (Québec : County)

Because the qualifiers are normally generic concepts that encompass the specific terms in the headings and because both the headings and the qualifiers are accessible in online retrieval, such headings in effect become reversed classed entries with the specific term preceding the generic term. A heading that contains a local place qualifier, such as **Left Bank (Paris, France)**, provides in effect a trilevel approach, i.e., the city section, the city, and the country. A heading that contains different types of qualifiers, such as **Auschwitz (Poland : Concentration camp)**, represents a multidimensional classed entry, i.e., Auschwitz as a part of Poland and Auschwitz as an instance of concentration camps.

This fact, though interesting, has no implications for manual systems because of the limitations of linear access. But with multidirectional access in online retrieval, material can be gathered through the qualifier, thus providing what amounts to limited (i.e., bilevel) classed entry for those topics covered by headings that include generic qualifiers. Nevertheless, the thought of having any classed entries in a system based on the principle of specific entry is tantalizing. The theory of the alphabetical subject catalog prohibits classed entries, although a few have managed to creep into the Library of Congress system through subdivided headings that contain both generic and specific terms. Now, online access provisions permit the benefits of limited classed approach to material indexed under the Library of Congress subject headings system without substantial change in the system itself. The benefits could be great: recent online catalog use studies confirm a conviction long held by reference librarians, that users "frequently consult a term in the catalog that is broader than their topic of interest" and that they sometimes input a request that contains both a generic and a specific term.[15] So far, opportunities for this sort of access are confined to a few categories of materials, those that are systematically given qualifiers. The opportunities for bilevel access that qualifiers afford, however, are a good argument for increasing their use.

Precoordination

The Library of Congress subject headings system is basically a precoordinated system. Nonetheless, in many cases the postcoordinate approach is used; multiple headings are used to represent a single, complex subject:

Title: *Effect of Ferric Ion on Corrosion Resistance of Zirconium in HC1-A1C1₃* [hydrochloric acid — aluminum chloride] *Environment*

1. **Zirconium — Corrosion.**
2. **Iron ions.**
3. **Chlorides.**

In a manual catalog, in order to achieve specificity in such cases the searcher must scan all the records under one of the headings assigned and mentally combine or exclude search terms in order to single out the records that relate to all the relevant elements in the complex subject. In an online system, postcoordination can be achieved very easily through Boolean operations. Postcoordination provides satisfactory retrieval, for recall and precision both, in a great many cases. Of course, postcoordination, or the simple association of terms, cannot express relationships beyond what can be specified with proximity limits. When linking words or the order of terms in a string affect meaning, precoordinated strings are necessary for precision. CHEMICALS *AND* ADULTERANTS as a search statement will not distinguish material on chemical substances used (on purpose) as adulterants from material on foreign (adulterating) substances found in chemical solutions, nor will GRASSES *AND* CULTURE separate materials on lawn and pasture care from those on the impact of grasslands on cultural history. Such a list of examples can be easily continued: POISON *AND* PLANTS will get material on poisonous plants as well as that indexed under the heading **Plants, Effect of poisons on**; ART AND MUSIC is not the same as MUSIC IN ART. Obviously one cannot go so far as to claim that the ease of postcoordination in online systems removes the justification for precoordination in headings. But it can at least be said that a complex topic does not necessarily have to be represented by a precoordinated heading.

Nontopical Subdivisions

Most of the subdivisions in the Library of Congress subject headings system exist for the purpose of showing topical breakdowns. Many subdivisions are literally that: they represent subtopics of the subject covered by the main heading. Others represent aspects of the subject that are not purely topical: the historical time period treated, or the geographical setting. Finally, some subdivisions do not have to do with topic at all: they may show language of the text, document type (such as abstracts, bibliography, or specifications); publication form (such as facsimiles, juvenile films, or slides); periodicity of publication (such as periodicals or yearbooks); and time period of publication (such as **— Early works to 1800** or the date spans under certain headings like **Education; Readers**). These will be referred to as nontopical subdivisions.

Historically, a large number of the subdivisions in *Library of Congress Subject Headings* were introduced to subarrange large files under a single heading. In other words, they were devices for limiting. This was particularly true for nontopical subdivisions. In the MARC format, as already noted, the information these subdivisions carry is also coded in one or another MARC fixed field. (Some systems use codes for an even greater range of information than does MARC.) Furthermore, if there is a MARC code for a given piece of information, it is almost routinely used when a record is entered into a system. Nontopical subdivisions, on the other hand, are used relatively sparsely—particularly those for language and time period of publication. The existence in a record of coded information that duplicates what is shown by subdivision thus calls into question the continued value of nontopical subdivisions in headings on machine-accessible records.

CONCLUSION

In the online environment, features not available in manual systems remedy many of the shortcomings and insufficiencies of the Library of Congress subject headings system in manual catalogs. They also help to realize some of the potentials of the system that have not been fully explored in manual catalogs because of limitations such as linear access and the tedious process required for performing postcoordination manually.

Many of the principles that have governed the growth of the Library of Congress subject headings system take on different implications in the online context. The characteristics and features of online information handling increase the retrieval potential of the system but place different demands on it. The next chapter samples current professional opinion on *Library of Congress Subject Headings* and discusses how the system may be changed and improved to meet the challenge of the online age.

REFERENCES

[1]For example, Charles R. Hildreth, *Online Public Access Catalogs: The User Interface*, OCLC Library, Information and Computer Science Series, [1] (Dublin, Ohio: OCLC, 1982); Karen Markey, *The Process of Subject Searching in the Library Catalog: Final Report of the Subject Access Research Project*, OCLC Research Report Series OCLC/OPR/RR-83/1 (Dublin, Ohio: OCLC, 1983); Carol A. Mandel, with the assistance of Judith Herschman, "Subject Access in the Online Catalog" (Report prepared for the Council on Library Resources, 1981).

[2]Charles Goodrum and Helen Dalrymple, "Computerization at the Library of Congress: The First Twenty Years," *Wilson Library Bulletin* 57:118 (Oct. 1982).

[3]Karen Markey, *Subject Searching in Library Catalogs before and after the Introduction of Online Catalogs*, OCLC Library, Information and Computer Science Series, 4 (Dublin, Ohio: OCLC, 1984), 77.

[4]Hildreth, *Online Public Access Catalogs*, 129.

[5]Pauline A. Cochrane, "Subject Access in the Online Catalog," *Research Libraries in OCLC: A Quarterly* 5:1-7 (Jan. 1982).

[6]Neal K. Kaske and Nancy P. Sanders, *A Comprehensive Study of Online Public Access Catalogs: An Overview and Application of Findings: Final Report to the Council on Library Resources,* vol. 3, OCLC Research Report Series OCLC/OPR/RR-83/4 (Dublin, Ohio: OCLC, 1983), 38-39.

[7]Hildreth, *Online Public Access Catalogs,* 132.

[8]Markey, *Subject Searching in Library Catalogs,* 84; Stephen E. Wiberley, Jr., "Reducing Search Results a High Priority," in Pauline A. Cochrane, "Modern Subject Access in the Online Age: American Libraries' First Continuing Education Course: Lesson Three," *American Libraries* 15:255 (Apr. 1984).

[9]Gerard Salton and Michael J. McGill, *Introduction to Modern Information Retrieval* (New York: McGraw-Hill, 1983), 4.

[10]Markey, *Subject Searching in Library Catalogs,* 84-85, 100, 114-115; Mandel and Herschman, "Subject Access in the Online Catalog," 24.

[11]Markey, *Subject Searching in Library Catalogs,* 109.

[12]Ibid., 98.

[13]Hildreth, *Online Public Access Catalogs,* 121; Markey, *Subject Searching in Library Catalogs,* 84.

[14]Hildreth, *Online Public Access Catalogs,* 121.

[15]Markey, *Subject Searching in Library Catalogs,* 56, 70.

12

FUTURE PROSPECTS

INTRODUCTION

As we look into the next decade and beyond, the question arises, Is there a future for the Library of Congress subject headings system? The central issue in the question is, Can a system originally designed for the manual card catalog be a viable tool in the online environment?

Many factors will determine what system will be the favored tool for subject access in online catalogs; not the least among these is economics. Maximum effectiveness is essential, too. Logical, philosophical, and theoretical considerations also apply. It cannot be denied that better systems than the Library of Congress subject headings have been devised, systems that are theoretically more satisfying. However, the question of whether to continue the present system or adopt another system is not purely academic.

In contemplating the future of *Library of Congress Subject Headings*, three courses seem possible:

1) Abandon the system completely in favor of another system

2) Let the system continue on the present course and see what happens, a sort of *que sera, sera* approach

3) Try to improve the current system and render it more logical and consistent, with rigorously defined rules that rest on an understanding of user needs and behavior, of the nature of catalogs, and of the principles of information retrieval

The first course is the most drastic one, but it is not totally inconceivable. It has been suggested that alternatives to the current system be seriously considered. PRECIS has been put forward as a possibility. Another alternative would be to develop a completely new system that would take advantage of the modern theory of subject analysis. The ideal time to replace the Library of Congress subject headings system would have been at the inception of the LC MARC database. There would then have been a clear separation between the automated catalog and the manual catalog. However, as it happened, there was a considerable span of time at the Library of Congress when the card catalogs and the MARC database overlapped. There are now more than two million records in the LC database that contain Library of Congress subject headings. To introduce a completely different or new system now would be a major economic burden.

An alternative to the first option is to do away with controlled vocabulary altogether in favor of natural language keywords. Although the keyword (free-text) approach is an important feature in online information retrieval, by itself it cannot fulfill all the requirements of information retrieval. Charles R. Hildreth has warned against total reliance on keyword searching in OPACs (Online Public Access Catalogs):

> To provide only keyword, post-coordinated searching in OPACs is a misguided design philosophy; where installed, such OPACs can do a real disservice to catalog searchers. Keyword/Boolean searching was designed primarily to facilitate free-text searching of uncontrolled vocabulary fields in document citations, such as titles and abstracts. It was never intended as a wholesale replacement for controlled-vocabulary, pre-coordinated searching, but, rather, as an adjunct and complementary form of access.

> Both search approaches are needed in online library catalogs. They can be integrated creatively to improve access.[1]

The question of the future of Library of Congress subject headings was explored recently by Pauline A. Cochrane and a number of guest writers in a series of essays published in *American Libraries*.[2] In this series, experts on subject access expressed their thoughts and opinions regarding subject access in the online age in general and the future of the Library of Congress subject headings in particular. With regard to the latter, Hans H. Wellisch, although critical of the system, says that "10 years from now we will still have LC headings and they will look pretty much the same as today." Wellisch sees economical considerations as dominant, and states further, "Implementing a different subject access system in an individual library or a region would require brains and money—commodities generally in short supply. Such a system would be economical only if the cost could be spread over all or most of the library community, and if it were implemented from a central point."[3]

Sanford Berman[4] also takes a positive position on the future of Library of Congress subject headings: "Frankly, it would be irresponsible to advocate the destruction of LCSH, even though proposed substitutes might be 'theoretically' purer and intellectually more appealing." The reasons for continuing support of the Library of Congress subject headings system, as stated by Berman, are:

1) most new systems—like PRECIS—would not mesh into existing files;

2) split files are anathema to maximum catalog use;

3) substitute schemes would still be no more effective than the people who apply them; and

4) all types of American libraries have an incalculable investment in an existing scheme like LCSH.

This view is echoed by Hildreth: "The LC list of subject headings is the nearest thing we have to a common subject vocabulary authority system in this country. It would be unrealistic to abandon LCSH in the online catalog environment."[5]

The second and third courses of possible future development suggested above, i.e., maintaining the status quo or attempting to improve the present system, are perhaps the more viable approaches in terms of economic feasibility. Many persons outside the Library of Congress have urged the Library to move toward greater efforts in improving, and in some areas revamping, the current system. In other words, the third course of development appears to be the most favored. Currently, the policy of the Library of Congress with regard to its subject headings system appears to be somewhere between the two: it is maintaining the system largely as is while gradually seeking improvements.

More than a decade ago Richard S. Angell, then chief of the Subject Cataloging Division, favored such a policy:

> The most reasonable path ... is considered to be the improvement of the list in its present terms.... This course provides the obvious advantages of orderly evolution. It also recognizes the fact that, during the course of its seven decades of growth, the list and the catalogs in which it is embodied have been of substantial service in the library community.[6]

In contemplating the future of *Library of Congress Subject Headings*, one must bear in mind the usefulness of the system not only for the Library of Congress but also for the many libraries in the United States and abroad that rely on the Library of Congress for cataloging data. Whatever system is adopted by the Library of Congress becomes the de facto national standard. If the Library of Congress subject headings system is to continue to serve libraries across the country, the needs of all types of libraries and of different forms of the catalog must be taken into consideration.

A code for subject headings is generally considered desirable, but the enormous energy and resources that would be needed to develop such a code makes a cautious approach essential. Those who witnessed the effort involved in formulating and implementing *Anglo-American Cataloguing Rules*, second edition (*AACR2*), apparently have little enthusiasm for calling for a subject headings code any time in the near future. The recent publication of *Subject Cataloging Manual: Subject Headings*,[7] intended mainly as a guide for subject catalogers, is a step toward standardizing if not actually codifying subject cataloging practice.

RECOMMENDATIONS

In recent studies of subject access in online catalogs, many recommendations for improvement have been put forward. Some of these deal with vocabulary, others with application. In discussing possible actions for improving the Library of Congress subject headings system, it is best to separate two fundamentally different operations: (1) the construction and maintenance of the list and (2) the policies governing how headings in the list should be assigned to documents. The first concerns terminology, the forms of headings and subdivisions, citation order, and the cross-reference structure—in other words, aspects of the list itself. The second concerns how the list should be used and encompasses questions on the depth of indexing, the extent of coextensivity, when to use subdivisions, whether to do generic posting, and (especially for individual libraries) how extensive cross-references should be. While at given levels of subject analysis the question of coextensivity is determined by the vocabulary, the other aspects of application are mainly a matter of cataloging policy. This may vary among the libraries or agencies that use the system. Nonetheless, because many libraries make use of Library of Congress MARC records, the Library's policies regarding assignment of subject headings set the patterns for subject cataloging in other cataloging centers, particularly in the United States.

In a climate of increasing interest in change, with constant suggestions for improvement being rained on the Library of Congress and springing up within it, it should be noted that the lack of action on a given recommendation is not necessarily, or even probably, a reflection of the Library's failure to recognize the problems or its inability to cope with them technically. Almost any change would be time-consuming and costly to implement; availability of personnel and other resources is always a determining factor in whether to proceed with a new course of action. Furthermore, it may be that a given change in the current system would be advantageous in highly sophisticated online systems but detrimental in the manual environment or in online catalogs with less sophisticated features. In such cases the Library of Congress must proceed with caution, deferring the change until there are alternatives for those libraries that need them. Finally, not all changes are of equal urgency or significance; the Library, perhaps with the assistance of the profession, will need to work out priorities.

Thus, with regard to problems and recommended changes, it should be clear to the reader that there often is no perfect solution. The following discussion attempts to raise questions and discuss or propose possible changes and to point out the pros and cons of various suggested solutions. It will also set forth some recommendations.

Vocabulary

Terminology

Terminology is the aspect of Library of Congress subject headings that has received the severest criticism over the years. The three main issues in the question of terminology are specificity, currency, and common usage (i.e., how well a heading for a topic matches the terms chosen by most users for that topic).

Specificity

As discussed in chapter 2, in the Library of Congress system term specificity is determined largely by literary warrant; specific terms are introduced into the system as required for cataloging books or for preparing cross-references. Because headings are used to represent the overall contents of books, many highly specialized and narrow terms are precluded. As a result, the degree of term specificity is, in many areas, broader than that in an indexing vocabulary designed for use with journal articles in a specialized field, e.g., *Medical Subject Headings* and *ERIC Descriptors*.

Whether the Library of Congress system should introduce narrower or more specialized terms depends on its purpose. If the Library of Congress were to expand its policy of representing the overall content of books to representing parts of books and journals as well, the specificity of its terms would have to change accordingly.

Currency

There are two aspects to the issue of currency: updating obsolete and obsolescent terms and introducing new terms. Much of the criticism of *Library of Congress Subject Headings* has been directed at the lack of currency of many of its terms. In the past the Library often seemed reluctant to update terminology because of the intensive labor involved in changing headings in the existing cataloging records. What was done reflected priorities (the best use of available resources) rather than a lack of awareness on the part of the Library staff. In recent years the Library of Congress has increased its rate of updating terminology. Each issue of the *Supplement to LC Subject Headings* contains many revised headings.

It has been pointed out that changing headings in the online catalog need not involve as much work as in a manual catalog: a heading can be changed in a single operation rather than through repetitive labor. However, this observation assumes that the subject authority file of a given system is linked to its bibliographic records or that global changes can be made. Systems with such capabilities are rarer than is generally assumed. For example, in updating the heading Aeroplanes to **Airplanes** in the Library of Congress catalogs, the change in the card catalog was completed long before the change could be effected in the MARC database. In any case, updating terminology is more a technical and financial problem than a philosophical one. With proper design of online catalogs and more sophisticated computer software, it is safe to predict that the situation will improve.

With regard to currency of terminology, Berman makes two proposals for improvement: prompt recognition of new topics and validation of still unestablished old topics.[8] New topics are not always incorporated promptly, and many long-recognized topics are still not represented in *Library of Congress Subject Headings*, because a subject heading is brought into the system only when required by a book in hand. In other words, the introduction of new headings is closely tied to day-to-day cataloging operations. To implement Berman's proposals would require that subject catalogers at the Library of Congress deliberately go out of their way to search for new topics. An administrative problem then arises. Again, priorities must be determined for the best use of available resources and personnel. One possibility is to have librarians outside of the Library of Congress suggest new headings. Even then, however, new headings would have to be validated by the Library of Congress if the system is to remain under its control. Perhaps this idea could be tried; *Library of Congress Subject Headings* would then grow in much the same way as the name authority file that is being built with contributions from other libraries as well as by the Library of Congress.

Before this suggestion can be implemented, there must first be a way to ensure that contributing catalogers understand Library of Congress subject cataloging policies and practice. The recently published *Subject Cataloging Manual* provides detailed guidance on many details but lacks a set of well-defined underlying principles. Nor is it comprehensive enough to serve as a cataloging code.

Common usage

In addition to currency, another aspect of terminology is how well the terms used in the subject headings system match the terms most likely to be sought by users. In many senses, this matter is an aspect of the problem of currency. On the basis of recent online public catalog studies, Karen Markey found that "users had problems finding the right subject heading."[9] Several factors may account for failure in matching terms. One is that the users often use terms that are too general or too specific. Another cause is the obsolete subject headings. Yet another is the fact that, among synonymous terms, the user's term often does not match the one used in the heading. The problem of matching terms is an old one; Charles A. Cutter's great concern with usage demonstrates this fact. The difficulty of determining usage was discussed in chapter 2 of this book. One possible solution is to rely more on the documents being cataloged to generate terms used in the headings. The PRECIS system is an example of document-generated terminology: subject to synonym control, each entry string is generated from and tailor-made for the document in hand. And, to a certain extent, this is what the Library of Congress does now as a first step in establishing a new heading. The approach requires rigorous control over synonymous terms, and, in time, over term obsolescence.

The power of keyword searching on words in titles alleviates to a certain extent problems with lack of currency or failure to reflect common usage. Many subject indexes rely entirely on keyword display based on article titles or abstracts. Titles of documents that are expressive of content increase the effectiveness of keyword title access. Furthermore, this benefit is not available only to online catalog users; generous use of partial-title-added entries, to bring potentially useful access terms into filing position, can have much the same effect in the manual environment. Helpful as keyword searching can be, however, few theorists advocate abandoning the use of controlled vocabulary in library catalogs. Keyword access to terms in titles can be an adjunct to systematic indexing, but no more.

True, it is no easy task to maintain an indexing vocabulary at peak effectiveness at all times. Nevertheless, in spite of the many acknowledged difficulties in doing so, there seems general professional agreement that serious attempts must be made to render *Library of Congress Subject Headings* more receptive to terminology that is current, familiar to users, and compatible with the literature and with other tools of subject analysis.

Forms of headings

In the Library of Congress subject headings system, phrase headings, headings with qualifiers, and headings with subdivisions have sometimes been used for similar functions in the past. The time facet is usually expressed by means of a period subdivision, but sometimes by an adjectival modifier. The space facet, usually represented by a geographic subdivision, has previously also appeared in the form of [Topic] in [Place]. The qualifier is most frequently used for distinguishing between homographs, but it has also been used in place of a subject subdivision or an inverted adjectival heading, e.g., **Infants (Newborn)**, and sometimes to give context for an obscure term. Syntactical relationships are expressed by relational words such as *and, of, in, for*, or *as*, and sometimes by subdivisions or adjectival phrases, e.g., **Grooming for men; Sheep — Grooming**.

In recent years efforts have been made to tighten or normalize the forms of headings, for example, eliminating [Topic] in [Place] types of headings, limiting the use of qualifiers, and cutting down on the use of conjunctive phrases such as **Hotels, motels, etc.** The immediate problem is how to cope with existing headings in the old pattern when a change is made. When obsolete headings are canceled and replaced by current forms, all existing records bearing the obsolete headings should be updated. This is being done currently at the Library of Congress to records in the MARC database. It is not just the Library of Congress's own catalogs that matter here, but also the question of whether other libraries using the system are able to cope with the changes. It is hoped that time and technological improvements in online systems will eventually alleviate the problem.

For forms of headings, it may be helpful to determine and distinguish between the functions and usage of each type of heading. For example, the time and space facet may be best represented by subdivisions. The same is true for aspects, processes, and actions on the subject. Subdivisions may also be used to express certain phase relationships, such as effect or influence (e.g., **Air — Pollution — Physiological effect; Shakespeare, William, 1564-1616 — Influence — Scott**), application or tool (e.g., **Small business — Data processing**), and bias (e.g., **Sun — Religious aspects**). Much effort has been devoted recently by the Library of Congress to normalizing headings in these categories.

Some of the approaches mentioned above are already present in the Library of Congress system, but as is demonstrated by the examples involving the word *grooming* given above, there is considerable inconsistency. Making all usage consistent and uniform would render the system easier to apply in cataloging and easier to use in retrieval.

For headings with qualifiers, as mentioned in chapter 11, the inclusion of a generic term in a specific heading provides the possibility for a bilevel approach in online retrieval. This is an area worth exploring, because of the additional access points it affords. Currently, the bilevel approach can be used in retrieval of categories of headings to which generic or geographic qualifiers are regularly added, such as specific place names, and is particularly helpful in systems in which cross-references are inadequate. But it is less useful in categories of headings to which qualifiers are added only selectively for distinguishing between homographs or identifying obscure or highly technical terms.

Uniform headings and entry elements

The principle of uniform heading has served very useful purposes in the card catalog over the years, particularly in terms of economy and of the capacity to bring together works on the same subject. On the other hand, it has also been recognized that the principle significantly limits the number of access points per record. In recent years the principle has been gradually relaxed; the use of duplicate entries for a subject has increased. In online systems with keyword searching on headings, it should no longer be necessary to make duplicate entries containing the terms arranged in different orders, e.g., **United States—Foreign relations—France; France—Foreign relations—United States**.

If access points are no longer determined by the entry element (initial word) in online retrieval, then citation order, i.e., the order of words or elements in a complex heading, may be based on logical or syntactical considerations rather than on the choice of the "significant" term. Except in cases in which the order of the elements in the heading affects its meaning, both the application of the system by catalogers and indexers and the learning and use of the system by users may be facilitated by adopting consistent methods and patterns in ordering the individual elements (adjectival modifiers, subdivisions, etc.) in a particular type of heading. For example, with regard to word order, Berman recommends "the gradual conversion of all inverted forms to natural order headings to achieve consistency and eliminate uncertainty."[10] However, such an approach is feasible only in systems that allow keyword access to headings. In a system in which the initial word alone is indexed and matched with the user's input term, the entry element still has significance. Therefore, the question of citation order should be considered along with and in the framework of the design of the online catalog or retrieval system with regard to methods of indexing and matching of terms.

Distinguishing between topical and form headings

In *Library of Congress Subject Headings*, a number of headings represent both form and topic. Some examples are **Biography; Almanacs; Encyclopedias and dictionaries**, when used as main headings, as well as headings representing literary or artistic forms. In some cases a distinction is made between form and topic:

Form	*Topic*
Biography	**Biography (As a literary form)**
Essays	**Essay**
Short stories	**Short story**
Symphonies	**Symphony**
Poetry—Collections	**Poetry—History and criticism**
[Language] literature	**[Language] literature—History and criticism**

Occasionally such a heading is used only as a topical heading and not as a form heading. For example, the headings **Bibliography; Periodicals**; etc., are assigned to works discussing these forms but not to individual specimens of such forms. In other words, they are used as true subject headings.

In still other cases, identical headings are used to represent works about a particular bibliographic or artistic form *and* individual specimens of such forms. Examples are **Almanacs; Encyclopedias and dictionaries;** headings representing certain artistic genres (e.g., **Painting; Drawing; Sculpture**); and certain legal headings (e.g., **Peace treaties; Trials** [for proceedings as well as works discussing the trials]). In such cases the failure to make the distinction is a violation of the principle of unique heading, i.e., each heading represents only one subject or concept. In retrieval, using a heading of this sort will call up works both *in* and *about* the particular form. Furthermore, the lack of consistency in the formation and assignment of form headings creates difficulty for the cataloger and the user. Steps should be taken to normalize form headings, with an effort to distinguish between form and topic.

Subdivisions

In online retrieval subdivisions not only provide subarrangement of large files and make the headings more specific, they also provide additional access points. As discussed in chapter 11, certain functions originally allocated to subdivisions can be performed more effectively in online systems by limiting according to information in the MARC fixed fields. This is true for form subdivisions that show document types, period subdivisions indicating dates of publication, language subdivisions indicating language of the text, and, to a limited extent, indirect geographic subdivisions. Serious consideration should be given to maximizing the use of fixed-field information. It is a remarkably efficient base for searching and is carried on all records; thus, for language-of-text and date-of-publication information especially—which appears in only a few subdivisions—it is a device of superior effectiveness as well. Of course, the timing of changes in these areas will be crucial, because removing such subdivisions from subject headings will have adverse effects on manual catalogs. Nonetheless, in long-range planning, these possibilities should not be overlooked.

Those forms of documents not represented in the document type field may still require representation in subject headings. One alternative is to bring out the form in a separate heading. For example, all publications in the form of concordances may be assigned the heading **Concordances**, which may then be retrievable by itself or in conjunction, through the use of a Boolean operator, with a subject or subjects.

Even if the functions of some categories of subdivisions were taken over by fixed-field codes, many headings with multiple subdivisions would remain in the list. Does the citation order of subdivisions matter for such headings? Should there be rules of precedence among different types of subdivisions, perhaps even among subcategories of a given type? The point was made earlier that, useful as a standard citation order for subdivisions is for manually consulted headings, in the online environment citation order does not affect searching efficiency in most cases; with multidirectional access a given term can be searched wherever it appears in a heading. Nevertheless, in terms of expressiveness, citation order does matter when it affects meaning; this holds for both environments. There is another consideration for online systems, and that is the desirability of thesaurus display. Users looking for full headings—because they know they will get fewer false drops if they submit valid and appropriate headings—are best served by a thesaurus that is internally consistent. Without rules for how multipart headings should be put together, there can be no pattern by which a user could quickly scan the list. Furthermore, without such rules chances are increased that a given string will be ambiguous.

Geographic subdivision in the Library of Congress system, particularly indirect subdivision, has generated a great deal of debate and discussion in the past because of its inconsistent use and the numerous exceptions in application. The policy of indirect subdivision should be reconsidered in view of online retrieval characteristics. As discussed in chapter 11, the original purpose of using indirect subdivision, i.e., collocating material on a larger geographic area, can be carried out by using the geographic qualifier that is added to a local place name. In other words, the name of a larger geographic area may be accessed either when it follows the local place name as a qualifier or when it precedes the local place name as the interposing element in indirect subdivision. It is therefore recommended that indirect subdivision be abolished in favor of qualified direct subdivision in all cases. This would facilitate both the cataloging and access of information without losing the advantages originally ascribed to indirect subdivision. The move would have the advantage that the same form of geographic name could be used whether the name served as main heading or subdivision. This advantage can be seen in the following examples. The normal pattern is **Art—France—Paris; Art—California—San Francisco** [place in indirect subdivision] and **Paris (France)—Climate; San Francisco (Calif.)—Climate** [place as main heading]. In order to collect all records with headings relating to a particular place, therefore, users have to submit the name in two forms, in cases where abbreviations are used in the qualifiers. With the recommended change, geographic names in headings would follow the pattern of those in the list below, which features New York city—a place that is one of the few exceptions to the current policy of indirect subdivision.

> **Art—New York (N.Y.)**
> **Architecture—New York (N.Y.)**
>
> **New York (N.Y.)—Climate**
> **New York (N.Y.)—Economic conditions**

Another feature of the MARC record that has not been fully utilized for retrieval by geographic area is the fixed-field geographic area code (GAC), which designates locality in terms of broad areas that correspond generally to the gathering levels of indirect subdivision. Although most of the current online systems do not provide access through the GAC, it is a potentially useful access point that should not be ignored. One of the few systems that contain such a feature is DIALOG, which provides analogous access through a separate index called Geographic Location.

Precoordination or postcoordination

For representing complex subjects, there are three alternative approaches: precoordination, postcoordination, or a combination of the two. PRECIS is an example of a totally precoordinated system, in which a complex subject is represented by a single string containing as many terms as necessary to bring out all its component concepts or elements. Many of the online databases rely on postcoordination; the ERIC database is an example.

In a manual catalog a complex subject is ideally represented by a single multielement heading that brings together its various concepts or elements—in other words, by a precoordinated string. When component concepts or elements are presented by separate headings, a specific subject can be isolated only by scanning the records under one of the headings assigned and selecting those with headings for the other concepts or elements in the complex subject. In other words, a Boolean operation must be performed mentally. In an online system, specificity of a complex subject may be achieved with equal ease through precoordinated headings or by postcoordination (by means of Boolean operations on separate headings). The advantage of the latter, as pointed out by Jean Perreault,[11] is that documents may be retrieved on both the broad and the narrow level. The disadvantage, as discussed in chapter 11, is that relationships between concepts or subjects cannot be always properly expressed; the result is the retrieval of irrelevant documents.

As pointed out in chapters 2 and 8, the Library of Congress subject headings system is basically a precoordinated system in that for most complex subjects, concepts or elements are precoordinated into specific headings before or at the point of cataloging (if appropriate headings do not already exist). Nonetheless, in many cases, multiple headings are used, for instance

1. **Econometrics.**
2. **Time-series analysis.**

as opposed to a single heading such as Time-series—Econometric analysis. In view of the pros and cons of precoordination and postcoordination, a combination of the two, as is currently used at the Library of Congress, is probably still the most viable approach in the online environment. But because of online search capabilities, particularly keyword search and Boolean operations, greater reliance could be placed on postcoordination. On the basis of their findings, researchers who have studied online public catalogs favor postcoordinate searching as a feature of online catalogs.[12] It would be desirable to have a set of stated policies or guidelines indicating when precoordination is important. Precoordinated headings (both phrase headings and headings with subdivisions) are more effective than postcoordination in expressing relationships when the order of words affects the meaning of the heading or when relational or linking words are required to clarify or identify the relationships (for example, **Plants, Effect of gases on** and **Plants, Gases in; Plants, Effect of heat on** and **Plants, Heat production in; History—Philosophy** and **Philosophy—History**). On the other hand, greater reliance may be placed on postcoordination in cases in which the relationship is unequivocal or when the absence of linking words does not affect the meaning. For example, subjects such as Youth and drug abuse; Children and friendship are satisfactorily handled by assigning separate headings.

Length of headings

An aspect of subject heading structure that has not been discussed much in print but is an important issue in system design is the length of the string. Most of the subject headings in the Library of Congress system are relatively short, but there are many long ones. Long headings present a problem for some online systems, particularly with regard to vocabulary display or display of indexes. In some systems, for example, ORBIT of SDC, the maximum string length is only forty or so characters. This means that elements toward the end of a long string are truncated and users are cut off from the screening value the lost information might have for them. Eventually string length limits will undoubtedly be raised, with regard to both vocabulary display and file indexing. This problem must be addressed, not only by indexers, but also by systems designers.

From the users' point of view, the disadvantages of long strings are the necessity for almost total reliance on the thesaurus for those who want to submit exact searches, and the very large likelihood of input error. Recent online catalog studies indicate that search statements entered by most users in online subject searches are short, an average of 1.5 to 1.7 terms (i.e., words).[13]

The problem of long headings may be dealt with in a number of ways, some of which have already been discussed:

1) Eliminate subdivisions whose functions can be taken over by the limiting feature.

2) Treat certain subdivisions as independent specific terms by separating them from main headings and making them into separate headings, e.g., Great Blood Purge, 1934 instead of **Germany — History — Great Blood Purge, 1934**. In the attempt to simplify or shorten headings, it is important to ensure that neither specificity nor useful access points are sacrificed. Further study is needed to determine the optimal balance between consideration of string length and other factors, including specificity and expressivity.

3) Rely more heavily on postcoordination by representing elements of a complex subject with separate headings.

Cross-references

In a controlled vocabulary, cross-references assume the dual functions of providing access through synonymous terms and of connecting related subjects. In general, *see* references connecting synonymous terms are considered mandatory; they are required in almost all controlled vocabularies. A *see* reference represents an additional access point to each record that bears the index term referred to. Recent online catalog studies indicate that users need more *see* references to lead them from their search terms to valid subject headings.[14] A recent research project conducted by Cochrane[15] tested the feasibility of increasing *see* references, also called entry vocabulary, in *Library of Congress Subject Headings* through cooperative efforts. A number of participating libraries were invited to suggest *see* references to the Library of Congress Subject Cataloging Division. Many of the suggestions received so far have been added to the system, with the result that the entry vocabulary for subject access to MARC records has been greatly enlarged. However, if the operation is to continue smoothly and efficiently, Cochrane recommends that the control mechanism inside the Library of Congress for reporting back to participating libraries be altered, and that guidelines concerning the kinds of *see* references to be made be established. She also recognizes the need for additional personnel at the Library for such an undertaking.

One of the problems associated with establishing *see* references is how to determine when a particular term should be used as a *see* reference and when it should be established as a regular heading. This is particularly true for quasi-synonymous terms and for terms considered too narrow to be useful as headings. For example, should terms like Industrial hygiene libraries; Industrial safety libraries; Occupational safety libraries be included as *see* references to the heading **Occupational health libraries**, or should they be established as separate headings? This is a difficult problem to which there is probably no clearcut solution. A partial solution may lie in online system design. This possibility will be discussed later in this chapter.

In her recent study of online subject access, Cochrane[16] finds the use of the symbols *see, x, xx,* and *sa* confusing to users and suggests replacing them with USE, UF (used for), BT (broader term), NT (narrower term), and RT (related term) symbols used in most of the modern thesauri. This approach has been considered by the Subject Cataloging Division of the Library of Congress at various times in the recent past. However, because the conversion would require substantial labor and time, the suggestion has not yet been implemented. However, there is strong evidence that the Library of Congress is moving in this direction.

The policies governing *see also* references in *Library of Congress Subject Headings* in the past have not been rigorously defined, nor have the policies that existed been consistently followed. For hierarchically related terms, *see also* references have usually been made from the more general to the more specific term, but not always. For coordinate terms—those related in other ways than general/specific—reciprocal *see also* references, though required by the Library's policies, have not always been made. This is unfortunate, because it is only with reciprocal references that notational clues (the joint presence of the symbols *sa* and *xx*) are present to differentiate them from hierarchical references. As a result *Library of Congress Subject Headings* as it currently stands is a long way from being usable as a base for a related-term display as systematic and exhaustive as would be implied by the use of BT, NT, and RT.

The future, however, looks brighter. A move in the right direction was taken at the beginning of 1984, when the Library of Congress's Subject Cataloging Division began regularizing its practice for both hierarchical and related-term references—an important step toward normalizing the whole *see also* reference structure.

Properly structured *see also* references have great potential. Carried to perfection, they superimpose a classified structure on an alphabetical arrangement and thereby provide a dictionary or subject catalog with the best of both worlds. An ideal syndetic structure must be as tightly and logically constructed as a classification scheme; only with such a structure can one be sure that the hierarchy is complete and that there are no missing links or elements. By policy, as noted earlier, the Library of Congress already makes many *see also* references from broad to narrow, and to terms related in other ways. But to date the approach seems to have been to create cross-references on a heading-by-heading basis without attempting to fit concepts into a systematic structure. One possible approach is to use a classification scheme as a guide in making an overall hierarchical map of the Library of Congress system. Such a map would cover one kind of coordinate relationship, what might be called sibling relationships within a given hierarchy. It would not, however, cover relationships that cut across hierarchies. There is a great need for cross-references that provide, as F. W. Lancaster says, "associations that would not normally be indicated explicitly in a classified schedule,"[17] particularly one based on division by discipline. Some guidance to such associations could come from a device such as the relative index of a classification scheme; the rest would have to come, on a heading-by-heading basis, from observation of how topics co-occur in the literature.

Devices like the tree structures in *Medical Subject Headings (MeSH)* and the hierarchical clusters in *ERIC Descriptors* are apparently very useful to persons using indexes with such provisions. It is hoped that something analogous can eventually be developed for the users searching in files of records under the Library of Congress subject headings system.

Subject authority file

A subject authority file is a tool for catalog or database management. Ideally, it should contain a subject authority record for every complete ready-made heading that has been actually used in subject cataloging. A thesaurus, on the other hand, serves as a source of indexing terms. For a system that allows free combination of specified elements or categories of elements, as the Library of Congress system does to an increasing extent, a thesaurus lists individual index terms and gives the conditions for synthesis but does not normally list all the strings actually used. To help the indexer or the searcher select appropriate terms, each index term is accompanied by appropriate cross-references, definition or scope notes if any, and a history of the term if appropriate. From the beginning, *Library of Congress Subject Headings* (with some auxiliary tools) has served as both thesaurus and subject authority file for the Library's subject headings system. The distinction between the two has not been clearly made; the list has included some headings (e.g., established name headings and synthesized headings) a thesaurus would not list, and it has omitted many entries (e.g., headings with free-floating subdivisions) used on Library of Congress cataloging records that a subject authority file would include.

Establishing a separate thesaurus as a source of indexing terms, with cross-references and syntactical rules for synthesis, is something the Library of Congress may wish to consider. Such a list would facilitate greatly the work toward improving the cross-reference structure and any attempt to establish tree structures based on the headings.

In recent years the Library of Congress has been devoting considerable effort to developing an online subject authority file, a project that became feasible after a format for subject authority records was established as part of *Authorities: A MARC Format.*[18] Such a tool has great potential benefit for libraries in general as well as for the Library of Congress itself. In the development of the automated subject authority file and possibly a thesaurus, the following questions warrant consideration.

1) Should a record be created for each index entry, including those resulting from the combination of free-floating subdivisions? Such records would assist in the validation of subject entries assigned by cataloging agencies outside the Library of Congress and would aid in online retrieval. The increase in the number of records would of course add to the cost of the file, but,

because of the large number of synthesized headings already in the file, the increase should not be excessive.

2) Should history notes be provided? Until recently the Library of Congress did not need history notes on changed subject headings because it revised all records with superseded headings. But for libraries and databases with split files (some records under the old heading and some under the new), history notes are helpful in both cataloging and searching. Now, with the Library of Congress's card catalogs frozen, history notes would be useful to the Library itself as links from current headings to headings in the card catalogs. History notes could take the form of *see also* references or explanatory references.

There is another policy question for the architects of the online subject authority file, and that is whether individual authority records can be linked to MARC bibliographic records. This would be the ideal situation for any bibliographic system, because such linkage greatly facilitates changes and corrections. The technical capability is there; the obstacle is the cost of implementation. A linked system appears beyond reach for the 1980s, but it is an ideal that should not be lightly abandoned. The relative costs of different ways of carrying out various bibliographic operations change almost monthly, very often in favor of increasingly sophisticated online processes.

Application Policies

While the development and maintenance of the Library of Congress subject headings system is the sole responsibility of the Library of Congress, the application, i.e., the use of *Library of Congress Subject Headings* in cataloging or indexing, extends to libraries and agencies outside the Library. However, because Library of Congress cataloging records are used so widely by other libraries, the way subject headings are applied at the Library of Congress has become the de facto standard for subject cataloging. The Library's policies and practice are discussed in chapters 8 through 10 in this book. In the following pages some recommended changes are discussed.

Depth of subject cataloging

An area of subject cataloging policy that has been sharply criticized is the scarcity of subject headings assigned to each cataloging record. The general policy of summarization (i.e., assigning subject headings to cover the overall content of a book instead of individual parts of it) results in relatively few headings per document. As Marcia Bates points out, this economy of subject headings reflects the constraints of the manual catalog: "With more than one or two subject entries per book, card catalogs would have become cumbrously large—hard to use, hard to file in, hard to find room for. In the early days, catalog entries often had to be handwritten. The current subject heading system, therefore, was deliberately developed to be minimally redundant."[19] In online systems, on the other hand, additional access points do not affect the bulk of the catalog, but they definitely do improve recall in searching. Many writers and critics of the Library of Congress subject headings system have deplored the scarcity of subject headings on cataloging records and have urged the Library of Congress to increase the number of headings assigned.[20]

In the recent past several suggestions have been made that, if implemented, would make a difference in the number and nature of the subject headings on Library of Congress cataloging records. One example of a different approach is the Subject Access Project at Syracuse University, an experiment in augmenting MARC records with subject terms selected from tables of contents and back-of-the-book indexes.[21] Such an augmentation would represent a fundamental change in the Library of Congress's cataloging policy with regard to the depth of subject indexing, with a concomitant increase in the specificity of access terms. If and when the Library of Congress considers expanding its subject headings assignment policy, the following issues should be examined:

1) *Criteria for selection of headings.* The first question is: On what basis are the additional subject headings to be assigned—on individual chapters in the book, on individual units in a collection of writings, on individual articles in a journal, or on detailed analysis similar to back-of-the-book indexing? A further question is: Should all materials in the collection receive the same depth of treatment? The answer will have enormous financial implications. Subject headings based on individual units of a work are analytic entries similar to multilevel description in descriptive cataloging. If multilevel subject analysis is adopted, another question is how the subject headings assigned to each level (the entire work, parts of the work, sections within a part, etc.) should be labeled or stored in separate fields.

2) *Precision of search results.* A large number of access points per record will no doubt result in high recall. On the other hand, it may also decrease precision, because irrelevant or less useful materials will be retrieved. Stephen E. Wiberley points out the pitfalls of too much information being retrieved: "In designing systems that provide increased access, we must take into account the potential for information overload. (Markey reports that currently nearly 20 percent of online catalog users say they find too much information)."[22] The important question is: What is the optimal depth of indexing?

3) *Redundancy of access points.* The capability of keyword searching in online systems often makes duplication of access points in the same record redundant. A term in a subject heading assigned to a record may occur more than once in the subject fields or may be identical to a keyword or phrase in another searchable field (e.g., main entry, title, or contents note), or the term may be equivalent to a limiting feature, such as document type. The duplication does not increase the accessibility of the record, and so is helpful only when the searching is limited to subject fields. When the Library of Congress subject headings system eventually serves mainly online systems, the redundancy question should be reexamined.

Similar questions that apply to depth of indexing must be raised about other enhancements that have been recommended, in exhaustivity of indexing and in generic posting. These issues will be examined below.

Exhaustivity of indexing

It has been claimed that the Library of Congress's subject cataloging should be more exhaustive. The term *exhaustivity of indexing* refers to the extent to which aspects and elements of a complex subject are covered in a heading or set of headings. For example, PRECIS index strings are relatively exhaustive compared to Library of Congress subject headings: the PRECIS rules for string construction call for representing individual facets of a subject and also allow adjectival and prepositional phrase qualification of concept terms. Exhaustivity of indexing is not the same as depth of indexing; the former refers to the representation of individual facets and elements of a complex subject, while the latter concerns the representation of subunits (individual chapters, articles, etc.) of a bibliographic item. Regarding the exhaustivity of applying subject headings, Berman suggests that the Library of Congress expand its "assignment policy to include headings for literary genres and for thematic topics applied to individual novels, plays, and other literature."[23] If Library of Congress subject cataloging were made more exhaustive, a decided increase in the number of access points per record would result. Such a policy would have enormous economic implications in terms of the labor and time required. Again, the problem is not purely a technical one.

Generic posting

It has been a general policy in subject cataloging to assign a heading whose meaning closely approximates a summary statement of the content of the document in hand. The ideal situation is one in which document and heading are coextensive. In reality, there is a lot of generic posting, or assigning a broader heading than would be ideal. A generic heading is typically assigned (1) when a specific heading is not available because it cannot be established for some reason or because (usually in the case of other libraries using *Library of Congress Subject Headings*) it has not yet been established by the Library of Congress and (2) in addition to the specific heading when a broader context for a given heading is considered desirable, as in the case of assigning biographical headings, i.e., [**Class of persons** or **Discipline**] – **Biography**, to individual biographies in addition to the individual personal name headings.

The first circumstance raises the question of whether a heading of the appropriate level of specificity should be created. This is a question of thesaurus development, not of application. On the other hand, whether both broad and narrow headings should be assigned a given document *is* an application question. Generic posting is a response to demands for access at different hierarchical levels, and there have been many calls for the Library of Congress to do more of it. Is it the best way? If so, how many levels are appropriate? Should a work on beagles receive the headings **Hounds; Hunting dogs; Dogs; Canis** in addition to the heading **Beagles (Dogs)**? Or should reliance be placed on hierarchical *see also* references, with generic posting reserved for cases in which context cannot easily be denoted any other way? These are questions the profession must attempt to answer.

Online Catalog Design

It will take more than improvements in the indexing language and changes in policies on application to give users optimal online subject access to information in books and other library materials. Two important additional areas for improvement are user interface features and the nature of the catalog itself — particularly what it covers. The former is our major focus in this section, but a few words are in order first on the nature of the catalog.

Changes in the nature of the catalog

Traditionally, library catalogs have been limited to entries for books and serials cataloged by the library; in some cases, even, whole sets of books have been treated as if they were a single entity. There have often been separate catalogs for different types of materials, such as children's books or government publications; records of material in the process of being added to the collection have not always been available to the public; and patrons could find out if a particular book were available for checkout only by going to the shelves or having it paged. In the manual environment, such arrangements are advantageous: for special materials, limited-scope catalogs are easier to consult, and a catalog that mixed in-process and circulation records with cards for cataloged books would be cumbrous and well-nigh incomprehensible to anyone but librarians — besides being virtually impossible to maintain.

The picture is different in the online environment. Because records do not have to be consulted serially, a very large file does not present the same sort of hindrance to efficient searching as it would in card form. Different kinds of entries — in-process or circulation records, for instance, or material in other libraries in the same network — can be easily identified, and the limiting feature described earlier can be used to confine searches to a given category or to refine or expand searches. The MARC format, in fact, already provides almost all the codes that could conceivably be needed for this. In a given sitting, from one terminal, a library user who has identified some titles he or she wants to see (and, to arrive at the list, quite likely benefitted from online search features that would not have been available in a card catalog) can find out things like whether the items are on the shelf; if not, when they are due to be returned; if they are ordered when they are likely to be on the shelves; and so on. Furthermore, as far as technological considerations apply, periodical indexes and other online reference services, and the online catalogs of distant libraries or library networks, could be linked to the home system databases. Thus, again in one sitting and using one terminal, a user could access almost the whole universe of publicly available information.

To a harried library director trying to raise money even for a fairly limited online catalog, the foregoing projection, particularly the part about links, may seem so far in the future as to strain credibility. Yet the picture is not unrealistic. A great deal of work has been done already on incorporating in-process records and circulation information into some online public access catalogs. The larger question, what the online age implies for the nature of the catalog and of the information services libraries should try to provide, has attracted considerable attention from theoreticians and other library professionals at conferences and in the literature. Many are also thinking about what is needed in preparation for a larger role for online catalogs.

Cochrane, for instance, has pointed out the need for standardization in loading records into various online catalogs and for uniformity in respect to user commands.[24] The latter will be particularly important in a world in which different types of databases are linked.

Aids for users

Our main concern here, however, is not the relatively distant future, but how the online catalogs we have now, or can expect to have soon, can be made easier to use. Most users apparently find the online catalog a congenial tool.[25] At the same time, all the recent catalog use studies published to date indicate that failures in subject searching are very high measured against what could have been retrieved. Most users have difficulty finding the proper search terms, a few do not find them at all, and few are able to make full use of a system's capabilities for refining or expanding their searches.[26] All the online catalog use studies have strongly recommended that help be given.

Online thesaurus display

Access to cross-references seems to be the most pressing need. Because simple mismatches of vocabulary account for a large proportion of search failures, users particularly need *see* references. And, because searches on terms that are too broad are very common, they need *see also* references, to an only slightly lesser extent. A desirable first step, therefore, would be to put *Library of Congress Subject Headings* online. There are different ways to do this, varying in both cost and sophistication. The cheapest and simplest would be to mount a snapshot of the *Library of Congress Subject Headings* database, indexed by first words only; this could be produced (and remounted) on the same schedule as the COM (fiche) product. Such a step would do no more than give users a convenient way to look up what is available to them now in the microfiche version of *Library of Congress Subject Headings*, with no help in interpreting the list, but it would be a start. Keyword display of the same list, or allowing it to be searched by keywords (not the same thing), would increase its potential usefulness. Among other advantages, keyword access to a thesaurus obviates the need for some *see* references. Given the size of *Library of Congress Subject Headings*, neither of the alternative keyword measures would be simple to implement, but each is straightforward from both machine and intellectual standpoints; the latter, however, would require careful programming to lessen the likelihood of long, virtually meaningless sequences centering on terms that occur very frequently.

A temporary expedient would be to excerpt the *see* references from *Library of Congress Subject Headings* (on the same quarterly basis that the microfiche is produced) and display that file for online consultation. With that list users would at least have easy access to lead-in vocabulary.

A more ambitious undertaking respecting thesaurus display would be to provide clustered groupings of authorized terms—both multilevel hierarchical clusters of headings along with their broader and narrower terms, and coordinate clusters of headings related in other ways. In earlier discussions it was pointed out that a great deal of editorial work is needed before the syndetic structure of *Library of Congress Subject Headings* can serve as an adequate base for such displays. Their potential helpfulness, however, should not be overlooked.

Another shortcoming in *Library of Congress Subject Headings* from the searcher's point of view deserves mention here. It does not routinely list headings that result from application of the various free combining principles — subdivisions under pattern headings or in the free-floating lists, for instance, or headings of the form **[Topic] in literature**. This circumstance has received little attention in the searching literature, yet these omissions can be detrimental. Searchers accessing large files need to know how they are subdivided if they are to winnow them down efficiently, and skipping to promising subdivisions is not as easy in online searching as it is in traditional catalogs that are well provided with guide cards. Incompleteness here is one problem, but even more serious is the implication that because a synthesized heading is not listed it is not used. Fuller information on provisions for synthesis, therefore, is an apparent need. There is great potential for online assistance here, although to date no concrete proposals have apparently been put forward.

Automatic vocabulary control

Some functions of *see* references can be accomplished through truncation or stemming, and others through keyword access — neither, however, goes very far in solving the entry vocabulary problem. A sophisticated and very user-friendly way of handling *see* references in the online environment is to make them invisible. Equivalent terms are linked within the system, and users receive full output whether they put in the right term or not. This is the synonym operation referred to in chapter 11. *See also* references could also be linked to headings, so that they could be presented, directly or through a "Do you want to see related terms?" dialog, whenever one of the linked terms was submitted. Few online library catalogs have features of this sort; an exception is the New York Public Library, which has used hidden *see* referencing from the early days of its automated system.

Many online reference services have term-control devices that can serve as models. For example, in the STAIR system developed by IBM, *see* references are handled through automatic substitution, called synonym operator.[27] When a synonym not used as a valid indexing term is entered by the searcher, the system automatically substitutes the valid term and retrieves relevant documents listed under that term. In CITE, a prototype online catalog at the National Library of Medicine, the system automatically checks the user's input terms against the database's searchable title and subject indexes and *Medical Subject Headings (MeSH)* and performs an "intelligent" stemming of the input terms.[28] This feature of automatic substitution and stemming is also available in the Legislative Information Files (indexed by *Legislative Indexing Vocabulary Terms*) in the Library of Congress's SCORPIO system, although it is not yet available in the LCCC file for books in the same system.

Online help messages

The studies mentioned several times in chapters 11 and 12 show that online catalogs have been received with considerable enthusiasm. It is clear that many catalog users at least have no trouble getting started. From the information the same studies uncovered about low proficiency in taking advantage of online system features, however, it can be predicted that not even all the measures noted above will be enough. There appears to be a need for online teaching devices: help screens, interactive search diagnostics, teaching packages—the first two integrated with the catalog itself, the tutorials as a separate program. Here, as for other online features, nonlibrary systems offer models. The CAI (computer-assisted instruction) field has shown what can be done with interactive diagnostic routines. The best of the packages that introduce complex software for microcomputers furnish good patterns for tutorials. So do the training manuals prepared by some of the online reference services.

CONCLUSION

The Library of Congress subject headings system is a viable subject access tool in the online environment. Many of its current recognized shortcomings are mitigated, not exacerbated, by the properties of online information processing systems. How well the Library of Congress subject headings system fares in the new environment will depend on how well it adapts to new requirements and, in particular, how well it capitalizes on the special features of online retrieval.

Chapter 11 has outlined and discussed the online features considered to have the most potential for improving access to material indexed by Library of Congress subject headings, and this chapter has pointed out the steps the Library of Congress might consider taking to benefit from online provisions. It would be unrealistic to expect changes to be effected rapidly. There are crushing financial constraints. Furthermore, the Library of Congress is aware of its responsibilities to the overall library community; it cannot initiate changes that would be efficacious only in very sophisticated systems without making sure that there are workable alternatives for libraries without such facilities. Nonetheless, in its planning the Library of Congress should not confine its view to the short-term future only. Many changes that seem infeasible now may be practicable—and perhaps essential to the continued viability of *Library of Congress Subject Headings* as an indexing system—sooner than one might expect.

REFERENCES

[1]Charles R. Hildreth, "To Boolean or Not to Boolean," *Information Technology and Libraries* 2:237 (Sept. 1983).

[2]Pauline A. Cochrane, "Modern Subject Access in the Online Age," *American Libraries* 15:80-83, 145-150, 250-255, 336-339, 438-442 (Feb.-June 1984).

[3]Hans H. Wellisch, "Subject Access Mess Is a Political Problem," in Pauline A. Cochrane, "Modern Subject Access in the Online Age," 254.

[4]Sanford Berman, "Proposal for Reforms to Improve Subject Searching," in Pauline A. Cochrane, "Modern Subject Access in the Online Age," 254.

[5]Charles R. Hildreth, "LCSH Needs Hierarchical Restructuring," *American Libraries* 15:529 (July/Aug. 1984).

[6]Richard S. Angell, "Library of Congress Subject Headings—Review and Forecast," *Subject Retrieval in the Seventies: New Directions: Proceedings of an International Symposium*, ed. Hans (Hanan) Wellisch and Thomas D. Wilson (Westport, Conn.: Greenwood Publishing Company, 1972), 161.

[7]Library of Congress, Subject Cataloging Division, *Subject Cataloging Manual: Subject Headings*, prelim. ed. (Washington, D.C.: Library of Congress, 1984).

[8]Berman, "Proposal for Reforms to Improve Subject Searching," 254.

[9]Karen Markey, "Thus Spake the OPAC User," *Information Technology and Libraries* 2:383 (Dec. 1983).

[10]Berman, "Proposal for Reforms to Improve Subject Searching," 254.

[11]Jean Perreault, "Library of Congress Subject Headings: A New Manual," *International Classification* 6:162 (1979).

[12]Karen Markey, *Subject Searching in Library Catalogs Before and After the Introduction of Online Catalogs*, OCLC Library, Information, and Computer Science Series 4 (Dublin, Ohio: OCLC, 1984), 67.

[13]Ibid., 67-70.

[14]Ibid., 84; Carol A. Mandel with the assistance of Judith Herschman, "Subject Access in the Online Catalog" (A report prepared for the Council on Library Resources, Aug. 1981), 23.

[15]Pauline A. Cochrane, "LCSH Entry Vocabulary Project" (Final report to the Council on Library Resources and to the Library of Congress, Mar. 1983).

[16]Cochrane, "Modern Subject Access in the Online Age," 147.

[17]F. W. Lancaster, *Vocabulary Control for Information Retrieval* (Washington, D.C.: Information Resources Press, 1972), 16.

[18]Library of Congress, *Authorities: A MARC Format* (Washington, D.C.: Library of Congress, 1981).

[19]Marcia J. Bates, "Factors Affecting Subject Catalog Search Success," *Journal of the American Society for Information Science* 28:168 (May 1977).

[20]Berman, "Proposal for Reforms to Improve Subject Searching," 254; Mandel and Herschman, "Subject Access in the Online Catalog," 22; Markey, *Subject Searching in Library Catalogs*, 43.

[21]Pauline Atherton, *Books Are for Use: Final Report of the Subject Access Project to the Council on Library Resources* (Syracuse, N.Y.: Syracuse University, School of Information Studies, 1978).

[22]Stephen E. Wiberley, Jr., "Reducing Search Results a High Priority," in Cochrane, "Modern Subject Access in the Online Age," 255.

[23]Berman, "Proposal for Reforms to Improve Subject Searching," 254.

[24]Cochrane, "Modern Subject Access in the Online Age," 83.

[25]Markey, *Subject Searching in Library Catalogs*, 2.

[26]Ibid., 72-73.

[27]Gerard Salton and Michael J. McGill, *Introduction to Modern Information Retrieval* (New York: McGraw-Hill, 1983), 37-38.

[28]Tamas Doszkocs and John E. Ulmschneider, "A Practical Stemming Algorithm for Online Search Assistance," in *National Online Meeting Proceedings—1983*, comp. Martha E. Williams and Thomas H. Hogan (Medford, N.J.: Learned Information, 1983), 93-106.

APPENDIXES

APPENDIX A:
GLOSSARY

Alphabetical subject catalog. A catalog containing subject entries based on the principle of specific and direct entry and arranged alphabetically. Cf. Alphabetico-classed catalog; Classed catalog; Dictionary catalog.

Alphabetico-classed catalog. A subject catalog in which entries are listed under broad subjects and subdivided hierarchically by topics. The entries on each level of the hierarchy are arranged alphabetically. Cf. Alphabetical subject catalog; Classed catalog; Dictionary catalog.

Analytical subject entry. Subject entry for part of a work. Also called subject analytic.

Annotated Card Program. A Library of Congress program for cataloging children's materials that differs from regular cataloging by the addition of a summary note and additional subject headings assigned from *Subject Headings for Children's Literature.*

Authority record. *See* Name authority record; Subject authority record.

Biographical heading. A heading used with biographies that consists of the name of a class of persons with appropriate subdivisions, e.g., **Physicians — California — Biography; Poets, American — 19th century — Biography**.

Biography. A special genre of works consisting of life histories of individuals, including those written by the individuals themselves, i.e., autobiographies. Cf. Collective biography; Complete biography; Individual biography; Partial biography.

Chain. A series of subject terms from different levels of a hierarchy, arranged either from general to specific or vice versa.

Chronological subdivision. *See* Period subdivision.

Citation order. The order in which elements in a compound or complex subject heading or in a heading with subdivisions are arranged.

City doubling. Library of Congress's policy to assign an additional entry under the name of a city when a work in certain subject categories has been assigned a heading of the type **[Topic]** – **[City]**.

City flip. Library of Congress's previous practice of reversing the citation order between topic and place in some headings when the place involved was at the city level, e.g., **Fountains – California**, but Los Angeles (Calif.) – Fountains.

Class catalog. *See* Classed catalog.

Class entry. A subject entry consisting of a string of hierarchically related terms beginning with the broadest term leading to the subject in question.

Classed catalog. A subject catalog consisting of class entries arranged logically according to a systematic scheme of classification. Also called class catalog, classified subject catalog, systematic catalog. Cf. Alphabetical subject catalog; Alphabetico-classed catalog; Dictionary catalog.

Classified subject catalog. *See* Classed catalog.

Coextensive heading. A heading that represents precisely (not more generally or more specifically) the subject content of a work.

Collective biography. A work consisting of two or more life histories. Cf. Individual biography.

Complete biography. A biography that covers the entire life story of an individual. Cf. Partial biography.

Cross-reference. A direction from one term or heading to another in the catalog. Cf. *See* reference; *See also* reference; *Refer from* reference; Explanatory reference; General reference; Specific reference.

Depth of indexing. The degree to which individual parts of a publication are represented in indexing.

Diaries. Registers or records of personal experiences, observations, thoughts, or feelings, kept daily or at frequent intervals.

Dictionary catalog. A catalog in which all the entries (author, title, subject, series, etc.) and the cross-references are interfiled in one alphabetical sequence. The subject entries in a dictionary catalog are based on the principle of specific and direct entry. The term, when used in reference to the subject entries, is sometimes used interchangeably with the term *alphabetical subject catalog*. Cf. Alphabetical subject catalog; Alphabetico-classed catalog; Classed catalog.

Direct subdivision. Geographic subdivision of subject headings by name of a local place without interposition of the name of a larger geographic entity.

Downward reference. A reference from a broad term to a narrow one. Cf. Upward reference.

Duplicate entry.
1) Entry of the same heading in two different forms, e.g., **United States — Foreign relations — France**; **France — Foreign relations — United States**.

2) Assignment of two headings to bring out different aspects of a work. Frequently, one of the headings is a specific heading and the other a general (also called generic) heading subdivided by an aspect, e.g., **Bluegrass** and **Grasses — Scandinavia** for a work about Bluegrass in Scandinavia.

Exhaustive indexing. The practice of assigning indexing terms or subject headings to represent all significant concepts or aspects of a subject. Cf. Summarization; In-depth indexing.

Explanatory reference. A reference providing explanatory statements with regard to the heading involved. It is used when a simple *see* or *see also* reference does not give adequate information or guidance to the user.

Facet analysis. The division of a subject into its component parts (facets). Each array of facets consists of parts based on the same characteristic, e.g., language facet, space facet, time facet.

Festschrift. A collection of two or more essays, addresses, or biographical, bibliographical, and other contributions published in honor of a person, an institution, or a society, usually on the occasion of an anniversary or birthday celebration.

Film. A generic term for any pictorial medium intended for projection, including motion pictures, filmstrips, slides and transparencies, videotapes, and electronic video recordings.

First-order political division. A geographic unit representing a political division under the national level. The names of the first-order political divisions of certain countries are used in geographic qualifiers or indirect subdivisions instead of the name of the country.

Form heading. A heading representing the physical, bibliographical, artistic, or literary form of a work, e.g., **Encyclopedias and dictionaries; Essays; Short stories; String quartets.**

Form subdivision. A division of a subject heading that brings out the form of the work, e.g., **— Periodicals; — Bibliography; — Collected works.**

Free-floating phrase. A phrase that a subject cataloger may combine with a valid heading to form a new heading without establishing the usage editorially.

Free-floating subdivision. A subdivision that may be used by a cataloger at the Library of Congress under any existing appropriate heading for the first time without establishing the usage editorially.

General reference. A blanket reference to a group of headings rather than a particular heading. Example:

> **Nicknames**
> *sa subdivision* Nicknames *under subjects, e.g.,* Kings and rulers — Nicknames; *also special nicknames, e.g.,* Hoosier (Nickname), Uncle Sam (Nickname).

Cf. Specific reference.

Geographical heading. A name heading representing a place or an entity closely associated with a place (e.g., a park, a forest, a tunnel, etc.). Cf. Jurisdictional name heading; Nonjurisdictional name heading.

Geographic qualifier. The name of a larger geographic entity added to a local place name, e.g., **Cambridge (Mass.); Toledo (Spain).**

Geographic subdivision. A subdivision by the name of a place to which the subject represented by the main heading is limited. Cf. Direct subdivision; Indirect subdivision.

Hierarchical reference. A *see also* reference from a broad term to a narrow one.

History card. *See* Information reference.

In-depth indexing. The practice of assigning indexing terms or subject headings to represent individual parts of a publication. Cf. Summarization; Exhaustive indexing.

Indirect subdivision. Geographic subdivision of subject headings by name of country, constituent country or county (Great Britain), state (United States), province (Canada), or constituent republic (U.S.S.R.) with further subdivision by name of state (other than United States), province (other than Canada), county (other than Great Britain), city, or other locality. Cf. Direct subdivision.

Individual biography. A work devoted to the life of a single individual. Cf. Collective biography.

Information reference. A record providing information concerning the history of a heading. It was used previously with headings for corporate bodies that had undergone name changes. Now successive *see also* references are made instead. Also called history card.

—

Inverted heading. An adjectival or prepositional phrase heading with the words rearranged in order to bring the significant noun to the initial position.

Jurisdictional name heading. A geographic heading representing a political or ecclesiastical jurisdiction. Entities that belong to this category include countries, principalities, territories, states, provinces, counties, administrative districts, cities, archdioceses, and dioceses. At the Library of Congress jurisdictional name headings are established by the Descriptive Cataloging Division in accordance with *AACR2*.

Jurisdictional qualifier. A term (enclosed in parentheses) indicating type of jurisdiction, added to a geographic name in order to distinguish between places of the same name, e.g., **New York (State)**. Also called political qualifier.

Juvenile film. A film intended for children through the age of fifteen.

Juvenile work. Works intended for children through the age of fifteen (or through the ninth grade).

Literary warrant. The use of an actual collection of material or body of literature as the basis for developing an indexing or classification system. In the case of *Library of Congress Subject Headings*, the literary warrant is the Library's collection.

Liturgy. Prayers, rituals, acts, and ceremonies used in the official worship of a religion or denomination, public or private.

Local subdivision. *See* Geographic subdivision.

Model heading. *See* Pattern heading.

Multiple heading. A heading with a modifier followed by a bracketed series of similar modifiers ending with the word *etc.*, e.g., **Authors, American, [English, French, etc.]**. This device was used previously by the Library of Congress to illustrate how a heading may be modified. The practice of establishing multiple headings was discontinued in 1979.

Multiple subdivision. A subdivision in *Library of Congress Subject Headings* that incorporates bracketed terms, generally followed by the word *etc.*, e.g., **Subject headings — Aeronautics, [Education, Law, etc.]; Names, Personal — Scottish, [Spanish, Welsh, etc.]**. This device is used to indicate that similar subdivisions suggested by the terms enclosed in brackets may be created.

Name authority record. A record of a personal, corporate, or jurisdictional name heading that shows its established form and indicates the cross-references made to the heading. Cf. Subject authority record.

Nonjurisdictional name heading. A geographic heading representing an entity other than a jurisdiction. Typical nonjurisdictional name headings include those for rivers, mountains, parks, roads, etc.

Nonprint heading. *See* Unprinted heading.

Partial biography. A work that presents only certain details of a person's life. Cf. Complete biography.

Pattern heading. A heading that serves as a model of subdivisions for headings in the same category. Subdivisions listed under a model heading may be used whenever appropriate under other headings in the same category. For example, **Shakespeare, William, 1564-1616**, serves as a model heading for literary authors; **Piano** serves as a model heading for musical instruments. Also called model heading.

Period subdivision. A subdivision that shows the period or span of time treated in a work or the period during which the work appeared. Also called chronological subdivision.

Political qualifier. *See* Jurisdictional qualifier.

Postcoordination. The representation of a complex subject by means of separate single-concept terms at the input stage and the retrieval of that subject by means of combining the separate terms at the search or output stage. Also called a coordinate system. Cf. Precoordination.

Precoordination. The representation of a complex subject by means of combining separate elements of the subject at the input stage. Cf. Postcoordination.

Qualifier. A term (enclosed in parentheses) placed after a heading for the purpose of distinguishing between homographs or clarifying the meaning of the heading, e.g., **Indexing (Machine-shop practice); PL/I (Computer program language); Juno (Roman deity); New York State.** Cf. Geographic qualifier; Political qualifier.

Red-to-black reference. *See* Subject-to-name reference.

Refer from reference. An indication of the terms or headings *from* which references are to be made to a given heading. It is the reverse of the indication of a *see* or *see also* reference and is represented by the symbols *x* (*see* reference from) and *xx* (*see also* reference from).

Reference. *See* Cross-reference.

Related-term reference. A *see also* reference that connects headings related other than hierarchically.

See also reference. A reference from a heading to a less comprehensive or otherwise related heading. It is indicated in *Library of Congress Subject Headings* by the symbol *sa*. Cf. Hierarchical reference; Related-term reference.

See reference. A reference from a term or name not used as a heading to one that is used.

Specific entry. Entry of a work under a heading that expresses its special subject or topic, as distinguished from an entry for the class or broad subject that encompasses that special subject or topic.

Specific reference. A reference from one heading to another. Cf. General reference.

Split files. Separate files of subject entries in a catalog under headings represented by current and obsolete terms that refer to the same subject. The device, adopted by the Library of Congress in 1975 to facilitate updating of terminology, is no longer used.

Subdivision. The device of extending a subject heading by indicating one of its aspects—form, place, period, topic. Cf. Form subdivision; Geographic subdivision; Period subdivision; Topical subdivision.

Subheading. A subordinate unit of a name heading that follows the main heading or another subheading and is separated from it by a period and two spaces, e.g., **United States. Congress. Senate.**

Subject. The theme or topic treated by the author in a work, whether stated in the title or not.

Subject analysis. The process of identifying the intellectual content of a work. The results may be displayed in a catalog or bibliography by means of notational symbols as in a classification system, or verbal terms such as subject headings or indexing terms.

Subject analytic. *See* Analytical subject entry.

Subject authority record. A record of a subject heading that shows its established form, cites the authorities consulted in determining the choice and form of the heading, and indicates the cross-references made to the heading. Cf. Name authority record.

Subject catalog. A catalog consisting of subject entries only; the subject portion of a divided catalog.

Subject heading. The term (a word or group of words) denoting a subject under which all material on that subject is entered in a catalog.

Subject-to-name reference. A reference from a subject heading to a name heading for the purpose of directing the user's attention from a particular field of interest to names of individuals or corporate bodies that are active or associated in some way with the field. Current Library of Congress policy requires only subject-to-corporate-name references. Also called red-to-black reference.

Summarization. The practice of assigning indexing terms or subject headings to represent the overall content of a document rather than individual parts of it. Cf. In-depth indexing; Exhaustive indexing.

Syndetic device. The device used to connect related headings by means of cross-references.

Synthesis. The representation of a subject by combining separate terms.

Systematic catalog. *See* Classed catalog.

Thesaurus. A list of indexing terms used in a particular indexing system.

Topical subdivision. A subdivision that represents an aspect of the main subject other than form, place, or period. Cf. Form subdivision; Geographic subdivision; Period subdivision.

Tracing. An indication of the access points that have been made for a particular cataloging record. These access points include descriptive and subject headings. On a Library of Congress record in a book or card catalog, they are recorded in a paragraph following the notes, with the subject headings listed first, each preceded by an arabic numeral.

Uniform heading. Use of one heading in one form only for a given subject.

Unique heading. The principle of using a heading to represent one subject or concept only.

Unprinted heading. A heading that is used in catalog entries but not listed in *Library of Congress Subject Headings*. Most headings consisting of proper names (including personal and corporate headings) and many music headings are unprinted headings. Also called nonprint heading.

Upward reference. A reference from a narrow term to a broader term. Cf. Downward reference.

APPENDIX B:
AUXILIARY PUBLICATIONS OF
LIBRARY OF CONGRESS
SUBJECT HEADINGS

Subject Subdivisions under
Names of Countries, Etc.

Preliminary Lists of Subject Subdivisions under Names of Countries or States, and of Subject Headings with Country Subdivisions. Washington, D.C.: Government Printing Office, 1906; 1908 (2nd issue).

Preliminary Lists of Subject Subdivisions: (A) under Names of Countries or States; (B) under Cities; (C) under General Subjects. Washington, D.C.: Government Printing Office, 1910 (3rd issue).

Preliminary Lists of Subject Subdivisions: (A) under Names of Countries, States, Etc.; (B) under Names of Cities; (C) under General Subjects. Washington, D.C.: Government Printing Office, 1916 (4th issue).

Subject Subdivisions: (A) under Names of Countries, States, Etc.; (B) under Names of Cities; (C) under General Subjects. Washington, D.C.: Government Printing Office, 1920 (5th edition); 1924 (6th edition [reprinted 1936]).

Period Subdivisions under Names of Places

Marguerite V. Quattlebaum, comp. and ed. *Period Subdivisions under Names of Places Used in the Dictionary Catalogs of the Library of Congress.* Washington, D.C.: Government Printing Office, 1950.

Marguerite V. Quattlebaum, comp. *LC Period Subdivisions under Names of Places.* 2nd ed. Washington, D.C.: Library of Congress, 1975.

Subject Headings with Local Subdivisions

Preliminary Lists of Subject Headings with Local Subdivision. Washington, D.C.: Government Printing Office, 1916; 1917 (2nd issue).

Subject Headings with Local Subdivision. Washington, D.C.: Government Printing Office, 1920 (3rd ed.); 1925 (4th ed.); 1935 (5th ed.).

Literature and Language Subject Headings

Preliminary List of Language Subdivisions. Washington, D.C.: Government Printing Office, 1910; 1912 (2nd issue).

Preliminary List of Literature Subject Headings. Washington, D.C.: Government Printing Office, 1913; 1915 (2nd issue). Third issue, 1917, with the title, *Preliminary List of Literature Subject Headings with a Tentative List for Shakespeare.* Washington, D.C.: Government Printing Office, 1917 (3rd issue).

Literature Subject Headings, with List of Shakespeare Collections and Language Subject Headings. Washington, D.C.: Government Printing Office, 1920 (4th ed.) 1926 (5th ed.).

Subject Headings for Children's Literature

Subject Headings for Children's Literature: A Statement of Principles of Application and a List of Headings That Vary from Those Used for Adult Literature. Washington, D.C.: Library of Congress, 1969.

Music Headings

Music Subject Headings Used on Printed Catalog Cards of the Library of Congress. Washington, 1952.

Guide to Subdivision Practice

Library of Congress Subject Headings: A Guide to Subdivision Practice. Washington, D.C.: Library of Congress, 1981.

Subject Cataloging Manual

Subject Cataloging Manual: Subject Headings. Prelim. ed. Washington, D.C.: Library of Congress, 1984.

APPENDIX C:
FREE-FLOATING FORM AND
TOPICAL SUBDIVISIONS*

— Abbreviations
— Ability testing
— Abstracting and indexing
— Abstracts
— Accidents
— Accidents — Investigation
— Accidents and injuries
— Accounting
— Acronyms
— Addresses, essays, lectures
— Administration
— Air conditioning
— Alcohol use
— Alumni
— Amateurs' manuals
— Analysis
— Anecdotes
— Anecdotes, facetiae, satire, etc.
— Anniversaries, etc.
— Anthropometry
— Antiquities
— Antiquities — Collection and
    preservation

— Appointment, qualifications,
    tenure, etc.
— Appointments, promotions,
    salaries, etc.
— Appropriations and expenditures
— Appropriations and expenditures
    — Effect of inflation on
— Archaeological collections
— Archival resources *(Indirect)*
— Archives
— Art
— Art collections
— Atlases
— Attitudes
— Audio-visual aids
— Audio-visual aids — Catalogs
— Auditing and inspection
— Authorship
— Autographs
— Automatic control
— Automation
— Awards
— Biblical teaching
— Bibliography
— Bibliography — Catalogs

*Library of Congress, Subject Cataloging Division, *Subject Cataloging Manual: Subject Headings*, prelim. ed. (Washington, D.C.: Library of Congress, 1984), H1095 (rev. 7/20/84).

—Bibliography — First editions
—Bibliography — Methodology
—Bibliography — Union lists
—Bio-bibliography
—Biography[1]
—Biography — History and criticism
—Biological control (Indirect)
—Bonsai collections
—Book reviews
—Books and reading
—Buildings
—Buildings — Conservation and restoration
—Buildings — Guide-books
—By-products
—Calibration
—Capture, [date]
—Care and hygiene (Indirect)
—Care and treatment (Indirect)
—Caricatures and cartoons
—Cartoons, satire, etc.
—Case studies
—Catalogs
—Catalogs and collections
—Censorship (Indirect)
—Census
—Centennial celebrations, etc.
—Certification (Indirect)
—Chapel exercises
—Charities
—Charts, diagrams, etc.
—Chronology
—Church history
—Circus collections
—Citizen participation
—Civil rights (Indirect)
—Claims vs. ...
—Classification
—Cleaning
—Code numbers
—Code words
—Coin collections
—Cold weather conditions
—Cold weather operation
—Collected works
—Collected works — Translations from [name of language]
—Collected works — Translations into [name of language]

—Collection and preservation
—Collectors and collecting (Indirect)
—Colonization (Indirect)
—Comic books, strips, etc.
—Commerce (Indirect)
—Communication systems
—Comparative method
—Comparative studies
—Competitions (Indirect)
—Composition
—Computer assisted instruction
—Computer programs
—Concordances
—Conduct of life
—Congresses
—Congresses — Attendance
—Conservation and restoration[2]
—Constitution
—Contracts and specifications (Indirect)
—Control (Indirect)
—Controversial literature
—Cooling
—Correspondence
—Corrosion
—Corrupt practices
—Cost control
—Cost effectiveness
—Cost of operation
—Costs
—Costume
—Cult
—Curricula
—Data processing
—Dating
—Decision making
—Defects
—Defects — Reporting
—Defense measures
—Dental care (Indirect)
—Design
—Design and construction
—Designs and plans
—Deterioration
—Dictionaries
—Dictionaries, Juvenile
—Dictionaries and encyclopedias
—Dictionaries, indexes, etc.

Footnotes to appendix C appear on page 388.

— Directories
— Directories — Telephone
— Discipline
— Discography
— Diseases *(Indirect)*
— Diseases and hygiene *(Indirect)*
— Documentation *(Indirect)*
— Drama
— Drawings
— Drug use
— Drying
— Dust control
— Dwellings
— Early works to 1800
— Economic aspects *(Indirect)*
— Economic conditions
— Education *(Indirect)*
— Electromechanical analogies
— Emigration and immigration
— Employees
— Employment *(Indirect)*
— Endowments
— Energy conservation
— Energy consumption
— Environmental aspects *(Indirect)*
— Equipment and supplies
— Estimates *(Indirect)*
— Ethnic identity
— Ethnological collections
— Ethnomusicological collections
— Evaluation
— Examinations
— Examinations, questions, etc.
— Exhibitions
— Experiments
— Facsimiles
— Family relationships
— Fees
— Fiction
— Field work
— Film catalogs
— Finance
— Finance, Personal
— Fire, [date]
— Fires and fire prevention
— Folklore
— Food service
— Forecasting
— Foreign influences
— Forms
— Fume control
— Genealogy
— Government policy

— Grading
— Graphic methods
— Guide-books
— Handbooks, manuals, etc.
— Health and hygiene *(Indirect)*
— Heating and ventilation
— Heraldry
— Herbarium
— Historiography
— History
— History — 16th century[3]
— History — 17th century[3]
— History — 18th century[3]
— History — 19th century[3]
— History — 20th century[3]
— History — Philosophy
— History — Sources
— History and criticism
— Homes and haunts *(Indirect)*
— Hospitals *(Indirect)*
— Housing *(Indirect)*
— Hygienic aspects *(Indirect)*
— Iconography
— Identification
— Illustrations
— In-service training *(Indirect)*
— Indexes
— Industrial applications
— Industries
— Influence
— Information services *(Indirect)*
— Insignia
— Inspection
— Instruction and study *(Indirect)*
— Instruments
— Intellectual life
— Intelligence levels
— International cooperation
— Interviews[1]
— Inventories
— Job descriptions
— Juvenile drama
— Juvenile fiction
— Juvenile films
— Juvenile literature
— Juvenile poetry
— Juvenile sound recordings
— Kings and rulers
— Kings and rulers — Children
— Kings and rulers — Genealogy
— Knowledge — [topic]
— Knowledge and learning
— Labeling *(Indirect)*

—Labor productivity
—Laboratories
—Laboratory manuals
—Language
—Language — Glossaries, etc.
—Language (New words, slang, etc.)
—Languages
—Legal status, laws, etc. *(Indirect)*
—Legends
—Lexicography
—Libraries
—Library
—Library resources *(Indirect)*
—Licenses *(Indirect)*
—Lighting
—Linear programming
—Literary collections
—Location
—Longitudinal studies
—Maintenance and repair
—Management
—Manuscripts
—Manuscripts — Catalogs
—Manuscripts — Facsimiles
—Manuscripts — Indexes
—Map collections
—Maps
—Maps — Bibliography
—Marketing
—Materials
—Mathematical models
—Mathematics
—Measurement
—Medals
—Medical care *(Indirect)*
—Medical examinations *(Indirect)*
—Meditations
—Membership
—Methodology
—Microform catalogs
—Military aspects
—Miscellanea
—Models
—Moisture
—Monuments
—Monuments, etc.
—Moral and ethical aspects
—Morality
—Museums
—Museums, relics, etc. *(Indirect)*
—Music
—Musical instrument collections

—Name
—Names
—Natural history collections
—Noise
—Noise control
—Nomenclature
—Notation
—Numismatic collections
—Nutrition
—Observations
—Observers' manuals
—Officials and employees
—Officials and employees — Attitudes
—Officials and employees — Bonding
—Officials and employees — Charitable contributions
—Officials and employees — Furloughs
—Officials and employees — Pensions *(Indirect)*
—Officials and employees — Registers
—Officials and employees — Residence requirements
—Officials and employees — Salaries, allowances, etc.
—Officials and employees — Travel regulations
—Origin
—Outlines, syllabi, etc.
—Packaging
—Packing
—Papal documents
—Passes
—Patents
—Pensions *(Indirect)*
—Periodicals
—Periodicals — Bibliography
—Periodicals — Bibliography — Catalogs
—Periodicals — Bibliography — Union lists
—Periodicals — Indexes
—Personnel management
—Philosophy
—Phonotape catalogs
—Photograph collections
—Photographs from space
—Physiological aspects
—Physiological effect
—Pictorial works

—Pipe lines
—Planning
—Platforms
—Poetry
—Political activity
—Political aspects *(Indirect)*
—Politics and government
—Popular works
—Population
—Portraits
—Portraits, caricatures, etc.
—Portraits, etc.
—Poster collections
—Posters
—Power supply
—Practice *(Indirect)*
—Prayer-books and devotions
—Preservation
—Presidents
—Presidents — Wives
—Prevention
—Price policy
—Prices *(Indirect)*
—Private collections *(Indirect)*
—Privileges and immunities
    (Indirect)
—Problems, exercises, etc.
—Production control
—Production standards *(Indirect)*
—Professional ethics
—Programmed instruction
—Prophecies
—Protection *(Indirect)*
—Psychological aspects
—Psychology
—Public opinion
—Public relations
—Publishing *(Indirect)*
—Purchasing
—Purification
—Quality control
—Quotations
—Quotations, maxims, etc.
—Rates
—Rating of
—Readers
—Records and correspondence
—Recreation
—Recreational use
—Recruiting
—Registers
—Rehabilitation *(Indirect)*
—Reliability

—Religion
—Religious life
—Remodeling
—Remote sensing
—Reorganization
—Repairing
—Research *(Indirect)*
—Research — Laboratories
—Research grants *(Indirect)*
—Retirement
—Reviews
—Rites and ceremonies
—Romances
—Rules and practice
—Safety appliances
—Safety measures
—Safety regulations *(Indirect)*
—Salaries, allowances, etc.
—Salaries, pensions, etc. *(Indirect)*
—Sanitary affairs
—Sanitation
—Scholarships, fellowships, etc.
    (Indirect)
—Scientific apparatus collections
—Scientific applications
—Seal
—Security measures
—Selection and appointment
—Sermons
—Services for *(Indirect)*
—Sexual behavior
—Siege, [date]
—Sieges
—Simulation methods
—Slang
—Slide collections
—Slides
—Social aspects *(Indirect)*
—Social conditions
—Social life and customs
—Societies and clubs
—Societies, etc.
—Sociological aspects
—Songs and music
—Sources
—Specifications *(Indirect)*
—Specimens
—Speeches in Congress
—Stability
—Standards *(Indirect)*
—State supervision
—Statistical methods

—Statistical services
—Statistics
—Statistics, Vital
—Storage
—Study and teaching *(Indirect)*
—Study and teaching—Supervision
—Study and teaching (Continuing education) *(Indirect)*
—Study and teaching (Elementary) *(Indirect)*
—Study and teaching (Graduate) *(Indirect)*
—Study and teaching (Higher) *(Indirect)*
—Study and teaching (Internship) *(Indirect)*
—Study and teaching (Preceptorship) *(Indirect)*
—Study and teaching (Preschool) *(Indirect)*
—Study and teaching (Primary) *(Indirect)*
—Study and teaching (Residency) *(Indirect)*
—Study and teaching (Secondary) *(Indirect)*
—Suicidal behavior
—Supply and demand
—Tables
—Taxation *(Indirect)*
—Teacher training *(Indirect)*
—Technique
—Technological innovations
—Terminology
—Testing

—Text-books
—Texts
—Themes, motives
—Therapeutic use
—Time management
—Tomb
—Tombs
—Toxicology *(Indirect)*
—Trade-marks
—Training of *(Indirect)*
—Translating
—Translating services
—Translations
—Translations from [name of language]
—Translations from [name of language]—Bibliography
—Translations into [name of language]
—Translations into [name of language]—Bibliography
—Transportation
—Travel regulations
—Trials, litigation, etc.
—Tropical conditions
—Union lists
—Valuation *(Indirect)*
—Video tape catalogs
—Vocational guidance *(Indirect)*
—Waste disposal
—Water consumption
—Water-supply
—Weight
—Weights and measures
—Yearbooks

---

[1]Not free-floating when used under names of disciplines.

[2]*(Indirect)* only in the case of art objects.

[3]Not free-floating when used under place names.

APPENDIX D: FREE-FLOATING FORM AND TOPICAL SUBDIVISIONS CONTROLLED BY PATTERN HEADINGS

HISTORY

Subdivisions Controlled by Pattern Headings for Wars*

PATTERNS: United States—History—Civil War, 1861-1865
World War, 1939-1945

—Addresses, essays, lectures
—Aerial operations
—Aerial operations, American, [British, etc.]
—Afro-Americans
—Almanacs
—Amphibious operations
—Anecdotes
—Anniversaries, etc.
—Anti-aircraft artillery operations
—Antiquities
—Armistices
—Art and the war, [revolution, etc.][1]
—Atrocities

—Autographs
—Balloons *(Indirect)*
—Baptists, [Catholic Church, etc.]
—Battle-fields *(Indirect)*

—Battle-fields—Guide-books
—Biography
—Biography—Dictionaries
—Biological warfare
—Blacks *(Indirect)*
—Blockades
—Bomb reconnaissance
—Buddhism, [Islam, etc.]
—Camouflage
—Campaigns *(Indirect)*
—Campaigns—Eastern[2]

---

*Library of Congress, Subject Cataloging Division, *Subject Cataloging Manual: Subject Headings*, prelim. ed. (Washington, D.C.: Library of Congress, 1984), H1200 (rev. 5/13/85).

Numbered footnotes to this section of appendix D appear on page 391.

389

— Campaigns — Western[2]
— Caricatures and cartoons
— Cartography
— Casualties (Statistics, etc.)
— Causes
— Cavalry operations
— Censorship *(Indirect)*
— Centennial celebrations, etc.
— Chaplains *(Indirect)*
— Chemical warfare
— Children *(Indirect)*
— Chronology
— Civilian relief *(Indirect)*
— Claims
— Collaborationists *(Indirect)*
— Collectibles *(Indirect)*
— Commando operations *(Indirect)*
— Communications
— Concentration camps *(Indirect)*
— Confiscations and contributions
   (Indirect)
— Congresses
— Conscientious objectors *(Indirect)*
— Conscript labor *(Indirect)*
— Cossacks
— Counterfeit money
— Cryptography
— Deportations from [region or
   country]
— Desertions *(Indirect)*
— Destruction and pillage *(Indirect)*
— Diplomatic history[3]
— Dogs
— Draft resisters *(Indirect)*
— Economic aspects *(Indirect)*
— Education and the war, [revolu-
   tion, etc.][1]
— Electronic intelligence *(Indirect)*
— Engineering and construction
— Equipment and supplies
— Evacuation of civilians *(Indirect)*
— Finance *(Indirect)*
— Flags
— Food supply *(Indirect)*
— Forced repatriation
— Foreign public opinion[4]
— Foreign public opinion, Austrian,
   [British, etc.][4]
— German Americans
— Giftbooks
— Governments in exile

— Graffiti
— Gypsies *(Indirect)*
— Health aspects *(Indirect)*
— Historiography
— Horses *(Indirect)*
— Hospitals *(Indirect)*
— Humor
— Iconography
— Indians
— Influence
— Japanese Americans
— Jews *(Indirect)*
— Jews — Rescue *(Indirect)*
— Journalism, Military *(Indirect)*
— Journalists
— Jungle warfare
— Language (New words, slang,
   etc.)
— Law and legislation *(Indirect)*
— Libraries
— Literature and the war, [revolu-
   tion, etc.][1]
— Logistics *(Indirect)*
— Manpower *(Indirect)*
— Maps
— Medical care *(Indirect)*
— Military currency
— Military intelligence *(Indirect)*
— Missing in action *(Indirect)*
— Moral and ethical aspects
— Motion pictures and the war,
   [revolution, etc.][1]
— Museums
— Music and the war, [revolution,
   etc.][1]
— Name
— Naval operations
— Naval operations — Submarine
— Naval operations, American,
   [British, etc.]
— Occupied territories
— Pamphlets
— Participation, Afro-American,
   [Indian, etc.]
— Participation, Female
— Participation, Foreign
— Participation, German, [Irish,
   Swiss, etc.]
— Participation, Jewish
— Participation, Juvenile
— Peace

— Personal narratives
— Personal narratives, American, [French, etc.]
— Personal narratives, Confederate
— Personal narratives, Jewish
— Photography
— Pictorial works
— Pigeons
— Poetry
— Portraits
— Postal service
— Posters
— Prisoners and prisons
— Prisoners and prisons, British, [German, etc.]
— Prizes, etc.
— Propaganda
— Prophecies
— Protest movements *(Indirect)*
— Psychological aspects
— Public opinion
— Radar
— Reconnaissance operations
— Reconnaissance operations, American, [German, etc.]
— Refugees
— Regimental histories[5] *(Indirect)*
— Registers
— Registers of dead *(Indirect)*
— Religious aspects
— Reparations
— Riverine operations
— Riverine operations, American, [British, etc.]
— Science
— Scouts and scouting
— Search and rescue operations *(Indirect)*

— Secret service *(Indirect)*
— Sermons
— Social aspects *(Indirect)*
— Societies, etc.
— Songs and music
— Sounds
— Sources
— Tank warfare
— Technology
— Territorial questions *(Indirect)*
— Theater and the war, [revolution, etc.][1]
— Transportation
— Treaties
— Trench warfare
— Trophies
— Underground literature *(Indirect)*
— Underground movements *(Indirect)*
— Underground movements, Jewish *(Indirect)*
— Underground printing plants *(Indirect)*
— Veterinary service *(Indirect)*
— War work *(Indirect)*
— War work — American Legion
— War work — Boy Scouts
— Work work — Catholic Church, [Methodist Church, etc.]
— War work — Churches
— War work — Elks
— War work — Red Cross
— War work — Salvation Army
— War work — Schools
— War work — Young Men's Christian Associations
— War work — Young Women's Christian Associations
— Women *(Indirect)*

---

[1]Use term appropriate for type of engagement, e.g., **United States — History — Revolution, 1775-1783 — Art and the revolution.**

[2]Use only under the headings: **World War, 1914-1918; World War, 1939-1945.**

[3]Use only under wars established directly under the name of the war. For other wars, use [country] — Foreign relations — [period].

[4]Do not use under the headings: **World War, 1914-1918; World War, 1939-1945.**

[5]For instructions on use of the subdivision — **Regimental histories,** see H1995.

LAW

Subdivisions Controlled by the Pattern Heading for Legal Topics*

PATTERN: **Labor laws and legislation**

- —Cases
- —Codification
- —Compliance costs
- —Criminal provisions
- —Digests**
- —Forms
- —Interpretation and construction

- —Language
- —Legal research***
- —Popular works
- —Research *(Indirect)*****
- —Terms and phrases
- —Trial practice

---

*Library of Congress, Subject Cataloging Division, *Subject Cataloging Manual: Subject Headings*, prelim. ed. (Washington, D.C.: Library of Congress, 1984), H1154.5, H1550, H1710.

Used under legal headings for monographic or serial works consisting of systematically arranged compilations of brief summaries of individual statutes, regulations, court decisions, or regulatory agency decisions on particular topics. It is *not* further subdivided by other form subdivisions such as —Collected works;** —**Periodicals;** —**Yearbooks;** etc.

***Used under legal headings for works which discuss the use of legal research tools such as court reports, codes, digests, citators, etc. in determining the status of statutory, regulatory, or case law on the topic in question. It is not further subdivided by place.

****Used under legal topics for descriptions of proposed research, including such details as management, finance, personnel, special projects, methodology, goals, etc.

LITERATURE

Subdivisions Controlled by the Pattern Heading for Literatures (Including Individual Genres)*

PATTERN: **English literature**

I. *PERIOD SUBDIVISIONS:*

Period subdivisions may be followed by topical and form subdivisions (section III), with the exception of those footnoted, but not by groups of authors subdivisions (section II). Period subdivisions are not used under headings for minor genres, i.e. genres other than fiction, drama, poetry, essays, and prose literature; nor are they used under inverted headings, e.g. **Detective and mystery stories, American**. In addition, period subdivisions are not free-floating under headings modified by parenthetical qualifiers for language, e.g. **Nigerian fiction (English)**.

The listed period subdivisions evolved from English literature practice and should be used only when appropriate for other literatures. If inappropriate, special periods should be established under individual literatures and genres.

Literatures and genres, except drama:
— **Middle English, 1100-1500**   — **18th century**
— **Middle English, 1100-1500 — Modernized versions** — **19th century**
— **Early modern, 1500-1700**   — **20th century**

Drama:
— **To 1500**   — **18th century**
— **Early modern and Elizabethan, 1500-1600**   — **19th century**
— **17th century**   — **20th century**
— **Restoration, 1660-1700**

II. *AUTHOR GROUP SUBDIVISIONS:*

Use the following free-floating subdivisions under any literature or major genre of a literature for author groupings that identify subordinate bodies of that literature. Any subdivision that also designates the literature is not valid under that literature, e.g. **English literature — Celtic authors**, but not **Celtic literature — Celtic authors**. Author group subdivisions may be followed by any topical or form subdivision from section III but may not be combined in a single heading with period subdivisions from section I.

---

*Library of Congress, Subject Cataloging Division, *Subject Cataloging Manual: Subject Headings*, prelim. ed. (Washington, D.C.: Library of Congress, 1984), H1156 (rev. 2/13/85). Numbered footnotes to this section of appendix D appear on page 395.

When establishing new subdivisions following this pattern, submit additional phrases for internal *national, ethnic,* or *religious* groups *only*. For other author groups, follow the pattern **Children's writings, English — [place]** or **Prisoners' writings, French — [place]**. However, for external author groups, i.e. those living outside the country normally associated with the literature to which they are contributing, use simple geographical subdivision, e.g. **German literature — Romania**.

The literatures of the newly independent nations of Africa, Asia, and the Pacific must be established with the national or regional group as an independent literature (using a parenthetical language qualifier if necessary), e.g. **African literature (French)**. Since these are no longer considered subordinate groups within the general body of literature in a language, do not formulate headings such as **French literature — African authors**.

— Armenian authors
— Basque authors
— Black authors[1]
— Buddhist authors
— Catalan authors
— Catholic authors
— Celtic authors
— Chinese authors
— Christian authors
— Christian Science authors
— Commonwealth of Nations authors
— Dravidian authors
— Foreign authors
— Irish authors
— Jaina authors
— Japanese authors
— Jewish authors
— Kirghiz authors
— Korean authors
— Luxembourg authors
— Malawi authors
— Maori authors
— Marathi authors
— Men authors
— Mennonite authors
— Minority authors
— Mormon authors
— Muslim authors
— Parsee authors
— Protestant authors
— Quaker authors
— Scottish authors
— Sindhi authors
— Ukrainian authors
— Untouchable authors
— Welsh authors
— Women authors

III.   *TOPICAL AND FORM SUBDIVISIONS:*

The following free-floating subdivisions may also be used under subdivisions from section I (periods) or section II (author groups) with the footnoted exceptions.

— Adaptations
— American influences[2]
— Anecdotes, facetiae, satire, etc.
— Appreciation *(Indirect)*
— Arab influences[2]
— Bibliography
— Bibliography — Catalogs
— Bibliography — Early
— Bibliography — First editions
— Bibliography — Methodology
— Bio-bibliography
— Book reviews
— Buddhist influences[2]
— Chinese influences[2]
— Christian influences[2]
— Chronology
— Classical influences[2]
— Competitions *(Indirect)*

- Concordances
- Criticism, Textual
- Dictionaries
- Discography
- Egyptian influences[2]
- European influences[2]
- Examinations, questions, etc.
- Exhibitions
- Explication
- Explication — Dictionaries
- Film and video adaptations
- Foreign countries
- Foreign countries — History and criticism
- Foreign influences[2]
- French influences[2]
- German influences[2]
- Greek influences[2]
- History and criticism
- History and criticism — Abstracts
- History and criticism — Addresses, essays, lectures
- History and criticism — Bibliography
- History and criticism — Collected works
- History and criticism — Congresses
- History and criticism — Periodicals
- History and criticism — Theory, etc.
- History and criticism — Yearbooks
- Illustrations
- Illustrations — Exhibitions
- Indexes
- Indic influences[2]
- Italian influences[2]
- Japanese influences[2]
- Manuscripts
- Manuscripts — Facsimiles
- Mediterranean influences[2]
- Memorizing
- Microform catalogs
- Musical settings
- Mycenaean influences[2]
- Oriental influences[2]
- Outlines, syllabi, etc.
- Periodicals
- Periodicals — History
- Persian influences[2]
- Philosophy
- Pictorial works
- Programmed instruction
- Psychological aspects
- Research *(Indirect)*
- Roman influences[2]
- Russian influences[2]
- Social aspects *(Indirect)*
- Societies, etc.
- Sources
- Spanish influences[2]
- Stories, plots, etc.
- Study and teaching *(Indirect)*
- Study and teaching — Audio-visual aids
- Study and teaching (Elementary) *(Indirect)*
- Study and teaching (Graduate) *(Indirect)*
- Study and teaching (Higher) *(Indirect)*
- Study and teaching (Secondary) *(Indirect)*
- Taoist influences[2]
- Themes, motives
- Translations from foreign languages
- Translations from foreign languages — History and criticism
- Translations from French, [German, etc.]
- Translations from French, [German, etc.] — History and criticism
- Translations into foreign languages
- Translations into foreign languages — History and criticism
- Translations into French, [German, etc.]
- Translations into French, [German, etc.] — History and criticism

[1]Not valid under headings for American literature or its genres.

[2]Not valid under period subdivisions or under headings for literatures identified in the subdivision.

Subdivisions Controlled by the Pattern Heading for Groups of Literary Authors*

PATTERN: Authors, English

The subdivisions listed below may also be used as free-floating subdivisions under period subdivisions.

- Anecdotes, facetiae, satire, etc.
- Archives
- Autographs
- Biography
- Biography — Careers
- Biography — Last years and death
- Biography — Marriage
- Biography — Youth
- Books and reading
- Caricatures and cartoons
- Children
- Chronology
- Correspondence
- Diaries
- Dictionaries
- Directories
- Fees
- Homes and haunts *(Indirect)*
- Indexes
- Interviews
- Journeys *(Indirect)*
- Manuscripts
- Political activity
- Political and social views
- Portraits
- Psychology
- Registers
- Relations with men
- Relations with women
- Religious life
- Wives

Subdivisions Controlled by the Pattern Heading for Individual Literary Authors**

PATTERN: Shakespeare, William, 1564-1616

TYPES OF HEADINGS DESIGNATED BY THE CATEGORY: Names of individual literary authors. *Examples:* **Dante Alighieri, 1265-1321; Tolstoy, Leo, graf, 1828-1910; Saki, 1870-1916; Dwivedi, Mahavir Prasad.** For subdivisions used under groups of literary authors, see list above. For subdivisions used under names of persons other than literary authors, see pp. 420-432.

---

*Library of Congress, Subject Cataloging Division, *Subject Cataloging Manual: Subject Headings*, prelim. ed. (Washington, D.C.: Library of Congress, 1984), H1155.2.

**Library of Congress, Subject Cataloging Division, *Subject Cataloging Manual: Subject Headings*, prelim. ed. (Washington, D.C.: Library of Congress, 1984), H1155.4 (rev. 08/02/85).

CONFLICTS: Any subdivision listed here can be used as a free-floating subdivision, if appropriate, under any heading belonging to this category. Do not continue to use a variant phrase or subdivision printed in *LCSH* that is equivalent to a subdivision on this list.

SPECIAL PROVISIONS:

1. Since the following list of free-floating subdivisions is intended to apply to all literary authors, certain subdivisions occur which would not logically occur under Shakespeare, e.g. **—Biography—Exile**. Such subdivisions have actually been needed and appropriately used under other literary authors, e.g. Brecht and Pushkin in this case.

2. The list of topics under **Shakespeare, William, 1564-1616—Knowledge** is virtually closed. Assign topics from that list even to the extent of using broader subdivisions for specific topics.

3. Use the free-floating phrase heading **[name of author], in fiction, drama, poetry, etc.**, as (1) a form heading for biographical belletristic works, including musical dramatic works such as operas, ballets, musical comedies, etc., about an individual literary author; or (2) a topical heading for works which discuss an individual literary author as a theme in belles lettres, including musical dramatic works.

> Acting, see **—Dramatic production; —Stage history**
> > For works limited to discussions of the acting of an author's plays, assign **Acting** as a second heading.
> **—Adaptations**
> > Use for discussions of adaptations as well as for collections of adaptations of the author's works. Do not use for texts of single adaptations. For discussions of the author's adaptation of the themes of others, see **—Sources**.
> > See also **—Film adaptations**.
> **—Addresses, essays, lectures**
> > Use as appropriate under the author's name, or under any topical subdivision, e.g. **—Religion—Addresses, essays, lectures**.
> **—Aesthetics**
> > Use for discussions of the author's philosophy of art or beauty, whether explicitly stated or inferred from his works. Includes the author's knowledge of the aesthetics of others.
> Allegory and symbolism, see **—Symbolism**
> **—Allusions**
> > Use for contemporary (author's life span) and early brief references to the author. For works on the author's use of allusions, see **—Criticism and interpretation; —Knowledge—[appropriate subdivision]; —Style; etc.**
> > See also **—Quotations**
> Ancestry, see **—Biography—Family**

— **Anecdotes**

Use for collections of brief narratives of true incidents from the author's life.

See also — **Allusions**

— **Anniversaries, etc.**

— **Anniversaries, etc., [date]**

Use for material dealing with the celebration itself. Do not use for works merely published on the occasion of an anniversary.

— **Anonyms and pseudonyms**

— **Appreciation** *(Indirect)*

Use for works on *public* response and reception, group opinion (positive or negative), praise, tributes, cult, etc. For works on scholarly reception or consisting of critical analysis or interpretation, see — **Criticism and interpretation**, except when it is necessary to bring out the place. For works on the author's impact on other persons, groups, movements, etc., see — **Influence.**

— **Archives**

Use for collections or discussions of documentary material or records relating to the author, including manuscripts, diaries, correspondence, photographs, bills, tax returns, or other items of historical interest. See also — **Correspondence;** — **Diaries;** — **Iconography;** — **Manuscripts;** — **Notebooks, sketchbooks, etc.**

— **Archives — Catalogs**

— **Art**

Use under authors living before 1400 A.D. for works consisting of reproductions of works of art depicting the author or works discussing such art. For authors living after 1400, see — **Portraits.**

Associates, see — **Friends and associates**

— **Authorship**

Use for works discussing the attribution of authorship.

See also — **Spurious and doubtful works**

— **Authorship — Baconian theory, [Burton theory, etc.]**

— **Authorship — Collaboration**

Autobiography, see — **Biography**

— **Autographs**

Use for collections or discussions of specimens of the author's autographs or handwriting.

— **Autographs — Facsimiles**

Autographs, Spurious, see — **Forgeries**

— **Bibliography**

Use for lists of publications by or about the author. Use also under any topical subdivision, e.g. — **Religion — Bibliography.**

See also — **Exhibitions;** [author. title] — **Bibliography**

— **Bibliography — Catalogs**

— **Bibliography — First editions**

— **Bibliography — Folios**

— **Bibliography — Folios. 1623, [1632, etc.]**

Bibliography — Methodology Do not use. Use: **1.** [author]. **2. Bibliography — Methodology.**

— **Bibliography — Quartos**

—**Biography**
  Use also for autobiographies.
  Biography—Ancestry, see —**Biography—Family**
—**Biography—Birth**
—**Biography—Careers**
  Use to cover the non-authorial aspects of authors whose biographies class in P regardless of their activity in other disciplines. To bring out the specific discipline or subject area, assign a second heading of the type: [author]—Knowledge—[subject], as appropriate, e.g.,
  1. **Williams, William Carlos, 1883-1963—Biography—Careers.**
  2. **Williams, William Carlos, 1883-1963—Knowledge—Medicine.**
  3. **Poets, American—20th century—Biography.**
  4. **Physicians—United States—Biography.**
  Do not use or propose headings of the type: **[author]—Biography— Journalistic career, [Medical career, Teaching career, etc.]**
  Biography—Character, see —**Biography—Psychology.** For works on moral aspects, see —**Ethics.**
  Biography—Chronology, see —**Chronology**
  Biography—Death and burial, see —**Biography—Last years and death**
  Biography—Descendants, see —**Biography—Family**
—**Biography—Ennoblement**
  Use also for coat-of-arms.
—**Biography—Exile** *(Indirect)*
—**Biography—Family**
  Use for works on the author's family or relations with family members. Use also for genealogical works about the author's ancestors or descendants.
—**Biography—Health**
—**Biography—Imprisonment** *(Indirect)*
—**Biography—Last years and death**
—**Biography—London life**
  May be unique to Shakespeare. Use for works about his middle years spent largely in London. Do not confuse with —**Homes and haunts— England—London.**
—**Biography—Marriage**
  See also —**Relations with men; —Relations with women**
  Biography—Old age, see —**Biography—Last years and death**
  Biography—Personality, see —**Biography—Psychology**
—**Biography—Psychology**
  Use for interpretation of the author's personality or character or for psychological insight into the author's life.
—**Biography—Sources**
  Do not assign this subdivision as a form subdivision to single original works.
  See also —**Correspondence; —Diaries**
—**Biography—Youth**
  Use for works about the author's life to approximately 25 years of age. Includes period of education generally.
  Birthday books, see —**Calendars, etc.** Assign **Birthday books** as a second heading.
  Bones, see —**Museums, relics, etc.; —Tomb**

— **Books and reading**
> Use for works dealing with written material known to have been seen by the author; his reading habits and interests; books borrowed from libraries or friends; etc.
> See also — **Knowledge — [appropriate subdivision]**; — **Library**

— **Calendars, etc.**
> See also — **Quotations**
> Canon, see — **Authorship**; — **Chronology**; — **Criticism, Textual**
> Careers, see — **Biography — Careers**

— **Caricatures and cartoons**
> Use for collections or discussions of caricatures or pictorial humor about the author.

— **Censorship**
> Centennial celebrations, etc., see — **Anniversaries, etc.**
> Character, see — **Biography — Psychology**; — **Ethics**

— **Characters**
> Use for works about the author's characters in general. For specific groups or categories of characters, see the list below and assign an additional heading, e.g.
>> 1. **Shakespeare, William, 1564-1616 — Characters — Children.**
>> 2. **Children in literature.**

— **Characters — Abandoned children**
— **Characters — Actors**
— **Characters — Artists**
— **Characters — Children**
— **Characters — Clergy**
— **Characters — Comic characters**
— **Characters — Criminals**
— **Characters — Daughters**
— **Characters — Dramatists**
— **Characters — Fairies**
— **Characters — Fathers**
— **Characters — Fools**
— **Characters — Gauchos**
— **Characters — Ghosts**
— **Characters — Giants**
— **Characters — Gypsies**
— **Characters — Heroes**
— **Characters — Heroines**
— **Characters — Indians**
— **Characters — Irish**
— **Characters — Jews**
— **Characters — Kings and rulers**
— **Characters — Lawyers**
— **Characters — Men**
— **Characters — Mentally ill**
— **Characters — Messengers**
— **Characters — Minnesingers**
— **Characters — Monsters**
— **Characters — Physicians**
— **Characters — Poets**

— Characters — Prisoners of war
— Characters — Revolutionists
— Characters — Rogues and vagabonds
— Characters — Saints
— Characters — Satirists
— Characters — Scientists
— Characters — Servants
— Characters — Single people
— Characters — Slaves
— Characters — Soldiers
— Characters — Teachers
— Characters — Valets
— Characters — Villains
— Characters — Welsh
— Characters — Women
— Characters — Youth
— Characters — [name of individual character], e.g. — Hamlet, [Margaret of Anjou, Sherlock Holmes, etc.]

> Use specific named characters in uninverted form, e.g. — Characters — Julius Caesar [*not* — Characters — Caesar, Julius] without establishing the usage editorially. If the character is a historical person, assign a second heading of the type [name], in fiction, drama, poetry, etc. If the character is fictitious, assign a second heading of the type [name] (Fictitious character). Headings of the latter type must be established editorially.

— Chronology

> Use for lists with dates of the author's life and/or works, as well as for discussions thereof.

— Cipher
— Collected works

> Use for collected works about the author. Do not use for the published collected works of the author. Use as appropriate under topical subdivisions, e.g. — Criticism and interpretation — Collected works.

Collections, see — Addresses, essays, lectures; — Collected works; — Periodicals

— Comedies

> Use for critical works only. Do not use under dramatists who principally write comedies, e.g. Molière.

Comic books, strips, etc., see [author's name], in fiction, drama, poetry, etc.

Commentaries, see — Criticism and interpretation

Companions, see — Friends and associates

— Concordances

> Use as a form subdivision for indexes to the principal words found in the author's works.
> See also [author. title] — Concordances

— Congresses

> Use as appropriate under the author's name or under any topical subdivision, e.g. — Criticism and interpretation — Congresses.

— **Contemporaries**

Use for works about persons flourishing during the author's life, but not necessarily in close contact with the author.

See also — **Friends and associates**

— **Contemporary England, [Contemporary America, Contemporary France, etc.]**

In each case, assign a second heading for history, social conditions, etc., of the country, as appropriate.

See also — **Homes and haunts**

— **Correspondence**

Use as a form or topical subdivision for letters from and/or to the author. In the case of an individual correspondent, assign a second heading for the correspondent.

— **Correspondence — Facsimiles**

— **Correspondence — Indexes**

Costume, see — **Dramatic production; — Stage history**

For works only on the costuming of an author's plays, assign **Costume** as a second heading.

— **Criticism, Textual**

Use for works which aim to establish authoritative texts, e.g. comparison of manuscripts and editions. Do not use for the critical explication of text. Do not further subdivide by — **History**.

See also **[author. title] — Criticism, Textual.**

— **Criticism and interpretation**

— **Criticism and interpretation — Congresses**

— **Criticism and interpretation — History**

— **Criticism and interpretation — History — 17th century**

— **Criticism and interpretation — History — 18th century**

— **Criticism and interpretation — History — 19th century**

— **Criticism and interpretation — History — 20th century**

Dance, see — **Knowledge — Performing arts**

Death and burial, see — **Biography — Last years and death**

— **Death mask**

Dialects, see — **Language — Dialects**

— **Diaries**

Use for collections or discussions of the author's diaries. Also use for individual diaries.

— **Dictionaries, indexes, etc.**

Do not use under author-title entries.

See also — **Concordances; — Language — Glossaries, etc.**

— **Discography**

Use for lists or catalogs of sound recordings by or about the author.

Drama, see **[author's name], in fiction, drama, poetry, etc.**

— **Dramatic production**

Includes aspects of stage presentation, e.g. acting, costume, stage setting and scenery, etc. For historical aspects of dramatic production, see — **Stage history.**

— **Dramatic works**

Use for criticism only. Do not use under authors who write principally drama, e.g. Shakespeare.

Dramaturgy, see — **Dramatic production; — Dramatic works; — Technique**

Dwellings, see —**Homes and haunts**
Editions, see —**Bibliography**
—**Editors**
Education, see —**Knowledge and learning**; —**Knowledge—Education**
Ennoblement, see —**Biography—Ennoblement**
—**Estate**
> Use for discussions of the aggregate of property or liabilities of all kinds
> that the author leaves for disposal at his death.
> See also —**Will**
—**Ethics**
—**Exhibitions**
> Use for catalogs and for checklist bibliographies which class in P.
> See also [author. title]—**Exhibitions**
Exile, see —**Biography—Exile**
Family, see —**Biography—Family**
Fiction, see [author's name], **in fiction, drama, poetry, etc.**
—**Fictional works**
> Use for criticism only. Do not use under authors who write principally
> fiction, e.g. Simenon.
> See also —**Prose**
—**Film adaptations**
> Use for discussions of motion picture productions.
Folklore, mythology, see —**Knowledge—Folklore, mythology**
Forerunners, see —**Sources**; —**Criticism and interpretation**
—**Forgeries**
—**Forgeries—Collier, [Ireland, etc.]**
> Use individual name for well-known forger as determined by scholars. Do
> not establish editorially. Use only the last name of the forger, and assign
> an additional heading for this person, e.g.
>> 1. Shakespeare, William, 1564-1616—Forgeries—Collier.
>> 2. Collier, John Payne, 1789-1883.
—**Friends and associates**
> Use for works about the author's circle of close and immediate contacts
> such as patrons, co-workers, companions, etc.
> See also —**Contemporaries**
Genealogy, see —**Biography—Family**
Glossaries, see —**Language—Glossaries, etc.**
Grammar, see —**Language—Grammar**
Grave, see —**Tomb**
—**Handbooks, manuals, etc.**
Handwriting, see —**Autographs**
Haunts, see —**Homes and haunts**
Health, see —**Biography—Health**
—**Histories**
> Has been used for discussions of English Chronicle plays; largely
> applicable only to Shakespeare, whose principal dramatic genres are
> comedy, tragedy, and history.
—**Homes and haunts** *(Indirect)*
> Use for discussions of places of residence or places to which the author
> made repeated visits. For voyages and travels, see —**Journeys**.

— **Humor, satire, etc.**
> Do not use as a form subdivision. Use only for critical works discussing the author's humor, irony, satire, etc.

— **Iconography**
> Use for works consisting of pictures or other visual images pertaining to the author, e.g. photographs, medals, relics, etc., usually treated collectively.
>
> See also — **Art;** — **Caricatures and cartoons;** — **Monuments;** — **Museums, relics, etc.;** — **Portraits**

— **Illustrations**
> Use for collections or discussions of pictorial representations of the author's works. Do not further subdivide by — **History and criticism.**
>
> See also **[author.   title] — Illustrations**

Illustrations, Comic, see — **Illustrations**

Imitations, see — **Parodies, imitations, etc.**

Indexes, see — **Concordances;** — **Dictionaries, indexes, etc.**

— **Influence**
> Use for the author's impact on national literatures or literary movements. Assign a second heading to identify the group or national literature influenced.

— **Influence — Pushkin, [Scott, Strindberg, etc.]**
> Use for the author's impact on a specific person. Use only the last name of the person influenced, and assign an additional subject entry for this person.

— **Interviews**
> Use for works consisting of transcripts of what was said during the course of interviews or conversations with the author on one or more occasions.

Itineraries, see — **Journeys**

Journals, see — **Diaries**

— **Journeys** *(Indirect)*
> Use for works about voyages and travels actually undertaken by the author. When — **Journeys** is further subdivided by place, assign an additional heading of the type: **[place] — Description** or **[place] — Description and travel**, as appropriate. For places of residence or places to which the author made repeated visits, see — **Homes and haunts.**
>
> See also — **Biography — Exile**

— **Juvenile films**
> Use also under other literary subdivisions as appropriate.

— **Juvenile literature**
> Use also under other literary subdivisions as appropriate.

— **Juvenile sound recordings**
> Use also under other literary subdivisions as appropriate.

— **Knowledge — [appropriate subdivision from list below]**
> Use this heading, which occurs only with a subdivision, for material dealing with the author's knowledge or treatment of themes or specific subjects. Use — **Knowledge and learning** for works on the author's education, learning, and scholarship in general.
>
> Use only with the following subdivisions. This constitutes a closed list.
>
> *Note:* See references are included only as suggestions for application. They are not intended to be definitive, and may not apply in all

situations. For every heading of the type [author] — Knowledge — [topic] assigned, assign a second heading [topic] in literature. The latter should be as specific as needed for the work in hand, e.g.

1. [author] — Knowledge — Botany.
2. Flowers in literature.

Knowledge — Aesthetics, see — **Aesthetics**

— **Knowledge — America, [Italy, Spain, etc.]**

Limited to countries and regions larger than countries. Designate a smaller geographic entity by means of a second heading, e.g. **London (England) in literature.**

Knowledge — Archery, see — **Knowledge — Sports and recreation**

— **Knowledge — Architecture**

— **Knowledge — Art**

Knowledge — Astrology, see — **Knowledge — Occult sciences**

— **Knowledge — Astronomy**

Knowledge — Bible, see — **Religion**

Knowledge — Birds, see — **Knowledge — Zoology**

— **Knowledge — Book arts and sciences**

— **Knowledge — Botany**

Knowledge — Catholic Church, see — **Religion**

— **Knowledge — Chemistry**

— **Knowledge — Commerce**

— **Knowledge — Communications**

Knowledge — Cosmography, see — **Philosophy;** — **Knowledge — Astronomy**

Knowledge — Costume, see — **Dramatic production**

Knowledge — Criticism, see — **Knowledge — Literature**

Knowledge — Discoveries (in geography), see — **Knowledge — Geography**

Knowledge — Dreams, see — **Knowledge — Psychology**

Knowledge — Drinking, see — **Knowledge — Sports and recreation;** — **Knowledge — Manners and customs**

Knowledge — Dueling, see — **Knowledge — Sports and recreation**

— **Knowledge — Earth sciences**

— **Knowledge — Economics**

— **Knowledge — Education**

Knowledge — Ethics, see — **Ethics**

Knowledge — Fishing, see — **Knowledge — Sports and recreation**

Knowledge — Flowers, see — **Knowledge — Botany**

— **Knowledge — Folklore, mythology**

Knowledge — Food, see — **Knowledge — Manners and customs**

Knowledge — Freemasonry, see — **Knowledge — Manners and customs**

Knowledge — Games, see — **Knowledge — Sports and recreation**

— **Knowledge — Geography**

Knowledge — Geology, see — **Knowledge — Earth sciences**

Knowledge — Heraldry, see — **Knowledge — Manners and customs**

— **Knowledge — History**

Knowledge — Honor, see — **Ethics**

Knowledge — Insanity, see — **Knowledge — Medicine;** — **Knowledge — Psychology**

Knowledge — Journalism, see — **Knowledge — Communications**

— **Knowledge — Language and languages**

— **Knowledge — Law**

—Knowledge—Literature
—Knowledge—Manners and customs
  Knowledge—Marriage, see —Knowledge—Manners and customs
—Knowledge—Mathematics
—Knowledge—Medicine
—Knowledge—Military sciences
—Knowledge—Music
  Knowledge—Mythology, see —Knowledge—Folklore, mythology
—Knowledge—Natural history
  Knowledge—Naval art and science, see —Knowledge—Military sciences
—Knowledge—Occult sciences
—Knowledge—Performing arts
  Knowledge—Philosophy, see —Philosophy
—Knowledge—Physics
  Knowledge—Plant lore, see —Knowledge—Botany; —Knowledge—Folklore, mythology
  Knowledge—Political sciences, see —Political and social views
  Knowledge—Printing, see —Knowledge—Book arts and sciences; —Knowledge—Technology
—Knowledge—Psychology
  For psychological studies of the author as a person, see —Biography—Psychology
  Knowledge—Religion, see —Religion
  Knowledge—Repentance, see —Religion
—Knowledge—Science
  Knowledge—Social sciences, see —Political and social views
—Knowledge—Sports and recreation
—Knowledge—Technology
  Knowledge—Theater, see —Knowledge—Performing arts
  Knowledge—Translating, see —Knowledge—Literature
—Knowledge—Zoology
—Knowledge and learning
  Use for works on the author's education, learning, and scholarship in general.
  See also —Knowledge—[appropriate subdivision], and topics used directly under the name of the author.
—Language
  Use for critical works dealing with the author's language in general on the linguistic rather than the artistic level. For works on language on the artistic level, see —Style. For works on specific linguistic topics other than those listed below, assign a second heading, e.g.
    1. Shakespeare, William, 1564-1616—Language.
    2. English language—Early modern, 1500-1700—Semantics.
—Language—Dialects
—Language—Glossaries, etc.
—Language—Grammar
—Language—Pronunciation
—Language—Punctuation
  Language—Style, see —Style
  Language—Versification, see —Versification
—Language—Word frequency

Last years, see —Biography—Last years and death

Legends, see —Anecdotes; —Allusions

—Library
Use for works about the author's personal library. Use also for discussions of single books in the libraries of authors whose library history is scarce.
See also —Books and reading

—Library—Catalogs

—Library—Marginal notes

—Library resources *(Indirect)*
Use for works describing the resources or special collections available in libraries for research or study about the author.

—Manuscripts
See also —Archives; —Autographs; —Correspondence; —Diaries; —Notebooks, sketchbooks, etc.

—Manuscripts—Catalogs

—Manuscripts—Facsimiles
See also —Autographs—Facsimiles

Marginalia, see —Scholia

Marriage, see —Biography—Marriage

Men, see —Relations with men

—Miscellanea
Use for collections of curiosa relating to the author as well as for texts written in question and answer format.

—Monuments *(Indirect)*
Use for works about monuments erected in honor of the author.
See also —Museums, relics, etc.; —Tomb

Moral ideas, see —Ethics

—Moving-picture plays
Use for commentaries on film scripts written by the author.

Moving-pictures, see —Film adaptations

—Museums, relics, etc. *(Indirect)*
Use for works about museums devoted to the author. Also includes works on disinterred bones.
See also —Archives; —Death mask; —Tomb

Music, see —Knowledge—Music

—Musical settings
Use as a form subdivision for musical scores or sound recordings in which the writings or words of the author have been set to music.

Mysticism, see —Religion

—Name
Use for discussions of the history, orthography, etymology, etc. of the author's name.
See also —Anonyms and pseudonyms

Natural history, see —Knowledge—Natural history

—Notebooks, sketchbooks, etc.
Use for collections or discussions of the author's notebooks, sketchbooks, etc. Also use for individual works.

Outlines, syllabi, etc., see —Study and teaching—Outlines, syllabi, etc.

Pageants, see —Anniversaries, etc.; —Dramatic production

Paraphrases, tales, etc., see —Adaptations

—Parodies, imitations, etc.
>Use as both a form and critical subdivision for imitations, either comic or distorted, of the author's works. Do not use under author-title entries.

Patriotism, see —Political and social views; —Contemporary England, [Contemporary America, Contemporary France, etc.]; and/or Patriotism in literature

—Periodicals
>See also —Yearbooks

Personality, see —Biography—Psychology

—Philosophy
>See also —Aesthetics; —Ethics; —Political and social views; —Religion

Pictorial works, see —Iconography; —Art; —Portraits

—Plots
>Use for summaries and discussions of plot development for drama and fiction. For poetry, see —Summaries, arguments, etc.

—Poetic works
>Use for critical works only. Do not use under authors who write principally poetry.

Poetry, see [author's name], in fiction, drama, poetry, etc.

—Political and social views

—Portraits
>Use for collections or discussions of portraits of authors living after 1400 A.D., including portrait sculpture. For authors living before 1400, see —Art.
>See also —Caricatures and cartoons; —Death mask

Prohibited books, see —Censorship

Pronunciation, see —Language—Pronunciation

—Prophecies
>Use for works about prophecies made by the author.

—Prose
>Use only for criticism of prose works or passages. Do not use under authors who write principally prose, e.g. Thomas Mann.

Pseudonyms, see —Anonyms and pseudonyms

Psychological studies, see —Biography—Psychology; —Criticism and interpretation.

—Publishers

—Quotations
>Use for collections or discussions of the author's quotations.
>See also —Calendars, etc.

—Radio and television plays
>Use for commentaries on scripts written by the author.

Reading habits, see —Books and reading

Relations with editors, see —Editors

Relations with family, see —Biography—Family

Relations with friends and associates, see —Friends and associates

—Relations with men
>Use for works on intimate associations.

—Relations with men—John Doe, [Harry Smith, etc.]
>Use names in uninverted form without establishing them editorially. Assign a second subject entry for the person.

Relations with publishers, see —Publishers

— **Relations with women**
  Use for works on intimate associations.
— **Relations with women — Charlotte von Stein, [Charlotte Buff, etc.]**
  Use names in uninverted form without establishing them editorially.
  Assign a second subject entry for the person.
  Relics, see — **Museums, relics, etc.**
— **Religion**
  Satire, see — **Humor, satire, etc.**
— **Scholia**
  Use for marginal annotations, explanatory comments or remarks,
  especially on the text of a classical work by an early grammarian.
  Sepulchral monument, see — **Tomb**
— **Settings**
  Sketchbooks, see — **Notebooks, sketchbooks, etc.**
  Social views, see — **Political and social views**
— **Societies, etc.**
  Use for works discussing societies or organizations devoted to or special-
  izing in the author.
— **Songs and music**
  Use as a form subdivision for collections or single works of vocal or
  instrumental music about the person. For the author's knowledge of
  music, see — **Knowledge — Music**
— **Songs and music — Discography**
— **Songs and music — History and criticism**
— **Sources**
  Use for discussions of the author's sources of ideas or inspiration for his
  works. Do not assign to single original works. For discussions of adapta-
  tions by others of the author's works, see — **Adaptations.**
  See also **[author. title] — Sources**
— **Sources — Bibliography**
— **Spiritualistic interpretations**
  Use for works classed in BF1311.A-Z (Special topics, including names of
  individual literary authors).
— **Spurious and doubtful works**
— **Stage history** *(Indirect)*
— **Stage history — To 1625**
— **Stage history — 1625-1800**
— **Stage history — 1800-1950**
— **Stage history — 1950-**
  Stage presentation, see — **Dramatic production; — Stage history**
  Stage setting and scenery, see — **Dramatic production; — Stage history**
  For works only on stage setting and scenery of an author's plays, assign as
  a second heading **Theaters — Stage-setting and scenery; Moving-pictures —
  Setting and scenery;** or **Television — Stage-setting and scenery.**
— **Study and teaching** *(Indirect)*
  Use for methods of studying or teaching about the author.
— **Study and teaching — Outlines, syllabi, etc.**

—**Style**
> Use for discussions of rhetoric; figures of speech, e.g. imagery, metaphor, simile, etc.; and artistic use of language in general. —**Technique** is a larger concept. For works on specific linguistic topics, e.g. nouns, verbs, adjectives, syntax, pronunciation, etc., see —**Language**.
> See also —**Symbolism**

—**Summaries, arguments, etc.**
> Use for summaries and discussions of action in poetic works. For drama and fiction, see —**Plots**.

Supernatural element, see —**Knowledge—Occult sciences**

—**Symbolism**

—**Technique**
> Use for discussions of structural and formal elements in drama, fiction, and narrative poetry; the art of writing, e.g. general construction, asides, soliloquies, unities, dramatic irony, scene structure, stream-of-consciousness, etc.
> See also —**Style**; —**Versification**

Textual criticism, see —**Criticism, Textual**

Themes, motives, see —**Criticism and interpretation**

Themes, motives—[specific topic], see —**Knowledge—[specific topic]**

Theology, see —**Religion**

—**Tomb**
> Use for works about the author's grave, interred bones, etc. For works on disinterred bones, see —**Museums, relics, etc.**

—**Tragedies**
> Use for critical works only. Do not use under dramatists who write principally tragedies, e.g. Racine.

—**Tragicomedies**
> Use for critical works only. Do not use under dramatists who write principally tragicomedies.

—**Translations**
> Use for history and criticism or collections of translations. Do not use as a form heading for single translations. Do not further subdivide by —**History**.

—**Translations, French, [German, etc.]**

Translators, see —**Translations**

Travesties, see —**Parodies, imitations, etc.**

—**Versification**
> Use for discussions of the author's technique of writing verse; the structural composition of poetry, including rhythm, rhyme, alliteration, etc.
> See also —**Style**

Voyages and travels, see —**Journeys**

—**Will**
> Use for discussions of the author's legal declaration regarding disposition of his property or estate at his death.
> See also —**Estate**

Women, see —**Relations with women**

—**Yearbooks**

Youth, see —**Biography—Youth**

MUSIC

Subdivisions Controlled by the Pattern Heading for Music Compositions*

PATTERN: **Operas**

I. *PERIOD SUBDIVISIONS***

—To 500
—500-1400
—15th century
—16th century
—17th century
—18th century
—19th century
—20th century

II. *MUSICAL FORMAT SUBDIVISIONS****

—Parts
—Parts (solo)
—Piano scores
—Piano scores (4 hands)
—Scores
—Scores and parts
—Scores and parts (solo)
—Vocal scores
—Vocal scores with accordion
—Vocal scores with continuo
—Vocal scores with guitar
—Vocal scores with harpsichord
—Vocal scores with organ
—Vocal scores with piano
—Vocal scores with piano (4 hands)
—Vocal scores with piano and organ
—Vocal scores with pianos (2)

III. *TOPICAL AND FORM SUBDIVISIONS:*

—Analysis, appreciation
—Bibliography
—Bibliography—Catalogs
—Bibliography—Graded lists
—Cadenzas
—Discography
—Discography—Methodology
—Excerpts****
—Excerpts, Arranged****
—First performances *(Indirect)*
—History and criticism**
—Instructive editions
—Instrumental settings
—Interpretation (Phrasing, dynamics, etc.)
—Librettos
—Programs

---

*Library of Congress, Subject Cataloging Division, *Subject Cataloging Manual: Subject Headings*, prelim. ed. (Washington, D.C.: Library of Congress, 1984), H1160.

**Not used for collections of compositions by only one composer or for separate music compositions or under headings for folk, popular, and non-Western music.

***Not used under headings for music of special seasons, occasions, styles, etc., where the medium is not directly implied, e.g., **Christmas music; Country music; Te Deum laudamas (Music);** etc., or under headings for categories of works which are generally published in only one format, e.g., hymns, compositions for one instrument, and songs and choruses without accompaniment or with the accompaniment of only one instrument or two keyboard instruments.

****Used only under form headings. May be further subdivided by musical format subdivisions.

—Scenarios
—Simplified editions
—Stage guides
—Stories, plots, etc.
—Teaching pieces
—Thematic catalogs
—Themes, motives, Literary

Subdivisions Controlled by the Pattern Heading for Musical Instruments*

PATTERN: Piano

—Catalogs, Manufacturers'
—Catalogs and collections *(Indirect)*
—Chord diagrams
—Construction
—Dictionaries
—History
—Instruction and study *(Indirect)*
—Instruction and study—Fingering
—Instruction and study—Juvenile
—Instruction and study—Pedaling
—Keys
—Maintenance and repair
—Methods
—Methods—Group instruction
—Methods—Juvenile
—Methods—Self-instruction
—Methods (Jazz, [Rock, Bluegrass, etc.])**
—Orchestra studies
—Performance
—Practicing
—Strings
—Studies and exercises
—Studies and exercises—Fingering
—Studies and exercises—Juvenile
—Studies and exercises—Pedaling
—Studies and exercises—(Jazz, [Rock, Bluegrass, etc.])**
Tuning

---

*Library of Congress, Subject Cataloging Division, *Subject Cataloging Manual: Subject Headings*, prelim. ed. (Washington, D.C.: Library of Congress, 1984), H1161 (rev. 11/12/85).

When assigning the subdivision —Methods** or —**Studies and exercises** qualified by a particular style of popular music, assign as a second heading the style of music subdivided by —**Instruction and study**, e.g.

1. Banjo—Methods (Bluegrass)
2. Bluegrass music—Instruction and study.

1. Guitar—Studies and exercises (Rock)
2. Rock music—Instruction and study.

RELIGION

Subdivisions Controlled by the Pattern Heading for Religions*

PATTERN: Buddhism

—Apologetic works
—Apologetic works—History and criticism
—Catechisms
—Charities
—Controversial literature
—Creeds
—Customs and practices
—Discipline
—Doctrines
—Doctrines—Introductions
—Education *(Indirect)*
—Essence, genius, nature
—Government
—History
—History—To ca. 100 A.D.
—History—19th century
—History—20th century
—History—Philosophy
—Influence
—Liturgical objects

—Liturgy
—Liturgy—Texts
—Missions *(Indirect)*
—Origin
—Prayer-books and devotions
—Prayer-books and devotions—Tibetan, [English, etc.]
—Prayer-books and devotions—History and criticism
—Psychology
—Relations
—Relations—Christianity, [Islam, etc.]
—Sacred books
—Sacred books—Hermeneutics
—Sacred books—Introductions
—Sacred books—Language, style
—Sacred books—Preservation
—Sacred books—Quotations
—Social aspects *(Indirect)*
—Study and teaching *(Indirect)*

Subdivisions Controlled by the Pattern Heading for Sacred Works (Including Parts)**

PATTERN: Bible

—Abridgments
—Accents and accentuation[1]
—Addresses, essays, lectures
—Anecdotes, facetiae, satire, etc.
—Antiquities
—Appreciation
—Authorship
—Authorship—Date of authorship
—Bibliography
—Biography

—Biography—Sermons
—Canon
—Canon, Catholic vs. Protestant
—Caricatures and cartoons
—Chronology
—Chronology—Charts, diagrams, etc.
—Collected works
—Comic books, strips, etc.
—Commentaries
—Commentaries—Facsimiles

---

*Library of Congress, Subject Cataloging Division, *Subject Cataloging Manual: Subject Headings*, prelim. ed. (Washington, D.C.: Library of Congress, 1984), H1185.
**Library of Congress, Subject Cataloging Division, *Subject Cataloging Manual: Subject Headings*, prelim. ed. (Washington, D.C.: Library of Congress, 1984), H1188.
Numbered footnotes to this section of appendix D appear on page 415.

—Comparative studies
—Concordances
—Concordances, English
—Concordances, English—
  American Revised
—Concordances, English—Douai
—Concordances, English—
  Jerusalem Bible
—Concordances, English—Living
  Bible
—Concordances, English—Moffatt
—Concordances, English—New
  American Bible
—Concordances, English—New
  American Standard
—Concordances, English—New
  International
—Concordances, English—New
  World
—Concordances, English—Revised
  Standard
—Concordances, French, [German,
  etc.]
—Copies, Curious
—Criticism, Form
—Criticism, interpretation, etc.
  (Indirect)
—Criticism, interpretation, etc.—
  Bibliography
—Criticism, interpretation, etc.—
  Censorship
—Criticism, interpretation, etc.—
  History
—Criticism, interpretation, etc.—
  History—Early church,
  ca. 30-600
—Criticism, interpretation, etc.—
  History—Middle Ages,
  600-1500
—Criticism, interpretation, etc.—
  History—Modern period,
  1500-
—Criticism, interpretation, etc.—
  History—16th century
—Criticism, interpretation, etc.—
  History—17th century
—Criticism, interpretation, etc.—
  History—18th century
—Criticism, interpretation, etc.—
  History—19th century
—Criticism, interpretation, etc.—
  History—20th century
—Criticism, interpretation, etc.,
  Jewish[1]

—Criticism, Redaction
—Criticism, Textual
—Devotional literature
—Dictionaries
—Dictionaries, Juvenile
—Editions, Curious
—Evidences, authority, etc.—History
  of doctrines
—Examinations, questions, etc.
—Extra-canonical parallels
—Folklore
—Geography
—Geography—Maps
—Geography—Maps—To 1800
—Handbooks, manuals, etc.
—Harmonies
—Harmonies—History and criticism
—Harmonies, English, [French,
  German, etc.]
—Harmonies, English, [French,
  German, etc.]—History and
  criticism
—Hermeneutics
—Historiography
—History
—History Bibles
—History of Biblical events
—History of Biblical events—Fiction
—History of Biblical events—Poetry
—History of contemporary events
—History of contemporary events—
  Fiction
—Homiletical use
—Illustrations
—Indexes
—Influence
—Influence—Civilization, Medieval
—Influence—Civilization, Occidental
—Inspiration
—Inspiration—History of doctrines
—Interlinear translations
—Interlinear translations, English,
  [French, etc.]
—Introductions
—Islamic interpretations
—Juvenile literature
—Juvenile poetry
—Language, style
—Legends
—Liturgical lessons, Dutch, [English,
  etc.]
—Liturgical use
—Manuscripts

— Manuscripts — Catalogs
— Manuscripts — Facsimiles
— Manuscripts — Paragraphs
— Manuscripts, English, [Latin,
　Aramaic, etc.]
— Marginal readings
— Meditations
— Memorizing
— Miscellanea
— Numerical division
— Outlines, syllabi, etc.
— Parables
— Paragraphs
— Paraphrases
— Paraphrases — History and
　criticism
— Paraphrases, English, [French,
　German, etc.]
— Paraphrases, English, [French,
　German, etc.] — History and
　criticism
— Periodicals
— Philosophy
— Picture Bibles
— Prayers
— Prayers — History and criticism
— Prefaces
— Prophecies
— Prophecies — Chronology
— Prophecies — [subject of
　prophecy]
— Psychology
— Publication and distribution
　(Indirect)

— Publication and distribution —
　Societies, etc.
— Quotations, Early
— Quotations in rabbinical
　literature[1]
— Quotations in the New
　Testament[1]
— **Reading** *(Indirect)*
— **Reference editions**
— **Relation to Matthew, [Jeremiah,
　etc.][2]
— **Relation to the Old Testa-
　ment, [Mark, Psalms, etc.][3]
— Sermons
— Sermons — Outlines, syllabi, etc.
— Societies, etc.
— **Study** *(Indirect)*
— **Study** — Catholic Church
— Terminology
— Text-books
— Theology
— Thumb Bibles
— Translating
— Use
— Use in hymns
— Versions
— Versions, African, [Indic,
　Slavic, etc.][4]
— Versions, Baptist
— Versions, Catholic
— Versions, Catholic vs. Protestant
— Versions, Hussite
— Versions, Jehovah's Witnesses

---

[1]Use only under **Bible. O.T.** or individual books of the Old Testament.

[2]Use only under individual books of the Old Testament. Make a duplicate entry under the reverse, e.g. **1. Bible. O.T. Psalms — Relation to Jeremiah. 2. Bible. O.T. Jeremiah — Relation to Psalms.**

[3]Use only under individual books of the New Testament. Make a duplicate entry under the reverse, e.g. **1. Bible. N.T. Matthew — Relation to Psalms. 2. Bible. O.T. Psalms — Relation to Matthew.**

[4]Assign the adjectival qualifier for groups of languages only. For works on translations of the Bible into individual languages, assign: **Bible. [language] — Versions.**

APPENDIX E:
SUBDIVISIONS TO BE
FURTHER SUBDIVIDED BY PLACE*

—Abnormalities
—Abscess
—Adjuvant treatment
—Ambrosian rite
—Antiochene rite
—Appreciation
—Archival resources
—Armed Forces
—Armenian rite
—Balloons
—Biography—Imprisonment
—Biological control
—Blacks
—Boundaries
—Byzantine rite
—Byzantine rite, Greek
—Byzantine rite, Melchite
—Byzantine rite, Romanian
—Byzantine rite, Ruthenian
—Byzantine rite, Ukrainian
—Calcification
—Campaigns
—Cancer
—Care and hygiene
—Care and treatment
—Catalogs and collections
—Censorship
—Certification
—Chaldean rite
—Children

—Civil rights
—Civilian relief
—Collaborationists
—Collectibles
—Collectors and collecting
—Colonial forces
—Colonization
—Commando operations
—Commerce
—Competitions
—Complications and sequelae
—Concentration camps
—Confiscations and contributions
—Conscientious objectors
—Conscript labor
—Conservation
—Conservation and restoration
    [only when used under fine arts
    headings other than
    Architecture]
—Contracts and specifications
—Control
—Cost-of-living adjustments
—Counseling of
—Criticism, interpretation, etc.
—Cult
—Cysts
—Dental care
—Desertions
—Destruction and pillage

*Library of Congress, Subject Cataloging Division, *Subject Cataloging Manual: Subject Headings*, prelim. ed. (Washington, D.C.: Library of Congress, 1984), H860.

— Dialects
— Diplomatic and consular service
— Disease and pest resistance
— Diseases
— Diseases and hygiene
— Diseases and pests
— Dislocation
— Disorders
— Documentation
— Draft resisters
— Economic aspects
— Education
   [only when used under classes
   of persons, ethnic groups (ex-
   cept Indians), or religious
   bodies]
— Electronic intelligence
— Employment
— Environmental aspects
— Estimates
— Evacuation of civilians
— Exile
— Finance
   [only when used under wars]
— First performances
— Food supply
— Foreign economic relations
— Foreign relations
— Foreign service
— Forgeries
— Fractures
— Gallican rite
— Government ownership
— Government policy
— Gypsies
— Health and hygiene
— Health aspects
— Home care
— Homes
— Homes and haunts
— Horses
— Hospital care
— Hospitals
— Hospitals and asylums
— Housing
— Hygienic aspects
— In-service training
— Infarction
— Infections
— Information services
— Institutional care
— Instruction and study
— Jews

— Jews — Rescue
— Journalism, Military
— Journeys
— Labeling
— Law and legislation
— Legal status, laws, etc.
— Library resources
— Licenses
— Logistics
— Losses
— Malabar rite
— Malpractice
— Manpower
— Maronite rite
— Medical care
— Medical examinations
— Mental health
— Mental health services
— Military intelligence
— Military relations
— Missing in action
— Missions
— Monuments, etc.
— Mozarabic rite
— Museums, relics, etc.
— Mutilation, defacement, etc.
— Nursing
— Officials and employees
   [only when used under coun-
   tries, etc.]
— Oriental rites
— Palaces
— Patients
— Pensions
— Performances
— Political aspects
— Practice
— Prices
— Private collections
— Privileges and immunities
— Production standards
— Professional ethics
— Protection
— Protest movements
— Provincialisms
— Psychiatric care
— Public buildings
— Publication and distribution
— Publishing
— Radiography
— Reading
— Regimental histories
— Registers of dead

—Registration and transfer
—Rehabilitation
—Relations
   [only when used under places]
—Relations (diplomatic)
—Reporting
—Reproduction
   [only when used under fine arts
   headings]
—Research
—Research grants
—Road guides
—Safety regulations
—Salaries, pensions, etc.
—Scholarships, fellowships, etc.
—Search and rescue operations
—Secret service
—Service stations
—Services for
—Side effects
—Social aspects
—Specifications
—Spoken English
—Stage history
—Standards
—Storage—Diseases and injuries
—Study
—Study and teaching
—Study and teaching (Clinical
   education)
—Study and teaching (Continuing
   education)
—Study and teaching (Elementary)
—Study and teaching (Graduate)
—Study and teaching (Higher)

—Study and teaching (Internship)
—Study and teaching (Preceptor-
   ship)
—Study and teaching (Preschool)
—Study and teaching (Primary)
—Study and teaching (Residency)
—Study and teaching (Secondary)
—Surgery
—Syphilis
—Taxation
—Teacher training
—Territorial questions
—Tournaments
—Toxicology
—Training of
—Transplantation
—Transportation—Diseases and
   injuries
—Treatment
—Tuberculosis
—Tumors
—Ulcers
—Underground literature
—Underground movements
—Underground movements, Jewish
—Underground printing plants
—Valuation
—Veterinary service
—Vocational education
—Vocational guidance
—War work
—Weed control
—Women
—Wounds and injuries

The following subdivisions may be further subdivided by place, with interposition of place between the main heading and the topical subdivision:

— Archival resources
— Catalogs and collections
— Collectors and collecting
— Conservation and restoration
— Documentation
— Forgeries
— Information services
— Library resources

— Mutilation, defacement, etc.
— Private collections
— Research
— Study and teaching
    [and all parenthetically quali-
    fied forms of this subdivision]
— Teacher training
— Vocational guidance

APPENDIX F:
FREE-FLOATING SUBDIVISIONS
USED UNDER NAMES OF PERSONS*

— **Abdication, [date]**
— **Abstracts**
— **Adaptations**
Use under individuals such as artists or composers for discussions of adaptations by others of their creative works. For discussions of an individual's adaptations of themes from others, see — **Sources**.
— **Addresses, essays, lectures**
— **Adversaries**
Use for discussions of contemporaries who opposed the person's point of view or work.
— **Aesthetics**
Use for discussions of the individual's philosophy of art or beauty, whether explicitly stated or inferred from his creative works.
— **Alcohol use**
Use for works about the person's use or abuse of alcohol.
See also — **Drug use**
Allegory, see — **Symbolism**
Ancestry, see — **Family**
— **Anecdotes**
Use for collections of brief narratives of true incidents from the individual's life.
— **Anniversaries, etc.**
— **Anniversaries, etc., [date]**
Use for works dealing with the anniversary celebration itself. Do not use for works merely published on the occasion of an anniversary.

---

*Information provided by the Subject Cataloging Division, Library of Congress. For free-floating subdivisions used under names of literary authors, see appendix D.

—Appreciation *(Indirect)*

Use for works on public response and reception, praise, etc. of the person's artistic works. Use under persons active in the fine arts, music and performing arts. For works consisting of critical analysis or interpretation of artistic works without biographical details, see **—Criticism and interpretation.** For works on public opinion about the person, see **—Public opinion.** For works on the person's impact on other persons, groups, movements, etc., see **—Influence.** For works on systems of beliefs and rituals connected with divine persons or saints, see **—Cult.**

—Archaeological collections

Use according to H1427 for works about the person's collections of archaeological items or artifacts.

—Archives

Use for collections or discussions of documentary materials or records relating to the person's public or private activities, including manuscripts, diaries, correspondence, photographs, or other items of historical interest.

See also **—Correspondence; —Diaries; —Iconography; —Manuscripts; —Notebooks, sketchbooks, etc.**

—Archives—Catalogs

—Art

Use under persons living before 1400 A.D. for works consisting of reproductions of works of art depicting the person, or works discussing such art. For persons living after 1400, see **—Portraits.**

—Art collections

Use according to H1427 for works about the person's own art collection.

—Art patronage

Use for works about the person's support and patronage of the arts.

—Assassination

—Assassination attempt, [date]

—Assassination attempts

Associates, see **—Friends and associates**

Attitude towards [specific topic], see **—Views on [specific topic]**

—Authorship

Use for discussions of the validity of attributing authorship of works to the person. For discussions of the person's literary ability and accomplishments, see **—Literary art.**

Autobiography, use **[name of person].**

—Autographs

Use for collections or discussions of the person's autographs or handwriting.

—Autographs—Facsimiles

Autographs, Spurious, see **—Forgeries**

—Bibliography

Use for lists of publications by or about the person.

—Bibliography—Catalogs

—Bibliography—Microform catalogs

Biography, use **[name of person].**

—Birthplace

Bones, see **—Museums, relics, etc.; —Tomb**

— **Bonsai collections**

Use according to H1427 for works about the person's collection of bonsai.

— **Books and reading**

Use for works dealing with written material known to have been read by the person, his reading habits and interests, books borrowed from friends or libraries, etc.

See also — **Library**

Burial, see — **Death and burial**

— **Captivity, [dates]**

Use for works discussing periods in which the person was held captive in bondage or confinement, especially under house arrest, as a hostage, or in battle. Do not use under persons also known as literary authors. For works discussing periods in which the person was actually imprisoned in a correctional institution or prisoner of war camp, see — **Imprisonment, [dates]**.

See also — **Exile, [dates]**; — **Kidnapping, [date]**

— **Career in [specific field or discipline]**

Use for works limited to describing events in the person's occupational life or participation in a profession or vocation. Assign an additional heading for the field. Do not use under persons also known as literary authors. For works discussing the person's actual substantive contributions or accomplishments in a specific field or topic, whether made as a result of a vocation or an avocation, see — **Contributions in [specific field or topic]**.

See also — **Resignation from office**

— **Caricatures and cartoons**

Use for collections or discussions of caricatures or pictorial humor about the person.

Cartoons, satire, etc., see — **Caricatures and cartoons**; — **Humor**

— **Catalogs**

Use under artists and craftspersons for works listing their art works or crafts which are available or located in particular institutions or places.

See also — **Archives—Catalogs**; — **Bibliography—Catalogs**; — **Bibliography—Microform catalogs**; — **Catalogues raisonnés**; — **Discography**; — **Exhibitions**; — **Film catalogs**; — **Library—Catalogs**; — **Manuscripts—Catalogs**; — **Manuscripts—Microform catalogs**; — **Phonotape catalogs**; — **Slides—Catalogs**; — **Thematic catalogs**; — **Video tape catalogs**

— **Catalogues raisonnés**

Use for comprehensive listings of an artist's or craftperson's works in one medium or all media, usually chronologically or systematically arranged, and accompanied by descriptive or critical notes.

Centennial celebrations, etc., see — **Anniversaries, etc.**

Character, see — **Ethics**; — **Psychology**; — **Religion**

— **Childhood and youth**

Do not use under persons also known as literary authors.

— **Chronology**

Use for works which list by date the events in the life of the person.

— **Circus collections**

Use according to H1427 for works about the person's collections of circus items.

— **Claims vs. ...**
> Use for works about the legal claims filed by the person. Complete the subdivision with the name of the jurisdiction against which the claim was brought.

— **Clothing**

— **Coin collections**
> Use according to H1427 for works about the person's coin collections.

— **Collected works**
> Use for collected works about the person. Do not use for the published collected works of the person.

> Commentaries, see — **Criticism and interpretation**

> Companions, see — **Friends and associates**

— **Concordances**
> Use as a form subdivision for indexes to the principal words found in the writings of the person.

— **Congresses**

— **Contributions in [specific field or topic]**
> Use for works discussing the person's actual substantive contributions or accomplishments in a specific field or topic, whether made as a result of a vocation or an avocation. Also use for discussions of the person's philosophy or system of thought on a particular topic which he propounded or imparted to others. Use this subdivision to bring out one specific field or topic for a person active in more than one field, or to bring out subtopics or aspects of a particular field to which an individual contributed. Assign an additional heading for the field or topic. Do not use this subdivision for a work discussing the person's general contributions in the discipline or field with which he is solely or primarily identified. Assign the person's name without subdivision in such cases. Do not use under persons also known as literary authors. For works limited to describing events in the person's occupational life or participation in a profession or vocation, see — **Career in [specific field or discipline]**.

— **Coronation**

— **Correspondence**
> Use as a form or topical subdivision for the letters from and/or to the person. Assign an additional heading for individual correspondents.

> Costume, see — **Clothing**

— **Criticism and interpretation**
> Use for works consisting of critical analysis or interpretation of the person's artistic works or endeavors without biographical details. Use this subdivision only under persons active in the fine arts, music, and performing arts. For works on public response and reception, praise, etc. of the person's artistic works, see — **Appreciation**.

> Crowning, see — **Coronation**

— **Cult** *(Indirect)*
> Use under divine persons, saints, or persons worshipped for systems of beliefs or rituals associated with the person.

— **Death and burial**
> Use for works on the person's death, funeral, and burial, including his last illness. Do not use under persons also known as literary authors.
> See also — **Assassination**; — **Tomb**

— **Death mask**

Devotional literature, see — **Prayer-books and devotions**

— **Diaries**

Use for collections or discussions of the person's diaries. Also use for individual diaries.

— **Dictionaries, indexes, etc.**

See also — **Concordances**

— **Disciples**

Use for works discussing persons who received instruction from the individual or accepted his doctrines or teachings and assisted in spreading or implementing them.

— **Discography**

Use for lists or catalogs of sound recordings by or about the person.

See also — **Phonotape catalogs**

Diseases, see — **Health**

— **Drama**

Use as a form subdivision for plays and musical dramatic works, including operas, ballets, musical comedies, etc., about the person. Do not use under persons also known as literary authors. For criticism or discussions of plays, etc. about an individual, assign **[name of person], in fiction, drama, poetry, etc.** as a topical heading.

— **Dramaturgy**

Use under composers for discussions of their technique in writing operas and other dramatic works. Do not use under persons also known as literary authors.

— **Drug use**

Use for works about the person's use or abuse of drugs.

See also — **Alcohol use**

Dwellings, see — **Homes and haunts**

Early life, see — **Childhood and youth**

Education, see — **Knowledge and learning**

— **Employees**

Use for works discussing persons employed by the individual, including household servants, etc.

Enemies, see — **Adversaries**

— **Estate**

Use for discussions of the aggregate of property or liabilities of all kinds that a person leaves for disposal at his death.

See also — **Will**

— **Ethics**

Use for discussions of the individual's ethical system and values.

See also — **Religion**

— **Ethnological collections**

Use according to H1427 for works about the person's ethnological collections.

— **Ethnomusicological collections**

Use according to H1427 for works about the person's ethnomusicological collections.

— **Exhibitions**

Use for works about exhibitions on the life or work of the person, including catalogs of single exhibitions.

—**Exile, [dates]** *(Indirect)*
 Do not use under persons also known as literary authors.
—**Family**
 Use for discussions of the person's family or relations with family members. Also use for genealogical works. Assign an additional heading for the name of the family. Do not use under persons also known as literary authors.
—**Fiction**
 Use as a form subdivision for works of fiction about the person. Do not use under persons also known as literary authors. For criticism or discussions of fiction about a person, assign **[name of person], in fiction, drama, poetry, etc.** as a topical heading.
—**Film catalogs**
—**Finance, Personal**
 Use for discussions of the person's financial affairs.
 See also —**Estate;** —**Will**
 Folktales, see —**Legends**
—**Forgeries**
 Use for discussions of forgeries of the person's creative works or signature. In the case of individual forgeries, assign an additional heading for the name of the forger.
—**Freemasonry**
 Use for works discussing the person's membership or participation in the Freemasons.
 Frequented places, see —**Homes and haunts**
—**Friends and associates**
 Use for discussions of the person's close and immediate contacts such as companions, co-workers, etc.
 See also —**Adversaries;** —**Disciples;** —**Employees;** —**Relations with [specific class of persons or ethnic group]**
 Funeral, see —**Death and burial**
 Genealogy, see —**Family**
 Grave, see —**Tomb**
 Handwriting, see —**Autographs**
—**Harmony**
 Use under composers for works discussing their uses of harmony.
 Haunts, see —**Homes and haunts**
—**Health**
 Use for works about the person's state of health, including diseases suffered and accounts of specific diseases. Do not use under persons also known as literary authors. For accounts of specific diseases assign an additional heading of the type: **[disease]—Patients—[place]—Biography.**
 See also —**Alcohol use;** —**Drug use;** —**Mental health**
—**Herbarium**
—**Homes and haunts** *(Indirect)*
 Use for works discussing the person's home or dwellings, favorite places, or places he habitually frequented.
 See also —**Birthplace;** —**Journeys;** —**Palaces**

— **Humor**
Use as a form subdivision for humorous writings about the person. Do not use under persons also known as literary authors. For pictorial humor, see — **Caricatures and cartoons**.

— **Iconography**
Use for works consisting of pictures or other visual images relating to the person, including portraits, portraits of family and friends, views of birthplace, etc.
See also — **Art**; — **Caricatures and cartoons**; — **Numismatics**; — **Portraits**
Imitations, see — **Parodies, imitations, etc.**

— **Impeachment**

— **Imprisonment, [dates]**
Use for works discussing periods in which the person was actually imprisoned in a correctional institution or a prisoner of war camp. Do not use under persons also known as literary authors. For works discussing periods in which the person was held captive in bondage or confinement, especially under house arrest, as a hostage, or in battle, see — **Captivity, [dates]**.
See also — **Exile, [dates]**

— **Inauguration, [date]**
Indexes, see — **Concordances**; — **Dictionaries, indexes, etc.**

— **Influence**
Use for works discussing the person's impact on other persons, groups, movements, etc. Assign an additional heading for the person or group influenced. For works on public response and reception, praise, etc. of the person's artistic works, see — **Appreciation**.
Interment, see — **Death and burial**
Interpretation, see — **Criticism and interpretation**

— **Interviews**
Use for works consisting of transcripts of what was said during the course of interviews or conversations with the person on one or more occasions.
Journals, see — **Diaries**

— **Journeys** *(Indirect)*
Use for works about voyages and travels undertaken by the person. When the subdivision is further subdivided by place, assign an additional heading of the type: **[place] — Description** or **[place] — Description and travel**, as appropriate.
See also — **Exile, [dates]**

— **Juvenile drama**
Do not use under persons also known as literary authors.

— **Juvenile fiction**
Do not use under persons also known as literary authors.

— **Juvenile films**

— **Juvenile humor**
Do not use under persons also known as literary authors.

— **Juvenile literature**

— **Juvenile poetry**
Do not use under persons also known as literary authors.

— **Juvenile sound recordings**

— **Kidnapping, [date]**

— **Knowledge — [topic]**
Use for works discussing the person's knowledge of a specific topic, whether explicitly stated or inferred from his life and work. Also use for discussions of the person's educational background in a specific topic. Assign an additional heading for the specific topic. Under literary authors, further subdivision of — **Knowledge** is restricted to subdivisions listed in H1155.4 (see pp. 405-406). For works on the person's opinions or attitudes on a specific topic, whether explicitly stated or inferred, see — **Views on [specific topic]**.

— **Knowledge and learning**
Use for works about the person's formal or informal learning or scholarship in general. For knowledge or learning of specific topics, see — **Knowledge — [topic]**.

— **Language**
See also — **Literary art**; — **Oratory**

Last illness, see — **Death and burial**

Leadership, Military, see — **Military leadership**

Learning, see — **Knowledge and learning**

— **Legends**
Use as a form subdivision for stories about the person which have come down from the past and which are popularly taken as historical though not verifiable. Do not use under persons also known as literary authors.
See also — **Romances**

Letters, see — **Correspondence**

— **Library**
Use for works discussing the person's own library.
See also — **Books and reading**

— **Library — Catalogs**

— **Library resources** *(Indirect)*
Use for works describing the resources or special collections available in libraries for research or study about the person.

— **Literary art**
Use for discussions of the person's literary ability and accomplishments. Do not use under multi-career persons who are also recognized as literary authors. Under persons who are also recognized as literary authors, use appropriate subdivisions from H1155.4. For discussions of the validity of attributing authorship of specific works to the person, see — **Authorship**.

— **Literary collections**
Use for literary anthologies about the person which involve two or more literary forms. Do not use under persons also known as literary authors. For anthologies in one literary form, see the form, e.g. — **Drama**; — **Fiction**; — **Poetry**.

Litigation, see — **Trials, litigation, etc.**

— **Manuscripts**
Use for works discussing writings made by hand, typewriter, etc., by or about the person. Do not use for individual works in manuscript form.
See also — **Archives**; — **Autographs**; — **Correspondence**; — **Diaries**; — **Notebooks, sketchbooks, etc.**

— **Manuscripts — Catalogs**

— **Manuscripts — Facsimiles**

— **Manuscripts — Indexes**

—Manuscripts—Microform catalogs
—Map collections
> Use according to H1427 for works about the person's collections of maps.

—Medals
> Use for works about medals issued to commemorate the person.

—Meditations
> Use as a form subdivision for works containing descriptions of thoughts or reflections on the spiritual significance of the person's life or deeds.

—Mental health
> Use for works discussing the person's state of mental health, including mental illness and accounts of specific mental disorders. Do not use under persons also known as literary authors. For accounts of specific disorders or situations, assign an additional heading of the type: [disease]—Patients—[place]—Biography; Psychotherapy patients—[place]—Biography; etc.

—Military leadership
—Miscellanea
> Use for collections of curiosa relating to the person as well as for texts about the person in question and answer format.

—Monuments *(Indirect)*
> Use for works about monuments erected in honor of the person.
>
> See also —Museums, relics, etc.; —Shrines; —Tomb

Motives, themes, see —Themes, motives
—Museums, relics, etc. *(Indirect)*
> Use for works on museums devoted to the person. Also includes works on disinterred bones.
>
> See also —Archives; —Death mask; —Shrines; —Tomb

Music, see —Songs and music
—Musical instrument collections
> Use according to H1427 for works about the person's collections of musical instruments.

—Musical settings
> Use as a form subdivision for musical scores or sound recordings in which writings or words of the person have been set to music.

—Name
> Use for discussions of the history, orthography, etymology, etc. of the person's name.

—Natural history collections
> Use according to H1427 for works about the person's collections of natural history items or specimens.

—Notebooks, sketchbooks, etc.
> Use for collections or discussions of the person's notebooks, sketchbooks, etc. Also use for individual works.

—Notebooks, sketchbooks, etc.—Facsimiles
—Numismatic collections
> Use according to H1427 for works about the person's numismatics collections.
>
> See also —Coin collections

— **Numismatics**
Use for works discussing the representation of the person on coins, tokens, medals, paper money, etc.
See also — **Medals**
Opponents, see — **Adversaries**
— **Oratory**
Use for works discussing the person's public speaking ability.
— **Outlines, syllabi, etc.**
— **Palaces** *(Indirect)*
— **Pardon**
Use for works about the person's legal release from the penalty of an offense.
— **Parodies, imitations, etc.**
Use as both a form and topical subdivision for imitations, either comic or distorted, of the person's creative works.
Patronage of the arts, see — **Art patronage**
— **Performances** *(Indirect)*
Use under performing artists or performers of all types for works about their performances. Also use under composers, choreographers, etc. for works about performances of their compositions or works.
— **Periodicals**
See also — **Yearbooks**
Personal finance, see — **Finance, Personal**
Personality, see — **Psychology**
— **Philosophy**
Use for discussions of the individual's personal philosophy. Do not use under names of philosophers.
See also — **Aesthetics**; — **Ethics**; — **Religion**
— **Phonotape catalogs**
— **Photograph collections**
Use according to H1427 for works about the person's collections of photographs.
Pictorial humor, see — **Caricatures and cartoons**
Pictorial works, see — **Iconography**; — **Art**; — **Portraits**
Place of birth, see — **Birthplace**
Places frequented, see — **Homes and haunts**
— **Poetry**
Use as a form subdivision for works of poetry about the person. Do not use under persons also known as literary authors. For criticism or discussions of poetry about a person, assign **[name of person], in fiction, drama, poetry, etc.** as a topical heading.
— **Political and social views**
Use for works discussing the person's political and/or social views in general. For works on specific topics, see — **Views on [specific topic]**.
— **Portraits**
Use for collections or discussions of portraits of persons living after 1400 A.D., including portrait sculpture. For persons living before 1400, see — **Art**.
See also — **Caricatures and cartoons**; — **Death mask**; — **Numismatics**; — **Posters**; — **Self-portraits**

— **Poster collections**
Use according to H1427 for works about the person's collections of posters.

— **Posters**
Use for collections or discussions of posters depicting the person.

— **Prayer-books and devotions**
Use as a form subdivision, particularly under divine persons or saints, for works of devotions directed to those persons whose help or prayers are requested.

— **Prayer-books and devotions — English, [French, German, etc.]**

— **Pre-existence**
Use for works discussing the person's existence in a previous state or life.
Professional life, see — **Career in [specific field or discipline]**

— **Prophecies**
Use for works about the prophecies made by the person.

— **Psychology**
Use for discussions or interpretations of the person's psychological traits, personality, character, etc. Do not use under persons also known as literary authors.
See also — **Mental health**

— **Public opinion**
Use for works about public opinion about the person. Do not use under persons also known as literary authors. For works on public response and reception, praise, etc. of the person's artistic works, see — **Appreciation**.
Public speaking, see — **Oratory**

— **Quotations**
Use for collections or discussions of the person's quotations.
Reading habits, see — **Books and reading**

— **Relations with [specific class of persons or ethnic group]**
Assign an additional heading for the specific group with appropriate subdivision if necessary. Specific subdivisions are established under literary authors. See H1155.4 (or pp. 408-409).
Relations with employees, see — **Employees**
Relations with family, see — **Family**
Relations with friends and associates, see — **Friends and associates**
Relics, see — **Museums, relics, etc.**

— **Religion**
Use for discussions of the person's religious beliefs and practices. Do not use under names of theologians.
See also — **Ethics**
Residences, see — **Homes and haunts**

— **Resignation from office**
See also — **Abdication, [date]; — Impeachment**
Rhetoric, see — **Literary art; — Oratory**

— **Romances**
Use as a form subdivision under names of historical or legendary figures for medieval tales based chiefly on legends of chivalric love and adventure. Do not use under persons also known as literary authors.
Satire, see — **Humor**
Sayings, see — **Quotations**
Scholarship, see — **Knowledge and learning**

—**Scientific apparatus collections**
>Use according to H1427 for works about the person's collections of scientific apparatus.

—**Seal**
>Use for works discussing the devices, such as emblems, symbols or words, used by an individual to authenticate his writings or documents.

—**Self-portraits**
>Use for reproductions or discussions of self-portraits by the person.

Sepulchral monument, see —**Tomb**

—**Sermons**
>Use as a form subdivision, particularly under divine persons or saints, for single sermons or collections of sermons about the person.

Servants, see —**Employees**

—**Sexual behavior**

—**Shrines** *(Indirect)*
>Use for works discussing structures or places consecrated or devoted to the person and serving as places of religious veneration or pilgrimage.
>See also —**Museums, relics, etc.**

Sketchbooks, see —**Notebooks, sketchbooks, etc.**

—**Slide collections**
>Use according to H1427 for works about the person's collections of slides.

—**Slides**

—**Slides—Catalogs**

Social views, see —**Political and social views**

—**Societies, etc.**
>Use for works discussing organizations devoted to or specializing in the person's life or work.

—**Songs and music**
>Use as a form subdivision for collections or single works of vocal or instrumental music about the person. For collections or single works in musical dramatic forms such as operas, ballets, musical comedies, etc., see —**Drama.**

—**Sources**
>Use for discussions of the person's sources of ideas or inspiration for his endeavors or creative works. For discussions of adaptations by others of an individual's creative works, see —**Adaptations.**

Spiritual life, see —**Religion**

—**Stories of operas**
>Use under composers for works discussing or summarizing the stories or plots of their operas.

—**Study and teaching** *(Indirect)*
>Use for works on methods of studying and teaching about the person.

Style, Literary, see —**Literary art**

—**Symbolism**
>Use for discussions of the symbols employed by the person in his creative works.

Tales, see —**Legends;** —**Romances**

—**Teachings**
>Use for works discussing in general the body of knowledge, precepts, or doctrines the person taught to others.

—**Thematic catalogs**
Use under composers for listings of the themes of their musical compositions. Do not use under persons also known as literary authors.

—**Themes, motives**
Use for discussions of the themes and motives in the person's creative works. Do not use under persons also known as literary authors.

—**Tomb**
Use for works about the person's grave, interred bones, etc. For works on disinterred bones, see —**Museums, relics, etc.**
See also —**Death and burial**

Travels, see —**Journeys**

—**Trials, litigation, etc.**
Use for proceedings or discussions of proceedings of civil or criminal actions to which the person is a party.

—**Video tape catalogs**

—**Views on [specific topic]**
Use for works on the person's opinions or attitudes on a specific topic, whether explicitly stated or inferred. Assign an additional heading for the specific topic. Do not use under persons also known as literary authors. For works on the person's knowledge of a specific topic, whether explicitly stated or inferred from his life and works, see —**Knowledge—[specific topic]**.

Views on aesthetics, see —**Aesthetics**
Views on ethics, see —**Ethics**
Views on politics and society, see —**Political and social views**
Views on society, see —**Political and social views**
Voyages, see —**Journeys**

—**Will**
Use for discussions of the person's legal declaration regarding the disposition of his property or estate.
See also —**Estate**

Writing skill, see —**Literary art**

—**Yearbooks**

Youth, see —**Childhood and youth**

APPENDIX G:
FREE-FLOATING SUBDIVISIONS USED UNDER NAMES OF PLACES*

— Abstracting and indexing
— Abstracts
— Addresses, essays, lectures
— Administrative and political divisions[1]
— Aerial exploration[1]
— Aerial photographs
— Air defenses
— Air defenses, Civil
— Air defenses, Military
— Altitudes[1]
— Anecdotes, facetiae, satire, etc.
— Annexation to ...[1]
— Anniversaries, etc.
— Antiquities[2]
— Antiquities — Collection and preservation[2]
— Antiquities, Buddhist[2]
— Antiquities, Byzantine[2]
— Antiquities, Celtic[2]
— Antiquities, Germanic[2]
— Antiquities, Hindu[2]
— Antiquities, Phoenician[2]
— Antiquities, Roman[2]
— Antiquities, Slavic[2]
— Antiquities, Turkish[2]

— Appropriations and expenditures
— Appropriations and expenditures — Effect of inflation on
— Archival resources (Indirect)
— Armed Forces[3,4] (Indirect)
— Autonomous communities[1,5]
— Bibliography
— Bio-bibliography
— Biography
— Biography — Anecdotes, facetiae, satire, etc.
— Biography — Dictionaries
— Biography — Portraits
— Book reviews
— Boundaries (Indirect)
— Buildings, structures, etc.[6]
— Cantons[1,5]
— Capital and capitol[1]
— Census
— Census — Law and legislation
— Census, [date]
— Census, [number], [date][7]
— Centennial celebrations, etc.
— Charters[8]
— Charters, grants, privileges[9]
— Church history

*This list, prepared in June 1985, supersedes the lists published in Library of Congress, Subject Cataloging Division, *Subject Cataloging Manual: Subject Headings*, prelim. ed. (Washington, D.C.: Library of Congress, 1984), H1135, H1145.

Numbered footnotes to this section of appendix G appear on pages 437-438.

— Civil defense
— Civil defense — Law and legislation
— Civilization
— Civilization — 16th century[1]
— Civilization — 17th century[1]
— Civilization — 18th century[1]
— Civilization — 19th century[1]
— Civilization — 20th century[1]
— Civilization — Philosophy
— Claims
— Claims vs. ...
— Climate
— Clubs
— Coast defenses[3]
— Collected works
— Colonial influence
— Colonies[3,10]
— Colonization[3]
— Commerce *(Indirect)*
— Commercial policy[3]
— Commercial treaties[3]
— Congresses
— Constitution[1]
— Constitution — Amendments[1]
— Constitution — Amendments — 1st, [2nd, 3rd, etc.][1]
— Constitutional history[1]
— Constitutional law[1]
— Constitutional law — Amendments[1]
— Constitutional law — Amendments — 1st, [2nd, 3rd, etc.][1]
— Constitutional law — Amendments — Ratification[1]
— Constitutional law, State[1]
— Constitutional law, State — Amendments[1]
— Court and courtiers[3]
— Court and courtiers — Food[3]
— Court and courtiers — Language[3]
— Cultural policy
— Defenses[3]
— Defenses — Law and legislation[3]
— Departments[1,5]
— Dependency on ...[3]
— Dependency on foreign countries[3]
— Description[11]
— Description — Aerial[11]
— Description — Guide-books[11]
— Description — Tours[11]

— Description — Views[11]
— Description and travel[12]
— Description and travel — Aerial[12]
— Description and travel — Guide-books[12]
— Description and travel — Tours[12]
— Description and travel — Views[12]
— Dictionaries and encyclopedias
— Diplomatic and consular service *(Indirect)*[3]
— Diplomatic and consular service — Privileges and immunities[3]
— Directories
— Directories — Telephone
— Discovery and exploration[3]
— Distances, etc.
— Drama
— Economic conditions
— Economic conditions — Regional disparities[1]
— Economic conditions — Statistics
— Economic integration[13]
— Economic policy
— Emigration and immigration[3]
— Emigration and immigration — Government policy[3]
— Empresses[3]
— Ethnic relations
— Executive departments
— Executive departments — Public meetings
— Executive departments — Reorganization
— Exiles[1]
— Exploring expeditions[3]
— Fairs
— Fiction
— Film catalogs
— Foreign economic relations *(Indirect)*[3]
— Foreign opinion[3]
— Foreign opinion, British, [French, Italian, etc.][3]
— Foreign population
— Foreign population — Housing
— Foreign relations *(Indirect)*[14]
— Foreign relations — Executive agreements[14]
— Foreign relations — Treaties[14]
— Foreign relations administration[14]

— Frontier troubles[1]
— Full employment policies[1]
— Gazetteers
— Genealogy
— Genealogy — Dictionaries
— Gentry[1]
— Gold discoveries[1]
— Government property
— Government publications
— Government vessels[3]
— Governors[15]
— Governors — Children[15]
— Governors — Election[15]
— Governors — Wives[15]
— Handbooks, manuals, etc.
— Historical geography
— Historical geography — Maps
— Historiography
— History
— History — Anecdotes, facetiae, satire, etc.
— History — Autonomy and independence movements[1]
— History — Bombardment, [date]
— History — Chronology
— History — Errors, inventions, etc.
— History — Partition, [date]
— History — Periodization[1]
— History — Philosophy
— History — [period subdivision, if established] — Philosophy
— History — Prophecies
— History — Siege, [date]
— History — Sources
— History, Comic, satirical, etc.
— History, Local[1]
— History, Local — Collectibles[1]
— History, Military
— History, Military — Religious aspects
— History, Naval[3]
— Imprints
— Industries
— Industries — Energy conservation
— Industries — Energy conservation — Law and legislation
— Industries — Environmental aspects
— Industries — Location
— Industries — Location — Environmental aspects

— Industries — Statistics
— Intellectual life
— International status
— Juvenile drama
— Juvenile fiction
— Juvenile films
— Juvenile humor
— Juvenile literature
— Juvenile poetry
— Juvenile sound recordings
— Kings and rulers[1]
— Kings and rulers — Children[1]
— Kings and rulers — Death and burial[1]
— Kings and rulers — Folklore[1]
— Kings and rulers — Genealogy[1]
— Kings and rulers — Heraldry[1]
— Kings and rulers — Journeys (Indirect)[1]
— Kings and rulers — Mistresses[1]
— Kings and rulers — Mothers[1]
— Kings and rulers — Mythology[1]
— Kings and rulers — Religious aspects[1]
— Kings and rulers — Sisters[1]
— Languages[16]
— Languages — Law and legislation
— Learned institutions and societies
— Library resources (Indirect)
— Lieutenant-governors[15]
— Literary collections
— Literatures[17]
— Manufactures
— Maps
— Maps — Bibliography
— Maps, Comparative
— Maps, Manuscript
— Maps, Mental
— Maps, Outline and base
— Maps, Physical
— Maps, Pictorial
— Maps, Topographic
— Maps, Tourist
— Maps for the blind
— Maps for the visually handicapped
— Military policy[3]
— Military policy — Religious aspects[3]
— Military relations (Indirect)

—Military relations—Foreign
   countries
—Militia[1]
—Militia—Mobilization[1]
—Miscellanea
—Moral conditions
—Name
—National Guard[3]
—National security[3]
—National security—Finance[3]
—National security—Finance
   —Law and legislation[3]
—National security—Law and
   legislation[3]
—Native races[3]
—Naval militia[1]
—Neutrality[3]
—Nobility[3]
—Nobility—Heraldry[3]
—Nonalignment[3]
—Occupations
—Occupations—Licenses
—Officials and employees *(Indirect)*
—Officials and employees—
   Accidents
—Officials and employees—
   Appointment, qualifications,
   tenure, etc.
—Officials and employees—
   Attitudes
—Officials and employees—
   Bonding
—Officials and employees—
   Charitable contributions
—Officials and employees—
   Discipline
—Officials and employees—
   Dismissal of
—Officials and employees—
   Foreign countries
—Officials and employees—
   Foreign countries—Foreign
   language competency
—Officials and employees—
   Furloughs
—Officials and employees—Job
   stress
—Officials and employees—Leave
   regulations
—Officials and employees—
   Pensions

—Officials and employees—Rating
   of
—Officials and employees—
   Registers
—Officials and employees—Resi-
   dence requirements
—Officials and employees—
   Salaries, allowances, etc.
—Officials and employees—Titles
—Officials and employees—Trans-
   fer of
—Officials and employees—Travel
   regulations
—Officials and employees, Alien
—Officials and employees,
   Honorary
—Officials and employees, Retired
—Officials and employees, Retired
   —Employment
—Peerage[1]
—Periodicals
—Photo maps
—Photographs from space
—Pictorial works[18]
—Poetry
—Politics and government
—Politics and government—
   Philosophy
—Politics and government—[period
   subdivision, if established]—
   Philosophy
—Popular culture
—Popular culture—Economic
   aspects
—Population
—Population, Rural[1]
—Population density
—Population policy
—Presidents[19]
—Presidents—Election[19]
—Presidents—Mistresses[19]
—Presidents—Mothers[19]
—Presidents—Wives[19]
—Princes and princesses[3]
—Proclamations[3]
—Provinces[1,5]
—Public buildings *(Indirect)*
—Public buildings—Access for the
   physically handicapped
—Public lands
—Public works
—Public works—Accounting

—Public works—Accounting—Law and legislation
—Public works—Law and legislation
—Queens
—Race relations
—Registers
—Relations *(Indirect)*
—Relations—Foreign countries
—Relief models
—Religion
—Religion—16th century
—Religion—17th century
—Religion—18th century
—Religion—19th century
—Religion—20th century
—Religious and ecclesiastical institutions
—Religious life and customs
—Republics[1,5]
—Research *(Indirect)*
—Road maps
—Royal household[3]
—Rural conditions[1]
—Scientific bureaus
—Seal
—Slides
—Social conditions
—Social life and customs
—Social policy
—Social registers
—Songs and music
—States[1,5]
—Statistical services

—Statistical services—Law and legislation
—Statistics
—Statistics, Medical
—Statistics, Vital
—Strategic aspects
—Study and teaching *(Indirect)*
—Study and teaching—Law and legislation *(Indirect)*
—Study and teaching (Continuing education) *(Indirect)*
—Study and teaching (Elementary) *(Indirect)*
—Study and teaching (Graduate) *(Indirect)*
—Study and teaching (Higher) *(Indirect)*
—Study and teaching (Preschool) *(Indirect)*
—Study and teaching (Primary) *(Indirect)*
—Study and teaching (Secondary) *(Indirect)*
—Sultans[3]
—Surveys
—Territorial expansion[3]
—Territories and possessions[3]
—Travel regulations[1]
—Trials, litigation, etc.
—Vice-Presidents[19]
—Vice-Presidents—Election[19]
—Voting registers
—Yearbooks
—Zoning maps

Also free-floating:

... in art
... in literature
... Metropolitan Area ([geographic qualifier]) (based on names of cities)
... Suburban Area ([geographic qualifier]) (based on names of cities)
... Region ([geographic qualifier]) (based on names of cities)

---

[1]Do not use under cities.

[2]Do not use under names of ancient or early cities established as subject headings.

[3]Use only under countries or under regions larger than countries.

[4]See H1159 for further subdivisions used under —**Armed Forces.**

[5]Use only when the name of the country itself is used as a geographic subdivision under a topical heading, e.g. **Law—Spain—Autonomous communities; Civil procedure—Switzerland—Cantons; Budget—Colombia—Departments; Civil service—Canada—Provinces; Law—Soviet Union—Republics; Elections—India—States.**

[6]Use only under cities, as described in H1334 and H1334.5.

[7]Use only under **United States.**

[8]Use only under states, counties, cities, etc. of the United States.

[9]Use under countries, etc. other than the United States, and under cities other than those of the United States.

[10]See H1149.5 for further subdivisions used under —**Colonies.**

[11]Use only under cities (other than ancient cities); use —**Description and travel** or —**Description and travel—[further subdivision]** under places larger than cities; use —**Pictorial works** under ancient cities.

[12]Do not use under cities; use —**Description** or —**Description—[further subdivision].**

[13]Use only under regions larger than countries.

[14]Use only under countries, or under regions larger than countries, as described in H1629.

[15]Use under regions, states, etc. of the United States and countries, etc. other than the United States. For works dealing collectively with the governors and lieutenant-governors of the states of the United States, use **Governors—United States** and **Lieutenant-governors—United States.**

[16]See H1154 for further subdivisions used under —**Languages.**

[17]See H1156 for further subdivisions used under —**Literatures.**

[18]Use only under names of ancient cities; use —**Description—Views** for all other cities. Under places larger than cities, use —**Description and travel—Views.**

[19]Use under countries, etc. other than the United States. Use **Presidents—United States** and **Vice-Presidents—United States** for works on presidents and vice-presidents of the United States.

FREE-FLOATING SUBDIVISIONS AND TERMS USED WITH NAMES OF BODIES OF WATER, STREAMS, ETC.*

- Alluvial plain
- Antiquities
- Barrages
- Bridges
- Channelization
- Channels
- Climate
- Delta
  [Used under rivers]
- Description and travel
- Discovery and exploration
- Drama
- Evaporation control
- Fertilization
- Fiction
- History
- Levees
- Name
- Navigation
- Navigation — Law and
  legislation
- Poetry
- Power utilization
- Recreational use
- Regulation
- Shorelines
- Temperature
- Water diversion
- Water level
- Water-rights

FREE FLOATING TERMS: The terms **Region, Watershed, Estuary,** and **Valley** may be added to existing headings for names of bodies of water to form free-floating phrase headings. If the existing heading has a parenthetical qualifier, add the term before the qualifier.

*Library of Congress, Subject Cataloging Division, *Subject Cataloging Manual: Subject Headings*, prelim. ed. (Washington, D.C.: Library of Congress, 1984), H1145.5 (rev. 6/24/85).

APPENDIX H:
PATTERNS OF CROSS-REFERENCES FOR PROPER NAMES

Cross-references for personal, corporate, and jurisdictional headings are made according to *Anglo-American Cataloguing Rules*, second edition (*AACR2*). References for individual subject headings are enumerated in *Library of Congress Subject Headings*. Following are patterns and examples of cross-references for certain types of subject headings (mostly nonjurisdictional geographic headings) gathered from *Library of Congress Subject Headings*, various parts of the *Subject Cataloging Manual*,* and information provided by the Subject Cataloging Division.

Ancient and Early Cities

Pattern

    [Name] (Ancient city) [or **(City)**]
       x   [Alternate ancient name(s)] (Ancient city)
             [or (City)]
           [Alternate modern name(s)] (Ancient city)
             [or (City)]
     xx **Cities and towns, Ruined, extinct, etc. –**
            [Modern country or **first-order division]**
            [Modern country or **first-order division] – Antiquities**

Examples

    Vulci (Ancient city)
       x   Volci (Ancient city)
     xx **Cities and towns, Ruined, extinct, etc. – Italy**
          Italy – Antiquities

---

*Library of Congress, Subject Cataloging Division, *Subject Cataloging Manual: Subject Headings*, prelim. ed. (Washington, D.C.: Library of Congress, 1984).

Great Zimbabwe (City)
x   Zimbabwe, Great (City)
xx   Cities and towns, Ruined, extinct, etc.—Zimbabwe
Zimbabwe—Antiquities

Animals

Pattern

[Name of animal] ([Generic qualifier])
xx   [Generic heading]

Examples

Dancer's Image (Race Horse)
xx   Race horses

Miss Baker (Monkey)
xx   Monkeys

Old Abe (Eagle)
xx   Eagles

Archaeological Sites

Pattern

[Name] Site ([Geographic qualifier])
x   [Alternate name(s)] ([Geographic qualifier])
xx   [Modern country or first-order division]—Antiquities

and, if applicable, one of the following:

xx   Caves—[Modern country or first-order division]
Kitchen-middens—[Modern country or first-order division]
Rockshelters—[Modern country or first-order division]

Examples

Hascherkeller Site (Germany)
xx   Germany (West)—Antiquities

Galaz Site (N.M.)
x   Galaz Ruin (N.M.)
xx   New Mexico—Antiquities

Wombah Site (N.S.W.)
x   Wombah Middens Site (N.S.W.)
xx   Australia—Antiquities
Kitchen-middens—Australia

Rigdon's Horse Pasture Cave Site (Or.)
> *x*   Horse Pasture Cave Site (Or.)
> *xx* **Caves—Oregon**
> **Oregon—Antiquities**

Building Details

Pattern

[Name of structure] ([Geographic qualifier])—[Name of detail]
> *x*   [Name of detail], [Name of structure] ([Geographic qualifier])
> [Alternate name(s)], [Name of structure] ([Geographic
> qualifier])
> *xx* **[Type of detail]—[Country or first-order division]**

Example

Yakushiji (Nara-shi, Japan)—Saito
> *x*   Saito, Yakushiji (Nara-shi, Japan)
> West Pagoda, Yakushiji (Nara-shi, Japan)
> *xx* **Pagodas—Japan**

Buildings and Other Structures

Pattern

[Name of structure] ([Geographic qualifier])
> *x*   [Alternate name(s)] ([Geographic qualifier])
> *xx* **[Type of structure]—[Country or first-order division]**
> **[Name of river] ([Geographic qualifier])—Bridges** [if a bridge]

Examples

I Ho Yüan (Peking, China)
> *x*   Summer Palace (Peking, China)
> *xx* **Palaces—China**
> **Parks—China**

Balmoral Castle (Grampian)
> *xx* **Castles—Scotland**

Cleveland Municipal Stadium (Cleveland, Ohio)
> *x*   Municipal Stadium (Cleveland, Ohio)
> *xx* **Stadia—Ohio**

Brooklyn Bridge (New York, N.Y.)
> *xx* **Bridges—New York (State)**
> **East River (N.Y.)—Bridges**

Pont-Neuf (Paris, France)
> *xx* Bridges — France
> Seine River (France) — Bridges

City Districts, Quarters, Sections

Pattern

[Name of district or section] ([Name of city])
> *x* [Alternate name(s) or forms of heading]

Examples

Left Bank (Paris, France)
> *x* Paris (France). Left Bank
> Paris (France). Rive gauche
> Rive gauche (Paris, France)

North End (Boston, Mass.)
> *x* Boston (Mass.). North End

Federal Hill (Baltimore, Md.)
> *x* Baltimore (Md.). Federal Hill

Comic Characters

Pattern

[Name of character] (Fictitious character)
> *xx* Comic books, strips, etc.

Example

Snoopy (Fictitious character)
> *xx* Comic books, strips, etc.

Dynasties

Pattern

[Name] dynasty
> *x* [Alternate name(s)]
> *xx* [Country] — History — [Period subdivision]

Examples

Gupta dynasty
> *xx* India — History — 324 B.C.-1000 A.D.

Achaemenid dynasty, 559-330 B.C.
x   Achaemenians
Achaemenidae
Achaemenids
Hakhamanishiya
xx   **Iran — History — To 640**

Entities within a City

Pattern

[Name of entity] ([Name of city])
x   [Alternate name(s) or form(s) of name]
xx   **[Generic heading] — [Country or first-order division]**

Examples

Boulevard du Temple (Paris, France)
x   Temple Boulevard (Paris, France)
xx   **Streets — France**

Promenade du Peyrou (Montpellier, France)
x   Peyrou (Montpellier, France)
xx   **Plazas — France**

Fontana di Trevi (Rome, Italy)
x   Trevi Fountain (Rome, Italy)
xx   **Fountains — Italy**

Geographic Features

Pattern

[Distinctive name] [Generic term] ([Geographic qualifier])
x   [Alternate name(s)] ([Geographic qualifier])
xx   **[Type of feature] ([Geographic qualifier]) — [Country or first-order division]**

Examples

Chablais Mountains (France)
x   Chablais, Massif du (France)
Massif du Chablais (France)
xx   **Mountains — France**

El Capitan (Calif. : Peak)
x   Capitan (Calif. : Peak)
xx   **Mountains — California**
Sierra Nevada Mountains (Calif. and Nev.)

Sound, The (Denmark and Sweden)
    x Oresund (Denmark and Sweden)
       Sundet (Denmark and Sweden)
       The Sound (Denmark and Sweden)
   xx **Sounds (Geomorphology) — Denmark**
       Sounds (Geomorphology) — Sweden

Rio Grande
    x Rio Bravo del Norte
   xx **Rivers — Mexico**
       Rivers — United States

Amazon River
   xx **Rivers — Brazil**
       Rivers — Colombia
       Rivers — Peru

Missouri River
       [river located in more than three first-order political divisions]
   xx **Rivers — United States**

Niger River
       [river located in more than three countries]
   xx **Rivers — Africa, West**

Salmon River, Middle Fork (Idaho)
    x Middle Fork, Salmon River (Idaho)
   xx **Rivers — Idaho**

Forth, Firth of (Scotland)
    x Bodotria (Scotland)
       Firth of Forth (Scotland)
   xx **Estuaries — Scotland**

Gods and Goddesses

Pattern

[Name of god or goddess] ([Ethnic adjective] deity)
    x [Alternate name(s)] ([Ethnic adjective] deity)
   xx **Gods, [Ethnic adjective]**

Example

Brahma (Hindu deity)
   xx **Gods, Hindu**

Gods and Goddesses from Classical Mythology

Pattern

[Name of god or goddess] (Greek [or Roman] deity)
    x [Variant form(s) of name) (Greek [or Roman] deity)
   sa [Equivalent god or goddess]
  xx [Equivalent god or goddess]
      Gods, Greek [or Roman]

Example

Athena (Greek deity)
    x Athene (Greek deity)
   sa Minerva (Roman deity)
  xx Gods, Greek
      Minerva (Roman deity)

Islands or Island Groups

Pattern

[Name of island or island groups] ([Geographic qualifier])
    x [Alternate name(s)] ([Qualifier])
      [Name in vernacular] ([Qualifier])
      [Uninverted form of name] ([Qualifier])
  xx [Name of group] ([Qualifier])
      [omit if same as name of jurisdiction]
      Islands [or Specific type of island] — [Country or first-order
        division]
      Islands of the [Name]
        [if island does not lie near its controlling
        jurisdiction]

Examples

Sitkinak Island (Alaska)
  xx Islands — Alaska

One Tree Island (Qld.)
  xx Coral reefs and islands — Australia
      Great Barrier Reef (Qld.)

Carry Bow Cay (Belize)
    x Carrie Bow Cay (Belize)
  xx Islands — Belize

Melos Island (Greece)
    x Milo Island (Greece)
      Nísos Mílos (Greece)
  xx Islands — Greece

Sapelo Island (Ga.)
    xx   **Golden Isles (Ga.)**
           Islands—Georgia

Easter Island
    x   Isla de Pascua
         Pascua Island
         Rapa Nui
         Rapanui
    xx **Islands of the Pacific**

Corregidor Island (Philippines)
    xx **Islands—Philippines**

South Georgia Island
    xx **Islands of the Atlantic**

National Groups in the United States

Pattern

[Nationality] Americans *(Indirect)*
    x [Nationality] Americans—United States
    xx **Ethnology—United States**
           [Nationality]—United States

Example

Italian Americans
    x Italian Americans—United States
    xx **Ethnology—United States**
           Italians—United States

National Groups in Other Countries

Pattern

[Nationality] *(Indirect)*
    xx **Ethnology—[Country of origin]**
           [Country of origin]
                [if entry element is different from national group name]

Examples

Germans
    xx **Ethnology—Germany**

Russians
    xx **Ethnology—Russian S.F.S.R.**
           Ethnology—Soviet Union
           Soviet Union

Noble Houses

Pattern

> [Name], [Title in English]
>   *x* [Title in English and Name in natural word order]
>   *xx* [Country] — Nobility

Examples

> **Devonshire, Dukes of**
>   *x* Dukes of Devonshire
>   *xx* **England — Nobility**

> **Parma, Dukes of**
>   *x* Dukes of Parma
>   *xx* **Italy — Nobility**

> **Toulouse, Counts of**
>   *x* Counts of Toulouse
>   *xx* **France — Nobility**

> **Gloucester, Earls of**
>   *x* Earls of Gloucester
>   *xx* **England — Nobility**

Parks, Reserves, National Monuments, Etc.

Pattern

> **[Name of entity] ([Geographic qualifier])**
>   *x* [Alternate name(s)] ([Geographic qualifier])
>   *xx* **[Generic heading] — [Country or first-order division]**
>   **National parks and reserves — [Country or first-order division,**
>   if a national park, etc.]
>   **[Name of larger entity** of which entity in question forms
>   a part]
>   **[Special topic]**

Examples

> **Vestvolden (Copenhagen, Denmark)**
>   *xx* **Moats — Denmark**
>   **Parks — Denmark**

> **City Park (New Orleans, La.)**
>   *xx* **Parks — Louisiana**

Parque Nacional de Ubajara (Brazil)
    x Ubajara National Park (Brazil)
    xx **National parks and reserves — Brazil**
        Parks — Brazil

Naturpark Pfälzerwald (Germany)
    x Pfalzerwald, Naturpark (Germany)
    xx **Forest reserves — Germany (West)**
        Natural areas — Germany (West)
        Parks — Germany (West)

Isle Royale National Park (Mich.)
    xx **Game-preserves — Michigan**
        National parks and reserves — Michigan
        Isle Royale (Mich.)

Appalachian Trail
    xx **Trails — United States**
            [located in more than three states]

Tiger Haven Reserve (India)
    xx **National parks and reserves — India**
        Wildlife refuges — India

Apalachicola National Forest (Fla.)
    xx **Forest reserves — Florida**
        National parks and reserves — Florida

Railroads and Trains

Pattern

[Name of railroad or train]
    xx **Railroads — [Country or larger area]**

Examples

Chicago Great Western Railroad
    xx **Railroads — United States**

Midland Railway
    xx **Railroads — Great Britain**

Orient Express (Express train)
    xx **Railroads — Europe — Express-trains**

Royal Houses

Pattern

[Name], House of
- *x* [Alternate name(s)]
- *xx* **[Country of origin or Country most closely identified with royal house] — Kings and rulers**

Examples

Anjou, House of
- *x* Angevins
  Angio, House of
  House of Angio
  House of Anjou
- *xx* **France — Kings and rulers**

Saxe-Coburg-Gotha, House of
- *x* Coburg, House of
  House of Coburg
  House of Saxe-Coburg-Gotha
- *xx* **Germany — Kings and rulers**

Habsburg, House of
- *x* Austria, House of
  Hapsburg, House of
  House of Austria
  House of Habsburg
  House of Hapsburg
- *xx* **Austria — Kings and rulers**

Streets and Roads

Pattern

[Name of street or road] ([Geographic qualifier])
- *x* [Alternate name(s)] ([Geographic qualifier])
- *xx* **Streets [or Roads or more specific heading] — [Place]**

Examples

Cumberland Road
- *x* Great National Pike
  National Road (Cumberland Road)
  Old National Road
  Old Pike
- *xx* **Roads — United States**
  United States Highway 40

United States Highway 40
   x Highway 40 (U.S.)
      Route 40 (U.S.)
      U.S. 40
      U.S. Highway 40
      United States Route 40
   xx **Roads — United States**

Yonge Street (Toronto, Ont.)
   xx **Express highways — Ontario**
       Streets — Ontario

Crêt-Vaillant (Locle, Switzerland)
   x Rue du crêt-Vaillant (Locle, Switzerland)
   xx **Streets — Switzerland**

Interstate 77
   xx **Express highways — United States**

Trials

Pattern

[Name] Trial, [City], [Date(s)]
   x [Alternate name] Trial, [City], [Date(s)]
   xx **Trials ([Topic]) or [War crime trials] — [Place]**

Examples

Black Panthers Trial, New York, N.Y., 1970-1971
   x Bomb Conspiracy Trial, New York, N.Y., 1970-1971
      New York 21 Trial, 1970-1971
      New York City Bomb Conspiracy Trial, 1970-1971
   xx **Trials (Conspiracy) — New York (N.Y.)**

Red Brigades Trial, Turin, Italy, 1978
   x Brigate rosse Trial, Turin, Italy, 1978
      Processo Brigate rosse, Turin, Italy, 1978
   xx **Trials (Political crimes and offenses) — Italy**
       Trials (Terrorism) — Italy

Tokyo Trial, 1946-1948
   x Tokyo War Crimes Trial, 1946-1948
   xx **War crime trials — Japan**

Works about Individual Works of Art
by Known Artists

Pattern

[Name of artist]. [English title of work]
    x [English title] ([Type of art])
    x [Vernacular title] ([Type of art])
   xx [Name of person depicted] — Art [or — Portraits, etc. or
      — Portraits, caricatures, etc.]

Examples

Renoir, Auguste, 1841-1919.   Luncheon of the boating party
    x Déjeuner des canotiers (Painting)
       Luncheon of the boating party (Painting)

Francesca, Piero della, 1416?-1492.   Baptism
    x Baptism (Painting)
       Battésimo (Painting)
   xx Jesus Christ — Baptism — Art

Works about Individual Works of Art
by Unknown Artists

Pattern

[Vernacular title of work] ([Type of art])
    x [Variant(s) of vernacular title] ([Type of art])
   xx [Form of art], [Nationality]

Example

Levensbron (Painting)
    x De levensbron (Painting)
       Fountain of living water (Painting)
   xx Painting, Flemish

APPENDIX I:
AUTHORITIES USED IN
ESTABLISHING HEADINGS

Biological Names*

(1) The authorities followed by the Smithsonian Institution's taxonomists.

(2) Work cataloged, when published by a renowned research institute. Use caution with foreign classifications which may conflict with American practice.

(3) Taxonomic lists issued by American societies or government agencies, such as the American Entomological Society, United States Department of Agriculture, Environmental Protection Agency, etc.

(4) General thesauri and classifications such as the McGraw-Hill *Synopsis*, FAO lists, Wilson's *Biological & Agricultural Index*.

(5) Webster's 3rd unabridged dictionary and other general reference books, textbooks, and field guides.

Family Names**

(1) *New Dictionary of American Family Names*

(2) United States, Census Bureau, *A Century of Population Growth*. Tables.

(3) Work being cataloged.

(4) *Suburban Maryland Telephone Directory for the Washington Metropolitan Area* (for determining the most common form of a name).

---

*Library of Congress, Subject Cataloging Division, *Subject Cataloging Manual: Subject Headings*, prelim. ed. (Washington, D.C.: Library of Congress, 1984), H1332 (rev. 12/01/84).
**Ibid., H1597 (rev. 8/02/85).

Geographic Names*

(1) U.S. Board on Geographic Names (Library of Congress inquires by mail or telephone (for CIP (Cataloging-in-Publication) Information)).
(2) *Columbia Lippincott Gazetteer of the World* (1962) (for variant forms of names)
(3) *Webster's New Geographical Dictionary* (1980) (for variant forms of names)
(4) *Rand McNally Commercial Atlas and Marketing Guide* (latest edition)
(5) *Encyclopaedia Britannica* (latest edition)
(6) *Encyclopedia Americana* (latest edition)
(7) Guidebooks and atlases for the specific region
(8) Work being cataloged

*Material distributed at Regional Institutes on Library of Congress Subject Headings, sponsored by ALA Resources and Technical Services Division, Library of Congress, and ALA/RTSD Council of Regional Groups, 1982-1984.

APPENDIX J:
FIRST-ORDER POLITICAL DIVISIONS
OF THE EXCEPTIONAL COUNTRIES*

First-order division	*Form in qualifier*
AUSTRALIA	
Australian Capital Territory	**(A.C.T.)**
New South Wales	**(N.S.W.)**
Northern Territory	**(N.T.)**
Queensland	**(Qld.)**
South Australia	**(S. Aust.)**
Tasmania	**(Tas.)**
Victoria	**(Vic.)**
Western Australia	**(W.A.)**
CANADA	
Alberta	**(Alta.)**
British Columbia	**(B.C.)**
Manitoba	**(Man.)**
New Brunswick	**(N.B.)**
Newfoundland	**(Nfld.)**
Northwest Territories	**(N.W.T.)**
Nova Scotia	**(N.S.)**
Ontario	**(Ont.)**
Prince Edward Island	**(P.E.I.)**
Québec (Province)	**(Québec)**
Saskatchewan	**(Sask.)**
Yukon Territory	**(Yukon)**

*Library of Congress, Subject Cataloging Division, *Subject Cataloging Manual: Subject Headings*, prelim. ed. (Washington, D.C.: 1984), H810 (rev. 2/05/85), H1334 (rev. 3/01/85).

First-order division	*Form in qualifier*

GREAT BRITAIN
[as qualifiers for headings for natural features]

First-order division	Form in qualifier
England	**(England)**
Northern Ireland	**(Northern Ireland)**
Scotland	**(Scotland)**
Wales	**(Wales)**

[as qualifiers for jurisdictional headings and headings for buildings, structures, etc.]

England

First-order division	Form in qualifier
Avon	**(Avon)**
Bedfordshire	**(Bedfordshire)**
Berkshire	**(Berkshire)**
Buckinghamshire	**(Buckinghamshire)**
Cambridgeshire	**(Cambridgeshire)**
Cheshire	**(Cheshire)**
Cleveland	**(Cleveland)**
Cornwall	**(Cornwall)**
Cumbria	**(Cumbria)**
Derbyshire	**(Derbyshire)**
Devon	**(Devon)**
Dorset	**(Dorset)**
Durham (County)	**(Durham)**
East Sussex	**(East Sussex)**
Essex	**(Essex)**
Gloucestershire	**(Gloucestershire)**
Greater Manchester	**(Greater Manchester)**
Hampshire	**(Hampshire)**
Hereford and Worcester	**(Hereford and Worcester)**
Hertfordshire	**(Hertfordshire)**
Humberside	**(Humberside)**
Isle of Wight	**(Isle of Wight)**
Kent	**(Kent)**
Lancashire	**(Lancashire)**
Leicestershire	**(Leicestershire)**
Lincolnshire	**(Lincolnshire)**
Merseyside	**(Merseyside)**
Norfolk	**(Norfolk)**
North Yorkshire	**(North Yorkshire)**
Northamptonshire	**(Northamptonshire)**
Northumberland	**(Northumberland)**
Nottinghamshire	**(Nottinghamshire)**
Oxfordshire	**(Oxfordshire)**
Salop	**(Salop)**
Somerset	**(Somerset)**
South Yorkshire	**(South Yorkshire)**
Staffordshire	**(Staffordshire)**
Suffolk	**(Suffolk)**

First-order division	Form in qualifier

England *(continued)*

Surrey	(Surrey)
Tyne and Wear	(Tyne and Wear)
Warwickshire	(Warwickshire)
West Midlands (England)	(West Midlands, England)
West Sussex	(West Sussex)
West Yorkshire	(West Yorkshire)
Wiltshire	(Wiltshire)

Ireland

Carlow	(Carlow)
Cavan (County)	(Cavan)
Clare	(Clare)
Cork (County)	(Cork)
Donegal (County)	(Donegal)
Dublin (County)	(Dublin)
Galway (County)	(Galway)
Kerry	(Kerry)
Kildare (County)	(Kildare)
Kilkenny (County)	(Kilkenny)
Laois	(Laois)
Leitrim	(Leitrim)
Limerick (County)	(Limerick)
Longford	(Longford)
Louth	(Louth)
Mayo	(Mayo)
Meath	(Meath)
Monaghan	(Monaghan)
Offaly	(Offaly)
Roscommon (County)	(Roscommon)
Sligo (County)	(Sligo)
Tipperary (County)	(Tipperary)
Waterford (County)	(Waterford)
Westmeath	(Westmeath)
Wexford (County)	(Wexford)
Wicklow (County)	(Wicklow)

Scotland

Borders Region (Scotland)	(Borders Region, Scotland)
Central Region (Scotland)	(Central Region, Scotland)
Dumfries and Galloway	(Dumfries and Galloway)
Fife	(Fife)
Grampian	(Grampian)
Highland Region (Scotland)	(Highland Region, Scotland)
Lothian	(Lothian)
Orkney	(Orkney)
Shetland	(Shetland)
Strathclyde	(Strathclyde)
Tayside	(Tayside)
Western Isles (Scotland)	(Western Isles, Scotland)

First-order division	*Form in qualifier*
Wales	
Clwyd	**(Clwyd)**
Dyfed	**(Dyfed)**
Gwent	**(Gwent)**
Gwynedd	**(Gwynedd)**
Mid Glamorgan	**(Mid Glamorgan)**
Powys	**(Powys)**
South Glamorgan	**(South Glamorgan)**
West Glamorgan	**(West Glamorgan)**
MALAYSIA	
Johor	**(Johor)**
Kedah	**(Kedah)**
Kelantan	**(Kelantan)**
Kuala Lumpur (Malaysia)	**(Kuala Lumpur, Malaysia)**
Malacca (State)	**(Malacca)**
Negeri Sembilan	**(Negeri Sembilan)**
Pahang	**(Pahang)**
Pinang	**(Pinang)**
Perak	**(Perak)**
Perlis	**(Perlis)**
Sabah	**(Sabah)**
Sarawak	**(Sarawak)**
Selangor	**(Selangor)**
Terengganu	**(Terengganu)**
SOVIET UNION	
Armenian S.S.R.	**(Armenian S.S.R.)**
Azerbaijan S.S.R.	**(Azerbaijan S.S.R.)**
Byelorussian S.S.R.	**(Byelorussian S.S.R.)**
Estonia	**(Estonia)**
Georgian S.S.R.	**(Georgian S.S.R.)**
Kazakh S.S.R.	**(Kazakh S.S.R.)**
Kirghiz S.S.R.	**(Kirghiz S.S.R.)**
Latvia	**(Latvia)**
Lithuania	**(Lithuania)**
Moldavian S.S.R.	**(Moldavian S.S.R.)**
Russian S.F.S.R.	**(R.S.F.S.R.)**
Tajik S.S.R.	**(Tajik S.S.R.)**
Turkmen S.S.R.	**(Turkmen S.S.R.)**
Ukraine	**(Ukraine)**
Uzbek S.S.R.	**(Uzbek S.S.R.)**
UNITED STATES	
Alabama	**(Ala.)**
Alaska	**(Alaska)**
Arizona	**(Ariz.)**
Arkansas	**(Ark.)**
California	**(Calif.)**

First-order division	*Form in qualifier*
UNITED STATES *(continued)*	
Colorado	**(Colo.)**
Connecticut	**(Conn.)**
Delaware	**(Del.)**
Florida	**(Fla.)**
Georgia	**(Ga.)**
Hawaii	**(Hawaii)**
Idaho	**(Idaho)**
Illinois	**(Ill.)**
Indiana	**(Ind.)**
Iowa	**(Iowa)**
Kansas	**(Kan.)**
Kentucky	**(Ky.)**
Louisiana	**(La.)**
Maine	**(Me.)**
Maryland	**(Md.)**
Massachusetts	**(Mass.)**
Michigan	**(Mich.)**
Minnesota	**(Minn.)**
Mississippi	**(Miss.)**
Missouri	**(Mo.)**
Montana	**(Mont.)**
Nebraska	**(Neb.)**
Nevada	**(Nev.)**
New Hampshire	**(N.H.)**
New Jersey	**(N.J.)**
New Mexico	**(N.M.)**
New York (State)	**(N.Y.)**
North Carolina	**(N.C.)**
North Dakota	**(N.D.)**
Ohio	**(Ohio)**
Oklahoma	**(Okla.)**
Oregon	**(Or.)**
Pennsylvania	**(Pa.)**
Rhode Island	**(R.I.)**
South Carolina	**(S.C.)**
South Dakota	**(S.D.)**
Tennessee	**(Tenn.)**
Texas	**(Tex.)**
Utah	**(Utah)**
Vermont	**(Vt.)**
Virginia	**(Va.)**
Washington (State)	**(Wash.)**
West Virginia	**(W. Va.)**
Wisconsin	**(Wis.)**
Wyoming	**(Wyo.)**

First-order division	*Form in qualifier*
YUGOSLAVIA	
Bosnia and Hercegovina	**(Bosnia and Hercegovina)**
Croatia	**(Croatia)**
Macedonia (Republic)	**(Macedonia)**
Montenegro	**(Montenegro)**
Serbia	**(Serbia)**
Slovenia	**(Slovenia)**

OTHER JURDISDICTIONS THAT ARE ABBREVIATED WHEN USED AS QUALIFIERS

Jurisdiction	*Form in qualifier*
British Virgin Islands	**(V.I.)**
New Zealand	**(N.Z.)**
Puerto Rico	**(P.R.)**
United States	**(U.S.)**
Virgin Islands of the United States	**(V.I.)**

APPENDIX K:
MARC CODING FOR
SUBJECT INFORMATION*

FIXED FIELDS RELATED TO SUBJECT

At the Library of Congress, subject catalogers are responsible for supplying information required for the fixed fields in the MARC record relating to the following:

Field	*Data*
008/22	Intellectual level
	Juvenile literature
008/25-27	Nature-of-contents code
008/30	Festschrift indicator
008/33	Fiction indicator
008/34	Biography code
043	Geographic area code

MARC codes for these fields with description are reproduced in the following pages.

---

*Library of Congress, Automated Systems Office, *MARC Formats for Bibliographic Data* (Washington, D.C.: Library of Congress, 1980, update no. 10, 10/11/84).

008/22   INTELLECTUAL LEVEL CODE

ƀ	Unknown or not applicable
a	Preschool
b	Primary
c	Elementary and junior high
d	Secondary (senior high)
e	Adult
f	Specialized (for special audiences, i.e., doctors, librarians, etc.)
g	General
j	Juvenile

008/25-27   NATURE OF CONTENTS CODE

ƀ	No specified nature of contents
a	Abstracts/summaries (aside from its own)
i	Indexes (aside from its own)
o	Reviews
b	Bibliographies
c	Catalogs
r	Directories
y	Yearbooks
s	Statistics
l	Legislation
w	Law reports and digests
g	Legal articles
v	Legal cases and case notes
h	Biography
d	Dictionaries
e	Encyclopedias
p	Programmed texts
f	Handbooks
n	Surveys of the literature in the subject area

008/30   FESTSCHRIFT INDICATOR

0	Not a festschrift
1	Festschrift

008/33   FICTION INDICATOR

0	Not fiction
1	Fiction

008/34   BIOGRAPHY CODE

ƀ	No biographical material
a	Autobiography
b	Individual biography
c	Collective biography
d	Contains biographical information

043 GEOGRAPHIC AREA CODE

       INDICATORS

          ᔆ   Indicator 1 - Undefined

            ᔆ   Indicator 2 - Undefined

             SUBFIELDS

                ‡a   Geographic area code

EXAMPLES

    [043]   ᔆᔆ‡an-us---‡ae-fr---‡aa-ja---
                       NOTE: Topic related to the U.S., France, and Japan.

    [043]   ᔆᔆ‡anl-----
    [651]   60‡aGreat Lakes region.
                       NOTE: Topic related to the Great Lakes region.

    [043]   ᔆᔆ‡afw-----
    [651]   60‡aAfrica, West‡xJuvenile films.
                       NOTE: Topic related to West Africa.

    [043]   ᔆᔆ‡aa-np---
    [650]   60‡aBuddha and Buddhism‡zNepal.
                       NOTE: Topic related to Nepal.

    [043]   ᔆᔆ‡ae--gx--
    [650]   60‡aMusic, Popular (Songs, etc.)‡zGermany.
                       NOTE: Topic related to Germany.

    [043]   ᔆᔆ‡an-us-md
    [650]   60‡aSlavery in the United States‡zMaryland.
                       NOTE: Topic related to Maryland.

    [043]   ᔆᔆ‡an-uso-‡an-usm--
                       NOTE: Collection of steamboat records relating to
                               steamboats operating in the Ohio and Mississippi
                               Valleys.

SUBJECT HEADING FIELDS

The following fields in the MARC record are used for Library of Congress subject headings:

    600   Subject-added entry — Personal name
    610   Subject-added entry — Corporate name
    611   Subject-added entry — Conference or meeting
    630   Subject-added entry — Uniform title heading
    650   Subject-added entry — Topical heading
    651   Subject-added entry — Geographic name

MARC codes for these fields with description are reproduced in the following pages.

```
600   SUBJECT ADDED ENTRY - PERSONAL NAME
         INDICATORS

                                  Indicator 1 - Type of personal name
         0                             Forename only
         1                             Single surname
         2                             Multiple surname
         3                             Name of family

                                  Indicator 2 - Subject heading list or authority
                                      file
         0                             LCSH/LC authority files
         1                             Children's subject heading (LC Annotated Card
                                          Program)
         2                             NLM authority files
         3                             NAL subject authority file
         4                             Source not specified
         5                             Canadian subject headings/NLC authority file
                                          English headings, except those to be
                                          considered LC
         6                             Repertoire ces vedettes-matiere/NLC authority
                                          file French headings
         7                             Source specified in subfield ‡2

            SUBFIELDS

               ‡a                      Name (surnames and forenames)
               ‡b                      Numeration (roman numeral or roman numeral
                                          and name used with the entry element of a
                                          forename heading)
               ‡c                      Titles and other words associated with the
                                          name
               ‡d                      Dates (of birth, death, or flourishing)
               ‡e                      Relator
               ‡f                      Date (of a work)
               ‡g                      Miscellaneous information
               ‡h                      Medium
               ‡k                      Form subheading
               ‡l                      Language
               ‡m                      Medium of performance (for music)
               ‡n                      Number of part/section (for music, this may
                                          be the serial, opus or thematic number or
                                          date used as a number)
               ‡o                      Arranged statement (for music)

               ‡p                      Name of part/section (of a work)
               ‡q                      Qualification of name (fuller form)
               ‡r                      Key (for music)
               ‡s                      Version
               ‡t                      Title (of a work)
               ‡u                      Affiliation
               ‡x                      General subdivision
               ‡y                      Chronological subdivision
               ‡z                      Geographic subdivision
               ‡2                      Source of heading or term
               ‡3                      Materials specified
               ‡4                      Relator code
```

EXAMPLES

[600]   10‡aShakespeare,
William,‡d1564-1616.‡thamlet.

[600]   00‡aElijah,‡cthe prophet.

[600]   10‡aBach, Johann
Sebastian,‡d1685-1750.‡tSuites,
‡mvioloncello,‡n8WV 1009,‡rC major.

[600]   10‡aShakespeare, William,‡d1564-1616,‡kin
fiction, drama, poetry, etc.

EXAMPLES (Continued)

[600]   10‡aShelley, Percy
             Bysshe,‡d1792-1822.‡tPrometheus misbound.

[600]   30‡aMcAllister family.

[600]   10‡aNixon, Richard M.‡q(Richard
             Milhous),‡d1913- ‡xPersonality.

[600]   00‡aJesus Christ‡xHistory of doctrines‡yEarly
             Church, ca. 30-600.

[600]   17‡aJones, Charles
             Francis,‡d1878-1935.‡2[Source code for
             WHO WAS WHO IN AMERICA]
                 NOTE: Subject added entry for an original or historical
                        graphic item.

[600]   14‡aBullard, Robert
             Lee,‡d1861-1947.‡tFighting generals.

[600]   10‡aKennedy, John F.‡q(John
             Fitzgerald),‡d1917-1963‡xAssassination.
                 NOTE: The previous two examples illustrate usage for a
                        manuscript collection and for a single modern
                        manuscript cataloged in accordance with
                        contemporary manuscripts practice.

[600]   00‡aAlexander,‡cthe Great,‡d356-323 B.C.
                 NOTE: A rare or literary manuscript cataloged following
                        AACR2.

[600]   14‡aFranklin, Gerald,‡cpersonnel
             manager,‡uCole
             Manufacturing,‡kmemoranda‡xRacial
             discrimination‡zUnited States

[600]   14‡aRandolph, Henry,‡cgrocer of Mercersville,
             NJ,‡ecorrespondent‡xMigrant labor‡y
             1920's
                 NOTE: The previous two examples illustrate usage for an
                        archival record unit described according to
                        archival practice and a records accession
                        controlled according to records management
                        practice.

[600]   10‡aPushkin, Aleksandr
             Sergeevich,‡d1799-1837‡(Museums, relics,
             etc.‡zRussian S.F.S.R.‡zMoscow‡xMaps.

```
610   SUBJECT ADDED ENTRY - CORPORATE NAME
      INDICATORS
                            Indicator 1 - Type of corporate name
              0             Surname (inverted)
              1             Place or place and name
              2             Name (direct order)

                            Indicator 2 - Subject heading list or authority
                              file
              0             LCSH/LC authority files
              1             Children's subject heading (LC Annotated Card
                              Program)
              2             NLM authority files
              3             NAL subject authority file
              4             Source not specified
              5             Canadian subject headings/NLC authority file
                              English headings, except those to be
                              considered LC
              6             Repertoire des vedettes-matiere/NLC authority
                              file French headings
              7             Source specified in subfield ‡2

          SUBFIELDS
              ‡a            Name
              ‡b            Each subordinate unit in hierarchy
              ‡c            Place (including a name of an institution
                              where conference held)
              ‡d            Date (of conference or meeting/of treaty
                              signing)
              ‡e            Relator
              ‡f            Date (of a work)
              ‡g            Miscellaneous information
              ‡h            Medium
              ‡k            Form subheading
              ‡l            Language
              ‡m            Medium of performance (for music)
              ‡n            Number of part/section/conference (for
                              music, this may be the serial, opus or
                              thematic number or date used as a number)
              ‡o            Arranged statement (for music)
              ‡p            Name of part/section (of a work)
              ‡r            Key (for music)
              ‡s            Version
              ‡t            Title (of a work)
              ‡u            Affiliation
              ‡x            General subdivision
              ‡y            Chronological subdivision
              ‡z            Geographic subdivision
              ‡2            Source of heading or term
              ‡3            Materials specified
              ‡4            Relator code

      EXAMPLES
        [610]       10‡aUnited States.‡bConstitutional
                      Convention‡d(1787)
        [610]       10‡aBaltimore (Ecclesiastical Province)
        [610]       10‡aLisbon (Archdiocese)
        [610]       10‡aAlexandria, Egypt (Patriarchate, Coptic)
        [610]       20‡aUnited Nations‡zAfrica.
        [610]       20‡aChouinard Art Institute.
        [610]       10‡aUnited States.‡bArmy‡xHistory‡yCivil War,
                      1861-1865.
        [610]       10‡aUnited States.‡bCongress.‡bSenate.
```

EXAMPLES (Continued)

[610]   10†aUnited States.†tConstitution.†n1st-10th
            amendments.

[610]   10†aFrance.†tBulletin officiel du registre du
            commerce et du registre des metiers.

[610]   20†aSt. John's Church (Georgetown,
            Washington, D.C.)

[610]   20†aArk Royal (Ship)

[610]   20†aHVJ (Radio station : Vatican City)

[610]   20†aOrthodox Eastern Church.

[610]   20†aYale University†xFaculty.
            NOTE: The previous two examples illustrate usage for a
                   manuscript collection and a single manuscript
                   cataloged in accordance with contemporary
                   manuscripts practice or a rare or literary
                   manuscript cataloged following AACR2.

[610]   24†aBrown University.†bOffice of the
            President.†1French†xForeign
            administrative exchange policy

[610]   10†aAugusta (Ga.).†bBoard of Health
            NOTE: The previous two examples illustrate usage for an
                   archival record unit described according to
                   archival practice and a records accession
                   controlled according to records management
                   practice.

---

611 SUBJECT ADDED ENTRY - CONFERENCE OR MEETING

      INDICATORS

                         Indicator 1 - Type of conference or meeting name
            0   Surname (inverted)
            1   Place or place and name
            2   Name (direct order)

                         Indicator 2 - Subject heading list or authority
                             file
            0   LCSH/LC authority files
            1   Children's subject heading (LC Annotated Card
                             Program)
            2   NLM authority files
            3   NAL subject authority file
            4   Source not specified
            5   Canadian subject heading/NLC authority file
                             English headings, except those to be
                             considered LC
            6   Repertoire des vedettes-matiere/NLC authority
                             file French headings
            7   Source specified in subfield †2

          SUBFIELDS

            †a   Name of meeting or place element
            †b   Number (of conference or meeting) [OBSOLETE]
            †c   Place (including a name of an institution
                             where conference held)
            †d   Date (of conference or meeting)
            †e   Subordinate unit in name
            †f   Date (of a work)
            †g   Miscellaneous information
            †h   Medium
            †k   Form subheading
            †l   Language

‡n   Number of part/section/conference (for music, this may be the serial, opus or thematic number or date used as a number)
‡p   Name of part/section (of a work)
‡q   Name of meeting following place element
‡s   Version
‡t   Title (of a work)
‡u   Affiliation

‡x   General subdivision
‡y   Chronological subdivision
‡z   Geographic subdivision
‡2   Source of heading or term
‡3   Materials specified
‡4   Relator code

EXAMPLES

[611]   20‡aNobel Conference‡n(1st :‡d1965 :‡cGustavus Adolphus College)

[611]   20‡aSymposium on Physical Activity and the Heart‡d(1964 :‡cHelsinki, Finland).‡tProceedings.

[611]   20‡aCanadian Open Golf Championship Tournament‡d(1968 :‡cToronto, Ont.)

[611]   20‡aConference on Technical Information Center Administration ‡n(3rd :‡d1966 :‡cPhiladelphia, Pa.)

[611]   20‡aSymposium on Glaucoma‡d(1966 :‡cNew Orleans, La.)

---

630   SUBJECT ADDED ENTRY - UNIFORM TITLE HEADING

     INDICATORS

                 Indicator 1 - Nonfiling characters
   b   Nonfiling characters not specified [OBSOLETE]
   0-9   Number of nonfiling characters

                 Indicator 2 - Subject heading list or authority file
   0   LCSH/LC authority files
   1   Children's subject heading (LC Annotated Card Program)
   2   NLM authority files
   3   NAL subject authority file
   4   Source not specified
   5   Canadian subject headings/NLC authority file English headings, except those to be considered LC
   6   Repertoire des vedettes-matiere/NLC authority file French headings
   7   Source specified in subfield ‡2

     SUBFIELDS

       ‡a   Uniform title heading
       ‡d   Date (of treaty signing)
       ‡f   Date (of a work)
       ‡g   Miscellaneous information
       ‡h   Medium
       ‡k   Form subheading
       ‡l   Language
       ‡m   Medium of performance (for music)

‡n	Number of part/section (for music, this may be the serial, opus or thematic number or date used as a number)
‡o	Arranged statement (for music)
‡p	Name of part/section (of a work)
‡r	Key (for music)
‡s	Version
‡t	Title (of a work)
‡x	General subdivision
‡y	Chronological subdivision
‡z	Geographic subdivision
‡2	Source of heading or term

EXAMPLES

[630]	00‡aDead Sea scrolls.
[630]	00‡aBible.‡pO.T.‡pJudges V.
[630]	45‡aThe Studio magazine.‡pContemporary paintings‡xPeriodicals.
[630]	00‡aBible.‡lEnglish‡xVersions.
[630]	00‡aUniversal Copyright Convention‡d(1952)
[630]	00‡aUkrainian weekly‡xIndexes‡xPeriodicals.
[630]	00‡aBulletin (Canadian Association of Medical Record Librarians : 1944)
[630]	00‡aRural Japan today.‡h[Filmstrip]
[630]	00‡aBible.‡pN.T.‡pRomans‡xGeography‡xMaps.

---

650   SUBJECT ADDED ENTRY - TOPICAL HEADING

INDICATORS

Indicator 1 - Specifies level of the subject term

♭	No information provided
0	No level specified
1	Primary term
2	Secondary term

Indicator 2 - Subject heading list or authority file

0	LCSH
1	Children's subject heading (LC Annotated Card Program)
2	MeSH
3	NAL subject authority file
4	Source not specified
5	Canadian subject headings
6	Repertoire des vedettes-matiere
7	Source specified in subfield ‡2

SUBFIELDS

‡a	Topical heading or place element
‡b	Name following place entry element [OBSOLETE]
‡c	Place
‡d	Active dates
‡e	Relator
‡x	General subdivision
‡y	Chronological subdivision
‡z	Geographic subdivision
‡2	Source of heading or term
‡3	Materials specified

EXAMPLES

[650]   ꜩ0ꜩaArtꜩxExhibitions.

[650]   ꜩ0ꜩaAstronauts.

[650]   ꜩ0ꜩaWorld War, 1939-1945ꜩxCampaignsꜩzTunisia.

[650]   ꜩ0ꜩaAmish.

[650]   ꜩ2ꜩaKidneyꜩxtransplantation.

[650]   ꜩ3ꜩaKalmyk cattle

[650]   17ꜩaCareer Exploration.ꜩ2ericd
[650]   17ꜩaCooks.ꜩ2ericd
[650]   27ꜩaFood Service Occupations.ꜩ2ericd
[650]   27ꜩaJunior High Schools.ꜩ2ericd
[650]   27ꜩaSimulation.ꜩ2ericd
                 NOTE: Primary and secondary subject content identifi

[650]   ꜩ7ꜩastress-relaxation.ꜩ2test
                 NOTE: No subject content level specified.

[650]   17ꜩaacoustic measurement.ꜩ2test

[650]   ꜩ0ꜩaSchool librariesꜩxJuvenile films.

[650]   ꜩ0ꜩaReal propertyꜩzMississippiꜩzTippah
             Co.ꜩxMaps.

[650]   ꜩ0ꜩaJews in WarsawꜩxMaps.

[650]   ꜩ0ꜩaBallads, AmericanꜩzHudson River Valley
             (N.Y. and N.J.)

[650]   ꜩ0ꜩaNational songs (Instrumental settings)

[650]   ꜩ0ꜩaMoving-picture musicꜩxExcerpts.

---

651 SUBJECT ADDED ENTRY - GEOGRAPHIC NAME

INDICATORS

ꜩ   Indicator 1 - Undefined

                Indicator 2 - Subject heading list or authority
                                   file
0   LCSH/LC authority files
1   Children's subject heading (LC Annotated Card
                      Program)
2   NLM authority files
3   NAL subject authority file
4   Source not specified
5   Canadian subject headings/NLC authority file
                      English headings, except those to be
                      considered LC
6   Repertoire des vedettes-matiere/NLC authority
                      file French headings
7   Source specified in subfield ꜩ2

      SUBFIELDS

      ꜩa   Geographic name or place element
      ꜩb   Geographic name following place entry
                         element [OBSOLETE]
      ꜩx   General subdivision
      ꜩy   Chronological subdivision
      ꜩz   Geographic subdivision
      ꜩ2   Source of heading or term
      ꜩ3   Materials specified

EXAMPLES

[651]   &0‡aKenwood (Chicago, Ill.)

[651]   &0‡aChelsea (London, England)

[651]   &0‡aLouisiana‡xPolitics and
         government‡xAnecdotes, facetiae, satire,
         etc.

[651]   &0‡aUnited States‡xHistory‡y1849-1877.

[651]   &0‡aSiena (Italy)

[651]   &0‡aCanada.
[651]   &0‡aCanada‡xBibliography.
[610]   10‡aCanada.‡bDept. of Agriculture‡xOfficials
         and employees.

[651]   &0‡aClear Lake (Iowa : Lake)

[651]   &0‡aNew York (N.Y.)

[651]   &4‡3Psychiatric admission
         records‡aPennsylvania‡bThree Mile
         Island‡xNuclear reactor
         safety‡y1975-1985‡zUnited States.

[651]   &0‡aTippah County (Miss.)‡xMaps.

APPENDIX L: ABBREVIATIONS*

Abbreviations that are part of name headings established according to descriptive cataloging rules are retained when these headings are used as subject entries. Relatively few abbreviations are used in forming subject headings. Following is a summary of Library of Congress policies relating to the use of abbreviations in subject headings.

Acronyms, Initialisms, Etc.

Acronyms and initials are used in subject headings when the concepts are known primarily in an abbreviated form, e.g., **DDT (Insecticide); MARC System; T-shirts.**

Ampersands

Ampersands are used only in corporate name headings and certain railroad headings:

Black & Decker Manufacturing Company (Towson, Md.)
C.S. Wertsner & Son
Dow, Jones & Co.
Chicago, Burlington & Quincy Railroad Company
Chicago, Burlington & Quincy Railroad

---

*Library of Congress, Subject Cataloging Division, *Subject Cataloging Manual: Subject Headings*, prelim. ed. (Washington, D.C.: Library of Congress, 1984), H36.

Dates

Anno Domini; Before Christ

The abbreviations A.D. and B.C. are used only after a specific year or span of years. A.D. is used only when the dates in question span both B.C. and A.D. The abbreviation B.C. is added to all dates before Christ. Examples include:

Egypt — History — 332-30 B.C.
China — History — Han Dynasty, 202 B.C.-220 A.D.

Circa

The abbreviation ca. is used in period subdivisions. It precedes the date or dates:

Church history — Primitive and early church, ca. 30-600
Hoysala dynasty, ca. 1006-ca. 1346
United States — History — Colonial period, ca. 1600-1775

Doctor; Doctor of [...]

The abbreviation Dr. or M.D. is used in headings containing personal names:

Dr. William's Library — Catalogs
Francis, John, Dr. — Art collections
Hartmann, Peter, Dr. jur. — Poster collections
Villeneuve, André, M.D. — Addresses, essays, lectures

Et cetera

The abbreviation etc. is used in subject headings and subdivisions:

Law reports, digests, etc. — United States
Surveying — Handbooks, manuals, etc.
Subject cataloging — Anecdotes, facetiae, satire, etc.

Geographic Qualifiers

Many geographic names are abbreviated when used as geographic qualifiers. A list of qualifiers that are abbreviated appears in appendix J. Examples include:

West (U.S.)
Harpers Ferry (W. Va.)
Harry S. Truman Dam (Mo.)
Kremlin (Moscow, R.S.F.S.R.)
Red River (Tex.-La.)

Mister; Mistress

The abbreviations Mr.; Mrs. are used in headings containing personal names, e.g., **Mr. A's Boy's Ranch — History; Mr. Lucky.   Trick dog training; Downing, Clyde, Mrs. — Art collections — Catalogs.**

Numerals

Cardinal numerals

Cardinal numerals are expressed or replaced by arabic or roman numerals only when reference sources indicate that the numeral in a specific phrase is not normally spelled out, e.g., **35mm cameras; 4-H clubs; TRS-80 Model III (Computer).**

Ordinal numerals

Ordinal numerals are abbreviated when they are not in the initial position in a heading or when reference sources indicate that the numeral in a specific phrase is not normally spelled out. Ordinal numerals are abbreviated in the form 1st, 2nd, 3rd, 4th, etc.:

20th Century Limited (Express-train)
Dacian War, 1st, 101-102
Dacian War, 2nd, 105-106
Church history — 3rd century
United States — Social life and customs — 20th century

Compare, however:

First of June, 1794, Battle of
Second grade (Education)

Saint (Including Foreign Equivalents)

The word *saint* or its foreign equivalents is abbreviated in the form of St. or St only in headings established as such according to descriptive cataloging rules:

Federal Reserve Bank of St. Louis
St. Louis post-dispatch
Eglise de St-Joachim (Saint-Joachim, Québec)

Saint Louis Museum of Fine Arts
Saint Lawrence River
Bellini, Giovanni, d. 1516.   Saint Francis in ecstasy

APPENDIX M: CAPITALIZATION*

General Policies

Initial letters of proper nouns and adjectives

The initial letter of a proper noun or adjective (except in scientific names of plants and animals; see discussion on p. 479) is always capitalized, regardless of its position in the heading, subdivision, or reference:

!Kung (African people)
*Naborr (Horse)
97 Sen (Fighter planes)
Tariff on X-ray equipment and supplies

Gosannen kassen ekotoba (Scrolls)
    x Hachiman Tarō ekotoba (Scrolls)

Jesus Christ—Attitude towards the Old Testament

Initial words

The initial letter of the first word of a subject heading, a subdivision, or a reference is always capitalized, except when reference sources indicate that it should be in lowercase:

Adolescent boys
    x Teen-age boys

*Library of Congress, Subject Cataloging Division, *Subject Cataloging Manual: Subject Headings*, prelim. ed. (Washington, D.C.: Library of Congress, 1984), H32.

Writing — Materials and instruments — Addresses, essays, lectures

Serbo-Croatian language — To 1500

Beauce (France)
    x La Beauce (France)

Cévennes Mountains (France)
    x Les Cévennes (France)

p-adic numbers

p-divisible groups

35mm cameras
    x   35 mm cameras

3-dimensional manifolds (Topology)
    See **Three-manifolds (Topology)**

Inverted headings, subdivisions, and references

In an inverted heading, subdivision, or reference, the word that would have been in the initial position if the heading, reference, or subdivision had been established in the natural word order is capitalized. Such words are preceded by a comma. Examples include:

Assumption of the Blessed Virgin Mary, Feast of the

Cities and towns, Ruined, extinct, etc.

Medicine, Magic, mystic, and spagiric

Merkem (Belgium), Battle of, 1918

Measuring instruments
    x Instruments, Measuring

United States — History, Naval

Parenthetical qualifiers

The initial letter of the first word in a parenthetical qualifier is always capitalized. In addition, proper nouns and adjectives and the first word following a colon within the qualifier are capitalized. Examples include:

Catholic Church — Relations (Canon law)
Chambri (Papua New Guinea people)
Drill (Agricultural implement)
Citizenship as point of contact (Conflict of laws)

Wu (The Chinese word)
Auschwitz (Poland : Concentration camp)
Thebes (Egypt : Ancient city)

Previously established headings with the first word in the qualifier in lowercase will continue to be used:

Brothers (in religious orders, congregations, etc.)
Corruption (in politics)
Hunting (in numismatics)
Survival (after airplane accidents, shipwrecks, etc.)
Shooters (of arms)
Drill (not military)
Catholic Church — Relations (diplomatic)

Hyphenated compounds

The second part of a compound is capitalized if it is a proper noun or adjective; otherwise, it is in lowercase, e.g., **Ecuador-Peru Conflict, 1981**; **Sabazius (Thraco-Phrygian deity); Twelve-tone system; Twenty-first century.**

Name Headings

Name headings established by descriptive catalogers at the Library of Congress are capitalized in accordance with *Anglo-American Cataloguing Rules*, second edition (*AACR2*) and Library of Congress policies. The following guidelines pertain to name headings established by the Subject Cataloging Division.

Family names

The proper name (or names) in a family name heading is capitalized, e.g., **Miller family; Wang family; Pasek Kayu Sêlêm family**. If the family name includes an initial particle such as De, Du, La, L', Von, Van, etc., the particle is also capitalized:

Baden family
   x Von Baden family

De Groot family
   x De Groote family

Named dynasties

The word *dynasty* is not capitalized, e.g., **Achaemenid dynasty, 559-330 B.C.**

Named systems, computer programs, projects, etc.

Any letter within a heading for a named system, computer program, project, etc., that appears as such in reference sources is capitalized:

4-H clubs	**Pac-Man (Game)**
Agent Orange	**RuneQuest (Game)**
DC-to-DC converters	**SdKfz 251 (Half-track)**
DDT (Insecticide)	**TA-2M (Computer program)**
IJssel Lake (Netherlands)	**WordStar (Computer program)**
MARC System	

Named events

All words except conjunctions, prepositions, and internal articles *a, an,* and *the* and their foreign equivalents in headings or references for named events are capitalized:

Abscam Bribery Scandal, 1980-

General Strike, Sri Lanka, 1953

Harpers Ferry (W. Va.) — John Brown's Raid, 1859
    x John Brown's Raid, Harpers Ferry, W. Va., 1859

Coal Strike, Colorado, 1913-1914

Transylvania (Romania) — History — Peasant Uprising, 1784
    xx **Peasant uprisings — Romania**

China — History — Ch'ing Dynasty Restoration Attempt, 1917
    x Ch'ing Dynasty Restoration Attempt, China, 1917

Certain types of named events, however, conventionally have never been established in accordance with the policy stated above. These exceptional patterns will continue to be followed when new instances of them are established. No new exceptions will be initiated. The exceptional patterns are as follows:

- — [...] colony, [Date]
- — [...] conquest, [Date]
- — Coup d'état, [Date]
- — [...] domination, [Date]
- — [...] dynasties, [Date]
- — [...] dynasty, [Date]
- — [...] intervention, [Date]
- — [...] invasion, [Date]
- — [...] invasions, [Date]
- — [...] movement, [Date]
- — [...] occupation, [Date]

—[...] period, [Date]
—[...] periods, [Date]
—[...] rule, [Date]

Examples include:

Painting, Chinese — Three kingdoms, six dynasties — Sui
dynasty, 220-618
Japan — History — Attempted Mongol invasions, 1274-1281
India — History — British occupation, 1765-1947
United States — History — Colonial period, ca. 1600-1775

Cultural and geological periods

Only the initial words in headings for cultural and geological periods are capitalized, e.g., **Bronze age; Iron age; Mesolithic period; Paleolithic period, Lower; Stone age.**

Named movements

Named movements are not considered proper names. Examples include:

Anti-Nazi movement
China — History — Reform movement, 1898
Ecumenical movement
Gay liberation movement
Pro-life movement
Stakhanov movement
Symbolism (Literary movement)

Named schools

For headings or subdivisions for named schools that refer to a group (as of painters, economists, architects) under a common local or personal influence that produces a general similarity in their work, only the initial letter in the first word and any proper name or adjective are capitalized, e.g., **Chicago school of theology; Classical school of economics; Marxian school of sociology; Flower arrangement, Japanese — Shōgetsudō Koryū school.**

Scientific names of plants and animals

All words in scientific names of plants and animals except the initial word are in lowercase, even if they incorporate proper nouns or adjectives, e.g.,

Anguilla japonica

Litchi chinensis
    x Nephelium litchi

Pinus sibirica
    x Pinus cembra sibirica

Geographic headings in English

Both generic and proper nouns and adjectives in geographic names in the English language are capitalized. These include names of places, regions, sites, metropolitan areas, and named geographic and geological features (including coasts, islands, rivers, valleys, watersheds, etc.). Examples include:

Alaska, Gulf of
Assateague Island National Seashore (Md. and Va.)
Atlantic Coast (Canada)
Beluga Lake (Alaska)
Boundary Waters Canoe Area (Minn.)
Dakota Aquifer
Death Valley (Calif. and Nev.)
Ionian Islands (Greece)
McKinley, Mount, Region (Alaska)
Peking Metropolitan Area (China)
Pennsylvania Dutch Country (Pa.)
Po River Valley (Italy)
Stone Creek Site (Alta.)
Tokyo Region (Japan)
Valley Forge National Historical Park (Pa.)
Washington Region

However, the word *regions* in the heading **Antarctic regions** and **Arctic regions** is in lowercase, e.g., **Black Coast (Antarctic regions); Coasts — Antarctic regions; Arctic regions — Aerial exploration.**

Non-English headings and references

The capitalization of non-English headings and references follows *AACR2* and reference sources. In cases of conflict, *AACR2* takes precedence. Examples include:

Tatar Strait (R.S.F.S.R.)
   x   Tatarskiĭ proliv (R.S.F.S.R.)

> *Strait* is capitalized in the English heading **Tatar Strait (R.S.F.S.R.)** because names of geographic features, regions, etc. are capitalized. The Russian word for strait, *proliv*, as part of the vernacular *see* reference, is in lowercase because it appears as such in Russian encyclopedias and because lowercasing is consistent with the capitalization rules for Russian geographic names in appendix A of *AACR2*.

Rite of spring (Ballet)
   x   Sacre du printemps (Ballet)

> Although the word *spring* appears uppercased in reference sources, both *printemps* and *spring* are lowercased because appendix A of *AACR2* requires that names of seasons be lowercased in both English and French.

Balkan Mountains (Bulgaria)
   x Stara planina (Bulgaria)

Bellini, Giovanni, d. 1516. Saint Francis in ecstasy
   x Saint Francis in ecstasy (Painting)
     San Francesco nel deserto (Painting)

Chang, Tse-tuan, fl. 1111-1120. Going up the river at Ch'ing-ming Festival time
   x Ch'ing ming shang ho t'u (Scroll)

Parc provincial des Laurentides (Québec)
   x Laurentides Provincial Park (Québec)
     Parc des Laurentides (Québec)
     Parc national des Laurentides (Québec)

Soester Scheibenkreuz (Sculpture)
   x Kreuztafel mit hölzener Scheibe (Sculpture)

Votivbild Kartause Cella Salutis zu Tuckelhausen (Panel painting)

Special Cases

Armed Forces

The word *forces* in the heading **Armed Forces** and in the subdivision **—Armed Forces** is capitalized, e.g., **Armed Forces—Civic action**; **United States—Armed Forces—Foreign countries**.

[...] countries

The word *countries* is in lowercase, e.g., **Arab countries—History—20th century**; **Canary Islanders—Foreign countries**; **Communist countries**; **European Economic Community countries—Economic conditions**.

Terms attached to dates

Anno Domini; Before Christ

The abbreviations A.D. and B.C. are capitalized, e.g., **China—History—Han dynasty, 202 B.C.-220 A.D.**

[...] century

The word *century* is in lowercase, e.g., **English literature—20th century**; **Twenty-first century**.

Circa

The abbreviation ca. in period subdivisions is in lowercase, e.g., **United States—History—Colonial period, ca. 1600-1775.**

APPENDIX N: PUNCTUATION*

The punctuation marks used in Library of Congress subject headings are listed below.

Apostrophe

Standard usage is followed.

Brackets

Square brackets are used in the printed list to indicate multiple headings and multiple subdivisions. They are not used in subject entries. Examples include: **Authors, American, [English, French, etc.]; Mysticism — Brahmanism, [Judaism, Nestorian Church, etc.].**

Comma

A comma is used

o   to separate parallel terms in a heading, e.g., **Hotels, taverns, etc.; Exercise — Handbooks, manuals, etc.**

o   to separate the noun from the modifier in an inverted heading, e.g., **Historical poetry, English; Plants, Effect of radiation on; Michigan, Lake**

o   to separate the surname from the forename of a person and to separate the name from the dates, e.g., **Shakespeare, William, 1564-1616**

*Library of Congress, Subject Cataloging Division, *Subject Cataloging Manual: Subject Headings*, prelim. ed. (Washington, D.C.: Library of Congress, 1984), H30.

o   to separate a basic heading that contains a comma or commas from a free-floating term or phrase in a combination heading, e.g., **Hotels, taverns, etc., in literature; Rudolf, Lake, Region (Kenya and Ethiopia); Shakespeare, William, 1564-1616, in fiction, drama, poetry, etc.** Compare, however, **Manhattan (New York, N.Y.) in art; Music halls (Variety-theaters, cabarets, etc.) in literature**.

Dash

A dash is used to designate a subdivision, e.g., **United States — History — Civil War, 1861-1865 — Campaigns**

Hyphen

In addition to its normal use in compound words, a hyphen is used to indicate a span of years or an open date:

Great Britain — Politics and government — 1964-1979
United States — Foreign relations — 1981-   — Periodicals
Skelton, John, 1460?-1529

Parentheses

Parentheses are used

o   to enclose a qualifier or a set of qualifiers:

Kwegu (African people)
Lake District National Park (England)
Wall Street (New York, N.Y.)
Sinaloa (Mexico : State)
Sextets (Piano, clarinet, violins (2), viola, violoncello)
Conference on Security and Cooperation in Europe (1980 : Madrid, Spain)

o   to enclose spelled-out forenames in a personal heading, e.g., **Eliot, T. S. (Thomas Sterns), 1888-1965.**

Period

A period is used

o   at the end of every tracing on a printed cataloging record, with the exception of tracings that end in a closing parenthesis or a mark of ending punctuation:

1.   Children's poetry, American.
1.   Adams, John, 1735-1826.

    1. Fonda, Jane, 1937-   .
    1. Great Britain — Economic policy — 1945-
    1. Elite (Social sciences) — Germany (West)
    1. Diet — Handbooks, manuals, etc.
    1. China — History — To 221 B.C.

o   as an abbreviation mark:

    Smith, J. J., 1910-
    Smedley, W. T. (William Thomas), 1858-1920
    Smith Creek Canyon (Nev.)
    C.O.D. shipments
    Bible. N.T. Matthew
    Russian S.F.S.R.
    Egypt — History — To 332 B.C.

o   to separate a subheading or subheadings from the main heading:

    United States. Dept. of the Interior. Water and Power
       Resources Service. Engineering and Research Center.
       Library — Periodicals

o   to separate a title or uniform title from the name in a name/title heading:

    Joyce, James, 1882-1941. A portrait of the artist as a
       young man
    United States. Declaration of Independence
    Wyeth, Andrew, 1917-   . Christina's world

BIBLIOGRAPHY

"AACR2 Changes." *Supplement to LC Subject Headings, 1981*. Washington, D.C.: Library of Congress, 1982.

American Library Association. Division of Cataloging and Classification. Committee on Subject Headings. "Bibliography of Subject Headings Lists 1938-1952." *Journal of Cataloging and Classification* 8:159-170 (Dec. 1952).

Angell, Richard S. "Library of Congress Subject Headings—Review and Forecast." *Subject Retrieval in the Seventies: New Directions: Proceedings of an International Symposium*. Edited by Hans (Hanan) ·Wellisch and Thomas D. Wilson. Westport, Conn.: Greenwood, 1972.

_____. "Standards for Subject Headings: A National Program." *Journal of Cataloging and Classification* 10:191-197 (Oct. 1954).

Anglo-American Cataloguing Rules. 2nd ed. Prepared by the American Library Association, the British Library, the Canadian Committee on Cataloguing, the Library Association, and the Library of Congress, and edited by Michael Gorman and Paul W. Winkler. Chicago: American Library Association; Ottawa: Canadian Library Association, 1978.

Atherton, Pauline. *Books Are for Use: Final Report of the Subject Access Project to the Council on Library Resources*. Syracuse, N.Y.: Syracuse University, School of Information Studies, 1978.

Austin, Derek. "The Development of PRECIS: A Theoretical and Technical History." *Journal of Documentation* 30:47-102 (March 1974).

_____. *PRECIS: A Manual of Concept Analysis and Subject Indexing*. 2nd ed. With assistance from Mary Dykstra. London: The British Library, 1984.

Austin, Derek, and Jeremy A. Digger. "PRECIS: The Preserved Context Index System." *Library Resources & Technical Services* 21:13-30 (Winter 1977).

Balnaves, John. "Specificity." In *The Variety of Librarianship: Essays in Honour of John Wallace Metcalfe*, edited by W. Boyd Rayward. Sydney: Library Association of Australia, 1976.

Bates, Marcia J. "Factors Affecting Subject Catalog Search Success." *Journal of the American Society for Information Science* 28:161-169 (May 1977).

_____. "System Meets User: Problems in Matching Subject Search Terms." *Information Processing and Management* 13:367-375 (Nov. 1977).

Berman, Sanford. "Do-It-Yourself Subject Cataloging: Sources and Tools." *Library Journal* 107(8):785-786 (April 1982).

_____. *Prejudices and Antipathies: A Tract on the LC Subject Heads Concerning People*. Metuchen, N.J.: Scarecrow, 1971.

_____. "Proposal for Reforms to Improve Subject Searching." In Pauline A. Cochrane, "Modern Subject Access in the Online Age: American Libraries' First Continuing Education Course: Lesson Three." *American Libraries* 15:254 (April 1984).

_____, ed. *Subject Cataloging: Critiques and Innovations*. New York: Haworth, 1985.

Betz, Elizabeth. *Subject Headings Used in the Library of Congress Prints and Photographs Division*. Washington, D.C.: Library of Congress, 1980 (distributed by Cataloging Distribution Services).

Bilindex: A Bilingual Spanish-English Subject Heading List: Spanish Equivalents to Library of Congress Subject Headings/Bilindex: una lista bilingüe en español e inglés de ebcabezanuebtis de materia. Oakland, Calif.: Spanish language database, 1984.

Bishop, William Warner. "Subject Headings in Dictionary Catalogs." *Library Journal* 31:C113-C123 (Aug. 1906).

Black, Henry. "An Approach to a Theory of Subject Headings." *College & Research Libraries* 7:244-248, 255 (July 1946).

Boll, John J. "From Subject Headings to Descriptors: The Hidden Trend in Library of Congress Subject Headings." *Cataloging & Classification Quarterly* 1(2/3):3-28 (1982).

Bonnici, Norbert. "PRECIS and LCSH in the British Library: Problems of Consistency and Equivalence." *Catalogue & Index* 56:9-11 (Spring 1980).

Brinkler, Bartol. "The Geographical Approach to Materials in the *Library of Congress Subject Headings.*" *Library Resources & Technical Services* 6:49-63 (Winter 1962).

Canada. Parliament. Library. *Répertoire des vedettes-matière. Subject Headings Used in the French Catalogue.* Ottawa: R. Duhamel, Queen's Printer, 1963.

Canadian Library Association. Technical Services Section. *A List of Canadian Subject Headings.* 1st ed. Edited by Joan Mitchell, Hazel I. MacTaggart, and Nicholas Krenta. Ottawa: Canadian Library Association, 1968.

Cataloging Service 1-125, June 1945-Spring 1978 (Washington, D.C.: Library of Congress, Processing Dept.).

Cataloging Service Bulletin 1- , Summer 1978- (Washington, D.C.: Library of Congress, Processing Services).

Chan, Lois Mai. "Alphabetical Arrangement and Subject Collocation in Library of Congress Subject Headings." *Library Resources & Technical Services* 21:156-169 (Spring 1977).

_____. " 'American Poetry' but 'Satire, American': The Direct and Inverted Forms of Subject Headings Containing National Adjectives." *Library Resources & Technical Services* 17:330-339 (Summer 1973).

_____. "The Period Subdivision in Subject Headings." *Library Resources & Technical Services* 16:453-459 (Fall 1972).

_____. "The Principle of Uniform Heading in Library of Congress Subject Headings." *Library Resources & Technical Services* 22:126-136 (Spring 1978).

Christ, John M. *Concepts and Subject Headings: Their Relation in Information Retrieval and Library Science.* Metuchen, N.J.: Scarecrow, 1972.

Clack, Doris. *Black Literature Resources: Analysis and Organization.* New York: Marcel Dekker, 1975.

Coates, E. J. *Subject Catalogues: Headings and Structure.* London, Library Association, 1960.

Cochrane, Pauline A. *LCSH Entry Vocabulary Project: Final Report.* Washington, D.C.: Council on Library Resources, 1983.

_____. "Modern Subject Access in the Online Age: American Libraries' First Continuing Education Course." *American Libraries* 15:80-83, 145-150, 250-255, 336-339, 438-442, 527-529 (Feb.-Aug. 1984).

_____. "Options for Automated Subject Access: A Personal Assessment." *Cataloguing Australia* 7(4):52-62 (Oct./Dec. 1981).

_____. "Subject Access in the Online Catalog." *Research Libraries in OCLC: A Quarterly* 5:1-7 (Jan. 1982).

_____. "Subject Retrieval: A Marriage of Retrieval Systems and Library Automation Efforts." *Cataloguing Australia* 7(4):2-13 (Oct./Dec. 1981).

Cochrane, Pauline A., and Monika Kirtland. *I. Critical Views of LCSH ... II. An Analysis of Vocabulary Control in the Library of Congress List of Subject Headings.* Syracuse, N.Y.: ERIC Clearinghouse on Information Resources, 1981.

Cochrane, Pauline A., and others. "Subject Retrieval in the 1980s." *Cataloguing Australia* 7(4):2-75 (Oct./Dec. 1981).

Coen, James A. "An Investigation of Indirect Subdivision by Place in Library of Congress Subject Headings." *Library Resources & Technical Services* 13:62-78 (Winter 1969).

Coetzee, P. C. "Syntactics and Semantics of the Subject Heading: An Essay in Catalogistics." *Mousaion* 21:1-41; 22:1-30; 23:1-30 (1957).

Colby, Robert A. "Current Problems in the Subject Analysis of Literature." *Journal of Cataloging and Classification* 10:19-28 (Jan. 1954).

Coté, J. P. "PRECIS et le système de vedettes-matière de la Library of Congress; vers une étude comparative globale." *Documentation et Bibliothèques* 25:11-21 (March 1979).

Cranshaw, J. "The Alphabetico-Classed Catalogue and Its Near Relatives." *Library Assistant* 30:202-211 (1937).

Cutter, Charles A. *Rules for a Dictionary Catalog.* 4th ed., rewritten. Washington, D.C.: Government Printing Office, 1904.

Daily, Jay E. "The Grammar of Subject Headings: A Formulation of Rules for Subject Heading Based on a Syntactical and Morphological Analysis of the Library of Congress List." Ph.D. diss., Columbia University, 1957.

_____. "Many Changes, No Alteration: An Analysis of Library of Congress Subject Headings, Seventh Edition." *Library Journal* 92:3961-3963 (Nov. 1, 1967).

_____. "Subject Headings and the Theory of Classification." *American Documentation* 8:269-274 (Oct. 1957).

Doszkocs, Tamas, and John E. Ulmschneider. "A Practical Stemming Algorithm for Online Search Assistance." In *National Online Meeting Proceedings—1983*, compiled by Martha E. Williams and Thomas H. Hogan. Medford, N.J.: Learned Information, 1983.

Dunkin, Paul S. *Cataloging U.S.A.* Chicago: American Library Association, 1969.

Eaton, Thelma. *Cataloging and Classification: An Introductory Manual.* 4th ed. Ann Arbor: distributed by Edwards Brothers, 1967.

Foskett, A. C. "Better Dead Than Read: Further Studies in Critical Classification." *Library Resources & Technical Services* 28:346-359 (Oct./Dec. 1984).

_____. *The Subject Approach to Information.* 4th ed. London: Clive Bingley; Hamden, Conn.: Linnet Books, 1982.

Frarey, Carlyle J. "Developments in Subject Cataloging." *Library Trends* 2:217-235 (Oct. 1953).

_____. "Practical Problems in Subject Heading Work: A Summary." *Journal of Cataloging and Classification* 8:154-158 (Dec. 1952).

_____. "The Role of Research in Establishing Standards for Subject Headings." *Journal of Cataloging and Classification* 10:179-190 (Oct. 1954).

_____. "Studies of Use of the Subject Catalog: Summary and Evaluation." In *The Subject Analysis of Library Materials*, edited by Maurice F. Tauber. New York: School of Library Service, Columbia University, 1953.

_____. *Subject Headings.* The State of the Library Art, vol. 1, part 2. New Brunswick, N.J.: Graduate School of Library Science, Rutgers— The State University, 1960.

_____, ed. "Symposium on Subject Headings." *Journal of Cataloging and Classification* 8:131-158 (Dec. 1952).

Gabbard, Paula Beversdorf. "LCSH and PRECIS in Music: A Comparison." *The Library Quarterly* 55:192-206 (April 1985).

Gjelsness, Rudolph H. "The Classified Catalog *vs.* The Dictionary Catalog." *Library Journal* 56:18-21 (Jan. 1, 1931).

Goodrum, Charles, and Helen Dalrymple. "Computerization at the Library of Congress: The First Twenty Years." *Wilson Library Bulletin* 57:115-121 (Oct. 1982).

Gorman, Michael. "Fate, Time, Occasion, Chance, and Change: Or, How the Machine May Yet Save LCSH." *American Libraries* 11:557-558 (Oct. 1980).

_____. "New Rules for New Systems." *American Libraries* 13(4):241-242 (April 1982).

Greenberg, Alan M. "Scope Notes in Library of Congress Subject Headings." *Cataloging & Classification Quarterly* 1(2/3):95-104 (1982).

Gull, C. D. "Some Remarks on Subject Headings." *Special Libraries* 40: 83-88 (March 1949).

Hanson, J. C. M. "The Subject Catalogs of the Library of Congress." *Bulletin of the American Library Association* 3:385-397 (1909).

Hardy, May G. "The Library of Congress Subject Catalog: An Evaluation." *Library Quarterly* 22:40-50 (Jan. 1952).

Harris, Jessica Lee. *Subject Analysis: Computer Implications of Rigorous Definition.* With a preface by Maurice F. Tauber and Theodore C. Hines. Metuchen, N.J.: Scarecrow, 1970.

Haykin, David Judson. "Let's Get Down to Fundamentals!" *Medical Library Association Bulletin* 36:82-85 (April 1948).

_____. "Project for a Subject Heading Code: Revised." Washington, D.C., 1957.

_____. *Subject Headings: A Practical Guide.* Washington, D.C.: Government Printing Office, 1951.

_____. "Subject Headings: Principles and Development." In *The Subject Analysis of Library Materials*, edited by Maurice F. Tauber. New York: School of Library Service, Columbia University, 1953.

Hennepin County Library. Cataloging Section. *Cataloging Bulletin*, no. 1- . Edina, Minn.: Hennepin County Library, 1973- .

Hickey, Doralyn J. "Subject Analysis: An Interpretive Survey." *Library Trends* 25:273-291 (July 1976).

Hildreth, Charles R. "LCSH Needs Hierarchical Restructuring." In Pauline A. Cochrane, "Modern Subject Access in the Online Age: American Libraries' First Continuing Education Course: Lesson Three." *American Libraries* 15:529 (July/Aug. 1984).

_____. *Online Public Access Catalogs: The User Interface.* Dublin, Ohio: OCLC, 1982.

_____. "To Boolean or Not to Boolean." *Information Technology and Libraries* 2:236-237 (Sept. 1983).

Holley, Robert P., and Robert E. Killheffer. "Is There an Answer to the Subject Access Crisis?" *Cataloging & Classification Quarterly* 1(2/3): 125-133 (1982).

Holmes, Robert R. "Introduction to the Seventh Edition of Subject Headings Used in the Dictionary Catalogs of the Library of Congress." *Library Resources & Technical Services* 12:323-329 (Summer 1968).

Horner, John. *Cataloguing*. London: Association of Assistant Librarians, 1970.

Hulme, E. Wyndham. "Principles of Book Classification." *Library Association Record* 13:445-447 (1911).

Immroth, John Phillip. *Analysis of Vocabulary Control in Library of Congress Classification and Subject Headings*. Littleton, Colo.: Libraries Unlimited, 1971.

International PRECIS Workshop. *The PRECIS Index System: Principles, Applications, and Prospects: Proceedings*. Edited by Hans H. Wellisch. New York: H. W. Wilson Co., 1977.

Jackson, Sidney L. *Catalog Use Study: Director's Report*. Edited by Vaclav Mostecky. Chicago: American Library Association, 1958.

_____. "Sears and LC Subject Headings: A Sample Comparison." *Library Journal* 86:755-756, 775 (Feb. 15, 1961).

Jouguelet, Suzanne. "A Network of Subject Headings: The Répertoire of Laval University Adapted by the Bibliothèque Nationale, Paris." *International Cataloguing* 12(2):17-19 (April/June 1983).

Kaiser, Julius O. "Systematic Indexing." In *Systematic Indexing*. The Card System Series, vol. 2. London: Pitman, 1911.

Kaske, Neal K., and Nancy P. Sanders. *A Comprehensive Study of Online Public Access Catalogs: An Overview and Application of Findings*. Final Report to the Council on Library Resources, vol. 3. OCLC Research Report Series, no. OCLC/OPR/RR-83/4. Dublin, Ohio: OCLC, 1983.

Kirtland, Monika, and Pauline Cochrane. "Critical Views of LCSH—Library of Congress Subject Headings: A Bibliographic and Bibliometric Essay." *Cataloging & Classification Quarterly* 1(2/3):71-94 (1982).

Lancaster, F. W. *Vocabulary Control for Information Retrieval*. Washington, D.C.: Information Resources Press, 1972.

_____. "Vocabulary Control in Information Retrieval Systems." *Advances in Librarianship* 7:1-40 (1977).

Library of Congress. *Library of Congress Name Headings with References*. Washington, D.C.: Library of Congress, 1974-1980.

Library of Congress. *Name Authorities: Cumulative Microform Edition*. Washington, D.C.: Library of Congress, 1983- .

Library of Congress. Automated Systems Office. *MARC Formats for Bibliographic Data.* Washington, D.C.: Library of Congress, 1980, Update No. 10, 10/11/84.

Library of Congress. Catalog Division. *Subject Headings Used in the Dictionary Catalogues of the Library of Congress.* 3rd ed. Edited by Mary Wilson MacNair. Washington, D.C., 1928.

Library of Congress. Processing Services. *Authorities: A MARC Format.* 1st ed. Washington, D.C.: Library of Congress, 1981.

_____. *Library of Congress Filing Rules.* Prepared by John C. Rather and Susan C. Biebel. Washington, D.C.: Library of Congress, 1980.

Library of Congress. Subject Cataloging Division. *Library of Congress Subject Headings.* 10th ed. Washington, D.C.: Library of Congress, 1986.

_____. *Subject Cataloging Manual: Subject Headings.* Prelim. ed. Washington, D.C.: Library of Congress, 1984.

_____. *Subject Headings Used in the Dictionary Catalogs of the Library of Congress.* 4th ed. Edited by Mary Wilson MacNair. Washington, D.C., 1943.

_____. *Subject Headings Used in the Dictionary Catalogs of the Library of Congress.* 5th ed. Edited by Nella Jane Martin. Washington, D.C., 1948.

Lilley, Oliver L. "Evaluation of the Subject Catalog: Criticisms and a Proposal." *American Documentation* 5:41-60 (1954).

_____. "How Specific Is Specific?" *Journal of Cataloging and Classification* 11:3-8 (Jan. 1955).

_____. "Terminology, Form, Specificity and the Syndetic Structure of Subject Headings for English Literature." Ph.D. diss., Columbia University, 1958.

Lipetz, Ben-Ami. "Catalog Use in a Large Research Library." *Library Quarterly* 42:129-139 (Jan. 1972).

Lipow, Anne Grodzins. "Practical Considerations of the Current Capabilities of Subject Access in Online Public Catalogs." *Library Resources & Technical Services* 27:81-87 (Jan./March 1983).

Lubetzky, Seymour. "Titles: Fifth Column of the Catalog." *Library Quarterly* 11:412-430 (1941).

McKinlay, John. "Australia, LCSH and FLASH." *Library Resources & Technical Services* 26:100-108 (April/June 1982).

_____. "Concerning Subject Authority Catalogues." *Library Resources & Technical Services* 16:460-465 (Fall 1972).

MacNair, Mary W. "The Library of Congress List of Subject Headings." *Bulletin of the American Library Association* 23:301 (1929).

McWilliams, Jerry. "Automatic Assignment of Pre-Coordinate Subject Headings from Free-Floating Descriptors." In *The Information Community: An Alliance for Progress: Proceedings of the 44th ASIS Annual Meeting, 1981*, vol. 18. White Plains, N.Y.: Knowledge Industry Publications, 1981.

Mandel, Carol A., with the assistance of Judith Herschman. "Subject Access in the Online Catalog." A report prepared for the Council on Library Resources, Aug. 1981.

Mann, Margaret. *Introduction to Cataloging and the Classification of Books.* 2d ed. Chicago: American Library Association, 1943.

Markey, Karen. *The Process of Subject Searching in the Library Catalog: Final Report of the Subject Access Research Project.* OCLC Research Report Series, no. OCLC/OPR/RR-83/1. Dublin, Ohio: OCLC, 1983.

_____. *Subject Searching in Library Catalogs Before and After the Introduction of Online Catalogs.* OCLC Library, Information and Computer Science Series, no. 4. Dublin, Ohio: OCLC, 1984.

_____. "Thus Spake the OPAC User." *Information Technology and Libraries* 2:381-387 (Dec. 1983).

Metcalfe, John. *Alphabetical Subject Indication of Information.* Rutgers Series on Systems for the Intellectual Organization of Information, vol. 3. New Brunswick, N.J.: Graduate School of Library Service, Rutgers University, 1965.

_____. *Information Indexing and Subject Cataloging: Alphabetical: Classified: Coordinate: Mechanical.* New York: Scarecrow, 1957.

_____. *Information Retrieval, British & American, 1876-1976.* Metuchen, N.J.: Scarecrow, 1976.

_____. *Subject Classifying and Indexing of Libraries and Literature.* New York: Scarecrow, 1959.

_____. "Tentative Code of Rules for Alphabetico-Specific Entry." In *Subject Classifying and Indexing of Libraries and Literature.* New York: Scarecrow, 1959.

Miksa, Francis. *The Subject in the Dictionary Catalog from Cutter to the Present.* Chicago: American Library Association, 1983.

Milstead, Jessica. "Natural versus Inverted Word Order in Subject Headings." *Library Resources & Technical Services* 24:174-178 (Spring 1980).

Mischo, William. "Library of Congress Subject Headings: A Review of the Problems, and Prospects for Improved Subject Access." *Cataloging & Classification Quarterly* 1(2/3):105-124 (1982).

Mostecky, Vaclav. "Study of the See-Also Reference Structure in Relation to the Subject of International Law." *American Documentation* 7:294-314 (1956).

Needham, C. D. *Organizing Knowledge in Libraries: An Introduction to Information Retrieval.* 2d rev. ed. London: A. Deutsch, 1971.

Norris, C. "MeSH—The Subject Heading Approach." *Aslib Proceedings* 33: 153-159 (April 1981).

Norris, Dorothy May. *A History of Cataloguing and Cataloguing Methods 1100-1850: With an Introductory Survey of Ancient Times.* London: Grafton, 1939.

Olding, R. K. "Form of Alphabetico-Specific Subject Headings, and a Brief Code." *Australian Library Journal* 10:127-137 (July 1961).

O'Neill, Edward T., and Rao Aluri. "Library of Congress Subject Heading Patterns in OCLC Monographic Records." *Library Resources & Technical Services* 25:63-80 (Jan./March 1981).

_____. *Research Report on Subject Heading Patterns in OCLC Monographic Records.* OCLC Research Report Series, no. OCLC/RDD/RR-79/1. Columbus, Ohio: OCLC, Research and Development Division, 1979.

Perreault, J. M. "Latest vs. Contemporaneous Place Names in Library of Congress Subject Headings." *Cataloging & Classification Quarterly* 1(2/3):29-69 (1982).

_____. "Library of Congress Subject Headings: A New Manual." *International Classification* 6:158-169 (1979).

Perreault, J. M., and Sanford Berman. *A Dialogue on the Subject Catalogue —J. M. Perreault: "A Representative of the New Left in American Subject Cataloguings": A Review Essay on Sanford Berman's "The Joy of Cataloging" with Response by Sanford Berman.* Urbana, Ill.: Illinois University, 1983.

Petersen, Toni. "The AAT: A Model for the Restructuring of LCSH (Art and Architecture Thesaurus)." *The Journal of Academic Librarianship* 9:207-210 (Sept. 1983).

Pettee, Julia. "The Philosophy of Subject Headings." *Special Libraries* 23:181-182 (April 1932).

_____. *Subject Headings: The History and Theory of the Alphabetical Subject Approach to Books.* New York: H. W. Wilson Co., 1947.

Prevost, Marie Louise. "An Approach to Theory and Method in General Subject Headings." *Library Quarterly* 16:140-151 (April 1946).

"Principles of the *Sears List of Subject Headings.*" *Sears List of Subject Headings.* 12th ed. Edited by Barbara M. Westby. New York: H. W. Wilson Co., 1982.

Ramakrishnan, M. N. "Adjectives in Subject Headings." *Herald of Library Science* 1:139-141 (July 1962).

Ranganathan, S. R. *Elements of Library Classification.* 3d ed. Bombay: Asia Publishing House, 1962, 82-89.

_____. "General Theory of Classification." *Abgila* 2:A25-A40 (1951).

_____. "Subject Heading and Facet Analysis." *Journal of Documentation* 20:109-119 (Sept. 1964).

Richmond, Phyllis Allen. "Cats: An Example of Concealed Classification in Subject Headings." *Library Resources & Technical Services* 3:102-112 (Spring 1959).

_____. *Introduction to PRECIS for North American Usage.* Littleton, Colo.: Libraries Unlimited, 1981.

_____. "Research Possibilities in the Machine-Readable Catalog: Use of the Catalog to Study Itself." *Journal of Academic Librarianship* 2:224-229 (Nov. 1976).

Russell, Keith W., comp. and ed. *Subject Access: Report of a Meeting Sponsored by the Council on Library Resources, Dublin, Ohio, June 7-9, 1982.* Washington, D.C.: Council on Library Resources, 1982.

Salton, Gerard, and Michael J. McGill. *Introduction to Modern Information Retrieval.* New York: McGraw-Hill, 1983.

Salton, Gerard, and C. S. Yang. "On the Specification of Term Values in Automatic Indexing." *Journal of Documentation* 29:351-372 (Dec. 1973).

Schabas, Ann H. "Postcoordinate Retrieval: A Comparison of Two Indexing Languages." *Journal of the American Society for Information Science* 33(1):32-37 (Jan. 1982).

Schaeffer, Rudolf F. "Delights and Pitfalls of Subject Cataloging." *Library Resources & Technical Services* 14:98-108 (Winter 1970).

Scheerer, George. "The Subject Catalog Examined." *Library Quarterly* 27:187-198 (July 1957).

Schwartz, Jacob. "A Dozen Desultory Denunciations of the Dictionary Catalogue, with a Theory of Cataloguing." *Library Journal* 11:470-477 (Dec. 1886).

Sears List of Subject Headings. 12th ed. Edited by Barbara M. Westby. New York: H. W. Wilson Co., 1982.

Seely, Pauline A. "Subject Headings Today." *Library Journal* 78:17-22 (Jan. 1, 1953).

Shera, Jesse H., and Margaret E. Egan. *The Classified Catalog: Basic Principles and Practices.* With a code for the construction and maintenance of the classified catalog by Jeannette M. Lynn and Zola Hilton. Chicago: American Library Association, 1956.

Sholtys, Pauline M. "Adapting Library of Congress Subject Headings for Newspaper Indexing." *Cataloging & Classification Quarterly* 4(4):99-102 (1984).

Sinkankas, George M. *A Study in the Syndetic Structure of the Library of Congress List of Subject Headings.* Pittsburgh: University of Pittsburgh Graduate School of Library and Information Sciences, 1972.

Steinweg, Hilda. "Punctuation in Library of Congress Subject Headings." *Library Resources & Technical Services* 22:145-153 (Spring 1978).

_____. "Specificity in Subject Headings." *Library Resources & Technical Services* 23:55-68 (Winter 1979).

_____. "Thought on Subject Headings." *Journal of Cataloging and Classification* 6:40-45 (Spring 1950).

Studwell, William E., Elaine Rast, and Cheryl Felmlee. "Library of Congress Subject Heading Period Subdivisions for Africa: Some Proposed Additions." *Cataloging & Classification Quarterly* 4(4):51-98 (1984).

"Subject Analysis: Summary Report: Subject Analysis Committee Subcommittee on Subject Headings for Individual Works of Art and Architecture." *RTSD Newsletter* 5:63-66 (Nov./Dec. 1980).

The Subject Analysis of Library Materials. Papers presented at an institute, June 24-28, 1952, under the sponsorship of the School of Library Service, Columbia University, and the A.L.A. Division of Cataloging and Classification. Edited by Maurice F. Tauber. New York: School of Library Service, Columbia University, 1953.

Subject Authorities: A Guide to Subject Cataloging. New York: Bowker, 1981.

"Subject Heading Code in Preparation." *College & Resource Libraries* 14: 216 (April 1953).

Subject Retrieval in the Seventies: New Directions: Proceedings of an International Symposium Held at the Center of Adult Education, University of Maryland, College Park, May 14 to 15, 1971. Edited by Hans (Hanan) Wellisch and Thomas D. Wilson. Contributions in Librarianship and Information Science, no. 3. Westport, Conn.: Greenwood, 1972.

Svenonius, Elaine. "Metcalfe and the Principles of Specific Entry." In *The Variety of Librarianship: Essays in Honour of John Wallace Metcalfe,* edited by W. Boyd Rayward. Sydney: Library Association of Australia, 1976.

Taube, Mortimer. "Specificity in Subject Headings and Coordinate Indexing." *Library Trends* 1:219-223 (Oct. 1952).

Taylor, Jed H. "Classification and Subject-Headings in the Small College Library." *Library Resources & Technical Services* 5:87-90 (Winter 1961).

Taylor, Kanardy L. "Subject Catalogs *vs.* Classified Catalogs." In *The Subject Analysis of Library Materials,* edited by Maurice F. Tauber. New York: School of Library Service, Columbia University, 1953.

Université Laval. Bibliothèque. *Répertoire de vedettes-matière.* 8-ème ed. Quebec: 1976.

Van Hoesen, H. B. "Perspective in Cataloging with Some Applications." *Library Quarterly* 14:100-107 (April 1944).

Vatican Library. *Rules for the Catalog of Printed Books.* Trans. from the 2d Italian ed. by the Very Rev. Thomas J. Shanahan, Victor A. Schaefer, and Constantin T. Vesselowsky. Edited by Wyllis E. Wright. Chicago: American Library Association, 1948.

Vickery, Brian C. "Systematic Subject Indexing." *Journal of Documentation* 9(1):48-57 (1953).

Wellisch, Hans. "Poland Is Not Yet Defeated: Or, Should Catalogers Rewrite History? With a Discourse on 'When Is an Island Not an Island?' " *Library Resources & Technical Services* 22:158-167 (1978).

Wepsiec, Jan. "Language of the Library of Congress Subject Headings Pertaining to Society." *Library Resources & Technical Services* 25:196-203 (April/June 1981).

White, John B. "On Changing Subject Headings." *Library Resources & Technical Services* 16:466-469 (Fall 1972).

Wiberley, Stephen E., Jr. "Reducing Search Results a High Priority." In Pauline A. Cochrane, "Modern Subject Access in the Online Age: American Libraries' First Continuing Education Course: Lesson Three." *American Libraries* 15:255 (April 1984).

Williams, James G. *Classified Library of Congress Subject Headings.* New York: Marcel Dekker, 1972.

Wilson, Patrick. "The End of Specificity." *Library Resources & Technical Services* 23:116-122 (Spring 1979).

Wright, Wyllis E. "Standards for Subject Headings: Problems and Opportunities." *Journal of Cataloging and Classification* 10:175-178 (Oct. 1954).

———. "The Subject Approach to Knowledge: Historical Aspects and Purposes." In *The Subject Analysis of Library Materials*, edited by Maurice F. Tauber. New York: School of Library Service, Columbia University, 1953.

INDEX